# VISION ON FIRE

# VISION
## ON
## FIRE

EMMA GOLDMAN ON THE SPANISH REVOLUTION

EDITED WITH INTRODUCTIONS BY
DAVID PORTER

COMMONGROUND PRESS                    NEW PALTZ, N.Y.

Credits: Photo of Goldman in Paris, 1937, given to Federico Arcos by Senia Fleshin; photo of Goldman addressing Hyde Park, London meeting and Goldman 2/8/35 letter to Max Nettlau reprinted by permission of Schocken Books Inc. from *Nowhere at Home: Letters from Exile of Emma Goldman and Alexander Berkman* by Richard and Anna Marie Drinnon, eds. (Copyright © by Richard and Anna Marie Drinnon); photo of Goldman addressing an indoor London meeting reprinted by permission of Wide World Photos, Inc.; photos of Goldman in N.Y., 1934, and addressing Hyde Park, London meeting, and photo-images of announcement of public meeting on Spain, 1/19/38, London and of 6/9/37 Goldman letter to Harry Kelly reproduced by permission of Rare Books and Manuscript Divison (Emma Goldman Papers), The New York Public Library, Astor, Lenox and Tilden Foundations; credits for all other Goldman material indicated in acknowledgements and sources pages.

Library of Congress number: 82-074015

Paperback ISBN: 0-9610348-2-3

Cover Design by Mike Finn

Typeset by The Print Shop, Hauppauge, N.Y. (IWW)

Printed by Celecom Corp., East Longmeadow, Mass.

Commonground Press
546 Albany Post Rd.
New Paltz, N.Y. 12561

The constructive work done here disproves [the] false accusation hurled against us by all sorts of people. . . . I feel it was worth all I have given to the Anarchist movement to see with my own eyes its first buddings. It is my grandest hour.

E.G., 11/30/36

I have been in a frightful depressed stated ever since the events in Barcelona. Spain had meant so much to me. It held out such hopes for the last years of my life. Now all that is gone by the board and I am left dangling in the air.

E.G., 6/8/37

I realize that when one is in a burning house one does not consider one's possessions, one tries to jump to safety even if it means death. The possessions of my comrades have been their sterling quality, their staunch adherence to fundamentals. But they are surrounded by consuming flames and they feel if they hold on to every part of their past they would lose everything.

E.G., 9/27/37

If ever there were a people who love liberty sufficiently to struggle for it, live it in their daily relationships and even die for it, the Spanish workers and peasants have demonstrated that they stand at the highest peak.

E.G., 1/14/40

# Acknowledgements

Most manuscripts emerge from the cooperation of many individuals, through many stages of conceptualization, research, writing and editing along the way. In a sense each work represents a small community of its own, though many participants have no contact with each other save through the author. I feel especially fortunate to have seen the community behind this book appear and grow over six long years. This in itself was an important satisfaction. Inevitably many of those involved must go un-named, since the list of those providing encouragement and assistance at various stages extends into dozens. However the role of some was crucial and should be stated. Unending thanks go to my fine companion Nancy Schniedewind for her consistent, many-sided support, patience and rekind-ling of energies over the half-decade on this path. Dave and Noelle also pro-vided constant inspiration through their own free spirits and endured with good humor and understanding the long hours of my preoccupation with the book. Among those true comrades who for years offered generous aid and encouragement without which this work might never have come to fruition, I especially want to thank Federico Arcos and Ken Mazlen. Much praise also to Geoff, Ted, Lew, Esther, Sam, Ahrne, Paul, Dennis, Bill and Elaine for their important and timely support at critical moments in the enterprise. Many others also joined this community through their careful readings, discussion and critiques, their encouragement about the worth of the project generally and their fine anarchist spirit. For the completed manuscript to emerge as a book, however, required a significant financial base. Here the generous support of Arthur Bortolotti was decisive. Finally, my thanks to Esther Pank and Riley Bostrom of The Print Shop for their fine advice and efforts in layout and typesetting.

Helpful research assistance was provided from the special collections staffs at the New York Public Library, the International Institute of Social History (Amsterdam), and libraries at the University of Michigan, Harvard University, Yale University, New York University and Radcliffe College. I must also thank Ian Ballantine, Emma Goldman's great-nephew and literary executor, as well as all the above institutions except the IISH for permission to quote from the Goldman material found. Unfortunately the quotation policy of the latter institution is far more restrictive than that of its archival counterparts in this country.

*Emma Goldman, New York City, 1934 (NYPL)*

*Emma Goldman, Paris, 1937 (Fleshin)*

Top:     *Buenaventura Durruti, 1936*
Bottom:  *International volunteers with the Durruti column of anarchist militia*

# Conversando con Emma Goldmann

E' già la seconda volta che Emma Goldmann, la ben nota propagandista anarchica, viene in Spagna. Accorse subito l'anno scorso, dopo le giornate di luglio, offrendo la sua solidarietà, intelligenza ed esperienza, a vantaggio della causa per cui lotta da cinquant'anni con fede, passione e sacrifici. E' pure la seconda volta che m'incontro con lei per scambiare qualche impressione in breve conversazione. E le ho chiesto :

— Potrei rivederti, Emma, non per una lunga intervista, ma per ben precisare il tuo pensiero pei lettori del *Risveglio anarchico* di Ginevra.

Senza esitare un secondo mi rispose :

— Volontieri. Prepara le tue domande, e possiamo incontrarci domani.

Infatti, all'ora fissata, ci troviamo in una

scevismo non è solo per la sua dittatura, bensì e sopratutto per negare ogni compromesso, i compromessi coi bolscevichi od altri, spingendo a negare l'anarchismo e ad oprare contro l'anarchia. Alla prova, la partecipazione dei nostri al governo ha dato i risultati più disastrosi. Anche non volendo essere assoluta nel giudizio, auguro che non si ripeteranno simili sbagli, a cui tutto si sacrifica, fede, dirittura, indipendenza, per ottenere nulla di nulla dagli improvvisati amici, per essere prima ricompensati con insulti e calunnie e poi, come ora, imprigionati, pugnalati, fucilati per di più.

— Vedi anche tu che adesso la CNT, malgrado il malumore che solleva tra i suoi affigliati, pratica troppo la consegna della non resistenza a tutte le provocazioni della reazio-

Top: *Portion of interview with Goldman in the Geneva anarchist paper,* Il Risveglio anarchico, *edited by Luigi Bertoni*

Bottom: *Newspaper note on Goldman and Souchy visit to* Nosotros, *the Valencia anarchist daily newspaper, September 18, 1937*

*Front page of the anarchist women's periodical,* Mujeres Libres: *"With work and arms, we, the women, will defend the liberty of the people"*

*Religious seminary transformed by the Catalan Libertarian Youth into a "people's university"*

Appeal to workers of the world to supply arms for the Spanish proletariat, in the New York anarchist periodical *Cultura Proletaria*

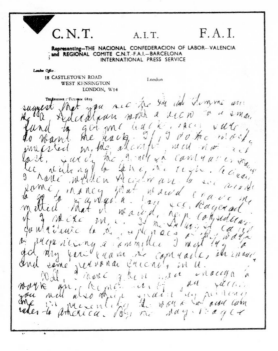

Top: *Page from Goldman's 6/29/37 letter to American anarchist Harry Kelly (NYPL)*

Bottom: *Handbill announcing a Goldman lecture after her second trip to revolutionary Spain (NYPL)*

*Goldman addressing a London meeting on the role of the CNT, January 18, 1937: on the left are Fenner Brockway and Ethel Mannin (Wide World Photos)*

*Anarchist militia in Barcelona prepare to leave for the front, 1936*

*Worker barricades, Barcelona, July 1936*

Left: Women in socialized textile factory
Right: Behind the front

Left:   *Children's colony established by anarchists on grounds of former aristocratic hotel*
Right:  *Peasants in collectivized farming*

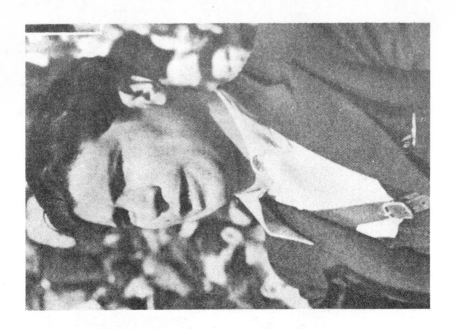

Left:   *Federica Montseny, 1936*
Right:  *Mariano R. Vázquez, 1936*

*Goldman speaking at Hyde Park (London) May Day demonstration, probably 1937; picture of Durruti is on her right (NYPL)*

*Visit to the front, October 1938: Alfonso Miguel, Lola Iturbe, José Carbó, Goldman, Martin Gudell, Pedro Herrera, Juan Molina, Gregorio Jover*

# *Contents*

# Preface

*Writings on Emma Goldman to date offer surprisingly little on her activism and views in the Spanish revolution.[1] To be sure, the years 1936-1939 were only a small part of her lifetime. Her effectiveness in that period as a speaker and organizer was crippled by forced exile from the United States, the social context where she was most at ease and had her greatest popular appeal.[2] Despite such qualifications, it is still fair to say that Goldman's life saw its great final test in Spain during the late 1930's. For one dedicated to the anarchist cause for half a century, having devoted such constant courage and energy, and having seen personally the wrenching tragedy of the authoritarian turn of the Russian revolution, Goldman viewed her own participation in the Spanish revolution as indeed "coming home after a lifetime of pilgrimage."[3]*

*For Goldman personally, Spain was a source of great revolutionary energy after so many draining years of activist effort and disappointment, an agony augmented by the trials of exile and the June 1936 death of her lifelong comrade Alexander Berkman. But beyond that, for Emma Goldman and the anarchist movement internationally, events in Spain represented the finest test to date of both the revolutionary effectiveness of a large-scale working-class anarchist movement and the viability of anarchism's vision of the new society. From personal and movement perspectives both (though for Goldman the two were virtually inseparable), Spain was the culmination, the summing-up and*

---

1. See footnote 1 at back of preface.
2. However she did maintain a constant stream of correspondence with friends and comrades in the U.S. (a major source indeed for the present book), contributed several articles on Spain to movement journals here and, during her last months of life in Canada, contacted many in the U.S. to raise money for the Spanish refugees.
3. Goldman 2/10/37 letter to William Jong (NYPL) (see the Sources section at the rear of the book for explanation of archival abbreviations). She also compared her emotions to those her "forbears must have felt when they entered the holy temple" (6/29/37 letter to Harry Kelly, NYPL).

*great final drama of her lifetime. As such, the experience deserves the atten-
tion which a book entirely devoted to her own writings from this period can
provide.*[4]

   *The first chapter begins with a general introduction of Emma Goldman for
those unacquainted with her lifelong quest for freedom. It continues with
outlines of her involvement with Spain from an early age and especially her
role during the Spanish revolution of the late 1930's. It concludes with an attempt to relate Goldman's discussion to our own current context of massive social crisis and efforts toward vast social transformation. Complementing these
several sections of the first chapter are introductions to subsequent chapters
and a chronological table of events in Spain. Together these should suffice to
guide readers through the more intricate material to follow. For those desiring more detailed information on names, terms, places and events, elaborate
footnote references are provided (lengthier footnotes at the end of each
chapter). However, through introductory comments of my own (marked with
a † symbol) before each Goldman quotation, the text is presented so as to
minimize the need to refer to that section for those who prefer uninterrupted
reading.*

   *To facilitate further ease of movement through the material, I list below and
briefly identify Goldman's chief correspondents and periodicals of publication
during this period. Letters to the thirteen persons indicated here account for
almost two-thirds of the entries in this book.*

| | |
|---|---|
| Stella Ballantine | *Goldman's niece and a movement associate during the several years before Goldman's forced exile from the U.S. in 1919.* |
| Tom Bell | *Anarchist activist in Scotland and the U.S. and a friend of Goldman for many years.* |
| Ben Capes | *A St. Louis anarchist activist converted to that cause by Goldman and subsequently one of her long-standing friends.* |
| Pedro Herrera | *General secretary of the FAI, the militant anar-chist federation in Spain.* |
| Harry Kelly | *A friend and movement associate of Goldman in the U.S. since 1896.* |
| Ethel Mannin | *British writer, member of the Independent Labour Party, close friend and associate of Goldman during the latter's efforts to publicize and gain support for the Spanish revolution.* |

---

4.  See footnote 4 at back of preface.

| | |
|---|---|
| Mark Mratchny | *Another veteran activist in Russia and the U.S., in the late 1930's editor of the Yiddish anarchist periodical* Freie Arbeiter Stimme *(N.Y.).* |
| Max Nettlau | *Austrian anarchist, author of many works on the international anarchist movement.* |
| Rudolf Rocker | *A veteran militant in Britain and Germany, a leading figure in the IWMA, the anarcho-syndicalist international; also a prolific writer on anarchism, especially after his exile to the U.S. following the Nazi rise to power.* |
| Helmut Rüdiger | *A leading German anarchist activist, also much involved with IWMA affairs, especially in its relations with Spanish anarchists in the late 1930's.* |
| Alexander Schapiro | *An influential Russian activist from before World War I, heavily involved with the IWMA while in exile in Germany and Paris.* |
| Mariano Vázquez | *General secretary of the Spanish anarcho-syndicalist organization, the CNT, with over two million members.* |
| Milly Witkop-Rocker | *A prominent anarchist activist in Britain and Germany; exiled with companion Rudolf to the U.S. in later years.* |

| | |
|---|---|
| Spain and the World | *A London periodical from 1936 through late 1938 edited by Vernon Richards; this was the first in a direct line of publications leading to* Freedom *(1945-present).*[5] |
| Spanish Revolution | *A New York-based periodical issued from 1936 to 1939 by anarchists supporting the struggle in Spain.* |
| Vanguard | *A New York anarcho-syndicalist periodical, 1932-1939.* |

*Specific indications of dates and contexts are provided in brief remarks preceeding each Goldman passage. The archival source for each document is shown in a separate section at the end of the book. (See that section also for the abbreviations used to cite particular archives in footnote references.)*

---

5. Several anarchist periodicals have used this title. The *Freedom* established by Peter Kropotkin and others in England in 1886 is the best known. This publication ceased by 1936.

*Unfortunately, only after the manuscript was complete did the International Institute of Social History (Amsterdam) unexpectedly indicate that they would not grant permission to quote more than minimal passages from each document chosen from their collection. Because these documents as a whole amount to a significant portion of the Goldman material and contribute important information on Goldman's perspective, I was forced to salvage these texts as well as I could under these arbitrarily restrictive conditions. Consequently, while some of the material was eliminated entirely, the more significant documents still appear in either extensively edited form alongside her other quotations throughout the book or as additional footnote information. In the former case, only a brief maximum allowable passage is quoted directly. Other significant passages are summarized or paraphrased before or after the direct quotations to indicate the content and tone of her actual remarks.*

*As Goldman was the first to recognize, her hastily typed correspondence had frequent errors or inconsistencies in spelling, grammar and punctuation. Throughout her texts in this book, I have tried to correct these to provide for easy reading without in any way altering the content of her original statements. Words added or eliminated for the sake of proper grammar or clarity are indicated through brackets and dots.*

*As was always true with Emma Goldman, her statements in this book are sure to arouse passionate responses from every reader. She expresses strong opinions on many subjects. No doubt many will feel surprised or offended by at least certain of her remarks. Hopefully, most also will feel moved by the intense satisfactions as well as pain of her involvement. I have tried to present the material in a responsible scholarly form, while simultaneously allowing Goldman to speak to the reader as directly as possible. At the same time, I have not sought to hide my own anarchist perspective and hope that in doing so the overall purpose, nature and readability of the book are much more consistent with Goldman's own intent.*

## Further Footnotes for Preface

1.  Beyond her own detailed autobiography, *Living My Life* (1931; rpt. N.Y.: Dover Publications, Inc., 1970), there are two book-length biographies of Emma Goldman in the English language. The best known, *Rebel in Paradise* by Richard Drinnon (Chicago: University of Chicago Press, 1961), devotes only one chapter out of thirty-three to her Spanish experience. The anthology of Goldman and Alexander Berkman letters which he and Anna Maria Drinnon edited more recently, *Nowhere at Home* (N.Y.: Schocken Books, 1975), reflects the same relative neglect. The second biography (addressed to a younger audience), *To the Barricades* by Alix Kates Shulman (N.Y.: Thomas Y. Crowell, 1971), gives slightly more attention (one out of twenty chapters), but in a relatively short book this is still frustratingly little. Likewise, Shulman's 398-page anthology of Goldman writings and speeches, *Red Emma Speaks* (N.Y.: Vintage Books, 1972), includes only one 11-page item on Spain. In contrast is the more recent Spanish-language biography by veteran anarchist militant and writer José Peirats, *Emma Goldman: Anarquista de ambos mundos* (Madrid: Campo Abierto Edi-

ciones, 1978). A full one-third of the book concerns Goldman's experience with Spain, however the work is not yet available in translation. Finally, there is one academic article by Robert W. Kern which devotes its entirety to the subject of Goldman and Spain ("Anarchist Principles and Spanish Reality: Emma Goldman As A Participant in the Civil War, 1936-39," *Journal of Contemporary History*, vol. 11, no.'s 2-3 [July 1976]). While providing welcome recognition of the significance of this phase of Goldman's life, unfortunately this article is marred by highly questionable interpretations and faulty scholarship.

4.  Following the fascist victory in 1939, Goldman strongly considered writing either a third volume of her autobiography (from 1928 on) or a new book devoted entirely to the Spanish experience (Goldman 7/31/39 letter to Angelica Balabanoff, NYU; Goldman 1/9/39 letter to Harry Weinberger, YAL; Goldman 9/12/39 letter to Liza [Koldofsky], NYPL; Goldman 10/7/39 and 11/20/39 letters to Herbert Read, NYU; Goldman 8/4/39 letter to Rudolf and Milly Rocker, AMS-R). Actually Goldman had considered as early as 1932 writing a whole book on rapidly changing Spanish politics and the anarchist movement in that country (Goldman 9/16/32 letter to Max Nettlau, AMS-G). The present work's heavy reliance on Goldman's personal correspondence follows consistently the method she used in preparing her own autobiography. While no doubt for the work on Spain she would have polished and edited her statements, she believed that "at no time does one reveal oneself so much as in one's intimate correspondence" (*Living My Life*, vol. I, p. vi; henceforth references to her autobiography will use the abbreviation of *LL*).

# CHRONOLOGY OF LEADING EVENTS

## 1936

| Spanish anarchists | Spanish politics and civil war | International context | Emma Goldman |
|---|---|---|---|
| | **February**<br>Left coalition wins elections, takes office | | |
| | | **March**<br>Germany occupies the Rhineland | |
| **May**<br>Saragossa congress of CNT | | **May**<br>Italy completes occupation of Ethiopia | |
| | | | **June**<br>Death of close comrade Alexander Berkman |
| **July**<br>Anarchists have leading role in blocking success of uprising<br>Formation of anarchist militia under Durruti and others<br>Anarchists lead collectivization effort, especially in Catalonia, Aragón and the Levante<br>FAI and CNT leaders decide to collaborate on new local and regional revolutionary coordination bodies for the economy and military effort | **July**<br>Rightist uprising met by massive popular resistance<br>Anti-fascist militia organized, move to front lines to confront Nationalist military<br>Collectivization of large sectors of economy in republican Spain by workers and peasants | **July**<br>German and Italian planes sent to Rightist insurgents, soon massive aid<br>France bans arms for Spain, initiates concept of "nonintervention" | |
| **August**<br>Catalonia region CNT agrees to eventually enter relaunched Catalan regional government | **August**<br>Nationalists launch first massive operational campaign<br>Spanish Communist party, under Comintern orders, states opposition to social revolution | **August**<br>Britain and France organize European "big power" adherence to "nonintervention"<br>Germany and Italy continue massive aid, despite pledge<br>First Soviet pressures on Spanish republican government | **August**<br>Invitation to come to Spain to assist in foreign propaganda |
| **September**<br>CNT national plenum chooses to join national government, recommends single military administration and obligatory military service<br>Catalan anarchists join Catalan regional government | **September**<br>Irún, San Sebastién and Toledo fall to fascists, attention focuses on expected massive attack on Madrid<br>Caballero government formed, choice made to pursue "democratic respectability" over revolution<br>Catalan government reorganizes, now supercedes revolutionary antifascist militia central committee | **September**<br>Execution of Zinoviev and Kamenev in Soviet Union<br>Soviet decision to become actively involved in Spain; first export of arms and cadres | **September**<br>Enters revolutionary Spain; begins observation tours, propaganda work |
| **October**<br>CNT-FAI in Catalonia signs pact with UGT-PSUC agreeing to coordination of collectivized sector by Catalan government | **October**<br>Local revolutionary committees in Catalonia replaced by municipal councils<br>Decree militarizing militia, incorporating into new "Popular Army"; only reorganized units will get arms<br>Fall of Madrid outer defense line | | |
| **November**<br>Anarchists join national government, head four ministries<br>New national committee of CNT formed, opposes traditional federalist working principles<br>Majority in Catalan anarchist youth congress oppose joining collaborative front with non-anarchist organizations<br>Anarchist leader Buenaventura Durruti killed in Madrid, massive demonstrations | **November**<br>National government leaves Madrid for Valencia<br>Intense battle of Madrid begins | **November**<br>Comintern-organized International Brigades arrive, join in defense of Madrid<br>Large amounts of Soviet arms now arrived<br>Germany and Italy officially recognize Franco's Nationalist regime | |
| | **December**<br>Communists force reorganization of Catalan government, with new power of Communists over police and supplies, elimination of POUM from government | **December**<br>*Pravda* favors purge of Spanish anarchists and "Trotskyists" as in Russia | **December**<br>Leaves Spain for London to begin propaganda and fundraising work as CNT–FAI representative |

# 1937

| | | | |
|---|---|---|---|
| | **February**<br>Communists begin political campaign against Largo Caballero because of his refusal to follow their advice<br>Fall of Málaga on southern coast | | |
| **March**<br>Opposition to collaboration becomes more visible in anarchist ranks, as with "Friends of Durruti" group in Barcelona<br>Last anarchist militia unit (the "Iron Column") accepts militarization officially | **March**<br>Battle of Guadalajara ends with first major anti-fascist victory | | |
| **April**<br>Violent Communist attacks on certain anarchists in Catalonia | **April**<br>Scandal of Communist secret police prisons becomes public<br>Caballero begins action against Communists in police and army | | |
| **May**<br>Anarchist leaders urge Barcelona anarchist street militants to lay down arms, though many of latter ready for decisive battle with their anti-fascist "allies"<br>CNT remains in new Catalan government<br>CNT national meeting votes against participation in new Negrín government<br>Catalan anarchist youth organization returns to traditional principles, opposing collaboration and compromise | **May**<br>Violent confrontation for several days in Barcelona (and elsewhere in Catalonia): Catalan government troops (under Communist and Republican orders) vs. anarchists and POUMistas; central government intervenes with troops<br>Communists, with Socialist and Republican allies, force fall of Caballero government, replacing him with Negrín<br>Negrín government seeks negotiation of truce with Nationalists<br>Beginning of government imposed censorship on critical political discussion; POUM paper suspended | | |
| | **June**<br>Government launches repression of POUM leaders, opens door to widespread arrests of revolutionaries<br>Fall of Bilbao on the northern coast | | |
| **July**<br>Ex-minister Montseny publicly attacks government repression and Moscow tyranny | | **July**<br>European powers completely abandon partial 1½ month effort to control outside intervention at Spanish borders | |
| **August**<br>National government dissolves anarchist Council of Aragón; sends troops to crush peasant collectives, give land to private owners, repress the anarchists | | | |
| **September**<br>Aragón CNT has new congress, relaunches the collectives | | | **September**<br>Arrives for second visit to revolutionary Spain, begins new round of visits throughout the republican sector |
| | **October**<br>Fall of Gijón and the Asturias to the Nationalists, giving them full control of the North<br>Transfer of national government to Barcelona | | |
| | **November**<br>New wave of anti-collectivist repression in Aragón, following the harvest | **November**<br>British government decides for *de facto* recognition of Franco regime | **November**<br>Returns again to London to continue former activities and launch London branch of SIA |
| **December**<br>Aragón peasant collectives relaunch activity after second wave of repression<br>Anarchist forces important element in the Teruel campaign | **December**<br>Republican forces capture Teruel, first and only important town taken from the Nationalists | | **December**<br>Participates in Paris congress of IWMA, at CNT request |

# 1938

**January**
CNT national economic plenum, demonstration of greater organizational centralization

**February**
Teruel recaptured by the Nationalists

**March**
CNT approves pact for unified program with the UGT, reformist and centralist in nature
Opposition mounts within the CNT and especially the FAI, as a favorable civil war outcome increasingly in doubt

**March**
Nationalist offensive rapidly overruns Aragón, parts of Catalonia and the Levante; first major collapse of a republican front

**March**
Nazi Germany takes over Austria; European climate moves toward war

**April**
Nationalist forces reach the ocean, dividing republican Spain into separate northeast and central zones
Negrín issues a 13-point program, basically seeking to restore pre-civil war society

**May**
CNT representative takes a ministry in Negrín government
Open split between CNT and FAI on Negrín program

**July**
Nationalists begin offensive in the Levante; Republican forces launch Ebro counteroffensive

**July**
Soviet Union indicates plans to remove its involvement in Spain

**August**
Decree for centralized state control over collectivized industrial units

**September**
Munich agreement gives free hand to Hitler in Czechoslovakia, indicates willingness of France and Britain to abandon other nations to fascism

**September**
Returns to Spain for final visit

**October**
National CNT-FAI meeting shows sharp divisions on collaboration and compromise

**October**
Opening of trial against POUM leaders

**October**
Attends POUM trial and CNT-FAI national meeting

**November**
End of battle of the Ebro, Valencia saved but republican forces exhausted

**November**
Returns to London

**December**
Nationalist offensive against Catalonia begins

# 1939

<table>
<tr>
<td>

**March**
Anarchist forces in the Madrid sector heavily involved in the coup against Negrín

</td>
<td>

**January**
Barcelona abandoned to Nationalist takeover

**February**
Nationalists complete takeover of Catalonia; mass of refugees flees to France

**March**
Negrín returns from France to central zone, appoints Communist military leaders
Coup against Negrín regime and Communists in Madrid, formation of National Council of Defense
Nationalist troops enter Madrid
General offensive by the Nationalists toward the sea; desperate evacuation efforts by republican forces

**April**
Fascist forces complete takeover of Spain

</td>
<td>

**March**
Nazi occupation of Czechoslovakia

</td>
<td>

**March**
Visits Paris to see Spanish anarchist refugees

**April**
Departs for Canada
Beginning of efforts there on behalf of Spanish refugees

</td>
</tr>
<tr>
<td></td>
<td></td>
<td>

**August**
Soviet pact with Nazi Germany

**September**
Germany and Russia invade and occupy Poland; Britain and France declare war on Germany

**November**
Russia invades Finland

</td>
<td>

**August**
50th anniversary of entering anarchist ranks

**October**
Begins efforts to save four Italian anarchists from political repression in Canada

</td>
</tr>
</table>

# 1940

**May**
Goldman has second stroke, dies in Toronto at age 70

# Introduction:

# Emma Goldman's Life and Involvement with Spain

*Those acquainted with Emma Goldman's life know that she was one of the most influential and self-revealing radical activists in the United States over the past one hundred years. For those not yet introduced to this woman, the first part of this introductory chapter provides a brief sketch of major events and forces in her life. Hopefully, the rest of this book will motivate such readers to pursue further the detailed lengthier descriptions already published.[1] Goldman's autobiography,* Living My Life, *provides an excellent description of anti-authoritarian politics and life-style, far more insightful than the usual outsider's account of radical history. Beyond the synopsis of her life offered below, the remainder of this chapter outlines the particular relationship between Goldman and Spain – throughout her years of political activism as well as during the Spanish revolution itself.*

*Emma Goldman was born in 1869 in Kovno (now Kaunas), Lithuania, part of the Russian Empire. Her mother's third daughter, she was the first child of a second marriage, her parents a Jewish couple soon to be innkeepers in the Baltic town of Popelan. Here and in the several other locales she moved to in her childhood, the roots for Goldman's radicalism appeared at an early age. Among contributing scars to her youthful consciousness were a tyrannical, physically abusive father, her parents' harsh treatment of inn-servants and maids, oppression of the local peasantry by state officials, bias and violent threats toward Jews, and the stifling authoritarianism of grade school. As a child, she already rebelled against immediate oppression in her family and school, stubbornly resisting as well the retaliations which followed. By her early teens, she read about and secretly admired the models of young Russian*

---

1. See references to several biographies of Goldman in footnote 1 of the Preface.

1

revolutionists, such as portrayed in Chernyshevsky's book, What Is To Be Done? By age sixteen, she had worked in glove and corset factories in St. Petersburg already for several years and had her first sexual relationship as well. Both experiences merely repeated for her the male authoritarianism and physical abuse endured earlier in other settings.

Longing to escape this stifling personal, economic and political atmosphere, Goldman – like many others – looked to America as a land of potential rebirth. Emigrating there with her sister in early 1886, she went immediately to Rochester, New York, where their oldest sister already was settled and married. Like other immigrants, she rapidly discovered the reality behind the glowing facade. Among other things, discipline in her garment factory job here even excelled that in St. Petersburg. Added to this, her own parents and younger brothers soon themselves also crossed the ocean, joining the three sisters in Rochester. Once again, Emma felt herself suffocating in the tight confines of the tense family enclosure. Desperate to escape, she married an immigrant fellow worker. Yet the two of them continued to live in the same house with her parents and her husband proved to be sexually impotent.

During this time, Goldman began reading newspaper accounts and attending public lectures on the socialist movement in the United States. Especially engrossing were details on the Chicago Haymarket bombing and the arrest and trial of eight anarchist activists in its wake.[2] Like many others at the time, she grew increasingly convinced of their innocence and the cruelty of the state and economic interests in pursuing their lives. With the climactic injustice of four executions, Emma Goldman was enraged. Confronting the nobility of the ideal these men represented against the tragic farce of her own daily existence, she welded together her personal and political frustration and anger in a solidified whole never to be broken. She soon took the radical steps of moving on her own to New Haven and later New York, abandoning her marriage and parents as well as a life of docile political conformity.

In New York by late 1889, Goldman had involved herself in regular anarchist discussion groups, meetings and demonstrations, associating especially with veteran activist, German immigrant Johann Most and the younger devoted Russian immigrant, Alexander Berkman.[3] Complementing her immersion in political activism were the first of many love relationships in her life – with Johann Most and with her communal living partners Berkman and his artist cousin Fedya.

Despite the personal satisfactions of shared daily lives and activism, she and her comrades soon began dreaming of return to Russia, where their own language and national background promised more effective conspiratorial activity. However, 1892 brought a major, well-publicized strike in

2. See footnote 2 at back of chapter.
3. See footnote 3 at back of chapter.

*Homestead, Pennsylvania against America's foremost steel magnate Andrew Carnegie.*[4] *With this event, Goldman and the others refocused their attention on revolutionary possibilities closer to home. When management's "dialogue" with steelworkers took the form of bloody repression, Goldman, Berkman and Fedya became furious. Determined to waste no time, the three boldly decided to attack the symbol and direct cause of this action, Carnegie's Homestead manager Henry Clay Frick. By so doing, they hoped to reinspire the steelworkers with a new spirit of resistance, a new determination to accept no compromise. Given the obvious atmosphere of labor unrest generally, the defiant will of the steelworkers, in turn, could hopefully precipitate a general revolution.*[5]

*With barely enough travelling funds even for one of their group, Berkman volunteered himself for the assassination mission, a task he never hoped personally to survive. On July 23, 1892, Berkman entered Frick's downtown Pittsburgh office and severely wounded but failed to kill his target. Berkman himself was quickly railroaded through the court process with totally inadequate defense and with no opportunity to explain publicly the motive for his action. The result was a devastating twenty-two year prison sentence.*[6] *In turn, Emma Goldman—eventually well-publicized as Berkman's comrade and lover[7]—became a nationally notorious focus of the capitalist press. As an arch-symbol of "diabolical foreign anarchism" and of radicalism in general, she was only too convenient a target for the ruling elite's efforts once again to frighten a politically-unsophisticated public.*

*For Goldman, the rapid events of Pittsburgh, the negative reaction of the public as well as by some anarchist comrades, and the prospective separation from her closest lover and comrade by an endless prison term were severe jolts to her consciousness. Her confident sense of appropriate political tactics was directly challenged. Homestead workers and the working class generally disbelieved, if they were not openly hostile to, the supportive intent of the attempted assassination. When even Johann Most, the mentor of Berkman and Goldman, mockingly denounced the action, Goldman reacted with a deep suspicion and antagonism toward all elites in the movement.*[8] *In turn, facing the long ordeal of separation and her comrade's personal suffering behind walls, Goldman was forced to new levels of independent maturity, personal*

4. See footnote 4 at back of chapter.
5. *LL*, I, 85-88; Berkman, pp. 4-7.
6. Goldman and Berkman both had expected a maximum sentence of seven years, based on the state law for attempted murder. This was a long period, no doubt, but they could at least hope for Berkman's survival. Instead, the prosecution presented a total of six indictments for this single action, thereby permitting the judge to impose sequential maximum penalties for each, amounting to twenty-two years. (*LL*, I, 103, 106-09.)
7. It was never proven by the authorities, however, that Goldman had conspired with Berkman about the assassination attempt.
8. See footnote 8 at back of chapter.

*and political assertiveness, and steel-willed endurance—quite beyond the ardent rebelliousness she already had shown.*

*Goldman thus emerged during the next several years as a well-known activist speaker and organizer in a variety of radical campaigns. Within only a few months, this new phase of New York-based activism culminated in her arrest for a fiery speech at a Union Square mass demonstration for the unemployed. In October 1893, she was sentenced to one year of imprisonment at Blackwell's Island. As was true for Berkman and everyone else behind bars, the intense oppressive conditions of prison were a direct test of her own personal strength.* [9] *But at the same time, Goldman now had space to reflect far more carefully on the past and future course of her own politics. Two elements especially in this setting consciously influenced her subsequent direction. In her own words, she was brought close "to the depths and complexities of the human soul" through the warm female comradeship of so many of her fellow prisoners—however tangled, inconsistent and apolitical their perspectives. At the same time, she was surprised by the liberal impulses of certain individuals on the staff, equally so by those of an unexpected concerned visitor John Swinton, past abolitionist activist and now editor-in-chief of the* New York Sun. *With Goldman's sensitive, constantly evolving, empathetic personality, both new types of encounter led her after prison to new assessments of political possibility.*

*Following her release, Goldman again flew into a whirlwind of political activism, as unrepentant as ever. Nevertheless, combining her prison-gained infirmary skills and social insights, she now also began a new practical pursuit as a private nurse. Soon realizing the importance of formal training for additional skills and of certification for better employment, she accepted her friend Fedya's offer to subsidize her travel and expenses for studies in Vienna. Still as much the anarchist as ever, however, before her arrival there in the Fall of 1895 she spent a month in Britain personally meeting local activists as well as several of the most influential figures of the international movement—Errico Malatesta, Louise Michel, and Peter Kropotkin.* [10] *In turn, the year in Vienna gave her not only advanced training for nursing and midwifery, but exciting exposure as well to the psycho-sexual theories of Sigmund Freud (she attended his lectures) and the new wave of iconoclastic European literature, including Nietzsche, Ibsen and Hauptmann.*

*Back in New York the following summer, Goldman resumed her activism in the context of a revived American movement. At the same time, she began practice as a professional nurse and midwife. By the following year, she embarked on a political lecture trip to the midwest, soon followed by a similar*

9.  Her account of these conditions is in *LL*, I, ch. 12.
10. See footnote 10 at back of chapter.

*cross-country tour, the first of many to follow. Opposing America's war with Spain, constantly supporting local labor struggles, advocating full equality for women and sexual emancipation generally—these were her main themes of concern as she visited one city after another, helping to re-energize and inspire the various local movements.*

*In 1899, while she was on tour in Detroit, friends of the movement there offered Goldman the chance to pursue advanced studies in medicine. As a youth she had aspired to be a doctor, but a grade-school religion teacher refused to pass on this rebellious student to the next level, thus denying her the potential opportunity. Now with nursing experience and a promise for five years of study support in Switzerland, she relaunched her professional aspirations. Travelling to Europe in late 1899, she was just in time to join a series of anti-war meetings denouncing British policy in South Africa. From Britain she went on to Paris where she acquainted herself with the French movement and participated in preparations for an international anarchist congress. Now, however, being informed of her political involvements en route to Switzerland, her "fellowship" sources from Detroit refused to continue support unless she promised to withdraw from further activism. For Goldman this was unthinkable, for years having seen the personal and political as one. Refusing outside constrictions on her own life, Goldman abandoned her plans of study. She made the best of her last days in Paris, however, through attending a tiny Neo-Malthusian meeting to discuss the new subversive topic of artificial birth control. Given her own first-hand exposure as a nurse and midwife to the agonies of unwanted pregnancies, as well as her general commitment to women's and sexual emancipation, she here first became determined to launch a birth-control campaign in the United States.*

*Such plans were delayed, however, because of a new unanticipated political context. Her several months of resumed anarchist lectures in this country came to an abrupt halt with the 1901 assassination of President McKinley and the vicious repressive atmosphere which followed. The assassin, Leon Czolgosz, was a working-class youth recently attracted to radical politics after bitter experiences growing up in an immigrant family in Cleveland. Moving quickly through disillusioning episodes with several socialist organizations in that city, he then exposed himself to the anarchist message, reading literature and personally attending a speech by Goldman on one of her tours. While calling himself an anarchist after his arrest, by no means had he had time to immerse himself deeply in anarchist thought or in comradeship within the movement. Nevertheless, Goldman saw in him the anguished personal rebel of her own life a decade before. Alongside French, Spanish and Italian emigré groups, and a small number of native-born American anarchists, Goldman was among the few anarchists in this country publicly to appeal for understanding of his background and motives (without, however, endorsing the political tactic he employed). Already denounced by*

*bloodthirsty politicians and the media as a prominent scapegoat in the case,*[11] *Goldman took a personally dangerous stance indeed. Yet what disturbed her most during these traumatic weeks was not the hostility of the authorities. This she had felt and defied before. Instead, she despaired at her isolation by many anarchist comrades, who were scared by her statements on behalf of Czolgosz or who openly attacked her and Czolgosz both. Again, now more than ever, she thus determined to pursue her own political path, regardless of any organizational or peer influence.*

*By 1906, she launched a new base of activity, one which proved more enduring and no doubt more influential than in the past. With a handful of collaborators in New York, she created a lively and unusually regular anarchist periodical called* Mother Earth. *Over the next decade, Goldman communicated here on a wide variety of current and general issues to an audience approaching 10,000 readers.*[12] Mother Earth *was the most influential anarchist periodical in the United States of its era, and perhaps at any time to the present. Beyond this, Goldman used her strong base in New York to launch a variety of other movement endeavors – ranging from political demonstrations and organization of a free school*[13] *to eventually forming the No-Conscription League in 1917. In the meantime, her constant travels and journalism encouraged many others throughout the country to take similar local action as well.*

*In the midst of all this, Goldman developed in 1908 a passionate and controversial relationship with iconoclast but non-anarchist Ben Reitman of Chicago, a stormy involvement which energized her personally but which alienated many movement comrades from her side.*[14] *With Reitman as a*

---

11. The viciousness of public attacks on Goldman was so great, quite possibly she also would have been executed in New York state had Illinois authorities granted her extradition. See Goldman's account of a later encounter with one member of the Buffalo prosecution team as one verification of that danger (*LL*,II, 559).

12. Drinnon, *Rebel in Paradise* (N.Y.: Bantam Books, 1973, paperback edition), p. 120. The entire collection of *Mother Earth* (1906-18) was reprinted in a single volume by Greenwood Reprint Corporation (N.Y.) in 1968. Some of the best of Goldman's own lectures, several of which had been reprinted in *Mother Earth*, were issued together in two editions of *Anarchism and Other Essays* by the Mother Earth publishing collective itself in 1910 and 1917. A reprint of the 1917 edition was published by Dover Publications, Inc. (N.Y.) in 1969. Seven more of her essays from *Mother Earth* appeared for the first time in book form in Shulman's anthology, *Red Emma Speaks*.

13. See footnote 13 at back of chapter.

14. Numerous were the movement individuals, including Berkman himself, who perceived this relationship as detracting from Goldman's potential activist energy and from Goldman's potential appeal because of Reitman's eccentric, crude and inconsistent behavior. The latter was seen not simply as a matter of personal taste, but as casting a bad light on the movement itself – as when Reitman at one point taught a Sunday School class in the *Mother Earth* office or chose to pocket some of the proceeds from her lectures. Though Goldman herself was extremely aware of such traits, she persisted with Reitman for so long precisely because of his intense emotional spontaneity as well as his definite talents as a road manager capable of organizing highly successful speaking tours. Indeed she regarded him as the first major lover in her life to truly value *both* the personal relationship and her movement activity with equal and simultaneous intensity. (*LL*, I, 421-23, 432-36.) For more detailed and interesting insights on this relationship, see Alice Wexler, "Emma Goldman in Love," *Raritan Quarterly Review*, Spring 1982, pp. 116-45.

*travelling manager to assist her during the next several years, Goldman par-*
*ticipated in the wave of local "free speech" campaigns precipitated by IWW*
*organizing efforts[15] and finally complemented her years of endorsing birth*
*control with promotion now of specific contraceptive methods.*

*The intensity of this period was enormous. For Goldman, as for many in the*
*movement in recent times, it was indeed this constant multi-dimensional*
*activism which gave her the greatest satisfaction yet. At the same time, the*
*dangers she faced should not be minimized. Arrested on numerous occasions,*
*almost lynched in San Diego in 1912 for her "free speech" efforts (Reitman was*
*kidnapped, beaten, tarred and tortured), she was indeed imprisoned in New*
*York for two weeks for providing birth control information in 1916.[16] Along*
*with Berkman,[17] she was the best known anarchist activist in this country at*
*the time and certainly one of the most famous radicals in general. As such, she*
*was subject to all the harassment and violent threats by government, the*
*capitalist press, and hostile individuals which such a role always brings in its*
*wake.*

*These intense years of activism culminated with the deepening crisis of*
*World War I and American moves toward entering the conflict. Strongly*
*rooted in anarchist traditions of internationalism and anti-militarism, both*
*Goldman and Berkman focused their significant prestige and skills on the*
*issue in 1917. Forming a No-Conscription League in New York which quickly*
*spread to other parts of the country, these two and several close anarchist and*
*liberal collaborators began a series of mass rallies and publicity campaigns*
*rapidly influencing directly or indirectly hundreds of thousands of Americans.*
*Negatively, the same campaign brought a final burst of governmental repres-*
*sion. On June 15, U.S. marshals raided the offices of Mother Earth and Blast*
*(Berkman's periodical); Goldman and Berkman were arrested for "conspiracy*
*against the draft." After a trial of one and a half weeks in which the two offered*
*their own eloquent defense,[18] each was found guilty, sentenced to prison for*
*two years and fined $10,000.*

*For Berkman, the harsh conditions of the Atlanta federal penitentiary after*
*fourteen earlier years behind walls were a blow to his health from which he*
*would never fully rebound. For Goldman, 21 months at the women's prison in*
*Jefferson City, Missouri, was a difficult sentence but not as severe. Among her*
*best friends there was Kate O'Hare, an active Socialist militant convicted*
*under the Espionage Law. With her and with many apolitical inmates,*

15. See footnote 15 at back of chapter.
16. See footnote 16 at back of chapter.
17. See footnote 17 at back of chapter.
18. Their brilliant effort to expose the sham of judicial process and to communicate their anarchist
    beliefs is described in *LL*, II, 615-23. Goldman's own eloquent concluding address to the jury
    was printed subsequently in pamphlet form by her comrades in the *Mother Earth* group. It is
    reproduced in Shulman, ed., *Red Emma Speaks*.

*Goldman found the commonly-endured oppression of prison a catalyst for warm communication, whatever their differences in the political realm.*

*It was during this confinement that revolutionary developments came to a climax in Russia. Already Goldman was enthralled by news of the initial upheaval there in early 1917. In prison, her spirits were all the more strengthened with any report on the revolution's continued survival and spread.[19] Indeed, it was during this time that she and Berkman both resolved to return to their native Russia (as had many anarchists in the United States and elsewhere), once released from prison. Unknown to them both, however, the federal government already prepared to remove that decision from their own realm of choice. As each finally emerged from their terms in September 1919, they were ordered to post bond by immigration authorities, pending the outcome of deportation hearings. As expected, the government ruled against them, scheduling their forced exile (with some 250 other radicals) for December 21, 1919. By late January, after a perilous four-week journey through stormy waters of the Atlantic and the North Sea in a barely reconditioned small boat,[20] Goldman and Berkman found themselves on their old native soil—now greeted at the border in the name of the new revolutionary regime.*

*I describe in more detail their subsequent experience in Russia in the introductions to Chapters Five and Nine below. Most important was the fact that both Goldman and Berkman arrived full of enthusiasm for their first direct exposure to a genuine revolutionary context. Unprejudiced, even good-willed toward the Bolsheviks,[21] they were quickly challenged by certain Russian anarchists to open their eyes to the rebirth of a new massive and oppressive state machine. Insisting on investigating and judging for themselves as always, Goldman and Berkman observed the new society through countless interviews with workers and militants (including Lenin, Trotsky and Zinoviev), daily street scenes, and encounters with the bureaucracy of Moscow and St. Petersburg. In addition, they travelled as far south as Odessa and as far east as Kiev. Increasingly disenchanted, they nevertheless hesitated to criticize openly the new regime while it was still under siege by domestic and foreign reaction. Only with the Soviet government's repression of the insurgent revolutionary Kronstadt commune in Spring 1921[22] did both of them decide to speak out. To do so publicly, however, even at that early date, meant risking imprisonment by the secret police, if not their very lives. After tense lengthy*

---

19. From prison at this time, Goldman wrote that she was confined only physically. Her thoughts and dreams were of the revolutions in Russia, Germany and Hungary—only these kept her alive (5/27/19 letter to "My dear, dear comrade" [probably Van Valkenburgh], UML).

20. Astonishing testimony to their effectiveness as organizers was the fact that crew members and soldier-guards on the *Buford* eventually offered to side with the prisoners in a mutiny and sail to Russia on their own (*LL*, II, 722).

21. See footnote 21 at back of chapter.

22. See footnote 22 at back of chapter.

*delays by the authorities, by the end of 1921, Goldman and her lifelong comrade again left their native land. This time, they brought with them the bitter taste of betrayed revolution, a taste they would never forget.*

*The ensuing fifteen years of forced exile were the bleakest period in Goldman's adult life. Residing first in Germany, she there observed at close hand the building of a new anarchist movement. Yet to her frustration, merely to keep her visa, she had to avoid any direct involvement of her own. After a year's stay in Britain, in 1924-25, desperate to protect her autonomy in the future, she accepted the generous marriage offer of an elderly Welshman, a longtime anarchist comrade and admirer. Enduring the official process so as to acquire British citizenship,[23] she at last had a reasonably secure home base and a passport for travel.*

*Unfortunately, Britain was not at all to her liking. British coldness to her politics — with her caustic and exhuberant direct speaking style and her continued public denunciation of the Soviet regime — was matched by Britain's increasingly unbearable winter weather. Following her Canadian visit in 1926-28, her brother and friends in North America helped her to obtain a small cottage at St. Tropez in southern France. There she worked until early 1931 painfully writing her autobiography, though constantly encouraged in the task by regular contact with Berkman who lived a still-harassed exile[24] in nearby Nice. Completing her book,* Living My Life, *she spent a good part of the next several years in seasonal migration from London to St. Tropez and back again, though also engaging in lecture tours of the continent and North America (including the United States for a frustratingly-brief 90 days in 1934).*

*Despite an endless stream of letters, articles and speeches which might have satisfied the energies of many others, for Goldman, lacking a clear enthusiastic locale for direct activism was unbearable. Indeed, her personal sense of isolation reflected the equally intolerable political context generally — with the growing mass popularity of authoritarian movements on the right and left both. In such a vacuum she suffocated, yet the strength of her ideal, her endless correspondence and her periodic contact with Berkman gave her the motivation to persist. In June 1936, however, the latter support*

---

23. She married James Colton, a militant anarchist coalminer she first had met in Glasgow in 1895. In the mid-1920's, the Foreign Office was expelling Communists from Britain. Goldman knew that temporarily (though Communists themselves were pressuring for her also to be expelled) her own presence was being tolerated because of her public critique of Russia. Her bad feelings about this tacit rationale and her sense that it depended also on her remaining uncritical of British politics caused her to accept marriage to gain her papers (Goldman 4/20/25 letter to Roger Baldwin, NYPL; Goldman 6/30/25 letter to Stella Ballantine, NYPL; *LL*, II, 973). Colton himself died in 1936.
24. According to Goldman, Berkman had to spend days every three months and a fortune in bribes to keep his French visa; even then, the outcome often remained doubtful to the final moment (3/17/39 letter to Rudolf Rocker, AMS-R).

*disappeared when Berkman took his own life after lengthy depression over his own pained exile and illness. For Goldman, the world had stopped. Only mechanically did she communicate with comrades in the United States and attempt to find a new home for Berkman's companion. Three weeks later full-scale revolution began in Spain.*

II

*July 1936 was not the first time Emma Goldman took notice of anarchism in Spain. More than thirty years before her own first brief trip there in 1928-29, she already had learned much about the conditions of that country, its people and the revolutionary movement.*

*Since the late 1860's, anarchist ideology and organizing flourished as much in Spain as in any other country in the world.*[25] *Political developments there gained frequent coverage in the North American movement press. In addition, both severe impoverishment and governmental repression caused significant Spanish emigration to the Americas well into the 20th century. Thus, a growing Spanish emigré community of comrades in the northeastern United States gave Goldman and other activists a direct sense of communication with Spain. Of equal significance, as a nurse and midwife on the East side of New York City, Goldman because acquainted with numerous Spanish immigrant families on a personal basis as well.*

*By her own account, Goldman's first public movement activity related to events in Spain was a meeting she, Harry Kelly and several others organized in 1896,*[26] *responding to news of a new wave of shocking governmental repression. The Montjuich prison torture of several hundred leftists*[27] *was a political scandal to the whole progressive spectrum in Europe and the Americas. Though Goldman and the others feared an empty lecture hall, the meeting in New York attracted well over a thousand people. When it was Goldman's turn to speak, apparently one of the undercover police sought to provoke her into demanding an immediate act of violent revenge against local Spanish diplomats. Goldman refused the bait. She did state, however, that if she were in Spain itself she indeed would try to kill the head of government responsible. When several weeks later a young Italian anarchist Michele*

25. See footnote 25 at back of chapter.
26. See footnote 26 at back of chapter.
27. In an atmosphere and scenario similar to the earlier Haymarket events in Chicago, following a bomb explosion during a religious procession in Barcelona, over 400 trade-unionists and anti-clerics, including some anarchists, were arrested (by order of General Weyler, notorious two years later for his barbarous repression in Cuba) and subjected to severe tortures in Montjuich prison in an attempt to extract confessions. Several went insane and died. After such ordeals, nearly a quarter of the prisoners were still brought to trial in early 1897. Though none was proven involved in the bombing, five were executed and most of the rest imprisoned once again.

*Angiolillo in fact did assassinate Prime Minister Cánovas, Goldman was beseiged by reporters seeking to link her to the action. Goldman of course was not involved. However, what was significant was her ability to identify strongly with the emotions of the Spanish movement whatever her distance from that country. This same passionate empathy was to surface again dramatically forty years later.*

*Goldman continued over the years to communicate publicly her concern with developments in Spain. She spoke at meetings on the Spanish-American War, where she denounced United States and Spanish policies alike in favor of Cuban independence. Similarly, she wrote articles and spoke out when the Spanish government launched new political repression during and after the bloody "Tragic Week" of Barcelona in 1909.* [28] *In honor of this latter event's most famous victim, libertarian educator Francisco Ferrer, Goldman, Berkman, Kelly and several others in 1910 co-sponsored the New York founding of a "Ferrer Association" based on the principles Ferrer himself had encouraged in his own network of schools in Spain.* [29]

*A decade later, in Russia, Goldman met directly with representatives of the large Spanish anarcho-syndicalist union, the CNT,* [30] *at the time of the Red Trade Union International congresses of July 1920 and July 1921. She no doubt also had further CNT contacts in Berlin during the December 1922 launching there of the anarcho-syndicalist International (the IWMA).* [31] *During that early period of CNT strength and following its spectacular resurgence with the end of the dictatorship and monarchy in 1931, Goldman was indeed fascinated and impressed with the unprecedented influence of the Spanish movement. From her own base of exile, she followed its destiny especially through letters from Rudolf Rocker, Max Nettlau, Alexander Schapiro and others in the international movement with close ties to the Spanish comrades, as well as through anarchist periodicals and more detailed published accounts.* [32]

*Goldman herself visited Spain in December 1928-January 1929, though for only three weeks and mainly as a tourist break from her exhausting work on the autobiography.* [33] *Despite the political dictatorship in Spain at the time, Goldman did visit with the Urales family—Federico, his companion Soledad Gustavo, and their daughter Federica Montseny—all of them well-known anarchist propagandists, though Goldman observed no revolutionary momentum on a broader scale. Within two years, the monarchy collapsed.*

28. See footnote 28 at back of chapter.
29. See footnote 29 at back of chapter.
30. See footnote 30 at back of chapter.
31. See footnote 31 at back of chapter.
32. See footnote 32 at back of chapter.
33. Unmentioned in previous biographies of Goldman, this trip is described in some detail in her letter to a "Friend" (Joseph Ishill), 1/25/29, UML (a slightly different early version of the same letter, dated 1/20/29, is in the collection at Harvard).

*Spanish politics again was open to a wide range of contending forces, not the least of which were the anarchists. Despite their severe repression under the dictatorship,[34] the Spanish comrades rapidly reconstructed at all levels their national labor federation, the CNT. At the same time, many local anarchist affinity-group networks worked together as an increasingly influential regional and national force, the FAI.[35] By 1932, Goldman already was so impressed from reports of events in Spain, she described them as perhaps "revolutionary"[36] and wrote to several friends that she hoped to spend the winter there instead of in France. In Spain, she could be closer to the dramatic process of change and even possibly prepare a book. (Still hoping as late as April 1933 to make that visit, she eventually gave it up for lack of funds. These she had hoped to raise through a speaking tour in Germany. With Hitler's takeover there, such a plan obviously became impossible.) Despite her enthusiasm about Spain then and during the next several years, Goldman wrote in a skeptical vein as well. To a good extent this latter sentiment had its roots in her Russian experience. But also it reflected particular contradictions she saw in the Spanish situation. Not the least of these were the continued subservience of women, as well as what she perceived to be anarchist abstention from the 1934 Asturian uprising, yet early 1936 interest in elections.[37] Nevertheless, in the early 1930's, to the extent Goldman saw hope for significant liberatory politics anywhere, it was in Spain.[38]*

## III

*Responding to periods of mass quiescence or apparent apathy, many anarchists over the years tried to maintain bearings by emphasizing at least their own personal integrity—that is, by living an individual life-style most consistent with anarchist ideals. Frequently it was also a time devoted to writing, to articulating in print their powerful vision however small the immediate audience. With eventual crises of war, economic depression, or simply generational change, rebellious discontent always reappeared. Large*

---

34. Outlawed early by the Primo de Rivera regime, large numbers of *cenetistas* were imprisoned or forced into exile. In sharp contrast was the experience of the reformist socialist UGT (Unión General de Trabajadores, General Union of Workers), which chose to collaborate with the Primo regime. Its leader Francisco Largo Caballero, so prominent later in the first year of the Spanish civil war, even became councillor of state in the government.
35. See footnote 35 at back of chapter.
36. See footnote 36 at back of chapter.
37. These three issues and Goldman's attitude toward them are explored in Chapters IV and VIII below.
38. It also should be noted that Goldman herself was well-known by this time among many Spanish anarchists as an influential writer. Cheap pamphlets of her translated essays had been issued by the Spanish anarchist press in the 1920's and 1930's, including writings on Russia, marriage and love, prostitution, and the liberated woman.

*numbers again consciously sought emancipatory alternatives. In these periods it was common for the same previously-uncompromising anarchists now enthusiastically to embrace activist political positions somewhere between their own traditional ideals and the unsophisticated mass consciousness.*[39] *After a decade or more of social isolation, if not direct repression, one naturally feels tempted to leap toward those signs of emerging new interest in one's ideas and ideals. To retreat at least slightly from one's past statements of position often is seen necessary to connect with and strengthen the perceived general libertarian impulse, however contradictory this latter may appear. Temptation is all the greater when the emerging movement is attacked by capitalist employers and the state. Finally, one may be that much more willing to compromise temporarily if one has confidence in the basic purity and strength of one's ideals. Indeed, sooner or later, as society again retreats from this period of emerging mass libertarianism, the same anarchists often themselves return to their original position; that is, through their life-styles and through their writings or other creative endeavor, they seek to maintain the clarity of their traditional vision.*

*In my view, this general pattern characterized probably the majority of anarchist militants and groups in the historical movement.*[40] *Furthermore, the same cycle no doubt applies all the more to other political activists and groups throughout the entire progressive spectrum.*[41] *It seems relatively easy to forego* certain *aspects of one's political vision, if all the rest seems close at hand or at least apparently on the way. What distinguishes anarchists from others is their unusual sensitivity precisely to the essential interrelationship of the several liberation goals, to that potential corruption of ends by the means, to the dangers of compromise. Whether compromise or change in one's strategy and tactics is seen as betrayal or as evolving wisdom is of course a debate which has wracked the movement continuously over the years. It is certainly a central theme of this book.*[42]

*For Emma Goldman, not only does the above pattern describe zig-zags in her own evolution over the decades as an anarchist, it also clarifies significantly her particular three years of changes and ambivalence concerning the Spanish revolution. For Goldman in the late 1930's, this overall cycle was condensed into yearly occurrences instead of decades. Three times she*

39. Thus, one who defended the traditional anarchist position of avoiding hierarchical organization might be willing, during a period of great mass activism, to militate within a movement group or context violating that principle if it seemed that many could be won to the anarchist perspective or that at least drastic new levels of repression could be fought.
40. See footnote 40 at back of chapter.
41. For those involved in movement activities in recent years, it is easy to imagine or recall attempts to act "responsibly" to attract support among those viewed as less advanced in political consciousness.
42. See further elaboration on this issue especially in the discussions on movement organization, collaboration, violence and the role of women, in the introductions to Chapters II, IV, VII and VIII below.

*moved first from a more purist critical and isolated stance to a generally en-
thusiastic endorsement of the Spanish anarchists, then subsequently back
again to her original position. Each of these three cycles coincided directly
with Goldman's own geographical and psychological movement between
Britain and Spain. From the distance and isolation of cautious, barely recep-
tive Britain,[43] Goldman moved to the super-charged energy and mass participatory social experimentation of revolutionary Spain,[44] only to return once
again to the bleakness of London.*

*In reading Goldman's thoughts from this period, therefore, one should
remember not only the chronological context of events in Spain—though of
course this is essential—but also the particular geographical-psychological
location of the writer. Goldman never lost her essential core commitment to
anarchism. Yet contradictions do appear. To some extent these are inevitable
in any one individual's attempt to analyze the immediate unfolding of epochal
events. Beyond this factor though, Goldman's differing assessments of individuals, policies, the revolution and the movement as a whole reflect also
the cyclical pattern described above. As with a fine novelist, ironically this
shifting overall combination of distancing and immediacy in Goldman's
writings adds much to the richness of her perspective, to the fullness of her attempt to describe and analyze the Spanish events, to the poignancy of her own
agony in attempting to maintain an authentic centered perspective through it
all.*

*Goldman visited Spain on three occasions during the revolution and civil
war, each time for a period of two to three months. The first visit was from
September 17 to mid-December 1936, thus well within the stage of greatest
revolutionary enthusiasm and initiative. Yet, as her writings reflect below,
already contradiction's within the revolution were beginning to become quite
clear. By the time of her next visit one year later (September 16 through
November 6, 1937), most of these contradictions already had exploded—in
the process seriously draining much of the revolution's strength. By the time of
her final visit (mid-September through early November 1938), there was little
hope for defeating the fascists, let alone for salvaging the revolution.[45]*

*Before her initial trip in 1936, Goldman was in southern France, despair-
ingly picking up the pieces of an exile life left hopelessly bleak with the death of
her comrade Berkman. First news of the outbreak of civil war and revolution*

43. Though she was not physically in Britain at the beginning of the Spanish revolution,
psychologically she was still in its spell.
44. As she expressed to comrades Rudolf and Milly Rocker on the occasion of her third visit to
Spain during the war: "I have the same feeling about my visits here as the two previous years.
Spain is too fascinating even if terrible in some respects. One cannot escape its sway. Like a
grand passion it holds me tightly clasped in her arms" (9/27/39 letter, AMS-R).
45. She also visited Paris for several days in March 1939 specifically to see her Spanish comrades—now in forced exile—for the last time before her departure to Canada.

*clearly shocked her out of that growing sense of futility.*[46] *Within several weeks her sense of personal loss became dwarfed by the immensity and seriousness of revolutionary struggle in Spain. Despite earlier criticism of the Spanish comrades, as near as she was and prepared for this battle by her own lifetime of militancy, it was essential for Goldman to join their efforts. A longtime friend and comrade in the German anarchist movement soon provided her the concrete steps for doing so. Augustin Souchy, then helping to organize CNT-FAI international propaganda from Barcelona, invited her on behalf of the Spanish movement to come contribute to their struggle as soon as she could.*[47] *After several frustrating delays, by mid-September she was on her way.*

*Goldman's reactions to the Spanish scene from this time on are the subject of the remainder of the book. During each visit most of her time was spent travelling to different zones of republican Spain, observing constructive social efforts as well as the front lines, talking with anarchists and non-anarchists alike, and comparing notes with other observers like herself who were in touch with developments all across the country. Inevitably she was overwhelmed by enthusiastic efforts at grass-roots social transformation, the widespread dedicated attempts to move directly toward the new society despite the enormous tension and sacrifices of war. Of the tragic demands and costs of the latter, Goldman also was very much aware. Additionally there were constant attacks on anarchist efforts and the social revolution generally by statist allies in the Popular Front coalition—liberal Republicans, Socialists and Communists. The enormous deadly hostility toward the anarchists from many of their "friends" on the Loyalist side, from the fascist insurgents and from the various foreign powers internationally simply made Goldman that much more sympathetic toward and enthusiastic for their cause. Disturbing compromise steps of the movement's leadership seemed less significant to her than the strength of the movement below and the vicious attacks from all sides.*

*During each visit, she felt moved literally to stay by her Spanish comrades to the end, in whatever capacity and whatever the outcome. Accepting the fact that age prevented her from physically fighting at the front lines, she offered to help with international propaganda (which she did during her first visit), to serve as a nurse, a canteen worker, or a child-care aide, or to propagate birth-control and new methods of hygiene.*[48] *Each time, however, her own in-*

46. ". . . I rejoice in the fortitude of my own comrades, the Anarcho-Syndicalists and the Anarchists. Their courage, their heroism has kept me from utter despair in the sorrow that has come to me. If only my old chum had held out a little longer he would have gained strength to go on in the magnificent display of our Spanish comrades" (Goldman 7/31/36 letter to John Powys, NYPL). However she still felt quite numbed by Berkman's death and envisaged her return to Britain or Canada, not joining the revolution in Spain (Goldman 8/8/36 letter to Harry Kelly, NYPL).
47. See footnote 47 at back of chapter.
48. Goldman 11/18/36 letter to Stella Ballantine, NYPL; Goldman 12/5/36 letter to Harry Kelly, NYPL; Goldman 11/22/36 letter to Mark Mratchny, UML.

*adequacies with the Spanish language[49] and the arguments of the Spanish that her greatest contribution would be to help with propaganda abroad persuaded her reluctantly to end her stay.[50]*

*With energy and enthusiasm recharged, upon first leaving Spain and over the next several months Goldman launched forth a new wave of activity in Britain, from organizing support groups and fund-raising events to her own public lectures and articles.[51] During this initial stage fresh from Spain, she was generally much less critical than a few months later toward the Spanish anarchists and the course of the revolution. At the least, she believed it was important carefully to explain why the movement's leadership in good faith rationalized their compromises in the way they did. Eventually, however, each time she found herself shivering in the cold physical, social and psychological climate of Britain[52] (and Canada during the last year of her life from early 1939 on[53]), in the same exhausting relative political isolation as before. In this context, Goldman tended once again to revert to a more critical stance and to a pessimism over short-range revolutionary prospects which this perspective implied.*

*As her writings in the rest of the book well illustrate, throughout these stages Emma Goldman sought at all times to maintain a personal honesty and dignity, a dedication to discovering political truth as well as she could and then living by those findings. She certainly was not the last to observe her own changes, her fluctuating moods and analysis. What is so commendable was her willingness to acknowledge to others the uncertainties which eventually all of us in both political and personal life must accept, and then, despite this, to continue as before to bring all of that clear purpose and great energy which she possessed to her lifelong struggle for meaningful human liberation.*

## IV

*The next seven chapters in this book (Chs. 2-8) are each constructed around Goldman's own writings (in chronological order) on specific major*

49. As she described it, during her first trip she knew not even the rudiments of Spanish. Though she got by on her French and with the help of translators, this was not adequate for sustained work in Spain (Goldman 2/16/37 letter to Van Valkenburgh, AMS-G). She subsequently never had enough time to concentrate on acquiring this language skill, though by the time of her last visit in late 1938 she at least could follow some of the Spanish dialogue around her.
50. She apparently never was convinced that this would be her best course. But her feeling of solidarity with those Spanish comrades she was most in contact with caused her to accept their judgement.
51. A number of her efforts are described in her comments in Chapter VI.
52. See footnote 52 at back of chapter.
53. See footnote 53 at back of chapter.

*issues.* [54] *The introduction to each chapter summarizes her thoughts on the subject and places her stand in the contexts of both the historical anarchist movement and her own life as an activist. Such an arrangement has several advantages. It permits separate and thus more concentrated focus on the key dynamics of the Spanish revolution itself. It also allows readers to perceive clearly how Emma Goldman responded emotionally and analytically to these issues as each one developed over time, and to understand the roots of these responses out of her life in the anarchist movement. We can thus better comprehend Goldman's own life, the Spanish revolution, and the historical anarchist movement, all at the same time. Most especially, beyond such historical insights, this arrangement by* issues *encourages readers to apply principles and lessons from this experience to contemporary efforts at radical social change in North America, Spain or anywhere else.*

*Coming from a comrade experienced with a half-century of militant struggle, Goldman's running commentary on the Spanish events combines passionate involvement in the immediate moment with careful reflection from a perspective of long-gathered revolutionary wisdom. Because the issues faced are fundamentally similar to those in current discussion on movement goals, strategies and tactics, it is as if Goldman herself is now at our sides. Whatever our response to her analysis (and she would be the last to force it upon us), it is her strong commitment to honest re-examination of valued principles and movement relationships, even in the midst and indeed because of the rapidly developing upheaval in Spain, that makes her a very human and welcome comrade for those of us in the confusing complexity of presentday struggle.*

*Her enthusiasm for both the heroic spirit of rebellion and the self-confident construction of a new society in the midst of death-filled turbulence reflects so well that tremendous energy felt by so many activists of the last two decades. To be sure, in affluent Western countries, presentday activists for the most part have not experienced the life and death extremes of the Spanish revolution. Nevertheless, the confrontation with militarist capitalism and the attempt to create defiantly new life-styles and communitarian alternatives in the midst of that battle are the same. Personally sensing through Goldman's writings the immediacy of wrenching social change, in both the enormity of sacrifice and the joy of new freedom, it is this which makes her remarks so poignant and which relates them more emphatically to the vivid realities of current activism. Needless to say, her commentary as well as her commitment in these texts is as fully emotional as intellectual and as such needs no apology. She never posed*

54. Necessarily there is some overlap between chapters on some of the more important issues. Logically this was inevitable. In assigning material to one chapter over another, I simply tried to select those locations most indicated by the weight of her concern in the given written context. Though I generally avoided breaking articles or letters into less than whole paragraphs (for inclusion in particular issue chapters), occasionally the length of (or abrupt transition within) a paragraph justified such a division.

*herself as a deeply philosophical writer. But the extent of her impassioned commitment to human liberation necessarily brought forth major issues of significant depth. These she tried to resolve, as most of us do, in the immediate context of highly-charged direct personal experience.*

*She reflects here on the realities of the Spanish and international contexts, on the twists and turns of Spanish anarchists trying desperately to retain their faith and integrity in the midst of hellish alternatives. Her thoughts are a solid and radical analytical effort to grasp the universals, the long-range implications out of the strange and deforming illuminated moments in the cross-fires of deadly battle. Here are the agonized and inspiring words of that rare individual committed to the most truthful analysis she is capable of—both for her own moral integrity and the survival of the revolutionary movement and project she holds so dear. From our own advantage of hindsight, certain of her perspectives may appear for some exaggerated or one-sided. As an anarchist committed to the notion that no final word is desirable or possible, Emma Goldman would be the last to suggest that any analysis, let alone her own, could completely withstand the rigors of time. But in directly confronting the issues of movement organization (Ch. 2), constructing the new society out of the old (Ch. 3), alliances and compromise with other political groups (Ch. 4), the extreme dangers of "authoritarian socialism" (Ch. 5), abandonment or hostile intervention from abroad (Ch. 6), the role of violence in social change (Ch. 7), and the place of women in the movement and new society (Ch. 8), Goldman demonstrates the vitality and usefulness of serious engagé intellectual effort. The Spanish comrades had such zeal and self-confidence, to her it was a constant wonder. Yet more than these are needed for the struggle. Without careful rational reflection on the daily and long-range implications of one's commitment, the movement unconsciously or through manipulation easily can be led astray.*

*For this reason, Goldman's commentary on the various issues mentioned is both a model for intellectual honesty in the midst of struggle and a specific body of reflections on issues still crucial for current movements of social change, anarchist and non-anarchist alike. Through these chapters, Emma Goldman is a comrade from the past reminding us of the greatest need constantly to attend to our principles, as well as informing us of particular strategies and tactics best reflecting the libertarian perspective. For those presently concerned, as we must be, with issues of sexism, violence, the international context, self-proclaimed vanguard groups on the Left, common front strategies, the relationship between "leaders" and other participants, and creating the new society, Goldman offers a still timely round of useful observations. While not intended as and by no means representing a comprehensive analysis of these issues, even when she wrote them, her critiques and descriptions provide enough leverage to stimulate our own deeper mutual- and self-critiques as we search for anti-authoritarian pathways of liberation.*

*Of equal importance to current principled resolution of specific issues is our ability to sustain a commitment to struggle over the long-range period. In Goldman's broader reflections on both the Spanish revolution as a whole (Ch. 9) and the nature of the anarchist movement generally (Ch. 10), we are exposed to an impassioned activist's attempt to maintain that balanced vision required—amidst the triumphs and tragedies of massive social upheaval, the greatness and failures of the movement. Her writings in this section are indeed a fitting conclusion to both her lifetime of activism and her particular experience with revolutionary Spain.*

## Further Footnotes for Introduction

2.  On May 4, 1886, anarchist activists involved in the Chicago labor movement organized a public meeting at Haymarket Square on behalf of striking McCormick Harvester workers. As the last speaker was concluding, police suddenly moved in forcefully to break up the gathering. A bomb was thrown, killing and wounding scores of persons, especially police. The latter then opened fire, apparently seeking to massacre most of the remaining crowd. Though its origin was never proved (quite possibly it was a provocation by the police themselves), the murderous explosion was then used by the police, the government and the press to justify an effort to decimate anarchist ranks and the radical labor movement generally. As with the "conspiracy trial" in Chicago some eighty years later, a combination of well-known and more obscure militants was brought for punishment before an openly-biased court. Convicted not by proved connection with the bombing, but only—as the prosecution itself admitted—to break up the movement, five of the Haymarket Eight were sentenced to die. Detailed accounts of these events can be found in various sources, including Henry David, *The History of the Haymarket Affair* (N.Y.: Russell & Russell, 2nd ed., 1958); Philip S. Foner, ed., *The Autobiographies of the Haymarket Martyrs* (N.Y.: Humanities Press, 1969); Lucy Parsons, ed., *Famous Speeches of the Eight Chicago Anarchists* (N.Y.: Arno Press, 1969); Carolyn Ashbaugh, *Lucy Parsons: American Revolutionary* (Chicago: Charles H. Kerr Publishing Co., 1976); and Bernard R. Kogan, ed., *The Chicago Haymarket Riot: Anarchy On Trial* (Boston: D.C. Heath & Co., 1969).
3.  Johann Most (1846-1906), a journalist and bookbinder born in Augsburg, Bavaria, was a rising popular leader in the left wing of the German Socialist Party in the 1870's, even serving a term in the German parliament. Imprisoned on various occasions, Most was finally forced into exile in late 1878 because of government persecution and party leadership reluctance to permit him further responsibility, given his views and popular following. From London, Most continued his fiery comments and appeals in his own social-democratic newspaper. In 1880, he was expelled from the German party itself by an increasingly cautious leadership. From this point, among the immigrant community in Britain and New York (from 1882 on), Most maintained his prominent reputation as a militant revolutionary speaker, writer and organizer—but now identified himself explicitly with the anarchist movement. Detailed English-language accounts on Most's life are found in Frederic Trautmann, *The Voice of Terror: A Biography of Johann Most* (Westport, Ct.: Greenwood Press, 1980); Andrew R. Carlson, *Anarchism In Germany*, vol. I—*The Early Movement* (Metuchen, N.J.: The Scarecrow Press, Inc., 1972); and an article by Goldman herself in *The American Mercury,* June 1926.
    Alexander Berkman emigrated from Russia to the United States in 1888, at the age of 17. Shortly thereafter he began anarchist activity within the immigrant movement in New York, at that time much influenced by Johann Most. His subsequent life as an anarchist in the United States and later exile was closely intertwined with that of Goldman herself and thus will be sketched out briefly in the present chapter. Currently the fullest English-language account of Berkman's entire life is in Goldman's own autobiography, though Berkman's powerful autobiographical account, *Prison Memoirs of An Anarchist* (1912; rpt. N.Y.: Schocken Books, 1970), covers best the period up through his release from prison in 1906.

4. The confrontation at Homestead developed from management's determination to break the strength of the steelworkers' union by reducing wages 18%, locking out the workers and insisting that each person reapply for jobs inside. When the workers refused such terms, a private force of Pinkerton guards was brought downriver to occupy the steelworks, intimidate the strikers and escort strikebreakers into the plant. When the Pinkertons opened fire on the aroused workers on shore, a bloody cross-fire ensued for several hours. Eventually the Pinkertons surrendered. A few days later, management succeeded in persuading the governor to declare martial law, occupying the town on July 12 with a large force of heavily armed militia. Even then, the strikers held together defiantly for another four months before having to give in. A good brief account of the Homestead strike appears in Jeremy Brecher, *Strike!* (Greenwich, Ct.: Fawcett Publications, Inc., 1972), ch. 3; more extensive descriptions are found in David Brody, *Steelworkers in America, The Nonunion Era* (N.Y.: Harper & Row, 1969) and Leon Wolff, *Lockout, The Story of the Homestead Strike of 1892* (N.Y.: Harper & Row, 1965).

8. *LL*, I, 98-99, 105-06, 109, 114. Goldman in fact was so furious over Most's public denunciation of Berkman's act and belittling of his serious intent that she wrote her first articles, fiery attacks from a rival anarchist journal, then came to a Most public lecture and literally whipped him when he refused to back down. This latter was an action she later came to regret.

10. Malatesta was the best-known figure in the Italian anarchist movement, with great influence internationally as well, from the 1870's through the 1920's. He died, under house arrest by the Mussolini regime, in 1932. (See Goldman's sketch of Malatesta in *LL*, I, 403-04.)

   Michel (1830-1905) was a progressive French activist who turned anarchist during forced exile for her prominent role in the Paris Commune of 1871. She remained as thoroughly unrepentant and militant in her beliefs and activity, with great popular support, from the time she returned until her death.

   After the death of Bakunin in 1876, the exiled Russian geographer and activist Kropotkin was generally acknowledged as the single most influential anarchist writer until his pro-Entente stand in World War I. Returning to Russia in 1917 after an exile of forty-one years, he died in 1921. His funeral in Petrograd was the occasion of the last open anarchist demonstration permitted by the Bolshevik regime.

13. The Ferrer Modern School, founded in New York City in 1911 and transferred to the intentional community of Stelton, N.J. (near New Brunswick) in 1915, was one of this country's most important early "free school" experiments. In sheer longevity it may indeed have the record, surviving many twists and turns until 1953. More detailed accounts of this experience are found in Chapter II of Laurence Veysey's interesting *The Communal Experience: Anarchist and Mystical Counter-Cultures in America* (N.Y.: Harper and Row, 1973) and in Paul Avrich's more recent *The Modern School Movement: Anarchism and Education in the United States* (Princeton: Princeton University Press, 1980).

15. In various locales in the American West, urged on by local businessmen, city officials attempted to suppress the energetic organizing efforts of the syndicalist IWW (Industrial Workers of the World) by passing laws against public speeches without a permit. Always the exponents and practitioners of direct action, IWW activists simply used this state tactic to their own advantage by then developing a new campaign over the issue of free speech itself — sure to draw greater publicity and support for the IWW than ever before. As emulated by later sit-in demonstrations of the Southern civil rights campaign in the 1960's, the local movement would attract militant supporters from all over, willing to offer their own one-minute test of the law before being arrested. With the jails eventually filled to overflowing and with mounting unfavorable publicity, quite frequently local authorities would then give in. Every book on IWW history has at least some coverage of this important aspect of its activity. One of the more extensive accounts is found in Philip S. Foner, *History of the Labor Movement in the United States*, vol. IV — *The Industrial Workers of the World, 1905-1917* (N.Y.: International Publishers, 1965), chs. 7-8.

16. Though on various occasions for 1½ years Goldman had lectured publicly on birth-control methods, surprisingly, given the laws of the times, she was not arrested and imprisoned until 1916. Yet again this event only resulted in far greater publicity and momentum for the birth-control movement than yet had been achieved. Not only did Goldman continue such efforts as part of the broader struggle, the general atmosphere of heightened exposure to this issue helped greatly in inspiring and supporting the more specialized campaign of Margaret Sanger and others already in progress. In the history of the evolution of this issue unfortunately Goldman's

efforts have been relatively neglected, a fact apparently attributable in part to Sanger's own disavowals at the time (*LL*, II, 590-91; a point also underscored in the recent extensive study by Linda Gordon, *Woman's Body, Woman's Right: A Social History of Birth Control in America* [N.Y.: Grossman Publishers, 1976], pp. 216-22).

17. Upon release from prison in 1906, Berkman went through an intense period of painful readjustment to outside society generally and the changes of Goldman and the movement in particular. Within a few months, however, he once again became extremely active in anarchist organizing—all the more effective now as a speaker and writer because of his reputation from the Homestead events and his long suffering in prison for the cause. For eight years closely involved as well with the *Mother Earth* collective in New York, he moved in 1914 to establish a separate workers' weekly in San Francisco, a fiery anarchist periodical, *The Blast*. Returning to New York again when the climate over the 1916 Mooney case became too repressive to continue in California, from that time onward he and Goldman again were associated closely in a variety of settings—federal trial and imprisonment during World War I, deportation to Russia, chosen exile from Russia to Europe in 1922 and painful forced isolation (because of the political terms of his visa) from the intense activism of the past until his death in 1936.

21. In her 1917 pamphlet *The Truth about the Bolsheviki* (N.Y.: Mother Earth Publishing Association) written just before entering prison, Goldman praised the Bolsheviks in high terms, defining them as "those revolutionists who represent the interests of the largest social groups, . . .who insist upon the maximum social and economic demands for those groups." She saw Lenin and Trotsky as having incorruptible integrity, converting from Marxist theory to an anarchist program because they recognized the impelling needs of the Russian people themselves.

22. Only the speed of Bolshevik repression prevented Goldman and Berkman from joining the Kronstadt rebels and sharing their ultimate fate. Goldman's account of this event appears in *LL*, II, 875-86 and in *My Disillusionment in Russia* (1923-25; rpt. N.Y.: Thomas Y. Crowell Co., 1970), chapter 27. Other useful accounts include Berkman's *The Kronstadt Rebellion* (Berlin, 1922), a pamphlet now reproduced in Berkman, *The Russian Tragedy*, comp. by William Nowlin (Montreal: Black Rose Books, 1976), and a chapter on Kronstadt in his *The Bolshevik Myth* (1925; rpt. N.Y.: E.P. Dutton, 1974), reprinted in Irving L. Horowitz, ed., *The Anarchists* (N.Y.: Dell Publishing Co., 1967), pp. 495-506; Voline, *The Unknown Revolution, 1917-1921* (1947; rpt. Detroit: Black and Red, 1974), pp. 439-538; Ida Mett, *The Kronstadt Uprising* (Montreal: Black Rose Books, 1971); Janis Bogdanow, *Ceux de Kronstadt* (Paris: Editions Gallimard, 1962) (a novel); Alexandre Skirda, *Kronstadt 1921: prolétariat contre bolchevisme (Paris: Editions de la Tête de Feuilles, 1971); Paul Avrich, Kronstadt 1921* (N.Y.: W.W. Norton and Co., 1974); and Avrich, ed., *The Anarchists in the Russian Revolution* (Ithaca, N.Y.: Cornell University Press, 1973), part nine.

25. For detailed English-language accounts of the Spanish anarchist movement up to the outbreak of revolution in 1936 see especially Murray Bookchin's excellent *The Spanish Anarchists: The Heroic Years, 1868-1936 (N.Y.: Free Life Editions, 1977); Gerald Brenan, The Spanish Labyrinth* (2nd ed., 1950; rpt. Cambridge, Eng.: Cambridge University Press, 1971); the lengthy historical background sketches in Gaston Leval, *Collectives in the Spanish Revolution* (London: Freedom Press, 1975); and José Peirats, *Anarchists in the Spanish Revolution* (Toronto: Solidarity Books, 1977). See also the shorter essay by Helmut Rüdiger, "The Origins of the Revolutionary Movement in Spain," in Albert Meltzer, ed., *A New World in Our Hearts: The Faces of Spanish Anarchism* (Sanday, Orkney Islands, Scotland: Cienfuegos Press, 1978). Four studies of more limited time-periods during these years are Temma Kaplan, *Anarchists of Andalusia, 1868-1903* (Princeton: Princeton University Press, 1977); Abel Paz, *Durruti: The People Armed* (Montreal: Black Rose Books, 1977) (covering the 1920's and '30's up to and including the first few months of the revolution); Jerome Mintz, *The Anarchists of Casas Viejas* (Chicago: University of Chicago Press, 1982) (focusing on the early 1930's); and Robert W. Kern, *Red Years, Black Years: A Political History of Spanish Anarchism, 1911-1937* (Philadelphia: Institute for the Study of Human Issues, 1978).

26. *LL*, I, 188-89. Harry Kelly was one of the first native-born American anarchists Goldman came to know. In his early twenties, Kelly moved from a socialist-leaning radicalism to anarchism after hearing a speech by English anarchist Charles Mowbray in Boston in 1894. He was later

a leading activist and organizer in the *Mother Earth* group and Stelton community for many years. (See more details on Kelly's life in Avrich, *The Modern School Movement.*) His own account of the 1896 meeting on Spain is found in his unpublished autobiography, "Roll Back the Years: Odyssey of A Libertarian" (in the John Nicholas Beffel manuscript collection of the Tamiment Library, NYU).

28. A spontaneous popular revolt occurred in Barcelona in July 1909 following the government's mobilization of working-class conscripts to fight in Morocco, an action seen as a direct provocation. Not only were anti-militarist feelings still strong from the disaster in Cuba a decade before, the action took place during a mounting climate of intense class confrontation and anti-clericism and was perceived as benefiting only business interests and the Jesuits. It is not surprising that the social explosion was as immense and destructive (primarily against property) as it was. In a few days, however, it was suppressed by the government with great bloodshed, with five official executions and hundreds of imprisonments to follow. See Joan Connelly Ullman, *The Tragic Week* (Cambridge, Mass.: Harvard University Press, 1968) for a detailed study of the event.

29. Though the Ferrer Association itself was founded in New York City in 1910 as a radical cultural center for adults, a Ferrer Modern School for children was included in its activities the following year. Abiding by the principles Ferrer himself developed in Spain (similar to many efforts in the "free school" movement in North America and elsewhere in the last two decades), in both projects learning was seen as a positive creative activity only if self-chosen. Thus even the educational community itself was organized on a self-managed basis. (See footnote 13 above.) The philosophy and practice of Ferrer's Modern Schools in Spain are presented in his *The Origin and Ideals of the Modern School* (N.Y.: G.P. Putnam's Sons, 1913). Goldman's own writing on his views and efforts as well as on the circumstances of his death, "Francisco Ferrer and the Modern School," is reproduced in her *Anarchism and Other Essays.* Further background on Ferrer's experience in Spain and a detailed discussion of the "modern school" movement in the United States are found in Avrich, *The Modern School Movement;* Sol Ferrer, *La vie et l'oeuvre de Francisco Ferrer* (Paris: Librairie Fischbacher, 1962) and William Archer, *The Life, Trial and Death of Ferrer* (London: Chapman and Hall, 1911).

30. The Confederación Nacional del Trabajo or National Confederation of Labor. Anarcho-syndicalism is that wing of the anarchist movement which views anarchist organizing through a coordinated, politically independent (not linked with parties) trade union movement as the best way both to bring about the social revolution (above all, through the general strike) and to coordinate economic life afterwards. Modelled after the French CGT but with roots as far back as the Spanish experience with the First International in the early 1870's the anarchist-led CNT became increasingly popular in rural and urban areas both, with greatest strength in northeastern Spain. With the economic prosperity Spain derived from its neutrality in World War I, the CNT broadened its base considerably and took an increasingly militant stance. By 1920 it already had more than a million members. Driven underground to a barely marginal existence under the Primo de Rivera dictatorship (1923-30), it re-emerged rapidly in the 1930's to become a very major economic and political force.

31. The International Workingmen's Association was an effort to provide coordination or at least communication among the various national anarcho-syndicalist organizations throughout the world. (As such it claimed at least direct spiritual links to the anarchist First International of the 1870's.) This goal was all the more desired as a conscious attempt to counteract the strong lure of the new Moscow-formed Red Trade Union International. At all times throughout the sometimes marginal existence of the IWMA up to the present, the Spanish CNT has been its largest national affiliate.

32. Goldman 1/25/35 letter to Albert de Jong, HAR; Goldman 5/9/37 letter to Max Nettlau, UML. The late 1930's correspondence of Goldman with Rocker, Nettlau and Schapiro was especially important and forms a crucial part of the Goldman text in subsequent chapters. Each of the three had extensive experience with the international anarchist movement. The attitude of each toward the Spanish revolution was clearly distinct from the others. Thus, Emma Goldman, who had known and corresponded with each for many years, could test and develop her own thoughts on Spain partly in response to the wide range of attitudes they represented.

Rudolf Rocker was well-known in the movement, his reputation based primarily on writing, speaking and organizing successes among the Jews of London's East End from the turn of the

century; similar efforts among the German working class during the 1920's; his key role in founding and leading the IWMA in Berlin; and his voluminous writings—especially *Nationalism and Culture* and those on the anarchist movement. Following the Nazi rise to power, Rocker fled to exile, soon coming to the United States where he died in 1958. For an indication of Goldman's own high estimation of his talents and perspectives, see her comments in Chapter X. Also, see her biographical sketch of Rocker written for *Freedom* (N.Y.), April 1933.

Max Nettlau was an Austrian-born anarchist who dedicated his life to researching and writing historical accounts of the movement. He died in Amsterdam in 1944.

Born in Turkey of Russian parents, Alexander Schapiro became an active anarchist in London around the turn of the century. With the 1917 revolution, he returned to Russia, engaged in anarchist propaganda and chose to fill positions for several years in the Bolshevik regime (in the Commissariat for Jewish National Affairs and later the Foreign Affairs Ministry). After increasing Bolshevik persecution of Russian anarchists, Schapiro chose exile where he joined in founding and developing the IWMA and campaigns to alleviate and publicize the plight of Soviet political prisoners. He continued in these efforts until his death in New York in 1946.

35. The Federación Anarquista Ibérica or the Iberian Anarchist Federation. Founded secretly in 1927, the FAI, like the CNT, was structured along confederal lines. Thus, FAI affinity groups (with usually about a dozen members) were linked by local federations, the latter by district and regional federations, and the last of these by a Peninsular Committee. Each federation was administered by an elected and recallable secretariat and committee, the latter with delegates from each lower unit. The committees were responsible for correspondence, administering organizational details and executing any tasks previously delegated by the federation assemblies to which they were accountable. Membership was secret and carefully selected, apparently numbering about 39,000 by mid-1936. Sharply condemning reformist syndicalist tendencies among the CNT's leadership and mass membership both in the early 1930's, the FAI was determined—through its militancy within the CNT—to alter its direction.

36. Goldman 9/8/32 letter to Joseph Ishill, HAR; Goldman 9/16/32 letter to Max Nettlau, AMS-G. Actually, already by June 1931 she had heard of such impressive activity by the Spanish anarchists that she hoped to spend at least that winter there, helping the comrades in any organizational way they saw fit. As she said, "I can see no hope of activity for myself in Europe, unless there is one for me in Spain" (6/20/31 letter to Rudolf Rocker, AMS-R).

40. Anarchists siding with Britain, France and the U.S. in both world wars, as well as collaboration (to varying degrees) of many anarchists with the Bolshevik regime in Russia and of anarchists in the Spanish anti-fascist coalition of the late 1930's (much of the subject of this book) are no doubt the leading examples of this tendency in anarchist movement history. But the much less dramatic, more invisible examples—such as anarchist participation in local hierarchically-organized anti-war groups in the 1960's—would equally prove the case.

I further elaborate on the dynamics of sustaining one's revolutionary vision in my article "Revolutionary Realization: The Motivational Energy" in Howard Ehrlich, et al., eds., *Reinventing Anarchy* (London and Boston: Routledge and Kegan Paul, 1979).

47. Souchy was another longtime anarchist militant with the IWMA with whom Goldman had had contact earlier in Germany. His original invitation was written August 18th. By this time, she already had begun to consider such a course herself and sought to inquire about the possibility with her prior acquaintance Federica Montseny. Goldman's immediate response to Souchy on the 21st indicated that she was "overjoyed" and "proud" to receive the invitation. "What grander, most worthy cause to devote my last years to than the heroic struggle going on in Spain now? I want to come with all my heart and to do whatever work will serve the Revolution most." Already, though, she understood that such service might require activity in England rather than in Spain. Souchy 8/18/36 letter to Goldman, AMS-G; Goldman 8/21/36 letter to Souchy, AMS-G.

52. Her frustration in the distance she felt was all the greater, sometimes to the point of real despair, when mail communication with her Spanish contacts repeatedly broke down—apparently through irresponsible writing habits and the failure of movement couriers to pass on the mail. Very frequently she would find her Spanish correspondents complaining of having heard nothing from her for a few weeks while in fact she might have written five or six letters during that same period, asking important questions of her own. In turn, she berated them for never replying to her desperate need for information and responses on particular issues.

(Problems of the mail and censorship also apparently prevented her from receiving opposi-tional anarchist letters and periodicals from Spain and France [Mollie Steimer 1/12/38 letter to Goldman, AMS-F; Abe Bluestein 1/4/38 letter to Goldman, AMS-F].) Perhaps even more significant was her lack of contact, at that distance, with the continuing constructive efforts of *grass-roots* anarchist militants in Spain, as opposed to the official propaganda lines and political compromise of CNT-FAI leaders at the top. It was the former exposure, of course, which gave her the immense energy she felt on each visit.

53. While for a time Goldman considered moving to Palestine from Britain, eventually she settled on a new journey to Canada—more from the desperate hope of gaining a new U.S. visa or at least being accessible to American visitors than from any optimism about a favorable pro-paganda climate in Canada itself. Only after her death from a second stroke in Toronto in May 1940 would the U.S. government grant Goldman a "visa," permitting her ashes to be brought to rest in Chicago's Waldheim Cemetery near the graves of the Haymarket martyrs who had in-spired her entrance to anarchist ranks some fifty years earlier.

# Chapter Two

# *The Spanish Anarchist Movement*

*The organized anarchist movement was larger and stronger in Spain in the 1930's than at any time, anywhere in the world. Awesome to outside observers such as Emma Goldman, the uniqueness of this force also raised serious questions. What were the nature and depth of its roots in Spain? What did the Spanish experience suggest about the possibilities of large-scale anarchist movements in general? Most basically, how could organizations such as the Spanish CNT and FAI maximize personal freedom and full use of individual potential, yet assure effective coordination and solidarity at the same time? Anarchists insist on creating the desired new society in the very process of confronting the old. Means must be similar to the ends. For this reason, appraisals such as Emma Goldman's about the nature and organization of the movement actually become appraisals of the likely new society as well. Obviously, such issues are just as important today as forty-five years ago. Currently, they are discussed in a wide variety of decentralized efforts, from alternative schools, cooperatives and communes to anti-authoritarian political movements, whether explicitly anarchist or not.*

*The Spanish anarchist movement itself never died, despite the military defeat in 1939 and the bloody repression by Franco which followed.[1] Though inevitably reduced in scale, guerrilla struggle and clandestine local organizing continued inside Spain all these long years. Meanwhile, thousands of anarchist exiles maintained their commitment in France, Mexico and other locations throughout the world. During the decade before Franco's death in 1975, anarchism gained a significant base also among the new generation of students and young workers. With the post-Franco regime, the CNT, FAI, libertarian youth and women's organizations, as well as autonomous anarchist groups and individuals, re-emerged publicly in massive numbers.[2] In this new context, the questions and*

---

1. See footnote 1 at back of chapter.
2. Estimates of membership in anarchist or anarcho-syndicalist organizations at present range in the hundreds of thousands, though there has been great fluctuation over the last several years.

*observations Emma Goldman and others articulated forty-five years ago are im-
mensely important for the future of Spain once again. Both the source of the movement's popular strength and the necessary organizational means to preserve and
expand it thus are debated passionately in Spain as elsewhere in the world. The present dialogue frequently echoes that of Emma Goldman and other anarchists in the
1930's and will again be important for the evolution of liberatory politics
everywhere.*

## II

*Emma Goldman's perspective on such issues in the late 1930's flowed clearly and
logically from her own statements and experiences before that period. For her, the
greatest strength of an anarchist movement came from the depth and clarity of consciousness held by its membership[3] as opposed to relying on decentralized struc-
tural arrangements primarily or alone. In her view, preserving personal integrity
in life-style and political practice was ultimately more important than the approval
of one's comrades in the movement. She herself maintained independent love relationships and shied away from deep involvement in anarchist movement organizations, though many anarchists she otherwise felt close to seemed clearly offended.[4]*

*On the other hand, she by no means insisted on purist autonomy in matters of the
movement. For example, she was willing and able to justify her own and others'
personal "leadership"[4a] roles in organizing and propaganda activity. (Indeed, some
anarchists then criticized her as too assertive, therefore perpetuating hierarchy.[5])
She also worked comfortably within small self-disciplined "affinity-group" contexts,
as in preparing the attempted assassination of Henry Clay Frick in 1892, regularly
editing* Mother Earth *(1906-1917), and in creating the No-Conscription League
before U.S. entry into World War I.*

*Concerning movement organization, she thus viewed with suspicion either pole
of the anarchist spectrum. Clearly, she disagreed with those isolated anarchist
purists who rejected any kind of leadership roles or organizational solidarity. Yet
she also criticized those seeking to structure the anarchist movement by a formula
approaching "democratic centralism."[6] Inevitably, she felt, such structures soon*

As was the case historically, hierarchical establishment and radical journals (such as the *New York
Times* and the *Guardian* respectively) avoid such a phenomenon as if nonexistent. The best English-
language sources on the current Spanish anarchist movement are still found in anarchist or anti-
authoritarian libertarian periodicals such as *Black Flag, Freedom* and the *Cienfuegos Press Anarchist
Review* in Great Britain, *Open Road* and *Our Generation* in Canada, and *Fifth Estate* and *Anarchist
News* (formerly *News from Libertarian Spain*) in the U.S.

3.  ". . . The total of the possibilities and activities of an organization is represented in the expression of
    individual energies" (*LL*, I, 402).
4.  See her comments on such problems between herself and the anarchist movement in *LL*, I, 425, and
    in Ch.X below.
4a. The meaning of the term "anarchist leaders" is controversial among anarchists. Goldman uses it with
    *both* positive and negative connotations, as in her 12/16/36 letter below. This ambiguity is reflected
    in her overall assessment of the Spanish movement.
5.  See footnote 5 at back of chapter.
6.  See footnote 6 at back of chapter.

*favored centralism over freedom. Goldman thus shares a common middle ground
with the vast majority of the historical anarchist movement. Within this majority,
her particular position of personally avoiding any organizational commitment
beyond the affinity-group level was common to smaller yet still very significant
numbers of anarchists. Apparently she, as many others, came to this stance from
both a disdain for the petty bickering between rival ideologues and a suspicion that
any political grouping—even an anarchist one—tends to encourage an insular,
constraining mentality.*[7]

## III

*Both basic themes of her organizational perspective appear in her descriptions of
Spanish anarchists during the revolution. On the one hand, Goldman tremendously
admired the movement's unprecedented size, impassioned consciousness and constructive self-discipline. Yet however strong these traits, she clearly recognized that
influential personalities of this movement—like any leaders—could be corrupted.*

*In this particular context, "corruption" at the least meant practice contradicting
traditional anarchist ideals. To counter the "political realism" she so painfully
observed among certain CNT-FAI "influentials," Goldman desperately looked to the
millions of members at the base. Despite whatever the leaders did in their "official"
capacities, she hoped that deep anarchist consciousness at the grass-roots level
would continue the movement in its constructive idealistic directions. At the same
time, however, Goldman also reluctantly but honestly admitted another contradiction. That is, that apparently the same cultural roots underlying Spanish anarchists'
great courage and idealism*[8] *also tragically nourished both their innocence in dealing with manipulative anti-fascist political "allies" and their inability, in some cases,
to carry out needed systematic organizational effort. Ultimately, she was led even
to doubt the depth of clear anarchist consciousness among the millions at the base
of the movement itself. As always, Goldman insisted on facing what to her seemed
the truth, no matter how agonizing the wound inflicted to her own long-cherished
anarchist dream.*

# General Observations

†*Six weeks into her first visit to revolutionary Spain (10/28/36), Goldman voices to
her niece Stella Ballantine both apprehension toward the leadership and tremendous admiration for the depth, enthusiasm and constructiveness of the Spanish
anarchist movement generally.*

One thing is certain: the Revolution is safe only with the people and peasants
not in Barcelona. It is as Sasha [Berkman] and I have always said: the best lost

7.  See her comments about this in Chapter X below.
8.  See footnote 8 at back of chapter.

their judgment and grit when in power.[9] . . .

. . . . . . . . . . . . . . . . . . . . . . . . . . . . . . . . . . . . . . . . . . .

. . . Our comrades are as human as all else, hence subject to misconceptions when they ascend to power. [However] they will not wield it for long because their aim is not the state but the independence and right of the people themselves. The Spanish are a race apart and their anarchism is not the result of books. They have received it with their mothers' milk. It is now in their very blood. Such people do not wield power for very long. But it is sad that they should ever have become a party to it. They were forced by the treachery of Madrid.[10] But they have gained nothing by it. Most of our comrades, especially in the provinces, are already decidedly against the Committee in Barcelona.[11] Well, darling, I still cling to my faith in the wonderful spirit of our comrades and to their  splendid constructive efforts. But the last few weeks have made me anxious and uneasy for the Revolution and the life and marvelous beginning made all over Spain since July 19th.

†*Two weeks later (11/14/36), Goldman elaborates further to her niece on the uniqueness and self-sufficient nature of the movement in Spain.*

The Spanish, though part of Europe, are the most un-European of any people I have ever met. They know nothing about the outside world, have not the slightest idea of the importance of outside propaganda, and what is more they resent any suggestion or interference from foreign comrades. Perhaps this self-sufficiency accounts for their capacity to organize their forces as they have all through the years. The CNT-FAI is a model of inner-discipline. Not one man would even think of refusing to carry out a decision of the organization. A case in point is Durruti, the most heroic figure in the struggle.[12] It was decided that he should take his Column to Madrid. He hated to comply. He had set his heart on taking Saragossa. But he went to Madrid realizing that this is the most important front now. Perhaps if our Spanish people were not so set

9. See Chapter IV for her detailed description of the compromises involved. Apparently, the "power" referred to by Goldman here is CNT-FAI participation and at first predominance in the quasi-governmental Antifascist Militia Committee in Barcelona, the "dual power" *de facto* replacement for the Catalan regional government after the successful anarchist-led armed resistance to the military coup attempt there in late July 1936. Similar organs were established throughout republican Spain at the local and regional levels.
10. See footnote 10 at back of chapter.
11. No doubt the "Committee" referred to here is the regional committee of the Catalan CNT, not the Antifascist Militia Committee which had already been succeeded on September 26 by the explicitly governmental "Generalidad Council" with continued anarchist participation.
12. Buenaventura Durruti (1896-1936), a leading popular FAI activist, was a major figure in organizing successful workers' resistance to the fascists in Barcelona. He immediately took responsibility for leading an armed column of 3000 anarchist volunteers to liberate Aragón and the major city of Saragossa to the west, an important center of anarchist strength. For further details on Durruti, see Goldman's remarks in this chapter below and the biography by Paz.

on their own, Anarchism might not have taken such roots here. It requires very considerable singleness of purpose to so inculcate a whole people with our ideas [that] the most simple peasant has them in his very blood.

†*Again to her niece (12/8/36), Goldman identifies tragic flaws in the movement produced by the very traits contributing to its greatness.*

They are so willing, our Spanish comrades, and so believing that one can achieve wonders. Their naiveté is the most beautiful side of the Spanish Anarchists. But also their shortcoming. They cannot understand that anyone should want to undermine their work when they are so willing to give others the fullest freedom. Alas, they are already paying heavily for their child-like faith. And heaven only knows how much more they will have to pay.

. . . . . . . . . . . . . . . . . . . . . . . . . . . . . . . . . . . . . . . . . .

I am sorry to say nothing came of the art exhibition.[13] The story is involved and I cannot write about it now. Partly it is due to the utter lack of decisiveness in the Catalan makeup. Though the Catalan comrades and not any others have saved Barcelona from Fascism. They are wonderful in revolutionary action. But in anything that requires system, promptness, or speed they are hopeless.

†*Expanding on the same theme to her niece just after her departure from Spain (12/16/36), Goldman attributes both the strength and weakness of the movement to a lack of solid leaders.*

In spite of many disappointments I have had and disagreements with some of the decisions of the CNT-FAI, I am miserable beyond words that I had to leave Spain. My heart and all my interests are there with the simple workers and the peasants who are the purist idealists I have known since the pre-revolutionary Russians. It is their purity and their idealism which is responsible for some of their mistakes. My one explanation for this inconsistency in the Spanish character is that the Revolution in Spain is absolutely and completely a proletarian Revolution without leadership of any sort. Hence its purity. Hence also its shortcomings.

†*To her longtime comrade Harry Kelly, Goldman asserts (6/29/37) that the immense constructiveness of the Spanish revolution owes itself to years of anarchist consciousness-raising and organization among workers and peasants.*

13. For two months Goldman tried to gather current Catalan art to exhibit in London upon her return. But a few days before her departure, the plan fell through, apparently because it was opposed by Left Republicans in the government.

More than the Russian Revolution, the Spanish is *our Revolution.* . . . [Our comrades] and no one else have and are suffering its labor pains. They and no one else have attempted what had never before been done—marvelous constructive work. The Russian Anarchists, what were they but a handful of refugees from other lands and exiles from prisons, unorganized and at each other's throat, more or less? No wonder they played such an insignificant part and that they permitted Lenin and his group to steal the wind from the revolutionary sails.[14] Not so the Spanish Anarchists. They had perfected a remarkable organization. In spite of all persecution, prison, torture they hammered away for 25 years about the importance of anarcho-syndicalism and Libertarian Communism until both became flesh of the Spanish militant workers and blood of their blood, and continues to be in spite of the blunders and compromises of the leaders of the CNT-FAI.

†*Responding to anarchist critics in France and elsewhere, Goldman states in a published article for* Spain and the World *(7/2/37) that Spanish anarchist leaders did not seek power for themselves and thus should not be viewed as corrupt or traitors to the movement. Nevertheless, she does see them as exercising faulty judgement and thus deserving of criticism.*

I can . . . understand perfectly the indignation of our French comrades and those in other countries against the CNT-FAI leaders. They have shown anything but clarity and judgment in dealing with their allies. My one objection to the manifesto issued by the comrades of the F.A.F. in France[15] is the charge of treachery and political corruption against the leading comrades in the CNT-FAI. Anarchists are but human, all "too human," and therefore as likely to betray their cause as other men and women, nor do I think that their revolutionary past would always save Anarchists from being inconsistent. It has not done so in the case of the erstwhile Bolshevik revolutionists. There is a difference however. Lenin and his party aspired to the dictatorship while the CNT-FAI have from the beginning of their inception repudiated dictatorship and have held high the banner of Libertarian Communism.

Whatever compromises the leaders of the CNT-FAI have made and are still making, no one—not even their bitterest enemies—can say that they did so for personal aggrandizement or because they wanted power.

For myself I find it impossible to believe that anyone of them have turned

14. For detailed descriptions of the evolution of Russian anarchism and its role in the revolution, see Avrich, *The Russian Anarchists;* Avrich, ed., *The Anarchists in the Russian Revolution;* and Voline, *The Unknown Revolution.*
15. She refers here to a manifesto highly critical of CNT-FAI compromises, published by the French Anarchist Federation in a special issue of their *Terre Libre* newspaper in June 1937. *Terre Libre* was published by André Prudhommeaux, Voline and others in Paris and Nimes. For more on Prudhommeaux and Voline see footnote 15 in Chapter IV.

traitors or have become corrupt politicians within the limited period of six months. I repeat that human nature is vulnerable, yet I cannot conceive [that] revolutionists of such courage, heroism and consecration as demonstrated all through the years in the Spanish Anarchist struggle by our outstanding comrades would so easily have become a prey to the lure of government position.

I hold no brief for the foolish belief that by entering ministries, Anarchists could hope to effect the course of the Spanish revolution. Or that by accepting the paralyzing conditions of Stalin our comrades would hasten the triumph of the anti-Fascist cause. Much less do I defend the weak stand taken by the leaders of the CNT-FAI in the tragic battle of May 3rd, 4th, 5th and 6th.[16] I certainly consider it an extraordinary reversal of the proud revolutionary stand always defended by the CNT-FAI to turn the other cheek, to call a retreat and to hold back the pent-up feelings of the rank and file by passive resistance. All this does not imply that we should be silent or not criticize. On the contrary, we should definitely state our disagreement and we should frankly and honestly call these comrades to account. However, I feel that Anarchists should be more careful than any other social groups to shout anathema against those who have served their cause all their lives or to crucify them at the first display of inconsistency.

Is there anyone of us who can truthfully say that he has always remained faithful to his ideas? For example our beloved comrade Peter Kropotkin. By his stand on the War[17] he was guilty of a breach of principle. His defense of the allies, his statement that if he were younger he would muster a gun, were diametrically opposed to Anarchism and to everything our great teacher had taught us about War as capitalist conquest and loot. We who were opposed to the world slaughter criticized our comrade and condemned his stand but it never occurred to anyone of us to charge Peter Kropotkin with treachery or corruption. What about ourselves? We were against the world war and some of us went to prison for our opposition to it. Yet, we immediately rallied to the support of the anti-Fascist war. We did so because we consider Fascism the greatest menace in the world, the poisonous contagion which disintegrates all political and social life. The Fascist countries as well as the Russian Dictatorship certainly prove this. One can still breathe in democratic countries, little democracy though they may have. One can still raise one's voice against

---

16. The tragic "May Days" of 1937 in Barcelona were a decisive turning point in the fate of the Spanish revolution. At this time, the most prominent CNT-FAI leaders (Montseny, Oliver and Vázquez) urged their own anarchist comrades, those thousands who were resisting government forces successfully, to give up their armed struggle in the streets against increasing statist (including Communist) control. This crucial event is referred to especially in Chapters IV, V and VII below. It is also described in various other sources, including the detailed account by eyewitness George Orwell in his *Homage To Catalonia* (London: Secker and Warburg, 1938), a book strongly endorsed by Goldman herself.

17. He supported the Entente against Germany, arguing that the latter was the severest threat to the existence and progress of liberty in Europe.

every political abuse and social inequity. One still has a certain amount of security to one's life and limb. All this is obliterated by Fascism. May it not be, therefore, that the comrades now held up for scorn and all kinds of cruel charges acted as they did because they felt and feel that everything must be concentrated on winning the anti-Fascist struggle? For it must be obvious to all thinking people that the revolution and all else will be lost if Fascism would win. We outside of Spain, we who do not face starvation and danger, should at least try to understand, if not to excuse, the motivations of the concessions and compromises made by the leaders of the CNT-FAI.

I wish to state emphatically [that] I stand today where I have stood all through my Anarchist life. I believe as fervently as I always have that affiliations with governments and political parties are inimical to Anarchism and harmful. I cannot however remain blind to the fact that life is more impelling than theories, that moments in the revolutionary struggle may arise when it requires superhuman will and the wisest judgment . . . to choose the right course. And as I myself am not all-wise nor can boast of super-human will, I cannot honestly say what I would have done had I been in the position of the Spanish comrades at the head of the CNT-FAI. For this very reason I am not prepared to accept the charges of treachery or political corruption against them, much as I disagree with their methods.


† *In this 10/24/37 letter to American anarchist Samuel Friedman during her second visit to revolutionary Spain, Goldman again stresses the immense depth of anarchist consciousness at the grass roots and contrasts this with anarchists stultifying in the bureaucracy.*


. . . My surprise here was not so much over what our people had lost in a political sense. My surprise is that they should still have so many achievements to their credit. Naturally I do not mean our comrades who work in offices and bureaus. That kind of occupation always tends to rusticate people. I have in mind the workers in factories and on the land. Their spirit and their dogged perseverance to go on building and perfecting collectives are something unknown in the history of revolutions. I know whereof I speak because I have covered very considerable ground between here [Barcelona] and Madrid—villages and towns—and I can assure you all that the accomplishments are truly formidable, especially if one bears in mind the obstacles in the way of our people, the hourly danger and the hardships. Until our comrades in other countries will demonstrate anything near so great I will not join those who are throwing stones at the CNT and the FAI. Not for a moment have I changed my position regarding any form of compromise. But my visit has taught me that in spite of everything the CNT-FAI are still the only organized moral force in the whole world that is articulating our dreams

and hopes in actions and not merely in words. Actually they are the only moral force that has taken deep roots in the workers and peasants to a degree far surpassing anything known in the history of our movement, perhaps ALL social movements. To see people holding on with iron will to the task of building Comunismo Libertario, and to do it with almost bare hands and every hindrance in their way is an inspiration one cannot easily forget.

† *Three months later (1/25/38) she writes to Abe Bluestein, a young American anarchist who helped with CNT-FAI foreign propaganda from Barcelona during most of 1937 and who became increasingly critical toward the end of his stay.*[18] *Here Goldman bluntly expresses her own contradictory attitude toward anarchist opposition within Spain.*

Do not think for a moment that because I am opposed to any public attack or criticism of our comrades I am also against the underground activities of the opposition.[19] I rather think it a healthy sign that such a thing exists. At the same time I urge that it could have waited until the hands of our people were untied – until the moment will come when they will no longer be harrassed by the whole world. Their work will then be effective and would hurt the struggle of the CNT-FAI less.

Having remained an old-time anarchist, [I] still believe in the right of the comrades to oppose what they consider wrong, even if they have to do so in a clandestine way. I dare say if I were in Spain taking their part in the front rank of the CNT-FAI, facing all their dangers and all their hardships, I should not be so magnanimous with the secret opposition. I don't mean to say that I would wish them to be arrested – indeed not; but I should use all my persuasive powers and all my reasoning to dissuade them from undermining the efforts of the CNT-FAI.

I do not agree with you when you say "to go on with the official CNT-FAI means to abandon the Spanish Revolution – to abandon the revolutionists in Russia and Spain, victims of the bolsheviks, and to abandon all those principles for which you have fought all your life and which still have to play their role in the social revolution throughout the world."

I believe that it was yourself who explained in your letter of June '37 and in your pamphlet that it is nonsense to speak of an "official CNT-FAI." Granted that the National Committee and the Regional Committee in Catalonia have acted arbitrarily, surely the 800 delegates from all parts of Spain are now in a position to settle with the National Committee,[20] dissolve it and send it about

18. He established the anarchist newspaper *Challenge* (1938-39) upon his return to New York. He is a present co-editor of *Anarchist News* (N.Y.).
19. See footnote 19 at back of chapter.
20. She refers here to the January 1938 national plenum of the CNT to discuss economic matters

its business. Or do you mean to say that the National Committee consists of 800 representatives? That of course would also be nonsense. Evidently the National Committee has to account to someone for its decisions; but in any event it is not a question of standing by the National Committee. If it were only that, I should not hesitate a moment to drop the work I am doing. To me it means standing by the millions of members of the CNT-FAI and by the revolutionary Spanish workers and peasants. That is the thing which you and Sania [Alexander Schapiro] seem to forget.

† *That Goldman still saw anarchist leaders potentially corrupted through exercising power is shown in this 8/16/38 letter to Welsh writer John Cowper Powys.*

You are quite right when you say Spain would be the most fertile soil for the experiment as planned by the Spanish Anarchists. The explanation for it is that the National Confederation of Labor and the Anarchist Federation of Iberia have demonstrated by act and example the practical possibilities of Anarchist-Communism. It will interest you to know that I found in some villages four generations steeped in Libertarian Communism. To them the idea was not merely on paper or in books, but a living force. I am sure it is this that differentiates the Spanish people from the masses elsewhere. They had the good fortune of being saved the corruption of parliamentarism and political intrigue. They relied on direct action and not on those in high places. Over and above all was the libertarian principle deeply rooted in the workers and peasants which would have no part of dictatorship. They knew perfectly well that once that step is made it is like rolling down a precipice—there is no halting on the way.

· · · · · · · · · · · · · · · · · · · · · · · · · · · · · · · · · · · · · · · · · · ·

The fact that my Spanish comrades "have suffered so long and so deeply themselves that perhaps they will find some way of guarding their liberty and their new creation, *and yet* of allowing their *intelligentsia* all the indulgence in the world to criticize" may not prove entirely true, for it is as old as the hills that the slaves of yesterday easily become the tyrants of tomorrow. No, it is not their suffering which will safeguard my comrades from curtailing intellectual freedom the moment they are at the helm of the new social order. Much rather is it their firm conviction that creative work in whatever form is

(described in detail by Peirats in his *La CNT en la revolución española* [Paris: Editions Ruedo Ibérico, 1971], III, ch. 27). At this meeting, despite occasional disagreements with its position, the CNT National Committee (CN) in fact consolidated its leadership role more than ever. For example, one of its propositions—calling for a single public ideological position within the movement press—apparently was approved without even demand for a vote. Similarly, the CN itself, against past precedent, prepared in advance its own position paper on each issue and participated actively in each debate. In the months which followed, there was increasing organizational centralization of the libertarian movement, though new opposition to the particular positions of the CN also increasingly was vocalized, especially by members of the FAI.

the only security of a rich social culture. (In proof I am sending you the latest issue of *Spain and the World*,[21] which contains a report on the Day of the Book celebrated in Barcelona, June 14th.) I believe fervently that Anarchism is the safest guarantee for intellectual freedom and "all the indulgence in the world to criticize." However, I do not claim infallibility for my Spanish comrades. They, too, may become tyrannical. My one hope is that the liberated masses may soon call the leaders to account. I can assure you of one thing: it is that when the new social order becomes a living reality and attempts the curtailment of intellectual freedom, I would cease to be a defender of that experiment.

†*During her 1937 trip to Spain, Goldman found little information on or contact with anarchist opposition. Her third trip revealed a drastic change, as she expresses in her 11/11/38 remarks to Rudolf Rocker.*

*Upon first arriving she was surprised to find such influential comrades as Herrera, Santillán, Montseny and Esgleas now completely opposed to the CNT national committee's endless concessions. Last year such people were in full support.[22] This time they submitted to Goldman an elaborate critique of the committee's mistakes as well as strong charges against the Negrín government[23] and the Communists. The same dossier was presented to anarchist delegates at the Barcelona plenum[24] during her last two weeks in Spain.*

*Although she found movement division quite deep, she reports also that both sides come together as a solid whole in the face of potential involvement by outsiders. This she regards as fortunate because an open split would destroy the CNT and FAI, a development their enemies would welcome. At the same time, she is confident that FAI opposition eventually will pressure morally the CNT to take a stronger, more effective stand against the Negrín regime and the Communists.*

*Despite these clashes, Goldman remains impressed with the outstanding courage and commitment shown at the plenum generally, at a time when Barcelona itself and the CNT headquarters were under bombardment. She reports that only several out of the large numbers of delegates left the meeting place for safety. The rest continued their discussion as intensely as ever, an attitude Goldman finds unequalled anyplace else in the world.[24a]*

21. This periodical was initiated in 1936 by Vernon Richards, a university student in London and son of Italian anarchist E. Recchione. Richards continued to publish it almost single-handedly through the end of 1938, though with contributed articles from various sources including Goldman herself. It was succeeded in early 1939 by *Revolt*, then later in the same year by *War Commentary*, and in 1945 by *Freedom*, a London anarchist publication still existing today and with which Richards is still associated.
22. See footnote 22 at back of chapter.
23. See footnote 23 at back of chapter.
24. A plenary meeting of the CNT-FAI was held in Barcelona, October 16-30, 1938. The FAI critique and the meeting generally are described in detail in Peirats, *Anarchists in the Spanish Revolution*, pp. 295-300.
24a.Goldman herself behaved consistently in the same way in the midst of the bombardments which occurred during her visits to Spain.

† *With the rapid collapse of republican Spain in early 1939,*[25] *the division and bitterness among Spanish anarchists became all the more obvious, especially in the extremely difficult conditions of exile in France. To her own agony, Goldman became personally exposed to these recriminations on her visit there in late March,*[26] *as she reports in a 3/31/39 letter to Milly and Rudolf Rocker.*

My dears, my dears, I find that the horrible collapse of the great beginning in Spain is as nothing compared with the sickening disintegration among the comrades. Not only is everybody against the other to the extent of threatening their lives, but the hatred, jealousies and greed rampant among the refugees smells to the heavens. The one question is "how does he live."

*Charges against CNT national secretary Mariano Vázquez*[27] *and others of the national committee were especially severe, but were also returned in kind. Thus, while hatred against bureaucratic and reformist tendencies in Vázquez are even more important than differences in policy, Vázquez in turn makes bitter accusations of his own, as in suggesting that Santillán is insane and comes from a background of mental illness.*
    *However Goldman especially is shocked at the degree of potential retaliation. Ironically it was Santillán himself who asked Goldman to warn Vázquez and his close associate Roca*[28] *of the danger of assassination. She also discovered the same threat toward García Oliver.*[29]

† *The final tragedy of the Spanish anarchists, their despicable condition as refugees in France, is summed up briefly by Goldman in a letter to Helmut Rüdiger on 8/4/39. In her view their suffering at present perhaps even overshadows the collapse in Spain. If she herself had to face the same constant humiliation, she would prefer to be shot by a firing squad.*

† *To her final months, Goldman continues to express highest admiration for the overall quality of her comrades from Spain (11/18/39 letter to Maximiliano Olay, a Spanish anarchist in New York).*

25. Catalonia was completely occupied by fascist forces by February 9, 1939. Madrid, Valencia and the remainder of the center and eastern zones were occupied by the beginning of April. With the collapse of each zone, hundreds of thousands of Spanish anarchists among others fled to exile—initially to France, the nearest land beyond Franco's deadly reach.
26. Goldman visited Paris at the time to gain one last direct contact with her Spanish comrades before crossing the ocean to Canada.
27. See footnote 27 at back of chapter.
28. Facundo Roca was a CNT representative in Paris.
29. Juan García Oliver was a militant anarchist from his early years. A passionate speaker, he was also an affinity-group comrade of Durruti and others from the early 1920's. In Largo Caballero's government, he was Minister of Justice. After Franco's victory, he eventually found exile in Mexico. See further Goldman comments on him below. García Oliver's own definitive autobiographical account is *El Eco de los Pasos* (Paris: Ruedo Ibérico, 1978).

Yes, I think our Spanish comrades are wonderful. In all the fifty years of my activities I did not find in our ranks any other group of people so beautifully generous, so eager to give and to help. People laugh at me when I tell them that when one asks a Spaniard for a cigarette he gives you the whole package and is insulted if you do not take it. In all my life I have not met with such warm hospitality, comradeship and solidarity. I know no other people who beat them.

## Particular Individuals

†*Goldman's assessments of particular Spanish anarchist leaders illuminate further both the nature of the movement itself and the particular dynamics of its policy during the revolution and civil war. Of all those she met in leading positions, none did she admire more than longtime militant Buenaventura Durruti, as she expresses in this letter to her niece during her first wartime visit to Spain (10/17/36).*

. . . The CNT-FAI consist of people who, whatever their missteps may be under the frightful danger they are facing, will never bow to any rigid authority. I felt this once more so strongly at the Aragón front where I spent two days [with] Durruti, one of our most daring comrades even under the old regime and now the spirit of the battle at this side of Saragossa. He is the most impressive personality I met here and the most flaming Anarchist. His men adore him, and yet he uses no force or barrack discipline to make them do almost anything and go through fire at his request. He said to me, "it will be a sad day for me and Anarchism if I should have to act in the capacity of a General, rule my column with iron force. I do not think that moment will ever come. The men at the front are my comrades. I live, eat, sleep and work with them, and share their danger. That works better than military rigidity." These were not mere phrases, darling. I spoke to the men and they substantiated every word.[30]

†*A month later, Durruti was dead. Goldman expresses the loss this represented for the Spanish movement, the revolution and the anti-fascist struggle in this eulogy published in* Spain and the World *(11/24/37).*

I find it impossible to write about our comrade Buenaventura Durruti in a few words or even in a long article. The wound his cruel death has struck the Spanish Revolution, the anti-Fascist struggle and all who knew and loved

---

30. A more detailed account of Goldman's mid-October discussion with Durruti and her visit literally to the front lines at Pina del Ebro is found in the 22-page sketch by Martin Gudell (her translator), "Emma Goldman in Spain" (NYU).

Durruti is still too raw to be able to detach oneself sufficiently to give an objective appraisement of his importance to the great events of 19th July and the gigantic work until his untimely end. Not that Durruti was the only outstanding personality in the valiant battle that nipped Fascism in the bud in Barcelona, and all of Catalonia. The great heroes of the battle are the Spanish masses. Herein lies the grandeur of the Spanish Revolution. It rose from the very bowels of the Spanish earth. It was entirely imbued with the collective spirit of the Spanish masses. It is therefore difficult to treat individual figures as separate and distinct from the force that swept over Spain on the 19th July.

If then I nevertheless consider our comrade Durruti the very soul of the Spanish Revolution it is because he was Spain. He represented her strength, her gentleness as well as her rugged harshness so little understood by people outside of Spain. It was this in the make-up of our dead comrade which so impressed me when I met him at the Front he and his gallant comrades were defending with their bare hands, but with a spirit that burned at red-white heat. There I found Buenaventura Durruti on the eve of an offensive surrounded by scores of people coming to him with their problems and needs. To each one he gave sympathetic understanding, comradely direction and advice. Not once did he raise his voice or show impatience or chagrin. Buenaventura had the capacity to put himself in the place of another, and to meet everyone on his own ground, yet retaining his own personality. I believe it was this which helped to create the inner discipline so extraordinary among the brave militias who were the pioneers of the anti-Fascist struggle. And not only discipline, but confidence in the man and deep affection for him.

The last tribute paid Durruti by half a million people[31] may not be an indication of the place he held in the minds and hearts of the masses. What proved more significant to me was to find the same admiration, the same love for our comrade a year after his death. One had but to mention the name to see faces transformed and people express the thought that the treacherous bullet that pierced Durruti's heart also struck the Revolution a frightful blow. Time on end I was assured that had Durruti lived the counter-revolutionary forces within anti-Fascist Spain would not have raised their ugly head, nor would they have succeeded in destroying so much of the revolutionary gains of the CNT-FAI. Durruti would have swept anti-Fascist Spain clean from all the reactionary and parasitic elements now restlessly trying to undermine the revolution.

I have already stated that in the stress and storm of Revolution the mass takes first importance. Yet we cannot get away from the fact that the individual too must play his part. And nothing decides the importance and significance of that part as the greatness of the personality that paves the way

31. At the funeral procession in Barcelona following his shooting by an unknown gunman on November 19, 1936 in Madrid. He died the following day.

and illumines the path the masses take. In this sense alone can one adequately appraise Buenaventura Durruti, his passionate love of freedom, the fiery revolutionist, the undaunted fighter who gave his all to the liberation of his people.

†*A second leading figure among the anarchists was Federica Montseny, whom Goldman first met in Spain in early 1929. Montseny was an extremely energetic and influential personality in the FAI, as Goldman makes clear in this late September 1936 letter to Rudolf Rocker.*

I saw and talked to Federica Montseny. She is the "Lenin" in skirts. She is idolized here. She is certainly very capable and brilliant but I am afraid she has something of the politician in her. She it was who helped to pass through the formation of the new Council which is replacing the Generalidad.[32] It is really only another name for the same thing. Let us hope the CNT will have no reasons to regret having entered into the Council as a governing body. However, I am very glad to see that Federica is such an intellectual, and organizing force. She works like a dog, 18 hours of 24.

†*But a few weeks later (11/3/36), she confides to Rocker that her fears of the compromising "politician" side of Montseny seem all the more justified.*

Well, dear Rudolf, I wish I could be more enthusiastic. It is not that I am of faint heart. It is that I cannot possibly believe in politicians no matter if they call themselves CNT-FAI. And some of them are that. Federica for instance. She has gone to the Right and she has a great influence here. She has become Minister of Health. What great achievement? It is all so sad.

†*To Mark Mratchny[32a] three months later (2/8/37), she appraises Montseny less critically than before though still she is very much aware of the latter's contradictions.*

32. The Council referred to here is the Antifascist Militia Committee. The Generalidad was the Catalan regional government. Anarchist participation in the former, a quasi-governmental body, was the first clear public endorsement of collaboration after July 19th. It was debated among and approved by a small group of leading CNT and FAI "influentials" in Barcelona. This crucial decision was never submitted for approval to the base membership, in fundamental violation of anarchist principles. Collaborationism and elitism within the movement complemented and re-enforced each other in an ever-more debilitating cycle through 1939.

32a Mark Mratchny (later Clevans) was an exiled Jewish anarchist from Russia, in the 1930's an editor of the Yiddish anarchist newspaper *Freie Arbeiter Stimme* (N.Y.). He had been an active militant in the Nabat anarchist confederation of the Ukraine during the Russian revolution, where Goldman met him in Kharkov in 1920. She later assisted in the difficult campaign to have Mratchny and other anarchists released from Soviet prisons in late 1921.

The address of Montseny[33] is also very illuminating, though I rather found her a bit too self-satisfied, and uncritical. I don't say that in any sense of condemnation. One whose whole life was spent in one sphere must be even more insular than most of the Spanish comrades who have lived in exile. Naturally she would see everything in roseate colors. Nevertheless, she is among the ablest of our people, and certainly the bravest.

† *To Milly and Rudolf Rocker, Goldman restates her critique of Montseny. Ironically, this letter is written on the very day (5/4/37) when, in the midst of Barcelona clashes between anarchists and their statist "allies," Montseny herself gave a radio appeal to anarchists to lay down their arms to preserve the coalition.*

. . . Only blind zealotry will deny that [Federica Montseny] among all the comrades is the most willing to compromise. I hope you understand, dear Rudolf, that I have no personal reason to say that Federica has gone more to the Right than any of the leading CNT-FAI members. Not only that but she is as dogmatic against any critical expression on the part of comrades in the FAI as anyone else.

*In Goldman's and others' opinion, Montseny's position of official responsibility has distorted her thinking. She finds this pitiful though not surprising, given what anarchists have always stated about the effects of political power. Nevertheless, she also does not doubt Montseny's sincerity and honesty and hopes that eventually she will turn around.*

† *In this letter to Max Nettlau five days later (5/9/37), now generally aware of the struggle in Barcelona, Goldman sees the attack on anarchists as a natural outcome of the mistakes made by Montseny, her fellow FAI militant and minister Juan García Oliver and others who began calculating as politicians instead of holding to basic anarchist principles.*

Now, while I am heart and soul with the struggle of the Spanish comrades, and while I have done my utmost to plead their cause, for which I would cheerfully give my life, I must insist that they are vulnerable: they have made terrible mistakes which are already bearing fruit. I hold Federica Montseny, García Oliver and several others of the leading comrades responsible for the gains made by the Communists and for the danger now threatening the Spanish Revolution and the CNT-FAI. My very first interview with these two comrades has shown me that they are on the "border-line" of reformism. I had

33. At Barcelona on January 3, 1937. This address was published as a pamphlet *Militant Anarchism and the Spanish Reality* (Glasgow: The Anti-Parliamentary Communist Federation, 1937). A large passage is quoted in Peirats, *La CNT . . .*, II, 115-19.

never met Oliver before, but I had met Federica in 1929. The change, since the Revolution swept her forward to the highest topnotch as leader, was only too apparent. I was strengthened in that impression every time I talked to her about the compromise she and the others had made. It was too obvious to me that these comrades are working into the hands of the Soviet government. That in showing their gratitude to Stalin and his regime (though why they needed gratitude in addition to the gold Stalin received for whatever he gave in arms,[34] I do not know), dire results were sure to follow. Incidentally, it also meant the betrayal of our comrades in the concentration camps and prisons of Russia.[35] I never saw a greater breach of faith with Anarchist principles than the joint "love-feast" of the CNT-FAI with the Russian satraps in Barcelona.[36] It was a sight for the gods, to see García Oliver and the Russian Consul competing with each other in the glowing tribute to the Soviet government, or the eulogies that appeared daily in the *Solidaridad Obrera*.[37] Not a word did the paper, or Oliver, or Federica have to say about the Russian people, about the fact that the Russian revolution has been castrated and that Stalin's henchmen are responsible for tens of thousands of lives. It was a disgraceful affair — unnecessary and humiliating! I have not written about this to anyone, dear comrade, although I felt indignation and could have cried out my contempt of the so-called leaders of the CNT-FAI.

· · · · · · · · · · · · · · · · · · · · · · · · · · · · · · · · · · · · · ·

Well, I am afraid we will probably not come to any understanding. You seem to feel about Federica and the Urales family as a mother does about her "chicks": nobody must touch them even remotely. I myself admired them for years; I admire her brilliant oratorical abilities, but I can say that she has feet of clay, and I can see no reason why it should not be admitted. She has gone terribly to the Right, and wearing a revolver in the belt does not make it any more Left. However, I am certain that the comrades [will] come to see that politicians, whether in pants or skirts, whether Anarchist or Socialists, must be watched. They will go from the fundamental principles as they always have in the past.

†*Her bitter attack on Montseny and Oliver continues in this 5/14/37 letter to Rudolf Rocker, now reflecting for the first time Goldman's knowledge of some of the crucial details of their roles in the Barcelona May Days.*

Since I wrote to you last week the frightful thing has happened, a thing most of

34. Arms shipments from the Soviet Union to the republican government began to arrive in mid-October 1936 in return for about $600 million in gold from the national treasury.
35. The Russian anarchist movement was decimated by police and military repression under Lenin, Trotsky and Stalin.
36. On the November anniversary of the Russian revolution.
37. The influential Barcelona daily newspaper of the CNT.

us foresaw, only I tried so hard to explain it rather than condemn at the outset. The pact with Russia in return for a few pieces of arms has brought its disastrous results. It has broken the backbone of Montseny and Oliver and has turned them into willing tools of Caballero.[38] I don't know whether you receive *Combat Syndicaliste*.[39] I am writing Mollie [Steimer][40] to send you the current copy. You will see that the murderous Stalin gang have killed Berneri and another comrade[41] and that they were back of the attempt to disarm the comrades of the CNT-FAI. Still more terrible to me is that Oliver and Montseny have called a retreat and have denounced the militant Anarchists, to whom the revolution still means something, as counter-revolutionists. In other words, it is a repetition of Russia with the identical method of Lenin against the Anarchists and S.R.'s who refused to barter the revolution for the Brest-Litovsk Peace.[42]

† *The energy expended by Spanish anarchists at all levels is typified in this description of Diego Abad de Santillán, a leading militant of the FAI (11/3/36 letter to Rudolf Rocker).*

Santillán is working for ten. He is frightfully worn out and nervous to the extreme. Elisa lives in constant fear about him. Their boy is in Argentina. Naturally she feels the separation frightfully. They send their greetings. Santillán told me it was impossible to translate the third part of your work[43] though he hopes to find someone who might do it. He is worked to death as I already said.

† *Despite attacks by some (such as her 2/23/37 correspondent here, Alexander Schapiro) on the competency of Santillán to hold an economic policymaking position, Goldman strongly defends his devotion and integrity as well as his need to learn through his own mistakes.*

You have always been antagonistic, unreasonably so, to Santillán. If I mistake not, you have expressed yourself even before the Revolution that he and a few

38. See footnote 38 at back of chapter.
39. The newspaper of the CGTSR (Confédération Générale du Travail Syndicaliste Révolutionnaire, the French anarcho-syndicalists).
40. See footnote 40 at back of chapter.
41. Italian anarchist Camillo Berneri and his comrade Barbieri were assassinated in Barcelona on the night of May 5, 1937. Because of Berneri's strong public criticism of CNT-FAI compromises and the statist forces they sought to appease, it is generally assumed that he and Barbieri were killed by armed Communists. See further details on Berneri in Chapter IV, footnote 15, as well as Goldman's elaborate remarks in Chapter X.
42. See footnote 42 at back of chapter.
43. Presumably she refers here to Rudolf Rocker's third volume of his autobiography. (It was eventually translated into Spanish, but not yet to date into English.)

others will have to be shot before the CNT can hope to succeed. In your letter you are positively vindictive against Santillán. True, he is no economist. But were the men in Russia economists who were placed in all sorts of councils? Did they not have to learn through experience by trial and error? Of one thing I am certain, even if I am not about Santillán's fitness in the economic council, and that is his stern honesty and consecration. I lived in his house and I saw his devotion. For the rest he will have to learn as we all do when the psychological moment comes. We should at least be willing to give Santillán a chance and not to make him the butt of scorn.

†*Over two years later (9/2/39), Goldman admits to Milly Rocker the limitations of Santillán in certain capacities. Despite his intellectual background and writing talents, he is incapable of effective practical activity. It is hardly surprising that he and Vázquez could not get along since the latter is just the opposite.*

†*In this first appraisal of CNT national secretary Mariano Vázquez (to Augustin Souchy, 7/27/37), Goldman strongly criticizes his defensive attacks on those who disagree.*

. . . Vázquez is of course a fool. He proves once more that the man risen to power is worse and more dangerous than the one born into it. The idea of Vázquez writing that the Russian Anarchists did not know danger, or that we are comfortably situated, hence have no right to judge compañero Vázquez. It is preposterous to say this of Voline, for instance, who is almost destitute.

*Believing that Vázquez probably would have said the same about Berkman as well, she finds it "scandalous" that charges are made against the revolutionary integrity of those who have devoted their lives to the movement.*

†*In a subsequent manuscript intended for publication (3/4/38), Goldman admits another side to Vázquez based on closer association with him during her late 1937 visit.*

In Valencia I again met comrades whom I had first encountered in Barcelona a year before. Owing to my activities for the National Confederaton of Labour and the Anarchist Federation of Iberia, I came to know Comrade Mariano Vázquez better. I admit my first impression of him in Barcelona was anything but favorable. He seemed to me to be blindly fanatical, rigid in his sectarianism and quite unsociable; but coming in closer contact with him during the short ten days in Valencia has convinced me that his savage wildness was only on the surface. Underneath was his large flaming spirit that lives and dreams only of the realization of the Revolution.

†*A more detailed description of Vázquez' contradictions and the impasse they produced among Spanish anarchist leaders appears in her 11/11/38 letter to Rudolf Rocker. She finds Vázquez a "typical proletarian," very honest and hard-working, but these qualities sharply contrast with his weaknesses. He thinks far too much of himself and his role and is abrasive and absolutely unyielding. It has now come to the point where even FAI leaders Herrera and Germinal de Sousa[44] have to communicate with him solely in writing.*

*For Goldman the bitterness and intolerance within the ranks left her "heartbroken," for she saw admirable qualities in most of those involved.*

† *The personality of Vázquez only fed the deeper policy clashes between the FAI and CNT, as indicated in this unpublished manuscript written in December 1938.*

I had come to Spain for two or three weeks and I wanted to leave. It had always been a painful wrench to depart from the comrades who had wound themselves round my heart with a thousand strings. I knew it would be even more painful this time, but I felt I should leave because the work of the CNT-FAI Bureau in London was left hanging in the air. The comrades of the Peninsular Committee of the FAI said they would not hear of it. I must remain for the two forthcoming plenums,[45] they said, where the difference which had arisen between them and the CNT Committee would be thrashed out. I wanted very much to be present at the session, but also I dreaded the outcome. I had read the material prepared by the Peninsular Committee, setting forth its opposition to the growing encroachment of the Negrín government on the libertarian achievements and the critical attitude to the timid stand of the National Committee. Not wishing to remain one-sided in my judgement, I had also listened to a long explanation of the steps taken by Comrade Mariano R. Vázquez. I realized that the relations between him and the comrades of the Peninsular Committee had become very strained. Not for a moment could I doubt the personal integrity of the contending comrades. I had found them all of sterling quality, deeply sincere and passionately devoted to the struggle. True, their tempermental differences had no doubt contributed to the quarrel.

Comrade Vázquez' rough-hewn manners and thunderous voice easily roused antagonism. I myself had at first been shocked by them until I learned to know his earnestness and his fine qualities back of his savage exterior. On the other hand was Comrade Pedro Herrera, thoughtful, tender and rather shy in his ways, though a fighter when need be; and all the other comrades. I was sure that the strained relations had deeper reason; the comrades of the Peninsular had begun to see that there is danger alone for the libertarian

44. A Portuguese exile, Germinai de Sousa was secretary-general of the FAI Peninsular Committee in 1938-39.
45. Actually, this was a joint plenum of the FAI and CNT in October 1938.

movement if the CNT and the FAI will not take a more aggressive and consistent stand. The comrades had reached the breaking point of their endurance of the maneuvers of Stalin's satraps. They had prepared a formidable dossier powerfully documented of some of the outrageous acts against the libertarian ranks. They felt the time had come to block their nefarious activities. I conceded the justification of the criticism and demands of our comrades of the FAI. Still, I felt like a hen for her chicks. I trembled for them.

† *Among Spanish anarchists in exile, attacks on Vázquez focused on his use of the CNT treasury. However, in her 4/24/39 letter to Milly Rocker, Goldman makes clear that Vázquez' problem in the realm of refugee relief stems from neglecting the individual. In fact she finds his insistence on using CNT money only for organization purposes and not for individual relief merely repeating the same mistaken emphasis made by Marxism.*

*She also regrets his tendency to compromise and cites Durruti as a far greater moral force. This, in turn, leads her to broader conclusions about the nature of the Spanish movement.*

In a measure we are paying for our belief that the masses as such can bring about fundamental changes. There never was a more proletarian revolution than the Spanish one, but there was a terrible poverty in great minds and strength of character. That was the real tragedy in Spain.

† *The tragedy of Vázquez' personal leadership was only magnified in Goldman's eyes by his accidental drowning in June 1939. In a 6/27/39 letter to Milly and Rudolf Rocker, she reflects further on his character and on her own ambiguous relationship with him.*

He had many faults: the most repelling was his gruffness with everybody, his brutal and abrupt manner and his fanatical adherence to the letter of organizational discipline. And yet I knew that he was tender and loving under his hard exterior. As to his honesty, he was of sterling quality, but as I say his fanatical organizational ways made him bureaucratic with people and overbearing.

*News of his death left her quite shaken, all the more since Martin Gudell reported that Vázquez recently described her as being "more than his mother" because of her rare ability to understand him as well as the Spanish cause.*[46]

46. Gudell was a Russian-born anarchist working with the CNT-FAI Foreign Propaganda Department in Barcelona during the late 1930's. He spent many hours translating and discussing with Goldman on her several visits to Spain, earning her high respect. Vázquez' final communication with Goldman before his death was very praising and apparently moved her a great deal, especially in the context of the tremendous turmoil Vázquez and the whole movement-in-exile were enduring at the time. A brief passage from the letter is reproduced in Drinnon, *Rebel in*

†*This final appraisal of Vázquez, in an 8/31/39 letter to his bitter critic Pedro Herrera, is perhaps even more significant in its appeal not to allow defeat to corrode the movement. One should analyze the plight of Spanish anarchism at the broader social level instead of solely through looking at personalities. It was in fact the international conspiracy against and lack of world proletarian support for the Spanish revolution which caused the essential mistakes made within Spain. Though individuals in the movement indeed made important errors, their positive service should not be forgotten.*

We must [reassess] our values and we must try to see that if mistakes were made all had a share in it and not merely this or that individual. This then is my attitude to Mariano. You and I can, I hope, remain the friends we have been all through the heroic struggle even if we do not agree in our appraisement of anyone of our comrades.

†*In this 12/27/37 letter to the* Toronto Star, *Goldman praises Cipriano Mera and García Vivancos, popular leaders of anarchist military columns.*

I appreciate deeply your tribute to my comrade Cipriano Mera.[47] He did all you say, and more. Next to Buenaventura Durruti, the people's idol, it is Mera whose valor has caught the imagination of the Spanish masses. Another of their heroes is the Anarchist García Vivancos, the hero of Belchite,[48] who freed that city from Franco's German and Italian forces. For this he was highly commended by General Pozas.[49] The latter though known as an arch-hater of Anarchism yet felt impelled to send Vivancos a message of appreciation.

Great as that achievement was, Vivancos—as I have just heard from an authentic source—has now followed it up with one still greater: for it was *GARCIA VIVANCOS who, with his 25th Division, which consisted of the 116, 117, and 118 Brigades, all CNT-FAI members, actually captured Teruel.*[50]. Vivancos is a born leader of men, and is greatly beloved by his men.

It is true to say that there are hundreds of such gallant men in Spain who

*Paradise* (paperback edition), pp. 386-87.

47. See footnote 47 at back of chapter.

48. Miguel García Vivancos was another longtime militant anarchist and affinity-group comrade of Durruti from the early 1920's. Belchite was captured on September 6, 1937.

49. See footnote 49 at back of chapter.

50. The capture of Teruel was completed on January 7, 1938 after a difficult battle of three weeks. It was the only important city recaptured by the anti-fascist forces during the entire civil war. With major Nationalist reinforcements, the steady battle of attrition favored Franco. The Nationalists took Teruel again on February 22 and thus established a continuing military momentum leading to total victory a year later.

have attained to magnificent heights by their bravery and courage in their fight against Fascism. Most of them were simple working men whose idealism and daring have proven stronger than German and Italian arms.

The greatest characteristic of the Spanish people is their selflessness. They do not want honors or medals. They find their supreme reward in the consciousness that by fighting Fascism they are not merely fighting for Spain alone but for the whole world, for the liberation of the people from that scourge.

†*In a 12/38 manuscript intended for publication, Goldman recalls the curiosity and intensity of another important anarchist militant and military leader, Gregorio Jover.*

Gregorio Jover[51] had been a close friend of Durruti and associated with him for years in their wanderings through Europe, their revolutionary exploits and the persecution they had endured from the governments of every country. Somehow I imagined Jover not merely the same commanding personality but also of the same heroic spiritual stature as Durruti. Great was my surprise therefore when on our arrival I found Jover looking more like a college professor than a military man. Indeed, his poise, reserve and quiet manner indicated the polished gentleman rather than the dare-devil who had once been considered a veritable terror by constituted authority. Comrade Jover at once proceeded to ply me with questions about the attitude of public opinion in England to the anti-Fascist struggle in Spain. A people so highly civilized, progressive and liberal as English men and women must needs understand the world-wide importance of the Spanish war. . . . He insisted that with the power of the press and the wireless, reaching to the remotest parts of the earth, the English people could not possibly have remained ignorant about what loyalist Spain is fighting for, nor the designs of Hitler and Mussolini in backing Franco. Spanish naiveté in European achievement and political affairs has always been a source of wonder to me. Still, I did not expect such childlike faith of Comrade Jover in the truth-telling or informative powers of the press and the radio. I pointed out that both are the great medium of the capitalist system, hence printed and radioed such news as their masters thought good for the people.

. . . . . . . . . . . . . . . . . . . . . . . . . . . . . . . . . . . . . . . .

Our real visit with Comrade Jover began when he returned from the hotel to his private office. There in the close circle of comrades—Gregorio Jover,

51. Gregorio Jover was yet another close associate of Durruti in the "Solidarios" (later "Nosotros") affinity group in the years before the revolution. An anarchist militia leader on the Aragón front in the initial months of the war, he subsequently became commander of the 28th Division. Later he became commander of one of the three army corps (the 10th) of the East.

Juan Molina, the former editor of *Tierra y Libertad,* his companion, Lola
Iturbe, a talented and ardent feminist,[52] Pedro Herrera, Martin Gudell and
several other comrades on the staff—I learned to know Gregorio Jover better
during that afternoon. I saw that back of the reserve was tremendous emotional strength and an ardent faith articulated in measured phrases only to better impress his hearers. There was, however, nothing studied or prepared in
his method. It was quite spontaneous—sparks from his own flaming spirit.
Our talk touched on every gamut of Spanish life, ideas and ideals, and the
supreme sacrifices already and still to be made by the people in order to win
the war. . . . The whole room was filled with his strength and his fire. We all
came under his spell and we would have continued all through the night. . . .

† *That the struggle of civil war and revolution also produced many disappointing
figures in the Spanish movement is clear from Goldman's description of an important
CNT leader, Horacio Prieto,[53] in her 8/4/39 letter to comrade Helmut Rüdiger.*

I was given to understand that before the Revolution [Horacio Prieto] was of
the ultra-fanatical revolutionary kind and that no method was revolutionary
enough for him. Imagine such a man retrograding into a reformer of the
palest soul. I simply cannot understand such a turn in mind, although it is
usually the case that extremists at one period in their lives become spineless
when faced with the least failure of their extreme ideas.

*His apparent indifference to the purpose of her own visits to Spain and a number of
other factors caused her to regard him as essentially "careerist" and, like some others
of the FAI and CNT, simply "too small" for the immense dimension of revolution.*
    *In her view, Orobón[54] had the greatest clarity and organizational skill of any an-
archist in Spain. It was a deep tragedy for the Spanish revolution that he died just
when his presence would have been most valuable.*

52. Juan Manuel Molina served alongside Jover and in the last stage of the war was Commissary of
    the 10th Army Corps. *Tierra y Libertad* was an influential Barcelona anarchist weekly, critical
    of political compromises in the Fall of 1936. Lola Iturbe was directly involved in many strikes
    and revolutionary activities and frequently contributed to the anarchist press. Her strong
    anarcha-feminist consciousness is reflected in writings from before the revolution down to the
    present. In 1974, she published a book of short sketches of women involved in the social
    struggle (cited in Ch. VIII).
53. See footnote 53 at back of chapter.
54. Valeriano Orobón Fernández was a young Spanish anarchist exile during the Primo de Rivera
    dictatorship. He worked closely for several years with Rudolf Rocker and the IWMA Interna-
    tional Bureau in Berlin. One of the leading writers and speakers for the CNT in the early years
    of the Second Republic, he was a strong advocate of anarchists joining a broad anti-fascist *and*
    revolutionary workers' alliance rather than acting on their own. He died of illness shortly
    before the beginning of the revolution. (See Peirats, *Anarchists in the Spanish Revolution,* pp.
    262-64.)

# Further Footnotes for Chapter Two

1.  Though hundreds of thousands of leftists fled to exile (primarily in France) before the borders were sealed, estimates of those murdered and imprisoned by the new regime in the first several years alone run as high as hundreds of thousands and over two million respectively. Of these, certainly a high proportion were anarchists. César Lorenzo, *Les anarchistes espagnols et le pouvoir, 1869-1969* (Paris: Editions du Seuil, 1969), ch. 12; Antonio Tellez, *Sabaté: Guerrilla Extraordinary* (London: Cienfuegos Press, 1974), p. 51; Hugh Thomas, *The Spanish Civil War* (N.Y.: Harper & Row, 1961), pp. 607-08.

    Good English-language sources on the overall post-1939 Spanish anarchist movement are not easily available. The Tellez book on Sabaté is a detailed account of an important anarchist guerrilla activist until his death in 1960. Translation of a similar study by Tellez, *Facerias*, is also under preparation by the same press. See also Miguel Garcia, *Franco's Prisoner* (London: Rupert Hart-Davis, 1972). Albert Meltzer, ed., *The International Revolutionary Solidarity Movement: 1st of May Group* (Sanday, Orkney Islands, Scotland: Cienfuegos Press, 1976) describes one aspect of Spanish guerrilla activity from 1960 on. Meltzer edited a subsequent anthology, *A New World In Our Hearts*, by the same publisher, in 1978. Though several of the articles concern the experience of the Spanish anarchists only through the 1930's, others deal with subsequent years of struggle all the way to the present. Several French-language sources covering overall developments include Octavio Alberola and Ariane Gransac, *L'Anarchisme espagnol et l'action révolutionnaire internationale (1951-1975)* (Paris: Christian Bourgois, 1975); the final portion of the Lorenzo book mentioned above; and a brief essay contribution by Freddy and Alicia, "Introduction à une étude du mouvement libertaire espagnole," to a collection, *Composition sociale du mouvement anarchiste*, edited by the Centre Internationale de Recherches sur l'Anarchisme in Lausanne, Switzerland, 1973 (published in book form as *Société et contre-sociéte chez les antiauthoritaires: communauté du travail du CIRA* [Geneva: Librairie Adversaire, 1974]). In Spanish, there are José Berruezo, *Contribución a la historia de la C.N.T. de España en el exilio* (Mexico City: Editores Mexicanos Unidos, 1967); Cipriano Damiano, *La resistencia libertaria* (Barcelona: Editorial Brueguera, 1978); Telesforo Tajuelo, *El M.I.L., Puig Antich y los G.A.R.I. (Paris: Ruedo Ibérico, 1977);* and an earlier edition of the book by Alberola and Gransac. The Spanish anarchist movement press, of course, continued to flourish from France and Latin America especially. Extensive collections of these publications exist in various libraries in the United States, including the New York Public Library and those at Brandeis University and the University of Michigan.

5.  She was quite aware of this perception, as her 8/9/36 letter to Philip (?) (NYPL) well indicates. In her autobiography, she admits to a tendency toward hasty appraisals of others, in part because of her whirl of activity (*LL*, II, 658, 665). Three critical statements by others are a Jo Labadie 8/3/11 letter to Goldman (UML), a 1933 letter from old associate Tom Bell to Alexander Berkman (quoted in Drinnon, *Rebel in Paradise* [paperback edition], pp. 389-90) and the interview with Sam Dolgoff in *Soil of Liberty* (Minneapolis), Spring 1982. Anarchist Joseph J. Cohen in his eulogy at the time of her death, "Emma Goldman – Valiant Fighter and Generous Soul! An Appreciation" (AMS-F), stresses the contrast between her nonyielding, dynamic and assertive exterior self (causing considerable friction with numerous anarchist comrades) and her warm generous personality shown to those in her private life. So also does Ethel Mannin in her sketch of Goldman in *Women and the Revolution* (N.Y.: E.P. Dutton & Co., 1939), p. 139.

6.  Leading proponents of such a model in 1926 were the Russian "Platformist" anarchists exiled abroad. Among the leaders of this group were Nestor Makhno and Peter Arshinov, prominent organizers in the anarchist-inspired mass revolution in the Ukraine from 1917 to 1921. Apparently the first English-language edition of their "Organizational Platform of the Libertarian Communists" was published as a pamphlet in 1972 by the North London group of the Organization of Revolutionary Anarchists. This was translated from a French edition published earlier that same year. Replies to this position by Goldman, Berkman and others in the 1920's are discussed in Jean Maitron, *Le mouvement anarchiste en France* (Paris: François Maspero, 1975), vol. II, pp. 81-82, and in Paul Avrich, *The Russian Anarchists* (Princeton: Princeton University Press, 1971), pp. 241-43.

8.  See the remarks of anarchist Gaston Leval in his *Espagne Libertaire: 1936-1939* (Paris: Editions du Cercle, 1971), pp. 61, 65-66 (the more recent English-language edition is *Collectives in the Spanish Revolution);* Gerald Brenan, *The Spanish Labyrinth*, chs. 7-8; and anarchist

Murray Bookchin's *The Spanish Anarchists*, ch. 5, for references by other observers to the deep cultural roots underlying the strength of Spanish anarchism by the 1930's. Even the Spanish CNT delegation to the December 1937 Paris meeting of the IWMA suggested the same "cultural" basis for their persistent determination to fight to the end (AIT [IWMA] minutes of the December 1937 meeting, p. 19, AMS-AIT Archives).

10. The various ways in which the anarchists' "allies" sabotaged the anti-fascist struggle and the revolution itself are described in Chapter V below. In this case, the "treachery of Madrid" refers to the government of Spain (by this date headed by Socialist Francisco Largo Caballero and earlier by liberal Republicans Santiago Casares Quiroga and José Giral) which failed to offer decisive resistance to the fascists, to a great extent for fear of the mounting wave of genuine social revolution. CNT-FAI leaders chose to appease the Madrid government by being very conciliatory toward non-anarchist forces in Catalonia, even though the anarchists there were clearly the dominant force in resisting and defeating the Right-wing uprising.

19. Referred to here are various groups and individuals within the Spanish anarchist movement but denied "official" recognition or status by the leaders of the CNT-FAI. The Barcelona "Friends of Durruti" affinity group was one notable example which especially attracted Goldman's curiosity (12/30/37 letter to Helmut Rüdiger, AMS-G). It was formed in early 1937 but was denied official FAI recognition because of its strong anti-collaborationist position. Its critique was well-publicized in the Barcelona May Days and for a time thereafter. The group is described in Paz; Carlos Semprun-Maura, *Révolution et contre-révolution en Catalogne* (Tours: Maison Mame, 1974); Burnett Bolloten, *La révolution espagnole: la gauche et la lutte pour le pouvoir* (Paris: Ruedo Ibérico, 1977) (the later English-language edition is *The Spanish Revolution: The Left and the Struggle for Power During the Civil War* [Chapel Hill: University of North Carolina Press, 1979]); and H. Chazé, *Chronique de la révolution espagnole* (Paris: Spartacus, 1979), a collection of articles published by a French Left Communist organization, the Union Communiste. A statement by the Friends of Durruti, "Towards A Fresh Revolution," was reproduced in 1978 by Cienfuegos Press in Britain and issued in pamphlet form. More on the Friends of Durruti can be found in their journal *Amigo del Pueblo* and in the notes of Hugo Oehler (Brandeis University manuscript collection), an American sympathizer of the Left Communist POUM in Barcelona at the time. A more prominent and "surfaced" opposition within the movement came from the Catalan Libertarian Youth. (See Peirats, *Anarchists in the Spanish Revolution;* Semprun-Maura; and their journal *Ruta.*) Also significant were several anarchist publications such as *Ideas, Acracia, Alerta!, Nosotros, Anarquía, La Noche,* and *Frente y Retaguardia,* as well as strong, anti-compromise sentiment within the anarchist military units, especially the "Iron Column" (later 83rd Brigade). Indications of the strength and perspective of the latter are found in Bolloten and *Protestation devant les libertaires du présent et du futur sur les capitulations de 1937,* a reprint of a long article published in *Nosotros* in March 1937 by an unidentified "Uncontrolled" anarchist militiaman (Paris: Editions Champs Libre, 1979) (much of this latter text is also quoted in Bolloten's book).

22. Opposition from FAI leaders strengthened from mid-1938 on. This evolution is described in some detail in Peirats, *Anarchists in the Spanish Revolution,* ch. 22.

Federica Montseny is the daughter of Soledad Gustavo and Federico Urales, two longtime anarchist activists and writers and veterans of the Montjuich imprisonment of 1896. She wrote and spoke abundantly for the movement in the years before 1936 and was regarded as a strong and influential defender of uncompromising anarchist principles. It therefore shocked many to see her rapidly endorse various concessions to statist forces from July 1936 on — including her own participation in the Caballero government as Minister of Health. In exile from 1939 on, she has continued to play a leading role in the CNT-FAI movement abroad. A relatively recent public critique by Montseny of her own and the movement's role in 1936-39 was written especially for Daniel Guérin, *Ni Dieu ni maître: anthologie de l'anarchisme* (Paris: François Maspero, 1970). Passages from an earlier (1951) critique by Montseny appear in Peirats, *La CNT . . .,* II, 212n. Also, see Goldman's further comments on Montseny in this chapter.

Diego Abad de Santillán was born in Spain in 1898. He became an anarcho-syndicalist militant while studying medicine in Argentina. Fleeing dictatorships there and in Uruguay in the early 1930's, he came to Spain again in 1933. There he became an influential writer and militant in the FAI. A strong force in pushing the CNT in Catalonia to collaborate with political parties and the state originally in late July 1936, he was also the chief CNT-FAI economic policymaker

for a time in Catalonia and held several other important functions as well. After several months of experience with collaboration, he came increasingly to view it as a mistake. His book *Por qué perdimos la guerra* (Why We Lost the War) was published in Buenos Aires in 1940. Goldman's further comments on Santillán appear below.

Pedro Herrera, a close associate of Santillán and a CNT and FAI militant on his own part, from July 1936 was on the Peninsular (in effect, the National) Committee of the FAI and its secretary for most of the war. He also participated in the second cabinet of the Catalan government, formed in December 1936. Goldman's further comments on Herrera also appear below.

Germinal Esgleas was a veteran CNT militant with years of struggle before the time of the revolution. In June 1937, he joined the Catalan regional government as Minister of the Economy. He was the close companion of Federica Montseny and with her occupied a leading position in the more orthodox, non-collaborationist wing of the CNT-in-exile after the war.

23. Juan Negrín, a minor Socialist politician before 1936, became Minister of Finance in the Caballero government. Later he became a thoroughly tractable ally of the Communists when they forced Caballero's removal in his favor in mid-May 1937. He continued as Prime Minister through the end of the war and as head of the government-in-exile until 1945.

27. Mariano Vázquez (1909-1939) was a CNT militant of the Construction Workers Union in Barcelona. On November 19, 1936 he stepped up from secretary of the Catalan regional CNT to become secretary-general of the National Committee. He remained an ardent defender of CNT centralization, discipline and compromising concessions with the anti-fascist allies even beyond the end of the war. Further Goldman comments on Vázquez appear below. A very favorable account of Vázquez is Manuel Muñoz Diez, *Marianet: Semblanza de un hombre* (Mexico City: Ediciones CNT, 1960).

38. Francisco Largo Caballero was the leader of the UGT (Unión General de Trabajadores), the Socialist-oriented rival to the CNT. Opportunistic enough to collaborate as part of the cabinet of dictator Primo de Rivera in the 1920's and fiercely anti-anarchist in the use of his repressive state powers as Minister of Labor in the early 1930's, he was imprisoned in 1934 by the right-wing government of Lerroux and there became acquainted with and enamored of Marxism and the works of Lenin for the first time. With organizational backing, a charismatic appeal and a new militant image from that time on, he eagerly assumed power as Prime Minister on September 4, 1936. Discarded by the Communists in mid-May 1937, he was forced out in favor of a more pliable Juan Negrín.

40. Mollie Steimer and her later companion Senia Fleshin were young Russian immigrant anarchists and antiwar activists in the U.S. during World War I. As many others of the day, they were strongly inspired by Emma Goldman's public speeches and articles on the war and other issues at the time (Mollie Steimer letter of 1/5/30 to Goldman, AMS-F). Fleshin himself for awhile even worked in the *Mother Earth* office (*LL*, II, 812). Like Berkman and Goldman, Steimer was imprisoned and deported to Russia for her activities. Soon after her arrival in late 1921, she met Fleshin who had come from the U.S. in 1917 and had worked with other Russian anarchists ever since. The two of them became openly critical of the Bolshevik regime, assisting other anarchists already in prison. Together, they also were imprisoned themselves. Deported from Russia in 1923, they became closely involved with Goldman and Berkman in Germany. From similar backgrounds and of similar views, the four became very close friends. Fleeing the Nazi regime, Steimer and Fleshin came to Paris in 1933. There they remained in the late 1930's, while strongly critical of CNT-FAI compromises in Spain. Again fleeing the fascists in 1940, they eventually found refuge and remained in Mexico. Steimer died in July 1980 and Fleshin several months later. See the section on Steimer in Margaret S. Marsh, *Anarchist Women: 1870-1920* (Philadelphia: Temple University Press, 1980). A detailed sketch of her life by anarchist historian Paul Avrich appears in *Anarchist News* (N.Y.), November 1980, and in *Black Rose* (Boston), no. 7 (Spring 1981). Goldman's descriptions of Steimer are found in *LL*, II, 666-67, 701-02, 704-06, 955-56.

42. Lenin pushed emphatically for a separate peace with Germany in early 1918, arguing that such was needed to provide time and space for the revolution in Russia while waiting for its outbreak in the rest of Europe. The humiliating terms of the Brest-Litovsk treaty, however, gave Germany full run over the relatively industrialized and agriculturally-rich Ukraine, and allowed them to concentrate more of their efforts on the western front. (21 years later, Stalin would repeat the same strategy to buy time through his pact with the Nazi. See Goldman's comments

on this in Chapters V and VI below.) Revolutionists in Russia were stunned, including a majority of Lenin's own comrades at the highest level of the Communist Party. Only after he personally threatened to resign and form a rival Communist Party if defeated did his comrades "approve." Critical anarchists and Socialist Revolutionaries in turn were arrested and imprisoned. In the Ukraine itself anarchist Nestor Makhno and others began a large-scale guerrilla insurrection which eventually liberated very substantial territory from the Ukrainian collaborationist regime, achieving various measures of social revolution at the same time. (See more on the Makhnovist revolution in Avrich's *The Russian Anarchists* and *The Anarchists in the Russian Revolution;* in Voline; in Peter Arshinov, *History of the Makhnovist Movement, 1918-1921* (1923; transl., Detroit: Black and Red, 1974); in Makhno's own *La Révolution russe en Ukraine (Mars 1917-Avril 1918)* [1927; rpt. Paris: Editions Pierre Belfond, 1970]; and in Michael Palij, *The Anarchism of Nestor Makhno, 1918-1921* [Seattle: University of Washington Press, 1977].)

47. Cipriano Mera was a CNT militant in the Madrid Construction Union and veteran of the December 1933 anarchist insurrection in Aragón. A talented leader of anarchist militia from 1936 on, he became a Lt. Colonel and commander of the 4th Army Corps in the Center region after his heroism at the battle of Guadalajara in March 1937. He became also a strong defender of the reintroduction of hierarchy and regular military discipline in the reorganized army (see Bolloten, pp. 346-48). At the same time, he made a famous public statement promising to go back to being a simple stonemason once the war was over. This he did, after a death sentence and imprisonment in Spain under Franco, then exile in France.

49. General Sebastián Pozas was named head of the Civil Guards after the February 1936 election victory of the Popular Front. He became Minister of Interior in the short-lived Giral government immediately after the July uprising by the Right. In October 1936 he became commander of the Army of the Center, shortly after that joining the Communist Party. Several months later, during the May fighting in Barcelona, he became commander of the Army of the East, including Catalonia and the Aragón front.

53. Horacio Prieto was a Basque anarchist militant who became CNT national secretary at the Saragossa national congress in May 1936. After strongly pushing for anarchist participation in the government of Caballero, he handed over his position to Vázquez with the achievement of his policy in November 1936. He continued to be a major CNT influence for collaborationism throughout the war, even arguing for the conversion of the FAI to a regular political party for that purpose. His perspective on Spanish anarchism was presented in a book apparently written by his son, César Lorenzo, *Les anarchistes espagnols et le pouvoir, 1868-1969.*

# Chapter Three

# *The New Society*

*At the heart of the anarchist faith is certainty in the immense rewards gained from fully pursuing the creative instinct. Freely to explore and recreate the natural and social environment potentially provides endlessly fulfilling modes of human existence. At best, work is simultaneously play, human interaction a mosaic of infinite, delightful combinations between the unique qualities of every individual. It is especially on the basis of their own experience that anarchists assume such vast potentials to exist for all. They have felt, not simply theorized, the heights attainable by "merely" being human—as individuals, in small groups, and in larger communities.*

*It is precisely an intense awareness of human potential which makes existing social conditions so painful. To experience the miseries of war, poverty, alienated labor, exploitation of one group by another, and even the co-optation of social change movements themselves is difficult enough. Yet all the more deeply enraging is to know that these conditions need not exist.*

*Traditionally, those in the anarchist movement were more willing than most to express this rage and to direct it consciously against those social targets most responsible for existing oppression. Yet the necessary change they envisioned was at such a pace and so all-encompassing that it was perceived by many as a direct personal threat, even to those on the Left. Liberals most often discounted anarchists, calling them pathological social misfits and indeed often joining in their repression. In turn, because anarchists insisted on opposing hierarchy in politics generally (most obviously, the state itself and centralized movements for change) non-anarchist radicals usually viewed them at best as useful only for the destructive tasks of revolution. More often they were simply convenient scapegoats to prove others' "respectability."*

*Even observers willing to acknowledge positive ideals in the anarchist movement most often rejected such visions as hopelessly unrealistic in modern society. Of course, utopians who refused even to speculate on how humans might arrange their lives after revolution deserved to be criticized. Such a position naively assumed that*

*everything would work out well and it would be best not to suggest possibilities now
which might inhibit the future. Yet few outside critics bothered to distinguish between this position and conscientious anarchist speculation.*[1] *For most, social
utopianism was idle daydreaming. It needed not to be taken seriously.*

*As in the past, anarchists currently most often suffer a bad image among 'pro-
gressives" on* both *counts—as either destructive negativists or irresponsible
dreamers. It is true that many people today admire revolutionary ideals; also,
decentralist, participatory social models are presently more fashionable than
before. Yet the traditional anarchist commitment to anti-authoritarian change
throughout economic, political and cultural realms all together is still dismissed by
most as naive and unattainable. However now also, as in the past, among the ranks
of liberals, 'democratic socialists" and Marxist communists alike, there is a hunger
for a more positive human image than any of these movements can offer. For such
individuals, the constructive experience of the Spanish revolution so enthusiastically endorsed by Emma Goldman in these pages should come as a welcome relief.
It is also an invitation for them to expand their own politics.*

# II

*For many years in the United States, Emma Goldman's name was publicly
synonymous with nihilistic violence. At the most dramatic level, not only was she
closely associated with Berkman's 1892 attempt on the life of Frick, she also was
portrayed in the yellow journalism of the day as encouraging Czolgosz' 1901
murder of President McKinley.*[2] *On the issue of effectively releasing legitimate
social rage, however, Goldman in fact by the latter date consciously had
moderated her own behavior and public stand. Thus, while she understood and
tried to explain the legitimate* human emotions *behind the violence of Czolgosz and
others, she no longer personally espoused such tactics for the anarchist
movement.*[3]

*However, massive upheaval against the whole oppressive social order was
another matter. She thus greeted the Russian revolution as an immensely positive
social development. Nevertheless, its first phase of spontaneous mass insurrection
and creation of new cooperative forms (factory councils, co-ops, and soviets) was
relatively brief. Under the dual impact of Bolshevik domination and armed foreign
and white Russian attacks, the revolution increasingly was smothered by an atmosphere of negativity and destruction, coercion and centralization. Seeing the*

1. Probably the best past work of this latter type was Peter Kropotkin's *Fields, Factories and
   Workshops* (2nd ed., N.Y.: Putnam's, 1913). Among the best such literature currently are
   Murray Bookchin's *Post-Scarcity Anarchism* (San Francisco: Ramparts Press, 1971), *Toward
   An Ecological Society* (Montreal: Black Rose Books, 1980) and *The Ecology of Freedom* (Palo
   Alto, Calif.: Cheshire Books, 1982). See also Giovanni Baldelli, *Social Anarchism* (Chicago:
   Aldine-Atherton, Inc., 1971).
2. So common was her media-fostered notoriety, parents would sometimes discipline their
   children with the threat of Emma Goldman "coming to get them."
3. Except in the case of obvious tyrants clearly hated by the masses (such as the czar in Russia or
   Prime Minister Cánovas in Spain). See further discussion of this issue in Chapter VII.

*ultimate logic of this direction when the Bolsheviks in 1921 bloodily suppressed the libertarian socialist Kronstadt commune, Goldman fully admitted the revolution's tragic failure. Leaving Russia for long years of wandering and empty exile, she openly denounced both the Bolshevik regime and its vociferous, organized supporters in the West. For her, revolution was still a cherished dream. Yet now more than ever, she saw that it had to be motivated and characterized by a thoroughly positive and constructive impulse. The destructive side of upheaval, though inevitable and necessary, should be only a subordinate stage or theme. Increasingly then, Goldman's own anarchist evolution led her to the point where only a massive positive social reconstruction could fulfill her vision of successful revolution.*[4]

## III

*It was this very process of seeing a new society constructed before her eyes that lifted Goldman to the heights of enthusiasm in the late 1930's. During her three trips through loyalist Spain, she insisted above all on visiting the collectivized economic units of city and countryside which embodied, or at least began to approach, the traditional anarchist ideal. Far more than the anti-fascist war, it was these efforts, together with the new educational models and social relief, which for her came to represent the brilliance of the Spanish anarchists, the heart and soul of the Spanish revolution.*

*Her own commentary on these efforts below reflects less of the objective balancing of strengths and weaknesses than we have come to expect from Emma Goldman. Undoubtedly this is because she recognized that, whatever their shortcomings, these constructive attempts at concrete practice were the most emphatic and articulate social statements of her own deepest aspirations. Small wonder that she chose to emphasize the affirmative here, saving her more critical words for an analysis of anarchist behavior in the explicitly political realm of the revolution. Understood in this light, her personal observations of this constructive side in Spain and her emphatic insistence on this as the essence of true revolution are useful and inspiring to those currently seeking the vast transformation of existing society.*

# General Observations

*†Already before her departure for Spain, Goldman writes enthusiastically to Milly and Rudolf Rocker (8/26/36) about the constructive model of revolution created by the Spanish anarchists.*

. . . I realize that armed defense is imperative against the armed attack of the black forces.[5] But I am much more interested in the constructive work our

4. See footnote 4 at back of chapter.
5. Goldman employs the term "black forces" here to indicate the Fascists (as with the Italian "blackshirts"). It was equivalent to referring to the Communists as "reds." Usage of both

comrades in Catalonia are doing, the socialising of the land, the organization of the industries. They may not be permitted to do so for long. But if they should be defeated they will yet have shown the first example in history *how Revolutions should be made.*

*†Barely in Spain for several days (9/19/36), Goldman describes to her niece the energizing effect of observing in person this massive social transformation.*

. . . I cannot possibly go into details about the situation after only three days in Barcelona. I can only say that I feel I have come to my own, to my brave and heroic comrades who are battling on so many fronts and against so many enemies. The most impressive of their achievements so far is the marvelous order that prevails, the work in factories and shops of those I have seen now in the hands of the workers and their organizations. Some of the places I visited and the houses requisitioned by our comrades for their different bureaus formerly belonging to the biggest concerns are in the same perfect condition as if no battle between life and death had happened in the streets of Barcelona. I think it is the first time in history that such stress is being laid on the superior importance of running the machinery of economic and social life as is being done here. And this by the much maligned, chaotic Anarchists, who supposedly have "no program" and whose philosophy is bent on destruction and ruin. Can you imagine what this means to me to see the attempt made to realize the very ideas I have stressed so passionately since the Russian Revolution? Why . . . it was worth all the travail, all the pain and bitterness of my struggle to have lived to see our comrades at work. I am too overjoyed, too happy to find words to express my exhaltation and my admiration for our Spanish comrades.

You understand, my dearest, that the primary effort of the CNT and FAI is to crush Fascism. But over and above they are also straining every nerve to demonstrate the possibility of a new social order along the lines of our ideas. No matter what the outside press, such miserable papers like the *Nation,* may say to belittle the contribution of the comrades in Barcelona and Catalonia, the CNT and the FAI are the moving spirit of the changes here. They are in control, they proudly declare they are aiming at far more than merely the battle against the black enemy and they are going to leave their roots, whatever happens, in the soil of the country and in the minds and hearts of its people. You can tell this to everybody for me, my dearest, and you can add that I want with all my heart to become a part, an active part, in any and every capacity in this grandiose battle for the triumph of our idea.

"political colors" is found, for example on p. 152 of Chapter V. Like the vast majority of radicals (and others) throughout her era, Goldman unfortunately also used "black" imagery, however unconsciously, with an offensive connotation for those of the black races.

*† The roots of creative revolution were embedded within the deep consciousness of the Spanish workers themselves. It was not a design imposed from above. This fact, based on weeks of investigation in republican Spain, validated more than anything else Goldman's lifelong faith in the viability of the anarchist ideal (11/30/36 letter to Roger Baldwin).*

One thing I can tell you already: the Revolution is safe with the workers and peasants of Catalonia, Aragón and the Levante. I know whereof I speak. I have travelled through these parts, have visited the collectivized towns and villages[6] and I have seen the spirit of the people. I know they are imbued with the ideal so many of us have [advocated] for a lifetime. I feel certain they will never be conquered. The most impressive phase of the Revolution to me is that it has no leaders, no great intellects. It is entirely a mass Revolution risen from the depth of the Spanish soil, the depths of the needs and aspirations of the workers. Never again will anyone dare to say Anarchism is not practical or that we have no program. The constructive work done here disproves this false accusation hurled against us by all sorts of people. Yes, my dear, I feel it was worth all I have given to the Anarchist movement to see with my own eyes its first buddings. It is my grandest hour.

*† One year later (11/11/37), in a letter to an unidentified U.S. comrade, Goldman expresses amazement that creative constructive activity persists stronger than ever, despite fierce obstacles and open sabotage against it.*

To deny the evils I found on my second visit to Spain would be a betrayal of my whole past and would ill-serve the Spanish comrades. Their losses are tremendous. And yet they do not weigh in the scale against their gains. I am not speaking only of their moral influence. I am speaking of the constructive work begun on the 19th of July which, in many instances, has grown, improved and has been perfected so much since last year. To me, it is miraculous for a people to go on building in the face of war, food shortage and a deadly political regime that has filled the prisons, destroyed some of the collectives and that disposes of all opponents in the dead of the night, thus endangering everybody's life who will not swear by the Stalin-Negrín regime.

I hope to write about the devastating march of the Lister and Marx brigades through some of the collectives in Aragón and of the havoc they left behind.[7] For the present, I only wish to say that even this savage siege has not dampened

---

6.  Augustin Souchy estimated that more than half the land in the republican zone was collectivized. Gaston Leval estimates a total of 1700 agrarian collectives. In the cities, the latter estimates Catalonia had 100% of industry and transportation collectivized; in the Levante, some 70%; and lower figures elsewhere. (Both authors are cited in Dolgoff, ed., *The Anarchist Collectives,* p. 71.)

7.  See footnote 7 at back of chapter.

the ardour and spirits of our comrades. Their spirit burns at white heat that gives them strength and determination to continue the process of building a new Spain. One must see their work and hear their story to realize that the revolution is far from dead. And that is enough to urge me to throw myself with renewed energy into the work abroad for the CNT-FAI.

† *Her mid-December 1937 speech to the IWMA congress in Paris reiterates the same theme.*

I returned to Spain with apprehension because of all the rumors that had reached me, after the May events, of the destruction of the collectives. It is true that the Lister and Karl Marx Brigades went through Aragón and places in Catalonia like a cyclone, devastating everything in their way; but it is nevertheless the fact that most of the collectives were keeping up as if no harm had come to them. In fact I found the collectives in September and October 1937 in better-organized condition and in better working order – and that, after all, is the most important achievement that must be kept in mind in any appraisal of the mistakes made by our comrades in Spain. Unfortunately, our critical comrades do not seem to see this all-important side of the CNT-FAI. Yet it is this which differentiates them from Lenin and his crowd who, far from even attempting to articulate the Russian Revolution in terms of constructive effort, destroyed everything during the civil war and even many years after.

† *Another year later, in the final months of the civil war (12/9/38), Goldman reports in a draft article that constructive activity is still as vigorous as before because it is in the workers' life-blood. She also clarifies that such activity is perceived as the first stages toward anarchism, not its full achievement.*

I was naturally interested to see how far the CNT-FAI were still the moral force in the ranks of the workers and peasants, and their influence in the industrial and agricultural life in Spain. This was the more essential because a number of comrades outside Spain are so easily susceptible to whatever derogatory reports about the CNT-FAI come to them. Now it is true that the war industries and the railroads have been nationalized.[8] It is also a sad fact that Negrín has turned over to the former owners the electrical plants, collectivized by the CNT-FAI immediately after July 19th, 1936. Yet even in the nationalized industries I found that the Spanish Anarchists were still very much in evidence. On the other hand, the collectives, such as transport, wood

8. That is, taken over by the state instead of remaining as workers' self-managed collectives (socialization).

industry, textile and garment workers, milk collectives and many more, continue to be manned by members of the CNT. The same holds good of the collectives on the land. Moreover this applies not only to Catalonia, which I was able to revisit, but to Castile, the Levante and the unoccupied part of Andalusia. I have this not only from our comrade, Augustine Souchy, but also from the many delegates from these parts who attended the plenum. Comrade Souchy has spent months in all these places and has collected an immense amount of material which he is now preparing for a book.[9] In other words, whatever thrusts the Spanish Revolution has received, and I know better than many other visitors to Spain how deep the wounds are, I must nevertheless insist that collectivization and socialization still represent the most potent revolutionary achievement of the Spanish Anarchists, and what is more to the point, even if Franco should possess himself of all Spain, which no one in the loyalist side considers possible, collectivization will continue. This, not only because of the influence of the CNT-FAI, but also for the reason that the idea of collectivization is deeply ingrained in the workers and peasants. One might even say collectivization is the very breath of their life.

Neither Lister's devastating march through the collectives in Aragón or the equally brutal destruction of other collectives by the Carl Marx Brigade, or the interference of the Government itself, had succeeded for long to keep the people from collectivization. I had ample proof of that last year, and perhaps more convincing demonstrations on my recent visit. For lack of space the few examples I will give must suffice, but before I do so I want to point out the childish claim of some comrades in America that collectivization is not Anarchism and that therefore our Spanish comrades had gone back on their ideals. Apart from the fact that these critics had never in their lives been called upon to demonstrate in practice their Anarchist theories, their enduring power and courage to face a whole world, it is necessary to point out to them that our Spanish comrades do not pretend that collectivization or socialization is Anarchism. They insist, however, that these two forms of reconstruction represent the first steps toward the realization of libertarian communism (Comunismo Libertario).[10] They are not only right, but they have proven the

9. The book which Souchy prepared from his notes on this and other visits was finally published as *Nacht über Spanien* (Darmstadt: Verlag die Freie Gesellschaft, 1957). English translations of several sections on collectivization appear in Dolgoff, ed., *The Anarchist Collectives*. An earlier work was Souchy's *Entre los campesinos de Aragón* (Barcelona: Tierra y Libertad, 1937). Abe Bluestein recently translated this work into English, *With the Peasants of Aragon* [Minneapolis: Soil of Lberty, 1982]). Since much of his material overlaps with impressions and information Goldman herself received from visits to many of the same collectives (often with Souchy himself), Souchy's works are appropriate companion readings for this chapter. The same is true of sections in another book published by a second 1936 traveller with Goldman, Hans Erich Kaminski, an anarchist sympathizer in exile from Germany. This work, *Ceux de Barcelone* (Paris: Denoel, 1937), includes some direct references to Goldman.

10. The vast majority—all but the pure individualists—in the historical and presentday anarchist movement no doubt would endorse the *general* social objective of libertarian or anarcho-communism as their broad goal. One brief common definition of that goal (from Berkman's

truism of Bakunin's[11] principle that revolution is not only the power of destruction but also the will to reconstruction. Only narrow-minded bigots in the Anarchist ranks will overlook the fact that our people were the first in the history of the social struggle and revolutions who have begun to reconstruct society in the midst of chaos and death, and in the face of a conspiracy of the democracies no less than of the Fascist countries. They have thereby set a glorious example to the international proletariat; for that and many other reasons the Spanish Anarchists have deserved better from their own comrades who pose as the only Simon Pure 100% Anarchists. All these people have done is to stab their Spanish brothers in the back.

# Socialized Industry

†*Her visit to a workers' self-managed champagne vineyard and bottling plant provides her the occasion to praise the positive rather than destructive attitudes of the Spanish proletariat (11/18/36 letter to her niece).*

Yesterday I visited the largest, most important champagne vineyards and industry in this country. It was founded in the 16th century and continued by a long line of the same family until the Revolution. It is the most modern and perfectly organized plant I have seen here. And would you believe it, the entire personnel including the manager are members of the CNT. The plant is now collectivized and run by the workers themselves. The manager, a comrade who fell on my neck when he learned my name, was quite surprised when I asked him whether the workers will have a chance to drink the champagne. "Of course," he said. "What is the Revolution for if not to give the workers what they never enjoyed?" Well, let's hope this will really be so. Meanwhile there are several million bottles of champagne that will most likely be used as a medium of exchange with the outside world for products Spain needs. Thus ten thousand bottles were sent to Russia a night before last. I suppose in exchange for the things Russia sent here. Fair exchange is no robbery. One thing is certain, the workers in Russia will not get a drop of the champagne. Here they can already get it. One sort, not so bad, only costs three pesetas[12] a bottle. That, however, is not the most interesting part. Rather is it the understanding and appreciation of the workers in Spain of the value of labor. I cannot say enough in that respect. Imagine people for centuries enslaved and poverty stricken leaving everything intact in the best of working

*What is Communist Anarchism?)* is: "the abolition of government, of coercive authority and all its agencies, and joint ownership—which means free and equal participation in the general work and welfare" (p. 196).

11. See footnote 11 at back of chapter.
12. In 1936, the Spanish peseta was worth about $ .326.

order without as much as a single bottle broken or anything destroyed. The friends who were with me (Germans) said, "In Germany the workers would have drunk as much as they could swill and the rest they would have destroyed." I rather think the Russian workers or many of them would have done the same. In a measure it would have been understandable of people who never enjoyed luxuries of any kind. But it does speak for the quality of the Spanish masses that they have such a constructive sense. They simply hate to demolish anything that represents labor. I have verified this in all factories, shops, stores and all other places I have visited. That gives me great hopes that when Fascism will be eradicated the workers will rebuild their country in half the time it has taken Russia. And it will be the workers themselves and not a political machine that will do it. If only Fascism will be exterminated. That is the rub. But here too one can only hope with every fiber of one's being.

†*In the midst of her second visit during the revolution, her 10/4/37 report to Ethel Mannin of a tour of the collectivized wood industry demonstrates Goldman's method of inquiry and the libertarian sentiments of the workers.*

I spent all day today going over the collectivized wood industry.[13] One can hardly credit it unless one can see it with one's own eyes how the workers go on at their task producing and perfecting their collective efforts surrounded by ever-present danger. And what optimism, what sublime faith. One completely forgets oneself and everything of a personal character amidst the life of the collective spirit of the masses. There is no power to destroy that. It is ingrained in the very texture of the Spanish masses. This realization strengthens my hope that whatever the mistakes and compromises of the CNT-FAI the Revolution is far from lost. Added to this is inborn dignity of the Spanish people and their utter fearlessness. You believe me, dearest, that I am not one to be content with the version I receive from the comrades who are at the head of the various committees in the collectives. I am too seasoned not to understand that no matter how honest and frank the best of us are, responsible positions create a certain psychology which must needs differ from the man at the bench and in the field who does the hardest labors. For this reason I naturally try to find out the reaction of the workers themselves. And I was inspired to find that they give a damn who is present, they speak their mind. They are not only not afraid but they simply feel their manhood too strongly to hide their reaction to the changes that had taken place here in the state machine. They look upon them with contempt because they know the political machine is transitory, the economic power of the people is the ultimate

13. In Barcelona. More on this experience can be found in Gaston Leval, *Espagne Libertaire, 1936-1939*, pp. 247-49.

deciding factor. To say therefore that coming here is as futile as going through Russia as a tourist is sheer ignorance of the independence and pride of the Spanish character. I am sure that the workers I spoke to today and ever since my return felt freer to speak out than workers in British or American factories. I was especially impressed with the replies to my question as to what actually had the workers gained by the collectivization. Would you believe it, the answer always was, first, greater freedom. And only secondly, more wages and less time of work. In the two years I was in Russia I never heard any workers express this idea of greater freedom. This seems to me to be a key to the intrinsic character of the Spanish workers, especially of the CNT-FAI. And that to me is the hope of the future development in this country.

†*Endlessly impressed with her Spanish comrades' energy and enthusiasm for economic reconstruction, in this 1/25/38 letter to Abe Bluestein, Goldman comments on their further creative planning for industrial development in the midst of the harsh civil war.*

Just think of it, dear Abe, here we are finding all kinds of fault with the stand taken by the CNT-FAI, discussing some article somebody wrote about the State, and all kinds of such things, and yet, our comrades in Spain can hold a conference attended by 800 delegates,[14] discussing not the State, nor the government, nor any political alignment; but economic reconstruction – the need of Spain's new economy, of getting rid of industrial undertakings that have failed and starting new industrial factories which hold out promise of success. Eight hundred sitting in conference and coolly discussing the economic reconstruction of Spain at a time when the cities are being bombarded, leaving in their wake hundreds of dead and mutilated, and when the war is waging at every front. Give me any other similar instance in history and I might not feel so determined to stand by the CNT-FAI.

†*In this excerpt from a published article (3/21/38), Goldman shares a more detailed glimpse of a self-managed textile factory visited during her second tour of revolutionary Spain.*

. . . We also had a chance to see the effect of the resourcefulness of CNT-FAI members in the industry [in Valencia]. An old monastery was turned into a modern workshop, employing large numbers of men, women and girls on the basis of mutual aid and cooperation. A group of unemployed workers of the same trade had undertaken the task of creating this new collective.

14. She refers to the national economic plenum of the CNT in Valencia in mid- to late January 1938, discussed in detail in Peirats, *La CNT* . . . ,III, 2-25.

It was all done by voluntary agreement, without one single worker having been coerced into it. While the venture had not yet reached perfection, the workers connected with it knew exactly what they wanted, and were pressing ahead in spite of all obstacles and imminent danger from bombardments. This collective factory was not merely for the production of things, but planned as a place for the physical and cultural life of those cooperating in the scheme. A dining room was in the midst of building; a dispensary, a lecture hall and reading room and ever so many other plans were already under way. We found a radio installed with connections to the shops where, while the women and girls were working, they could listen to the news, to good music or to their own moving song called "The Son of the People"; altogether a very remarkable undertaking by the workers themselves as a demonstration of what they will be able to do once Fascism is crushed and the road made free to the realization of the Revolution.

†*An intended article (12/9/38) following her third visit describes observations of another collective in the textile industry.*

My short stay in Spain did not permit me to visit even a small number of collectives, but those I succeeded in reaching showed that while a great deal of the collectives had been destroyed, many were working at high speed and were demonstrating the indestructibility of collectivization among the Spanish people. Among others I came upon a most unique collective of the textile and needle trade. It had been started by three members of the CNT. Now it can boast of a membership of thousands. Its factories are housed in a large modern building containing airy workrooms and offices. Neither the building nor a single piece of material has been expropriated; the comrades rented the house and are paying 50,000 pesetas annually for it. Also, they bought their stock of material and paid for it with hard cash. The majority of workers of this collective are women and girls. Owing to the shortage of electric power during the day, the work has to be done at night from 10 P.M. till 6 A.M. The advantage of this schedule is that street cars run more frequently at this time and the workers have the chance to ride to and from work.

I discovered in the head of the collective a Spanish comrade who had been in the United States. Evidently I needed no introduction to him. On the contrary, he knew all about my activities in America almost better than good Comrade A.S. [Souchy] who acted as my interpreter. He immediately proceeded to make me known to the workers in every room. He was sure the women and girls would be proud to know the pioneer fighter who had done so much "for us." I had to declare that I unfortunately had not been in a position to do something for the Spanish comrades, but that I wanted terribly to help them to the best of my ability now—that is why I am returning to Spain again

and again. It was embarrassing to go through with the ordeal of the numerous speeches our comrade-manager made in every room introducing Compañera Emma Goldman, but there was no stopping him. Besides the intermission and the speeches were greatly enjoyed by the women and girls, so I had to let them be.

As in everything else, so too when the Spanish comrades have a chance to display their conquests, they are so generous they cannot bear to let you miss any part, and so up and down we went the many stairs to every room in order to see the truly marvelous achievement of this collective. Needless to say, all the men and women employed in this collective are members of the CNT, each one socially conscious of the imperative necessity to triumph over Fascism. For the present the collective produces entirely for the front – wages range between 75 and 200 pesetas per week. Whatever surplus derived from the work is used to improve and perfect the building and machinery, for contribution to the care of the sick among the workers, and a very considerable contribution to educational and cultural efforts. . . .

## Collectivized Agriculture

†*In this published article (3/5/37), Goldman comments enthusiastically on a collectivized farm community, Albalate de Cinca.*

The superior quality of the Spanish Anarchist movement to those of other countries consists in the constructive preparatory work which our comrades had carried on almost from the very inception of the CNT. Some years ago, they sent a questionnaire to all their affiliated syndicates asking the workers how far they felt equipped to take over the industries, and manage them themselves, on the first day of the Social Revolution; how far they knew the resources and the cost of maintenance of the industries; and whether they felt able to take charge of the means of production and distribution. The Committee of the National Confederation of Labour was surprised to find how well the simplest workers and peasants understood the intricate machinery of the industrial system. In other words, the Spanish workers had years of experience and preparation for the supreme moment of a social revolution.

Aside of their economic preparation, they had been trained ideologically that it was not the creation of a formidable State machine but the capacity to produce for the needs of the whole community which guarantees the life and safety of the Revolution.

On July 19, 1936, the Spanish workers proved that they were prepared for the supreme moment. Since then they have also demonstrated in a masterly manner their pre-revolutionary schooling in the economic life of the country. While still fighting almost with bare hands – they at the same time proceeded

to expropriate the factories and shops – the entire transport system as well as the land – and they set to work to build a new mode of life out of the decadent conditions left by their economic masters.

In coming to Spain, I little dreamt that our Spanish comrades had proceeded with the constructive task to such a degree. I visited numerous large industries and was amazed at the capacity of the supposedly untaught workers to attend to the task in such an intelligent and able manner. And I was even more impressed with the spirit and ability of the peasantry in the villages I had visited to collectivize the land and to bring into being what they called "Comunismo Libertario."

The village Albalate de Cinca is a case in point. It is in the Province of Huesca – one of the most besieged fronts by the Fascists. Its population consisted of 5,000 – the majority of whom are CNT-FAI members. The leading spirits in the requisitioning of the land and the organization of work in common, are a comrade of seventy and his grandson, who is twenty-five. They have been steeped in the ideas and ideals of Anarchist Communism during three generations. It was no effort to them to carry into practice their long-cherished dream of working the land in common for the benefit of all.

The large estate belonged to one of the aristocratic parasites of whom there were many in Spain. He lived abroad, spending the large income that had been derived from the sweat and toil of the starving peasants. In 1929 he graciously offered his large possessions to the peasants in return for an exhorbitant rental. They took him at his word, but soon found that though they worked the land incessantly it did not yield enough to meet the demands of the man who owned the estate. They held out for a year and then refused to pay rent or taxes. As a result they were constantly persecuted by the henchmen of Primo de Rivera, then Dictator of Spain. With the advent of the Republic in '31, they were left in peace, but without any rights to the use of the land or without any material help to make it fertile, had they been permitted access to it. Then came the Revolution, July 19th, which spread like wildfire all through Spain and was most effective in Catalonia.

Among the first to interpret the Revolution in a constructive sense were the peasants of Albalate de Cinca. They set to work with a will and a whim which the outside world least expected of "crude and undeveloped peasants."

When I arrived in the beginning of October, barely three months after the heroic Catalan workers had driven Franco's gangs from their midst, these "crude and undeveloped" peasants had already succeeded in collectivizing part of the land and were working in a true spirit of Libertarian Communism. Actually, they showed more intelligence and better psychological perception than the men who had imposed dictatorship on the Russian workers and the peasants. They had realized the criminal blunder of driving their brothers into the collectives by Chekists[15] armed to their teeth. In their natural wisdom,

---

15. Soviet secret police.

our Albalate de Cinca comrades reasoned that it was their duty to demonstrate the superior quality of work in common. They told me "once we can prove to our brothers that collective labor saves time and energy, and brings greater results to each member of the collective, the peasants now standing aloof will join us."

I had occasion to verify the truism of this statement when I talked to some of the peasants outside of the collective. Fortunately, they did not know who I am, therefore did not have to make up their story to please me. In their simple way they expressed exactly the thought that had been elaborated for me by the Committee of the Albalate Collectives. They would "wait and see" how well collectivism worked, and would then decide whether to join it. The comrades have established three bodies that operate in Albalate de Cinca – a Council of Labor, of Food Supplies and of Defense. The three work in a federated way, of course. Federation is the very essence of the ideas and practice of the CNT-FAI.

It would be wrong to say that Albalate de Cinca is an anarchist commune in the full sense. The principle of labor, "from each according to his ability and to each according to his need" cannot yet be carried out to its full extent. The land has been lying too fallow too long and there is very little of modern machinery to work with. True, the first step of the collective was to buy a threshing machine and the most essential farm tools. But all that is still very primitive and therefore the land does not yield enough to satisfy all the needs of each member. Nevertheless, Albalate has succeeded in coming as near the principles of anarchist communism as hardly anticipated in the midst of danger and death from the bloodthirsty enemy and the defense of the Revolution. The means of livelihood are proportioned according to the size of each family. Whatever surplus realized is contributed to the anti-Fascist war and the Revolutionary struggle. It is indeed a remarkable feat to have achieved in the present situation.

What touched me deepest was the social awareness and the flaming spirit of the young generation in the collective. Not a thought of themselves; all their hopes and aspirations were concentrated on the great reconstructive work before them, the schools they wanted to build, the hospitals, libraries and museums they planned. Every youngster without exception was by far better read and better versed in social ideology than many of the young people in the large cities outside of Spain.

Whatever will become of the gallant struggle of the Spanish workers and peasants, and their advance guard, the CNT-FAI (they will, they must be victorious), the constructive experiment begun on July 19 will stand out as the most extraordinary example of how a Revolution should be made.[16]

---

16. A further description of this collective from Souchy's *Nacht über Spanien* is found in Dolgoff, ed., *The Anarchist Collectives*, pp. 133-34.

†*In an article published in* Spanish Revolution *(3/21/38 and 5/1/38), Goldman describes her impressions of collective farm organization in the region between Madrid and Valencia.*

Our next attention [in Madrid] was devoted to the Centre Federation of Peasants. It is housed in the private palace of a Count and is serving a much better purpose than when he was in possession. We collected a tremendous amount of data which Comrade A.S. [Souchy] is adding to his already monumental material on collectivization to form a book. I can only give a brief outline of the information given us by the Secretary of the Federation.

We learned that 700 syndicates and 300 collectives are affiliated with this Federation. The membership of the federation is 100,000. In view of the fact that the Federation had begun its work only a short time ago, it was amazing to see the amount already achieved. Thus the Federation has departments of statistics, propaganda, [and] interchange and sections dealing with oil, wine and all other kinds of provisions. We were taken into the scientific laboratory which, though not yet completed, already gave promise of an important and unique institution. The main stress laid there is on chemical and agricultural experiments and analyses. It is done with a view to improving and increasing the quality and quantity of output. In connection with this an experimental school for agricultural engineers was organized. The turnover from the 15th of July to the 15th of August, 1937 amounted to 11 million pesetas. This sum we were assured does not represent the full economic strength of the Federation because the local and territorial federations interchange among themselves and turn over to the Federation only the surplus of their products.

The Federation consists of two sections, laborers and small land-owners. The syndicates are very hospitable to the owners because they feel that eventually they will realize the superior method of working the land in the collective way than by individual drudgery. So much more could have been gathered from the interesting account of the Secretary had we but the time to remain long and make a thorough study of every detail of the ramifications represented by the Centre Federation of Peasants.

· · · · · · · · · · · · · · · · · · · · · · · · · · · · · · · · · · · · · · · · · · · · · · · · ·

On the 24th of September, 1937, we began our return trip to Valencia, visiting several collectives on the way. The largest and most important is in Azuquema, about 40 km. from Madrid along the road to Guadalajara. It has a population of only 1,500.

The collective is on the estate of the Count of Romanones. This grandee paid very little attention to the cultivation of that rich and beautiful estate consisting of 720 acres and known far and wide by the name of Miralcampo. The main occupation of Count Romanones was race-horse breeding for his own amusement. When the Revolution of the 19th of July broke out, this gentleman took to his heels and the peasants took possession of the estate,

which is now collectivized and employs 200 men.

The land through which the River Henares flows was flooded from time to time, gradually inundating the largest part of the land. Nevertheless the Count never took steps to check the danger. This has been accomplished by the workers themselves since they turned the estate to the use of all. Two engineers from the technical syndicate in Madrid were sent down to direct the harnessing of the river by means of filling in the inundated part with small stones and casing them in nettings of wire. These stones had to be brought to the river bed by means of a wheelbarrow which meant no end of difficult and hard labor; but every one of the members kept at the task with willingness and devotion. Certainly the accomplished task demonstrated the constructive capacity of the workers and held out hope for a great regeneration of Spain once Fascism will have been driven out of the country.

The old overseer of Miralcampo remained with the comrades in the collective. He took as much pride in looking after the variety of flowers, and perhaps more, than under his previous owner. He assured us that the work was much pleasanter because he had no master to drive him. He also assured us that the standard of life of the members of the collective, as well as that of the town of Azuquema, had greatly improved.

According to the European standards 350 pesetas a month is not very high; they are, however, infinitely higher than they were before the 19th of July when the peasants were paid 3 and 4 pesetas a day during the season and permitted to starve for the rest of the year. In addition to the amount paid, fully 50 per cent of the members of the collective eat together in the collectivized kitchen and pay 60 pesetas a month each. Children are given their food free.

. . . I have never before had a chance to be so close to the toilers of the soil and to enjoy their unspoiled and uncorrupted fellowship at the same table. It was indeed a great treat.

Here, too, I found several people who could speak French. One of them was the father of the Secretary of the collective, an old Anarchist who had lived a number of years in France. He constituted himself my guide and escort and explained everything in the minutest detail with great pride. Through him I learned that they work eight hours a day, that the richness of the soil had been increased; that before the 19th the crops realized 400,000 pesetas; now they exceeded a million.

The entire agricultural production of 1937 consisted of the following: 300 loads of melons; 250,000 kilos. of potatoes; 128,000 kilos. of barley; 175,000 kilos. of wheat; part of it had been sent to the Centre Federation of Peasants in Madrid, part to the front and the surplus for the needs of the collective. Of the crop in 1936, 125,000 pesetas worth of produce was contributed free of charge to the needs of Madrid. The comrade also spoke of the increase in livestock and in the quality of it. Among others, one of the members from Ganiz, a peasant who formerly tilled his own bit of ground,

had contributed 8 milking cows of the finest quality. The collective also has built its own bakery, rabbit hutches and chicken coops.[17]

There are two syndicates in the town of Azuquema. One belongs to the UGT. The other belongs to the comrades of the CNT. But as the workers of the former did not go in for collectivization of their land, quite a number of them are working in the collective of the CNT. Of course, a school was organized, not only for the children of the members but for the members themselves, as many of them had remained in illiteracy and ignorance until the 19th of July.

· · · · · · · · · · · · · · · · · · · · · · · · · · · · · · · · · · ·

We arrived in Telmes, a town of 1,780 inhabitants on the Madrid-Valencia road, in the afternoon. At the Secretariat of the CNT we were given the information we were seeking. We learned that until the 19th of July there was no organization of any kind, trade union or of a political nature, in that town. Today the CNT and the UGT have their own local syndicates, but it was the CNT members who organized a collective mainly composed of former small owners, numbering in all 435 members.

A tomato-canning factory had been turned over by its owner voluntarily. In the agreement with the collective he pledged himself not to demand the return of his machinery should he decide to leave the collective and in his presence the titles to his property were destroyed. True his motive was not entirely selfless; the poor man was head over his heels in debt amounting to 15,000 pesetas which he could not hope to repay in many years to come. By entering the collective he was relieved of that responsibility. The debt was paid for him. Partly out of self-interest and partly out of gratitude he now works as ardently as he did when the plant belonged to him.

The owners of an olive oil and soap factory followed the good example of their colleague from the tomato plant. Thus two-thirds of the members of the collective are former small owners. The rest are laborers. They now own the lands, tools, implements and livestock in common. The collective covers an area of 140 acres. The soil yields wheat, potatoes, corn, beans, barley, tomatoes, sweet peppers and olives. They own 15 cows, 60 goats and 100 mules. The collective has instituted family wages, arranged as follows: a married man receives 8 pesetas a day; a single person 6 pesetas; in addition married couples receive an additional allowance in cash and 125 kilos. of olive oil a year plus 40 kilos. for each child. The houses are municipalized.

The syndicates have their secretariat which consists of a council of economy composed of three sections — agriculture, manufacture of agricultural products, industry and one section of statistics and accounting.

---

17. Another brief description of this collective is found in Leval, p. 199. In a book published in Spain in 1968 and cited by Leval is another brief account, translated into English in turn in Dolgoff's book, pp. 150-51. Also see *Campo Libre*, July 30, 1937.

The structure of the syndicate is that of an organization performing a double function, that of production and consumption. The collective which is affiliated with the syndicate has a school attended by 70 children; 2 teachers, also members of the collective, work on the same principle as all the other members. All the material for the school is supplied free of charge.

I had a touching experience in this collective which shows the quality of the Spanish people in its most hard-worked and formerly enslaved and exploited ranks. The dwelling of the former owner of the tomato factory, though consisting only of two rooms, was spotlessly clean and had a few pieces of decent-looking furniture. I wondered whether all the population of the town had similar "luxurious" living quarters. I was assured by a comrade that this is not the case. He would take me to a place where a family of five were living in two stone rooms cut out of the rock, without windows, the air coming in during the day through the only opening, the door. It was really a cave, yet it was kept in the greatest order and with pathetic bits of crockery to give the place some color and to make up for never-penetrating sunshine.

I asked if I might wash my hands, as they had become quite soiled and we were going to have a meal before departing on our way to Valencia. The wife, who could not be more than 35, but looked 50 from frequent child-bearing and everlasting drudgery, brought a clean white towel and the last remnant of a piece of toilet soap which she undoubtedly cherished very much. It was her homage to me as a foreign comrade who, she had been told, would write about their struggle and their new hope. I should not have felt more deeply moved and honored by any token given me by people of wealth.

†*A 12/9/38 manuscript provides her impressions of the socialized milk production sector.*

My good old faithful friend, Augustin Souchy, who had been with me on many tours through Spain, took me on a tour of inspection of the socialized milk industry. Knowing how reliable and painstaking he is in taking notes, I cheerfully left this task to him during our visit to a number of the collectives. Part of the material here used comes from the copious notes he had taken. The credit for it is therefore his and not mine.

The socialized milk industry was reorganized by the workers of the CNT after July 19th, 1936, and placed on a modern and hygienic basis. This was the more necessary because the supply of milk in Barcelona had formerly been in the hands of small traders more interested in profits than the quality of the milk. In point of fact milk was adulterated with considerable admixtures of chemical substances. Cows were kept in filthy sheds without air, sunshine or a chance to be taken to pasture. As a result of it a large percentage of the cattle were tuberculous. In addition was the fact of outrageous exploitation of

the workers engaged in the milk dairies and industries. The reorganization was begun entirely under the guidance of the CNT. . . . As a result, *Industria Láctea Socializada* (Socialized Milk Industry) became a special branch of the food industry. Among the immediate steps taken was to create entirely new and modern methods to increase the quality and quantity of milk. Cooling stations were established. Seven of these were opened in Catalonia alone. The peasants from the surrounding villages bring the milk to the cooling stations. Here it is reduced to a temperature from 5 to 7 degrees above zero; put into thermos flasks, the milk reaches Barcelona at an even temperature.

We visited several cooling stations at Las Franquesa, Clot near Gerona, Satoville and La Perpetua de la Moguda, since renamed Granja Germinal. The first of these stations was placed in a former wine depot. It was completely renovated and equipped with machinery brought from Barcelona. Five men and five women were there, their wages being paid by their syndicate in Barcelona. It averages 160 pesetas per week. Instead of 30,000 litres of milk that could easily be cooled in this station, only 1,000 a day actually pass through the process. The reason for this was lack of fodder which unfortunately induced some peasants to slaughter a number of cows.

In Clot a large dairy factory was established and condensed milk and butter are being produced there. The entire produce is regularly taken by the military authorities for use at the front. In Clot we came upon an interesting case which, like so many other phenomena one meets, can only happen in Spain. Although the cooling station is collectivized, the widow of the former owner is being paid off the cost of the place in monthly rates; in addition she is permitted to keep her living quarters – much more comfortable I found than the homes of many workers in the large cities – and is also given a daily ration of milk. No wonder she assured me that she was very contented and that the Compañeros were most kind to her.

The estate of Satoville, about 50 kilometres from Barcelona, had been abandoned by its owner in the July days. He retired in safety to Barcelona, where he died in 1937. Although he was known to have Fascist leanings, he had in no way been molested. No doubt he ended his days hoping to his last breath that Franco would soon come to deliver him from the "Reds" who had turned his neglected estate into a well-organized and prosperous farm.

Ninety-four cows, many pigs and sheep, as well as chickens and rabbits, make up the livestock in Granja Germinal. Thirty-two hectares of land are under complete cultivation. Sixty peasants and an equal number of dairy workers are employed in this place, their pay averaging from 160 to 200 pesetas a week. Already this socialized venture has spent 90,000 pesetas on new cowsheds and other improvements to bring the estate up to date, and to make it yield returns it never had before.

We returned to Barcelona to visit the largest enterprise of the milk syn-

dicate. It is housed in the former Frigor Factory which manufactured milk by-products. All kinds of modern equipment in the way of pasteurizing machinery, butter churners, machinery for the production of cheese and yoghurt, skimming appliances and a new ice-cream producing plant had been established. In addition a number of model dairy depots were built for the retail sale of milk. Before July 19th this factory had a working capacity to produce 7,000 litres of milk daily. Now it could handle 100,000. The number of workers also had to be reduced from 350 to 200. The syndicates have reason to be proud of their great achievement. Far from that, they are most discontented because they cannot produce the increased amount of milk needed for the population in Catalonia. Formerly 200,000 litres of milk daily were used in Barcelona. Today 300,000 are necessary, owing to the great influx of refugees and the increase of the population. Formerly Catalonia used to buy large quantities of condensed milk in the north of Spain, now in the hands of Franco. Also large numbers of cows from Switzerland, Holland and the north of Spain used to be imported. All that has been made impossible since the beginning of the war. Another explanation for the famine in milk is to be sought in the calamity which had befallen Catalonia in May 1937. Owing to the plot against the CNT-FAI in Barcelona which resulted in the great disturbance, the former owners of the cattle evidently thought that the good old days had come back; they raided the collectives and led the cattle to their own sheds. When they realized that the syndicates were still in control they slaughtered their cows rather than give them back to the collectives. Yet with all the drawbacks, all the vicissitudes, the socialized milk industry stands out as a very great achievement. In point of truth, the milk syndicate has demonstrated that it was able to create a remarkable venture in a short period of months which had taken the peasant cooperatives in northern Europe decades to achieve.

# Education and Culture

†*As part of their overall efforts at social revolution, Spanish anarchists were committed to expanding educational opportunity on a libertarian basis, a theme Goldman shares here in this 10/10/36 letter to her niece.*

You will never think it credible, dearest, that in the midst of the nearing danger to Madrid and the Saragossa front [a] thousand delegates from every part of Catalonia foregathered to discuss the modern schools.[18] They argued

18. The "Modern School" movement in Spain was begun by anarchist educator Francisco Ferrer. See more on him in footnote 29 of Chapter I. Educational ideas discussed and implemented in Catalonia during the first months of the revolution are discussed in part in *L'Espagne Nouvelle*, no. 4 (May 8-15, 1937). See also Pere Solá, *Las escuelas racionalista en Cataluã* (Barcelona, 1976).

from morning until late at night. What do you think their argument [was] about? Nothing less than the safe-guarding of the federalist principles against any encroachment of centralization, Libertarian Communism against dictatorship. How can any one hope to crush such a people whose love of liberty is not merely acquired though reading, but is in their blood? No, whatever happens the CNT-FAI will not die, no matter what criminal forces are arrayed against them.

†*In this passage from an intended article (12/9/38), Goldman cites the importance of anarchist Puig Elías*[19] *in developing the libertarian schooling network.*

Some day soon I hope to find time to write a pen picture of Juan Puig Elías who is the real brain of the Ministry of Education and Culture.[20] I had met him for a short moment in 1936 at a Teachers' Conference attended by delegates from all over Spain, where he introduced his plan of La Escuela Nueva Unificada (the New Unified School) which was accepted by the entire assembly with enthusiasm and which has since been turned into fact.[21] Actually Comrade Puig Elías is one of the most outstanding modern pedagogues in the world, a man of wide culture and a profound psychological understanding of the life of the child. C.E.N.U. (the abbreviation of the new unified schools) has since come under the jurisdiction of the Generalidad [the Catalan government], but no amount of effort on their part has succeeded in eliminating the fundamental libertarian principles laid down by their originator. Comrade Puig Elías put me in [the] charge of his private secretary, Professor Mawa, the liveliest wire in all Spain. He is the man who can attend to a dozen jobs a day and still find time to respond to every request one makes with the utmost precision and in the friendliest manner. Thanks to this fine guide, I saw more in a few days of schools and colonies than I might have seen in several weeks.

†*In this passage from a 5/1/38 article, Goldman describes her exposure to a self-managed film-making collective.*

We did not omit to pay a call on our comrades of the Syndicate of Public Amusement [in Madrid]. We were fortunate in arriving just at the time when they were shooting a film called "Castilla se Libera" ("Castile has liberated

19. Juan Puig Elías created and directed the Escuela Natura (Natural School) for children on behalf of and supported by the Barcelona CNT textile workers. He persisted for nearly 20 years through various waves of government repression up to the time of the revolution. He died recently in Brazil.
20. See footnote 20 at back of chapter.
21. See footnote 21 at back of chapter.

itself"). The three scenes which were shown to us were splendidly done from every point of view and are of great value in showing to the outside world the constructive work carried on by the CNT-FAI in every part of anti-Fascist Spain. We were promised copies of the film for England and the United States as well as other countries in Europe.

My first experience as a movie star in my whole life I had at the studios of the Cine Española-Americana. We arrived just at the time when a Spanish fair was being filmed, with all the artists present in their different regional costumes. Among them were two most strikingly handsome young Spanish girls — dancers — who could well compare with Argentina and other great Spanish dancers, who are being paid phenomenal sums on the American stage. The manager, when he heard my name, rushed forward, embraced me as his own, and insisted that I must join the group of artists who were being filmed. I was never surrounded by a more colorful and intensely eager crowd of young people. Not only that, but he would have me greet Madrid in a few words so that they can reproduce it in sound. It was a very stirring event, my one regret being that I could not send my greetings to Madrid in Castilian, but Comrade A.S. did his best to get it as near as possible in his own quaint Spanish.

We learned that the leading artists of the collective — for it was a collective — receive the same salaries as before the 19th of July. The salary of the supporting cast, however, was increased. As far as one can get authentic answers in the presence of a manager, the artists all seemed satisfied with their lot. I do not mean to suggest that this manager was a fearsome person. He was but one with the others, *mostly members of the CNT*, who were in charge of the work from beginning to the very completion of the films they were making.


† *Goldman was deeply moved by anarchists' continued dedication to enriching popular culture in the midst of deadly conflict, as she describes in this 7/15/38 letter to Harry Kelly.*

[The most recent German bulletin[22]] contains a report of the celebration [the Spanish anarchists] had of [the] "Week of the Book." It brought tears to my eyes. Here are people condemned to death with all avenues closed in on them and their own comrades stabbing them in the back, subject to slow malnutrition, and yet they still think of culture and the value of good books. It is simply amazing.

22. She refers here to the German-language Bulletin of the CNT-FAI Foreign Propaganda Bureau, *CNT-FAI-AIT Informationsdienst.*

# Emergency Social Relief

† *Social relief for the large numbers of civilians whose lives were severely disrupted by the war was a crucial area in which Spanish anarchists could provide an alternative support network infused with libertarian principles. In this 12/10/37 article, Goldman describes her visit to one such effort.*

When I returned to Spain last September [1937] I promised myself to visit the colony for orphan and other children which had been organized by *España Libre* and supported by our comrades all over the world. Not the least among them the strenuous efforts made to raise funds by *Spain and the World*. . . . An Englishwoman who is very active in London on behalf of the refugees and her Spanish husband came to see me in Barcelona and they volunteered to take me to Gerona on their way to Figueras, their home town.

I arrived about 4 P.M. The [Durruti-Ascaso] colony[23] is situated in a magnificent park and in a spacious house which has ample accommodation for 200 children. Of them twenty are the orphans cared for by *Spain and the World*. These, as well as all the others, came from Madrid. The comrades who manage the colony consist primarily of a young Polish Jewish woman and a Frenchman supported by a staff of French and Spanish comrades. We came unannounced and unheralded. No preparation could have been made in advance. This gave me the chance to see the colony in its natural condition and daily routine. The dining room not being large enough to seat 200 children, the smaller kiddies were fed first, then those between seven and ten, and lastly the older ones. I was impressed and moved to see the pride of these kiddies when they showed their clean hands as they filed past the manageress of the colony. The dining room is sunny and airy with flowers on all tables, cheer emanating from every corner, cheer more necessary for the victims of Fascism than for children of normal conditions. The menu cards, illustrated with little flowers, give the menu of every day during the week.

The food is ample and wholesome. The dormitories, too, surprised me by their space, air and sunshine. The beds spotlessly clean – in fact every part of the house spoke of the efficiency and devotion of the comrades in charge of the children.

No less important were the playgrounds where the children romp in their leisure hours and after school. Our comrades had hoped to establish classes both indoor and outdoor in the colony; but it has now become obligatory to attend the government school. Fortunately the latter has not yet succeeded in

---

23. Along with Durruti, the colony was named for Francisco Ascaso, one of the close comrades of the former and of Vivancos, Jover and García Oliver in the "Solidarios" and "Nosotros" affinity groups. He was killed by gunfire during the street fighting in Barcelona against the military rebellion in July 1936. Regular accounts of the condition of this colony appeared in *Spain and the World*.

changing the splendid educational plans introduced at the large plenum of teachers which I attended in Barcelona in 1936. Nevertheless the colony has three teachers, one of whom is a comrade passionately devoted to the new approach and methods of modern education. The most gratifying impression was that the children are free and easy going and that there was no cringing before their elders. Perfect good fellowship and comradeship prevailed between our comrades at the head of the colony, the teachers and the children. There was no exhibitionism and showing off. No one imposed upon them the necessity to make believe. All in all, the colony made me wish that all the innocent victims of Franco might have similar care, attention and nourishment.

The readers of *Spain and the World* may justly ask if all refugee children are so well supplied and so splendidly taken care of as those in the Durruti-Ascaso colony. That is unfortunately so far not the case. It must however be borne in mind that Catalonia alone has two million refugees, men, women and children. In addition to its own population, then there is the need of sending food supplies to Madrid, as well as to feed the thousands of militias at the Aragón front; yet as far as it is within their power, our comrades of the CNT-FAI are doing their utmost to give to all children the necessities and care of life.

† *That Goldman herself was wholeheartedly committed to the significance of such work is indicated in her 2/14/38 letter to anarchist leader Pedro Herrera. She reminds him that she was bitterly disappointed in late 1937 to find refugee homes in such bad condition and to discover that little use was made of the money she had collected earlier in Britain for that realm. Only the establishment of an accountable relief organization, the SIA,[24] caused her to renew her own British relief efforts for refugees in Spain. But the money must be spent for its stated purpose.*

I don't want us to be like all the other organizations who collect tremendous amounts of money and use the largest part for their expenses of paid officers, travelling propagandists, etc., leaving a small percentage for suffering Spain. I am sure you will not mind my stressing this point. One must have a clear conscience to be able to awaken interest in people, especially when they are expected to contribute money.

24. The SIA was the International Anti-Fascist Solidarity organization, founded by the Spanish anarchists in 1937 to provide direct relief support for women and children refugees of the war. As Goldman points out below, relief fundraising for Spain in Western countries, including the United States, typically was dominated by Communists who then fed money and supplies to those sectors *not* under significant anarchist influence. The Spanish anarchists saw the SIA also as an important new avenue for publicity through which to encourage solidarity from large segments of the international proletariat previously unaware of the social revolution in Spain or the role of the anarchists. Following organization of SIA sections in Spain and Paris, Goldman accepted responsibility for developing a branch in London, during her Fall 1937 trip to Spain. By early 1938 she launched this effort publicly.

†*In this intended article following her final trip to Spain (12/9/38), Goldman describes the greatly expanded anarchist social relief program developed through their autonomous Solidaridad Internacional Antifascista organization and through their presence in the Ministry of Education. She also elaborates enthusiastically on a particular children's colony she visited in the Pyrenees.*

As the representative of the London section of SIA (International Anti-Fascist Solidarity) I was of course kept informed of the progress of the work of the comrades in Spain, but what I found on this visit was far beyond my expectations. As our Bulletin[25] contains a full report of the efforts of SIA I will not use up space to describe the extraordinary result of one year of a small group of dedicated people. Suffice it to mention here that SIA sections have spread like wildfire all through loyalist Spain, taking root in every city, town, village and hamlet. Everywhere along the road from Barcelona almost as far as Lérida, 250 kilometres away, SIA streamers with bold letters are stretched across so that no one can escape its existence. Nineteen children's homes and canteens, where colonies had not yet been established, popular restaurants, student lodgings, supplies of cigarettes, writing paper and soap to the various fronts, care of disabled militias, a hospital and dispensary treating an average of 80 patients daily, an ambulance with a staff of young nurses giving first aid to the victims of the daily frightfulness from the air, and alot more represent the magnificent achievement of the SIA. Further plans are in process of being carried out, largely due to the generous support from SIA sections in the United States, France and Sweden.

Without desire to underrate the activities of the other organizations and groups in Spain, I must say that SIA stands out as a veritable beehive. Our comrade, Lucía Sánchez Saornil, one of the most gifted women writers in Spain and an able organizer, with her secretary whom everybody calls by her given name, Christina, as well as Baruta,[26] head of the National Council of SIA, together with a staff of active young people, must be credited with the tremendous amount of work sponsored and carried on by SIA. In addition to all this there is a social welfare center, presided over by a very efficient comrade who had organized the maternity hospital in Barcelona in 1936 and who had been its guiding spirit until this spring. It is her function to minister to the health and needs of expectant mothers as well as mothers and infants in Barcelona and outside it.

. . . . . . . . . . . . . . . . . . . . . . . . . . . . . . . . . . . . . . . . . . . . . . .

Then there are the colonies created by Segundo Blanco and Juan Puig

25. The *SIA Bulletin of the English Section*, vol. 1, no. 4 (December 1938).
26. Enrique Baruta Vila and Lucía Sánchez Saornil were leading officials of the SIA. The former had been secretary to Montseny when she was Minister of Health. Sánchez Saornil was one of the originators of the "Mujeres Libres" (Free Women) newspaper and anarchist women's organization formed before the revolution. See further Goldman comments on her and this group in Chapter VIII below.

Elías since their entry in the Ministry six months ago. They are situated at Sitges, the former aristocratic summer place on the shore of the Mediterranean. Colonies housing 2000 children have already been created, and it is being stipulated that an additional 20,000 children should be established in that place. It is but just that the children of the drones who had built the magnificent houses and who never before were permitted to come anywhere near to them should now occupy the dwellings formerly the pleasure places of the Spanish grandees and the bourgeoisie. The children can now enjoy the soft beds, eat in sunlit dining rooms on white linen-covered tables, be taught in large, light and airy classrooms and have a chance to romp in the gardens and along the walk that separates the houses from the beach of the Mediterranean. It was indeed a feast for the eyes to see their young and healthy appetites served with decent food, consisting of soup, vegetables, salad and dessert, sometimes also meat. The motherly housekeeper in charge of the children told me with much glee that some militias from the front had sent them a whole sheep and some fruit for the children. This was not at all an exception, as I learned later. The Spanish militias from various divisions by no means satiated with food nevertheless managed to contribute in all sorts of ways to the colonies for refugee children. . . .

The most interesting visit with children happened in the very heart of the Pyrenees. My good guide, Professor Mawa, had told me about a colony there, but he wisely said nothing about the steep climb in order to reach the place. He probably thought that I would not have been so willing to visit it. By way of confession I have to own up that I was literally pulled up a mountain of 4,000 feet above the level of the sea, and this only with the help of Professor Mawa on the one side and the young son of Comrade Puig Elías on the other. A troupe of children singing lustily led the way. Another troupe with a cinema operator followed. I admit it was an exhausting feat, but I would not have missed it for worlds. On the very top of the mountain we found a small white peasant house and a patch of land. We were greeted by a large streamer which contained in bold letters the name of the colony — MON NOU (New World). Its credo read as follows:

"Children are the new world. And all dreamers are children; those who are moved by kindness and beauty, those in whose bosoms palpitates the love for liberty and culture and rejoice at the happiness of others; those who feel their hearts beat when they are able to mitigate a sorrow; they who abhor wickedness and for the good have their arms wide open at all times.

You who arrive: if you are sincere and possess a heart so big that your love for one being does not diminish the stock of your love and tenderness towards others; if you feel that freedom is the supreme objective and to attain it you work with enthusiasm imparting knowledge and culture among the little ones, please enter: you are a child.

You who arrive: if you have lost your faith in the goodness of man and fail to see a brother in your fellow creature; if selfishness and arrogance enclose and harden your heart; if ingratitude is part of your personality, do not come in: you are not a child."

Mon Nou is indeed a new world, not only in the letter but in the spirit as well. The life there is primitive and hard, cut off from the outside world, but a new world is being painfully born for these innocent victims of Franco's savagery, and the mother tenderly nursing the young plant is the companion of our comrade, Puig Elías. Her name is Señora Emilia Roca; she is not only mother, but teacher, friend and adviser to the thirty parentless children she has taken under her protecting wings.

Herself of peasant stock and the inheritor of the ancestral house and piece of land, Madame Roca has turned them into a sanctuary for children. She was a teacher by profession, but she gave up her position in order to be able to devote herself to the children who needed her most. Out of her earnings and those of Comrade Puig Elías she manages somehow to feed and clothe her wards. True, the government contributes bread rations and other provisions, but in no way sufficient to maintain the health and vigor of the thirty children. . . .

. . . The children had blessedly forgotten their past in the loving care and warm friendship of their new-found mother. They were full of play and frolic. They bathed in the swimming pool she had provided for them, their young bodies sparkling in the sun. They performed lovely Catalan and Spanish folk dances and songs. Young Puig Elías displayed remarkable dramatic feeling and talent in a heroic poem he recited. The smallest tot would not be outdone by him. She, too, must entertain the foreign guests.

The wildest hilarity came when the film operator began his job. The surprise of surprises when we unpacked our small gifts, chocolates, notebooks, colors for painting. It was a never-to-be-forgotten day. At the end, escorted by a group of older children, the son of our comrades on horseback proudly leading the way, we took leave of the guardian angel of Mon Nou. The descent proved no less arduous than the climb, but who cared? Not I, who had been filled to overflowing by the glowing day, the rich fount of love and generosity, the gaiety of the children and the ravishing mountain view.

# Collectivization in Exile

† *That self-managed collective forms were deeply desired by the Spanish anarchists is testified to by Goldman in this comment on refugee efforts even after Franco's victory (1/14/40 letter to U.S. labor leader David Dubinsky).*

A recent letter from Mexico in French you will find enclosed herewith. . . . This letter, as well as the one from Herrera, will show you that the Spanish workers and peasants while temporarily defeated can never be conquered. No sooner do they get to a place where they are permitted to breathe, they immediately set to work to create new life and new interest for themselves [through the establishment of producer cooperatives]. If ever there were a people who love liberty sufficiently to struggle for it, live it in their daily relationships and even die for it, the Spanish workers and peasants have demonstrated that they stand at the highest peak.

# Further Footnotes for Chapter Three

4. *LL*, II, 947; Goldman 5/13/31 letter to "My dear good comrade" (Max Nettlau), HAR; Goldman, *My Disillusionment in Russia,* ch. 33 ("Afterword"). Her view of the future post-revolutionary organization of society remained the same from her immediate post-Russian exile in 1922 until the Spanish revolution. Thus, in the latter book (written in 1922), she called for a syndicalist structure to organize production among industrial workers, co-ops to provide distribution and exchange links between town and countryside, and revolutionary cultural forces to inspire the anarchist vision generally. She stated the same themes in her 5/11/34 letter to William Jong (NYU), the first Goldman text in Chapter X. Another statement of this vision with which she clearly associated herself was in her comrade Berkman's *What Is Communist Anarchism?* (1929; rpt. N.Y.: Dover Publications, Inc., 1972). She wrote the introduction to the *Freie Arbeiter Stimme* edition of this work in 1937. Readers unfamiliar with the broad contours of constructive anarchist vision of the new society will find this an excellent introduction.

7. Communist-led anti-revolutionary repression which provoked the May days in Barcelona and forced the replacement of Caballero with Juan Negrín was followed within weeks by an attack in Aragón on anarchist-led rural collectives and the region's Defense Council (a body similar to that in Catalonia in late July 1936). On grounds of its "excessive autonomy" and "subversive" tendencies of "extremist" elements, the national government decreed the Council's dissolution, its replacement by a pro-Communist Republican governor, and the sending of Communist Enrique Lister's 11th Division to repress the local defense committees and anarchist organizations. The Marx Division (27th) and the 30th Division (Catalan separatists) followed with similar destructive efforts, all three units attacking the numerous peasant collectives and returning land and equipment to former landowners. The slanderous charges used to justify this campaign were typified by the detaining of the Defense Council president, anarchist Joaquín Ascaso, on grounds of smuggling gems. He was released after a month's imprisonment because there was no evidence to back the charge. At the same time, CNT-FAI leading committees ordered the three anarchist divisions on the Aragón front to refrain from counter-attacks. Despite such destruction, the creative anarchist spirit continued surging forth, forcing the government itself to recognize the collectives again temporarily in order for vital planting and harvest functions to proceed.

11. Michael Bakunin (1814-1876) was probably the single most influential writer-speaker-activist in the history of the anarchist movement. Though his own anarchist ideas did not finally coalesce until the last decade of his life, his exuberant rebellious personality was an influence in various liberation movements from the early 1840's onward. In the late 1860's and early 1870's, he was the quite successful rival to Karl Marx in the First International. An excellent selection of his writings, with a biographical sketch and comments, is Sam Dolgoff, ed., *Bakunin On Anarchy* (N.Y.: Alfred A. Knopf, 1972).

20. At this time, the Ministry was headed by Segundo Blanco, a longtime Asturian anarchist and veteran of the 1934 revolutionary insurrection. He was the sole anarchist to become a minister in Negrín's cabinet during the CNT's second attempt at official governmental collaboration at

the national level. He became Minister of Education on April 16, 1938. He supported Negrín to the end, which made him the focus of strong criticism from much of the anarchist movement.
21. According to official anarchist estimates, in one year the city of Barcelona added 82,000 schoolchildren and 151 new school units. Much attention was given to re-educating teachers themselves toward more "comradely relations with students and greater sensitivity to nature" (*España?* [Barcelona: CNT-FAI Office of Foreign Propaganda, Feb. 1938] and *Libro de Oro de la Revolución Española* [Toulouse: Propaganda Commission, MLE-CNT in France, 1946]). A lengthy, more detailed account is Caudal Pedagogico de la Revolución Española, *La Escuela Nueva Unificada* (Barcelona: Ediciones Españolas de la revolución, Sept. 1938).

# Chapter Four

# *Collaboration with Statist Forces*

*How much to join with other political forces to accomplish mutual goals was historically a crucial issue distinguishing anarchists from others in the movement for social change. It was equally significant in defining differences among anarchists themselves.*

*Collaboration, even for the most pure individualists, always was acceptable to anarchists if it was freely chosen, could be freely withdrawn, and was not aimed toward exploiting third parties. Examining how such qualifications are interpreted serves to clarify the more precise anarchist positions.*

*For anarchists, hierarchical institutions such as the state, church and big business are the opposite from, indeed the enemy of, free collaboration or association. Whatever functional reasons may have nourished their original roots, they long since had mystified such rationales simply to perpetuate their own power. On principle, therefore, with such institutions anarchists refuse to cooperate voluntarily. Even in the face of coercion, some anarchists maintain their autonomy to the point of risking their own lives. For anarchists, forced "collaboration" is fundamentally destructive whatever the context — in the capitalist labor market, a state prison or anywhere else. Though behind bars (of whatever sort), alert prisoners keep watchful eyes for opportunities to revolt and to destroy the oppressive hierarchy at hand. Anarchists traditionally differ from the liberal or socialist Left in refusing to join or legitimize any form of state structure — parliamentary or "revolutionary" in nature.[1] The same logic moves many (but by no means all) anarchists to oppose cooperating with those political movements clearly intending to replace existing hierarchy with one of their own, heralded as more "progressive."[2]*

1. See footnote 1 at back of chapter.
2. Examples of this type of progressive organization in the U.S. are the CIO trade unions which evolved from the "sit-in" militancy of the 1930's to the giant conservative bureaucracies of the present.

*It is at this point where anarchists most strongly differ among themselves. Given the hierarchical organization form and state power goal of most other Leftist forces, can anarchist cooperation with them against common enemies lead to a new overall social balance fundamentally less oppressive than before? Some anarchists say yes, some say no. Some pose the question on the basis of whether such cooperation is* strategic *(implying a medium- to long-range period) or whether it is* tactical *(momentary, thus more acceptable). Some see the problem as primarily a question of propaganda. Should anarchists immerse themselves in situations (such as parliamentary election campaigns or mass reformist movements) providing new access to far greater numbers of potential recruits? Or does such immersion always so confuse the image of what anarchists stand for that conversions will be few and/or superficial, while anarchists themselves, like all other politicians, will be corrupted by exercising unaccountable leadership?*

*Anarchist debate on this issue has been bitter and constant —from before the days of the First International (over a century ago) all the way to the present. In theory, the historical movement overwhelmingly rejected collaboration with the state, as well as any medium- or long-range collaboration with statist political movements. Yet contexts of crisis led many anarchists to link arms with other groups and even occasionally with governments to overcome a perceived greater common evil. Peter Kropotkin's endorsement of the Entente cause in World War I is only the most prominent example.[3] The scandal such behavior always produced among those anarchists with "clean hands" never failed to produce bitter denunciations. In any case, once the particular historical crisis subsided, the movement overwhelmingly returned to its orthodox non-collaborative position.[4]*

*In today's context of racist and sexist oppression, economic collapse, ecological disaster, imperialist domination and the nightmare of nuclear energy and nuclear armaments, major crises appear everywhere. Any one or several of these could potentially produce yet even greater despotism, deprivation and destruction than currently exist. As in earlier years, so in North American today, many anarchists therefore claim that they have no choice but to collaborate with others against the growing spectre of 1984. They argue that it is suicidal to maintain purist isolation from fellow inmates of an increasingly harsh societal prison. There will be no possibility of choice once a certain totalitarian "point of no return" is reached.[5] Others reply, again echoing earlier anarchists, that until death itself we must exercise our choice, our freedom, our unwillingness to compromise principles, at every moment. To put off the exercise of liberty to a later date, no matter how severe the present conditions, is to guarantee that it will be put off forever. Even if the worst of the present crisis is eventually overcome, those who survived through compromise will be unable to manifest and propagate the libertarian ideal. Of course human nature itself guarantees that new individuals in future generations will reassert a love of liberty, relaunching in their own way a new anarchist movement. Never-*

3.  As mentioned earlier, at the time Kropotkin was clearly the single most influential writer in the anarchist movement.
4.  See the lengthier discussion of these zig-zag tendencies in section III of Chapter I above.
5.  See footnote 5 at back of chapter.

*theless, that older generation which compromised will have lost irrevocably their own chance for fully meaningful lives.*[6]

*Spain in the late 1970's finally emerged from the vast desert of Franco's regime. It thus provides important contemporary evidence with which to weigh the relative merits of each side of this historical anarchist debate. Collaborationists and their opponents[7] vied for years with each other within the Spanish anarchist underground and exile movement. Each claimed its own approach the most effective, both for resisting police repression and for maintaining the anarchist tradition. To whom, then, does the present revived and specific nature of Spanish anarchism owe the most? And to what extent must the same issue of collaboration now be faced again—both to prevent a resurgence of reactionary power in Spain and to struggle more effectively, as part of the broader international movement, against the overall leviathan of sophisticated multinational corporate dominance? The present analyses and practice of Spanish comrades will be instructive to those everywhere who seek anti-authoritarian solutions to existing oppressive conditions.*

## II

*In her own anarchist evolution on this issue before the Spanish revolution, Emma Goldman travelled across nearly the entire spectrum of positions. Her early more individualist perspective[8] was shown in the assassination plot with Berkman, as well as in her subsequent attack on their ex-mentor Johann Most when the latter criticized Berkman's attempt. This more purist stance persisted also in her continued refusal to join anarchist movement organizations themselves. Nevertheless, the next two decades in America saw her deliberately reach out to liberal and socialist allies (as individuals and sometimes in temporary single-issue organizations) in various political efforts. Among such campaigns were protests against repression in Spain and czarist Russia, American bans on the entry of foreign radicals, repression of free speech and birth control, and conscription in World War I. Despite such collaborative experience, however, Goldman also clearly drew the line against supporting electoral campaigns by the same allies.[9]*

*For Goldman, the Russian revolution felt like the rise and tragic fall of a*

6.  Numerous statements of this perspective have appeared over the last several years, as in the Detroit periodical *Fifth Estate*, the British *Black Flag* and the French *Jeune Taupe!*.
7.  The various organizations and activities in either direction are too numerous to describe adequately in a footnote. Among the more useful sources for clarifying the nature of and principals in this conflict are those works cited in footnotes 1 and 2 of Chapter II.
8.  The term "individualist" is used here to indicate an attitude and behavior stressing immediate, defiant, individual self-responsibility. There is no legitimized leadership of some over others, no dependency on explicit structures or on group action instead of that by individuals.
9.  See her accounts of such campaigns and her position within them in *LL*. There she also makes clear that she rejected bids for her support by backers of populist presidential candidate William Jennings Bryan and of socialist Morris Hillquit, anti-war candidate for New York City mayor in 1917 (*LL*, I, 179-81; II, 636-37). (However, Goldman did join an exile section of the Russian Socialist Revolutionary party in the Lower East Side of New York in 1904 [*LL*, I, 359].)

*passionate love affair—multiplied a hundred times over. Originally entranced by Russia's apparent fulfillment of her lifelong revolutionary hopes, Goldman refused at first to endorse the negative critiques from anarcho-communists she met in Petrograd. Beyond that, she even accepted a minor cultural position within the government itself. Though increasingly aware of her Bolshevik allies' authoritarian behavior, she refused to criticize them publicly so as not to undermine the overall social revolution in the face of armed Rightist and foreign capitalist attacks. The Bolsheviks' violent suppression of Kronstadt finally caused her break. In late 1921 she left Russia itself, facing the bleak prospects of wandering exile among those few capitalist countries that would tolerate her presence. From temporary bases in Germany, France, Britain and Canada during the next decade and a half, both her bitterly personal sense of tragedy and her general anarchist political consciousness led her in print and in person to excoriate the revolutionary pretensions of the Soviet regime. For Goldman, her collaborationist fling with statist parties and even a government itself had been an immensely painful experience. Emphatically she returned to her pre-revolutionary orthodox position. As earlier in the United States, this did not preclude her willingness still to work with non-anarchists on single-issue campaigns—such as those on behalf of Russian political prisoners. Nevertheless, Goldman's uncompromising anti-Bolshevism caused most potential allies to shy away.* [10]

<h1 style="text-align:center">III</h1>

*It was hardly surprising when in early 1936 Goldman denounced suggestions for anarchists to collaborate in anti-fascist Left fronts. In the case of Spain, she was shocked at anarchists' apparent semi-official flirtation with the parliamentary electoral campaign. In her view, whatever the present threat from conservative and openly fascist forces, collaboration to this extent was a tragic sell-out of generations of courageous anarchist struggles and ideals.* [11]

*The death of her lifelong comrade Alexander Berkman in June 1936 sent Goldman into total despair. Facing a continued dreary and lonely exile existence, crying out with apparently little response against the world's rapid and mindless drift toward populist totalitarianism, she seriously questioned even her own ability to live on.* [12]

*Within two months, however, the immense anarchist-led revolutionary surge in Spain completely revived her spirit. Eagerly she accepted the CNT-FAI invitation to Barcelona. There, in a fully supportive atmosphere, she at last could work creatively to carry out precisely the ideals she had envisioned for so long. Her enthusiasm*

10. See footnote 10 at back of chapter.
11. Though adamant in criticizing any anarchist collaboration in electoral fronts, Goldman clearly also was ready to praise Communists and Socialists when, as in Austria in 1934, they fought back against fascist repression. In such cases, it was the potential and ideal of revolution itself under attack. In this context, Socialists and Communists were being forced to struggle for survival against the state and capitalism alike (Notes on her Brooklyn Academy of Music speech, 2/15/34, NYU).
12. Goldman 7/25/36 and 8/2/36 letters to Stella Ballantine, NYPL.

*was inevitable. Yet within days after her arrival, that political sensitivity of hers, honed to a fine edge by her Russian experience, again produced a strong anti-collaborationist critique. As she had warned in 1934 and early 1936,*[13] *the appeals of "realist politics" already were tempting toward major concessions most of the prominent Spanish anarchists she met.*

*From this point on through the end of the war, Goldman maintained an immensely uncomfortable, ultimately ambiguous position.*[14] *On the one hand, from her roots in anarchist tradition and the Russian revolution, she steadfastly proclaimed that anarchist collaboration with statist forces (the Left Republicans, Socialists, and Communists) and the government itself — however great the fascist menace — could only erode the strength and character of the anarchist movement in the present and future both. From this perspective, she fully agreed with the sharply critical voices of Voline, Schapiro, Berneri and Prudhommeaux, among prominent foreign anarchists.*[15] *She thus also was aligned objectively with anti-collaborationist anarchists in Spain itself, such as the Catalan Libertarian Youth movement and the "Friends of Durruti."*[16] *Her testimony below and in the following chapter provides abundant justification for this stand.*

*At the same time, she clearly distinguished between anarchist grass-roots and leadership levels. Additionally, her appreciation of the complexity of human motivation and her immense desire for anarchist survival and success left her at times pleading with others at least to understand the honest intention of Spanish anarchist leaders. In her view, they were concerned with revolutionary defense, not personal or movement power through the state. At the least, she felt that the entire Spanish movement should not be denounced and abandoned because of errors on the part of its leadership. In this stance and in her acceptance of the role of official CNT-FAI representative in London, she appeared to critics as at least a "collaborator with the collaborationists."*[17]

*Few were the anarchist critics who in fact refused any form of solidarity.*[18] *Yet Goldman went further than most in honestly exposing the agonizing personal dilemmas of this position. While agreeing with their negative critiques, she openly challenged even the most critical anarchists to claim that they themselves had never compromised in their personal lives and political practice or to prove their own infallible wisdom on every issue. In revealing her personal agony, of course, Goldman also reasserted the triumph of anarchist consciousness in her own life.*

13. Goldman 5/11/34 letter to William Jong, NYU, and the first two of her entries in this chapter.
14. As pointed out in Chapter I, section IiI, Goldman's zig-zag ambiguity on this issue tended to correlate with her psychological and geographical proximity to or distance from Spain itself.
15. See footnote 15 at back of chapter.
16. On those with an anti-collaborationist position within Spain, see Chapter II, footnote 19 above.
17. In London, Goldman herself "collaborated" with non-anarchist political organizations to a moderate degree — especially with the Independent Labour Party (the British party most closely aligned with the position of the Spanish left communist POUM), but even initially on one occasion (an exhibition of pictures of the Spanish revolution) with the Communists. Her bitter reaction to this experience and her cautious attitude generally toward cooperation even with the ILP is clearly stated below and in her remarks in Chapter VI. While officially accredited to be the CNT-FAI representative within the Catalan government (Generalitat) office in London, she set foot in it only briefly on two occasions. See footnote 45 below.
18. See footnote 18 at back of chapter.

*Her absolute unwillingness to flow with popular tides among even her own move-
ment comrades was deeply entwined with her fear of losing the priceless sense of
her own integrity.*

*Such assertive individuality obviously challenges the tolerance of any large-scale
political movement, especially in the midst of crises of revolution and civil war. Not
only to tolerate, but to encourage openly such autonomy is a qualitative step
beyond.*[19] *Yet surely it can be seen in hindsight that if Spanish anarchist leaders had
been more willing to listen to, seriously consider and attempt positively to respond
to strong anti-collaborationist sentiment—even if articulated by a minority
only—they would have increased chances for a more imaginative and successful
revolutionary offense and defense combined. Who can say that the subsequent
history of Spain would not have been drastically altered for the better if only the collaborationist "line" of the leadership had not remained so jealously protected from
effective challenge?*[20]


†*Two years before the outbreak of civil war and revolution, Goldman writes pro-
phetically to Ben (Capes?) (6/5/34) on the dangers of Spanish anarchist collaboration with Communist and Socialist forces.*

. . . It would be nothing short of a calamity if our comrades in Spain were to
affiliate themselves with the Socialists and the Communists. I am willing to
concede the Spanish Anarcho-Syndicalists may not prove strong enough to
withstand the tide of Fascism. But past experience has proven that Anarchists
have fared no better from Socialists, and certainly much worse from the
Bolsheviks, than they are likely to get if the Monarchy should be returned to
Spain. No group of people anywhere in the world who have at one time or
another consented to a united front with the Communists was able to maintain
its position against the insidious poison inculcated in their ranks. The Communists, like the Jesuits they are, always succeeded in undermining the position of these groups and in breaking their morale.

. . . . . . . . . . . . . . . . . . . . . . . . . . . . . . . . . . . . . . . . . . . . . . . . . . .

The reason some of the attempts of the Spanish Anarchists have failed are
the machinations of the Communists and the Socialists. They have done
everything in their power to interfere. They actually do not want the CNT to
succeed. For they know perfectly well that would be the end of their intrigues
and their methods. You speak of the Anarchists not being strong enough to
overthrow the reactionary regime. Perhaps the Spanish people are not ripe for
a revolution. If that should be the case the combined efforts of the Communists, the Socialists and the Anarchists would hardly avail. More and more
I come to the conclusion that revolutions cannot be artificially created, though
they may be directed for good or evil. In any event, it is more important that

19. Ideally an anarchist movement would not need even to raise such a question.
20. See footnote 20 at back of chapter.

the Anarchists should stand their grounds and remain true to their ideals than that they should pave the way for Socialist or Communist dictatorship.

I see no inconsistency in calling on progressive and liberal elements to fight Fascism. So long as these elements profess liberalism. But if they openly and brazenly stand for dictatorship it would seem suicidal to have truck with such people.

*†In this 4/2/36 letter to John Haynes Holmes (the liberal pastor of the New York Community Church) before the outbreak of civil war in Spain, Goldman presents her general perspective on "popular front" politics even in the midst of fascist threat.*

About the Radicals fighting among themselves, I do not know how that can be avoided, when the extremes are so great. In the olden days there was a possibility for, let us say, Socialists and Anarchists to combine on grave national and international issues, though they differed in their ultimate aims. But how is one holding Libertarian ideas to unite with Communists who represent the extreme opposite? Frankly, I could not possibly unite with them. Perhaps if I had not seen what the dictatorship has done to the Russian Revolution, I might be as credulous as to what Communists outside of Russia proclaim. But I have seen the "nature of the beast" and I am more than ever convinced that the extremes in the Socialist school will never meet.

You say, "preventing a united front against the enemy." Believe me, I know how vicious and dangerous Fascism is. But I fail to see that dictatorship from the Left is any less dangerous to progress. That is just the frightfulness of the situation. One wants to go with the Left, naturally. One has stood on the Left Bank all one's life, but what if the Left is going more and more to the Right, denying its birthright, willing to barter it away to the highest bidder? What if the Left is now more concerned in getting the goodwill of all the reactionary governments in the world rather than the support of international labor? It is indeed a spectacle for the gods to see the Soviet government clamor for sanctions, or being linked with the warring parties![21] Is that not a greater betrayal of the struggle for freedom and emancipation of the oppressed than anything the reactionary forces can do? Well, I for one shall continue to fight on both fronts—the Fascist as well as the Communist. Or shall I say: Fascism and the Stalin brand of Communism?

*†Responding (5/1/36) to an early 1936 questionnaire from the "Mas Lejos" anarchist group in Barcelona,[22] Goldman informs Eusebio Carbó,[23] one of its*

21. See footnote 21 at back of chapter.
22. See footnote 22 at back of chapter.
23. Eusebio Carbó, a longtime well-respected CNT militant, worked closely with IWMA

*members, of her continued strong stand against collaboration.*[24]

Your letter to Comrade Berkman of Feb. 27th reached him almost on the eve of an operation for which he had to go to the hospital. Since then, but for a few weeks at home, too ill to write to you, our comrade has undergone a second operation and is still in [the] hospital. . . .

. . . I have therefore decided to answer the questionnaire you sent to him. I do so on my own account. I am rather sure that our comrade would agree with my idea in this matter. But he will write you himself in due time. So please take this as my opinion.

*First*, the question as to whether the abstention from participation in elections is for Anarchists a matter of principle: I certainly think it is, and should be for all Anarchists. After all, participation in elections means the transfer of one's will and decisions to another, which is contrary to the fundamental principles of Anarchism.

*Secondly*, since Anarchists do not believe in the Jesuitic formula of the Bolsheviki that "the end justifies the means," it is but logical for Anarchists not to consider political participation as a "simple question of tactics," since such tactics are not only incompatible with Anarchist thought and principle, but also injure the stand of Anarchism as the one and only truly revolutionary social philosophy.

*Thirdly*, "can Anarchists, without scruple and in [the] face of certain circumstances, exercise power during a transition period?" I confess I was surprised to see such a question come from Spain, which has always stood out to us in all countries as the high water mark of Anarchist integrity and consistency. Even without the experience of the Russian Revolution and Soviet claims for the transition period, I should not have expected the Spanish Anarchists to be carried away by that term, in the name of which every crime against the Revolution has been committed by the Communist Party in Russia—the claims [that] power is inevitable during the transition period. Unless the comrades in Spain, now in favor of the same Jesuit contention, imagine that they are so much wiser and incorruptible than others, I cannot understand how they can possibly aspire to power.

From its very inception, Anarchism and its greatest teachers have maintained that it is not the abuse of power which corrupts everybody, the best more often than the worst men, but that it is the thing itself, namely *power*, which is evil and which takes the very spirit and revolutionary fighting

representatives in Spain such as Schapiro before July 1936 in criticizing apparently opportunistic, collaborationist tendencies within the CNT. He was the co-author with Schapiro of the critical report on the CNT for the April 1933 IWMA congress in Amsterdam.
24. Most of this same text later appeared as an article "Anarchists and Elections," *Vanguard*, June-July 1936. An earlier draft with similar wording on the same themes was her 4/24/36 letter to a "Comrade" of the New York Spanish anarchist group "Cultura Proletaria" (UML).

strength out of everybody who wields power. Does not Russian reality stand as a living example of this fact? Surely the Spanish Anarchists who now are willing to accept power and use it do not imagine themselves more heroic, more consecrated than the Russian masses who have fought and bled and died for the Revolution. Yet see what the snare of power during the transition period has done to the masses and to the Revolution. It has emasculated the Revolution and enslaved the masses. It has relegated [their] aims to the dim distance and has turned the transition stage into the aim in the name of which every crime in Russia is being justified by the masters of Russia and their followers. Precisely the same thing would happen to Anarchists were they to seize power. Not only would they *not* "hasten the march towards the realization of Anarchism," they would sink into the swamp of corruption and demoralization inherent in all power. Namely they would cling to power and forget their Anarchism. There is no reason whatever to believe that the Anarchist would not succumb to the same influence as the Socialists and Communists have.

However there is ample excuse for Marxians: since they believe in and propagate the State, they also believe in and propagate power. But how can the Anarchists, whose social philosophy repudiates the State, all political power, all governmental authority, in short every sort of power and authority over their fellow man, how *can* they take and exercise power? To me it is a denial of Anarchism and a most dangerous tendency which, if carried out, is likely to undermine whatever advance and recognition as a revolutionary fighting force the Anarchists in Spain have represented for so long. Moreover, if they should take power and use it (and power is here for no other purpose but to be used against the very masses who voted them into office), the Anarchists would do incalculable harm to the movement in Spain, and to us in the rest of the world. I am inclined to believe that the participation of some of our comrades in the election has already discredited our work.

Does this imply that I do not recognize the danger of Fascism, or do not appreciate the imperative necessity to fight it to the last degree? Nothing is farther away from my thoughts. What I do mean to say is this: if the Anarchists were strong enough to swing the elections to the Left,[25] they must also have been strong enough to rally the workers to a general strike, or even a series of strikes all over Spain. In the last analysis the capitalist class knows too well that officials, whether they belong to the Right or the Left, can be bought. Or they are of no consequence to their pledge. Whereas strong and determined

25. Despite lip-service to the traditional anarchist position of abstention, in fact the CNT and FAI engaged in no strong anti-electoral campaign as in the past. Indeed, many well-known anarchist militants openly announced in advance their intention to vote for the Popular Front slate, as an emergency "lesser evil" than the fascist-leaning Right and to bring the release of 30,000 political prisoners. Thus the February 1936 parliamentary elections brought a narrow victory to the Popular Front, in great part due to anarchist votes.

economic methods strike the capitalists in their most vulnerable spot—their material interests. That is the reason they dread the organized economic power of the workers. That is why they see in the general strike their deadly foe.

Now . . . was not the psychological moment for all Anarchists in Spain to have used their economic and direct action during the revolt of October 1934?[26] It was their bounden duty to join the workers and fight with them to the end. The excuse given at the time by the CNT for leaving the heroic masses in the Asturias to their fate was that it did not want to affiliate itself with the Socialists, with men like Caballero who so often had stabbed our comrades in the back. It was a poor excuse. But granted, for argument's sake, such an attitude was justified, how then could some of the Anarchists join the Socialists in elections? Frankly I cannot understand such reasoning. It was shortsightedness [about] the revolutionary situation rather rare in the history of Anarchists' activities. And it is precisely for this that the comrades who voted must have felt that they must undo what they had neglected to do in the last revolt of 1934. But they will pay for it dearly, I fear, if they are not already doing so.

I consider it a sorry distinction to have helped twenty Communists to office, to have established Communist activities in Spain, to have shown the other cheek to Caballero, so he CAN SLAP IT AGAIN when it suits his political purpose.

I understand that the comrades were largely motivated in their participation in the elections by their solidarity with the 30,000 political prisoners.[27] That was undoubtedly a very commendable feeling. But at the same time, their amnesty was but a short breathing spell, for it is already apparent that the new rulers in the saddle will not leave the prisons empty for very long. History certainly repeats itself. About thirty years ago or more, during black reaction in Italy with its prisons filled with politicals, our old comrade Merlino suggested to Malatesta that the Anarchists should participate in elections for the purpose of an amnesty.[28] Malatesta brilliantly disproved the efficacy of Merlino's argument. He pointed out that Anarchist participation in politics and in elections would merely forge additional chains for the new victims of those who will be returned to government offices. Malatesta did not have the living proof given by the traducers of the Russian Revolution; but he knew well enough what Socialists are capable of doing. The Spanish comrades have Russia before them. Yet they seem to have learned little or nothing from the events there.

---

26. See footnote 11 of Chapter VII for more details on this 1934 uprising and the anarchist role within it.

27. Thousands of anarchists were among those in prison by the beginning of 1936, following the several waves of earlier anarchist insurrections and the Fall 1934 Asturian revolt.

28. See footnote 28 at back of chapter.

In conclusion let me say, dear comrades, that though some of the Anarchists in Spain may be dazzled by the success of the Communists in different countries, it is yet true that they are but of the hour. The future belongs to those who continue daringly, consistently, to fight power and governmental authority. The future belongs to us and to our social philosophy. For it is the only social ideal that teaches independent thinking and direct participation of the workers in their economic struggle. For it is only through the organized economic strength of the masses that they can and will do away with the capitalist system and all the wrongs and injustices it contains. Any diversion from this stand will only retard our movement and make of it a stepping stone for political climbers.

† *In this first commentary (to Stella Ballantine, 9/11/36) on Spanish anarchist collaboration* after *the beginning of the civil war and revolution, Goldman clearly maintains her earlier position. She also indicates her dependence for details at the time on anarchist propaganda rather than first-hand knowledge.*

I had planned to prepare another statement as regards my attitude to the united front with the Communists. I do not mean I wanted it given publicity now. I had in mind anything that might happen to me. I should hate to give the Communists a chance to either claim me as having died in the arms of their church, or what is more likely to have them say I went to Spain to defend the Republic. But it occurred to me it will be more convincing if I send you such a statement from Spain after I have been there awhile. Besides, the Bulletin the comrades are sending me every week[29] has just arrived and it contains a definite statement by our people that they will never submit to either a Socialist or Communist government. They made that statement because of the Caballero Cabinet. They know from past experience that that man has turned them over to Rivera and the Lerroux government.[30] And he will, if given a chance, exterminate the Anarchists now even though that should kill the Revolution.

† *Within a few days of her arrival in Spain, to New York comrade Mark Mratchny, Goldman indicates for the first time (10/3/36) her own self-questioning, the softening of her previous absolute stand, on the issue of Spanish compromise and collaboration in a crisis situation. She also first states here her unwillingness to express any doubts about the Spanish choice in public.*

You too have lived through the tremendous reality of a revolution.

29. The CNT-FAI Foreign Propaganda Office in Barcelona published regular bulletins in Spanish, English, French and German editions. Most likely she refers here to the last of these.
30. See Chapter II, footnote 38 concerning Caballero's role in the Primo de Rivera dictatorship and under Prime Minister Manuel Azaña from 1931 to 1933.

You will know that every hour holds one breathless by its intensity and by its interest. Yet I have felt all along that I ought to write you something about the concrete achievements of our comrades. But so far it has been impossible for more than one reason. First I do not want to appear in our press or any other with alot of statements for which I am still far from being sufficiently informed. . . . I am here only 16 days. I have not the right to speak authoritatively, and I hate to speak merely out of my enthusiasm. Secondly because there are a number of things that seem incongruous and incompatible with the spirit and the traditions of the CNT, and even more so of the FAI. Until I have clarified these puzzling questions I prefer not to make my thoughts and feeling public.

I enclose a copy of my letter to Rudolf which is of course NOT for publication. It is only for you and Johanna. You will see that the negative sides of the situation here has not dampened my ardor or my profound faith in our Spanish comrades and my admiration for them. Still, all is not well and reconcilable with what I have worked for all my life. Time alone will tell who is correct. Just now I want nothing better than to help the comrades in their sublime efforts, especially the constructive side of their battle.

†*In a letter to longtime comrade Tom Bell[30a] the following day, Goldman explicitly identifies the fact of anarchist collaboration as the basic source of her misgivings. Already she sees the reality of dangerous sabotage by Socialist and Communist "allies," no longer merely a prophecy as before. (This theme is developed in detail in the next chapter.)*

. . . I am only too well aware that there are a number of incongruous and irreconcilable things with our ideas. The first among them is that the comrades should have joined the united front at all. It has inevitably led them to contradictory steps and it is already apparent that their allies are already proving a greater danger than Fascism. I hardly need point out who this enemy is. The growth of this villainous gang is due to the too much tolerance on the part of the CNT-FAI. Just because they wanted to show that Anarchists want to suppress no one unless discovered armed or those who are Fascists still abroad by the thousands, they have given the Socialists and Communists considerable carte blanche. The result is that these age-long enemies of our ideas are sabotaging right and left. And that they have grown into powerful organizations from nothing at all.[31] And in this to my mind lies the greatest

30[a].Tom Bell was a Scottish anarchist first met by Goldman in 1900 (*LL*, I, 262) and a continuing acquaintance after his emigration to the United States in 1905. Rudolf Rocker provides more biographical details in *The London Years* (London: Robert Anscombe and Co., Ltd., 1956), pp. 185-86. (This is an abridged and translated version of the second volume of Rocker's three-part autobiography.)

31. See footnote 31 at back of chapter.

danger for the CNT-FAI. However once a wrong step taken the retraction is not easy. Besides our comrades being men of their word, they cannot very well stop the pernicious and insidious counter-activities of their allies. Not now with the Fascist forces so near to Madrid.[32] The real struggle will only begin when this force has been smashed. So you see, my dear, the odds against our people, the luring betrayal surrounding them. With all that to consider it is the most commendable that they should go about their constructive labor as if there were no Judases and armed enemies within and without Spain.

†*After over a month in Spain (10/28/36), Goldman now expresses to her niece Stella Ballantine a deeper sense of tragic dilemma than ever before.*

. . . So many things happened the last few days I am sick at heart.[33] In fact if I had not been in the country and had not seen the revolutionary spirit of the people and their determination to fight for the Revolution to the last I should think Spain is going the way of Russia. Already many compromises have been made by our people that have led them in all kinds of unfortunate ways. Fortunately the Spanish people, especially the people of Catalonia, Aragón and the Levante are with the Revolution. They are invincible. But my heart is heavy and I feel overcome by grief.

†*Details on one source for her agony over anarchist collaboration appear several days later (11/3/36) in a letter to trusted comrade Rudolf Rocker. Not only specifying dangerous compromises (including anarchist participation in the government), she also perceives these as the beginning of ever-deeper contradiction of basic principles from which there may be no retreat.*

I found [your second letter] together with other mail on my return from a trip to Valencia and a number of collectivized villages. Müller-Lehning[34] was with me. Strangely enough we talked about the situation here almost verbatim as the contents of your letter. That before I read it. My dear, my dear, of course I am no doctrinaire. You should know that. I never was a fanatic, nor have I ever been blind to the fact that reality often puts all theories on their

32. Following the original military rebellion throughout Spain in July 1936 and its defeat in ⅔ of the country by the action of armed workers, more conventional battlelines and strategy soon emerged, roughly dividing the country in half from north to south. By the date of her letter, Franco's Nationalist army was rapidly approaching the outskirts of the capital, Madrid, for what he expected to be a quick victory and thus collapse of the republic.
33. Political developments in republican Spain were rapid indeed at the time. Consult the chronology for at least certain of the major events Goldman referred to in this statement.
34. See footnote 34 at back of chapter.

head. Still there are many things one cannot and should not do unless one is willing to deny everything one has stood for. I think you agreed with Sasha and me that the end does not always justify certain means. Well, my dear, that is the sad part here. The end evidently does justify the most impossible means. The tragic part is that the means, though contrary to everything we know of the glorious past of the CNT, far from having helped, have injured our comrades and their work beyond belief. And what is still more tragic is that there is no return to first principles. On the contrary, one is pulled deeper and deeper into the mire of compromise. Lest you think this is only my impression I have asked Lehning to write you. In addition, Berneri, one of our finest Italian comrades who is doing a tremendous work among the Italians who have come here to give up their lives at the front, has also prepared his attitude to some of the things I am sure you would object to. Later I will send you a copy of the statement.[35] Just now I can only repeat that the means used to move the heart of Caballero, far from having constructive results, have made the man more obdurate. He has sabotaged Catalonia and the CNT-FAI in a scandalous way and he continues doing so. Some of our comrades are realizing that. They know it was all in vain. But you know the old Tolstoy saying "once you roll down a precipice there is no halting on the way."

Even from the standpoint of joining the government the CNT-FAI is permitting itself to be treated like children. Thus they entered four new ministries.[36] But not the most important ones. Namely the Ministries of War and Finance. Caballero naturally keeps these for his satraps. And our people are as bound and fettered as before. However, you are right in your faith of the Spanish people and our comrades. I share that faith deeply and absolutely. I do so more every day when I get in touch with the workers in the factories and the peasants in the villages. The Revolution is safe with them because it has its roots in their hearts and their minds. My last trip has raised my spirit sky high. It is only in Barcelona where my heart sinks. I simply cannot be blind to the errors committed by our people. Yet even here I find as you do that the Spanish or Catalonian comrades are a race apart. . . . If only the situation were not so grave and so uncertain. It is this I know which is compelling the comrades to take certain steps that they themselves feel inconsistent. Thus the promise of Russia to send arms has turned the heads of several of our people. The *Soli[daridad Obrera]* began a campaign of eulogy of Russia that drove all of us to distraction. It was so stupid and so unnecessary

35. Berneri's statement was an original version of his eventual "Letter to Federica Montseny," published in the April 14, 1937 issue (no. 12) of his *Guerra di Classe* journal in Barcelona. It is reproduced in Camillo Berneri, *Guerre de classes en Espagne* (Paris: Spartacus, 1977) and in Daniel Guérin, *Ni Dieu ni maître* (paperback edition), vol. IV, 176-83. It is referred to by Goldman in more detail in Chapter X.
36. Federica Montseny became Minister of Health; Juan García Oliver, Minister of Justice; Juan López, Minister of Commerce; and Juan Peiró, Minister of Industry. They joined the government on November 4, 1936.

even from the point of diplomacy. Well, that was stopped, thank goodness. Still, a committee of 4 CNT, 4 Republican Left and 4 UGT was sent to Russia at the invitation from the Russian Consul here. It was only done to parade them during the festivities Nov. 7th. For no other reason. On the other hand every attempt to demand the release of our Russian comrades was shelved for "reasons of state." The same old story. Fortunately a splendid comrade, Martin [37] is his name, was sent along as interpreter. He is as honest as you can imagine, though a bit naive. A list of names including Znlz'[38] was sent along. But you and I know that it will have no effect. Had it been done publicly, as Sania [Schapiro] and I and several others demanded, it might have had an effect. It will have none privately presented to those dogs in Moscow.

The irony is that the few things in the way of arms sent by Russia went not to Barcelona, of course not. But to Madrid. And for such a thing it was worth to deny our anti-Soviet activities of 10 years. Believe me, I found it hard to swallow such a denial of our comrades in Stalin's concentration camps.

† *Two weeks later (11/14/36), she expresses further agony on this theme to Stella Ballantine. At the same time, she knows that it is primarily the war context which causes such compromise. Despite all, the Spanish working masses maintain an uncompromising revolutionary spirit.*

You will see by the copy of my letter to Mollie [Steimer] that all is not well. Our people are in a hornets' nest. And every day brings them further away from their old stand. Perhaps it is all in the day's work of war and revolution, especially war. I don't know. I only know that I find it difficult to reconcile myself to some of the steps taken by the CNT-FAI. But as I wrote Mollie the Revolution is safe with the Spanish masses. They are imbued with its spirit and they will fight like tigers for its realization. I do not mean to suggest that the leading comrades of the CNT-FAI have ceased to be what they had been through all their struggle. It is only the devastating war and the desperate need of exterminating the black pest that makes them consent to actions they had formerly repudiated. The danger is so great it is no wonder that they are staking their all on the last card.

37. Martin Gudell, referred to in footnote 46 of Chapter II.
38. Apparently she refers here to the widow of Erich Mühsam, German anarchist writer and activist who was murdered in a Nazi concentration camp in 1934. Zensl Mühsam subsequently escaped to what she expected to be haven in the Soviet Union, only herself to be imprisoned shortly thereafter. See Rudolf Rocker, *El camino de pasion de Zensl Muhsam: trece años prisionera de Stalin* (Buenos Aires?: Ediciones S.A.I., 1949?) and Roland Lewin, "Eric Muehsam, 1878-1934: The Man and His Work," *Cienfuegos Press Anarchist Review*, no. 3, pp. 84-86.

†*Now out of Spain, Goldman here summarizes to her niece (12/16/36) her conviction on the utter futility of collaboration.*

I found alot of mail, among them three letters from you. I haven't time to answer them all, especially your statement that you would unite with the devil to fight Fascism. I am afraid, my darling, I cannot agree with that. I know, and Spain is proving my position, that it does no good to combine with the "devil" or such forces that are diametrically opposed to the thing one wishes to achieve. Eventually such combine means the end of one's aims and makes it impossible for one to really gain anything.

†*Back in London, Goldman tried her best to explain the Spanish anarchist position, but new developments such as an anarchist proposal for concentration camps drove her constantly (as in this 1/1/37 letter) to demand that the CNT National Committee reassess their continuing drift from traditional principles.*

*She begins by reminding them of her own reluctance, while in Spain earlier, to push forcefully her own anti-collaborationist perspective.*

. . . Not knowing Spanish and not wishing to add to your responsibilities I never imposed my own ideas on the Spanish comrades. But the latest news of the creation of a concentration camp which García Oliver is supposed to have advised makes it impossible for me to keep silent. I know what a dangerous undertaking that is. What it has done in Russia.

*She goes on to point out that in Russia, as in Spain, the camps were established initially to deal with opponents to the revolution. They soon were used to eliminate all opposition to the Bolsheviks, based on revolutionary principles or not. She urges that they consider that potential and in any case that they send her more facts.*

†*Despite her own fundamental objections to collaboration, Goldman felt compelled to defend publicly the Spanish anarchists from accusations of treason. In this 1/5/37 letter to two New York anarchist periodicals (*Freie Arbeiter Stimme *and* Spanish Revolution*), she states her basic position of tolerance for the Spanish comrades in their effort to search out the most appropriate path through the frightful contradictions of the civil war. While clearly unwilling to endorse all the compromises of the Spanish anarchists to date, she does assert that their basic anarchist commitment remains unchanged.*

I said the part of the CNT-FAI in the Spanish struggle is hardly understood by the outside world. I fear even some of our comrades are still lacking in understanding of the colossal share our Spanish comrades had and have in the events there. I was led to this conclusion by the reports of the condemnation coming from our own ranks. In Holland, for instance, where some of the

pacifist Anarchists are carrying on a systematic attack on the CNT-FAI, heaping the same calumny and insults on their heads as the Fascists do. And from private correspondence I gather that our comrades in Spain are being charged with nothing short of treachery. That is very deplorable. To say the least it proves lack of understanding of the situation in Spain and the conditions under which the CNT-FAI are laboring. Perhaps I can put them right even if all the facts of the inner work of the so-called United Front cannot be given to the world. The truth has its own way of coming to the fore. Just at present we cannot oblige Franco and his backers. Nor is it necessary at present. Once Fascism will be defeated, as it MUST be, if the Revolution is to go on in its marvelous constructive work, all our comrades as well as the rest of the world will learn the truth. The truth of the gigantic share the CNT-FAI have played from their very inception until this day.

I hope I am still the old Anarchist and that I still believe in the necessity of criticism of steps taken that apparently look inconsistent with our ideas. I have never justified the notion that wrong acts committed by one's own comrades should be ignored more than when committed by our opponents. And if I know anything of the comrades of the CNT-FAI I can say with certainty that they themselves would be the last to expect complete acceptance of anything they have done with which we cannot agree in full. They do however expect our comrades outside of Spain to acquaint themselves with the real situation and the steps imposed on them by the factors working in their country. These factors left our comrades only one of two alternatives, either dictatorship or direct participation in the government. Never before was a revolution and its leading organization so scandalously sabotaged as in Spain. In point of truth the sabotage was systematic and flagrant enough to jeopardize the rescue of Madrid from the Fascist hordes. It was only [through] the decision of the CNT to take a responsible share of the government that Madrid was made ready in the eleventh hour for the defense since known to the whole world as one of the most heroic battles in history. For it was only when the government betook itself to Valencia that the real drive against the Fascist gangs, equipped with every sort [of] German and Italian arms,[39] could be undertaken. As on the 19th of July, so in Madrid, the people themselves, the dumb inarticulate masses, undertook the defense of Madrid and with it the defeat of Franco and his hirelings. Let it be understood by all comrades that the CNT was not at all unaware that Anarchists in ministries are an anomaly. But in the first place government and ministries do not mean the same thing to the Spanish

39. By November 6, when the republican government moved from Madrid to Valencia, Franco's military already had received decisive German and Italian military support: quickly transporting large numbers of the insurgent armies originally from Morocco to Spain, supplying initial arms and men, and promising to deliver significant arms, ammunition and troops over the longer range. Indeed such support in war materials, advisors and soldiers did begin arriving in large quantities in November.

Anarchists as [they do] to Europeans or Americans. They are mere makeshifts to them to be thrown overboard at will. In the second place it means the safety of Madrid, in fact the safety of Spain. Only the future will tell whether the CNT acted wisely or not. For the present it should suffice our comrades outside of Spain to know that the next step to entering the ministries was armed revolt against the sabotage that had been going on for months on the part of some of the allied parties that had joined the United Front.

I have already stated that our comrades had but one of two things to choose, dictatorship or the widest possible freedom for all their so-called friends in the anti-Fascist struggle. I am glad to say the CNT-FAI chose the latter. It may seem an exaggeration when I say that Catalonia today is the freest place politically in the world. But for the Fascists, every party enjoys unlimited freedom of speech, press and assembly. In fact some of them are interpreting liberty to mean license. They have requisitioned the most conspicuous buildings, they hold forth until all hours of the night in loud speakers and meetings. They have daily parades in military form and music. They do pretty much what they damn please, including intense preparation for the happy hour when they might be strong enough to put our comrades to the wall. True they will have as much luck in that as Franco has so far. But the fact remains, this is their greatest dream. I have often felt and expressed that such tolerance as the CNT-FAI shows may bring disastrous, grave results. And yet I had to agree that this danger is preferable to dictatorship. While the CNT-FAI does not believe in all the public mummery the others practice, they are not blind to the danger, they are prepared for it. But so deep rooted is their faith [in] freedom that they would rather endure the daily annoyances that would test the patience of saints than to forcibly prevent those who must rely on other methods to win adherents. Our people feel that Anarchism and Libertarian Communism are so ingrained in the Catalan workers and peasants they need no public shows to rouse their enthusiasm and devotion. This will have to do for the present as proof that far from having betrayed our ideas the CNT-FAI are today the only gallant fighters and defenders of them. Actually, they are the only large group of people in the world who still love liberty enough to struggle and die for it. I feel therefore that whatever our regrets may be of our Spanish comrades having entered ministries or having made other mistakes we have no right in judging them at least until Fascism has been crushed. At present there is only one menace, that is Fascism by whatever name it goes. Everything else must wait. Our duty outside of Spain is to help our comrades, to help the anti-Fascist battle with material and moral support. To help the women and children evacuated from the various fronts.

† *In another letter to* Spanish Revolution *published at the same time (1/8/37), Goldman speaks of the general menace from collaboration, but refuses to denounce*

*the Spanish anarchists' good faith or to suggest another alternative.*

Fascism is bad enough indeed, but the worst, by far, is the enemy within. . . . For long it has not been possible to thus speak out, but now the sabotage has gone so far that silence would be cowardly, nay criminal. . . . It has been felt up to now that the knowledge of any rift would be grist for the Fascist mill. However, the danger from all sides is too great for further diplomatic consideration.

There are many inexplicable things to be taken under consideration in this terrible welter of slaughter. First of all is the question why the comrades should have joined the United Front at all, for it has led, and inevitably was destined to lead them into the most contradictory steps and is daily proving a graver danger than Fascism itself. The growth of the villainy of the enemy from within is due to too much tolerance from the CNT-FAI in order to show that anarchism would suppress no one but armed or avowed Fascists—hence they have given the Socialists and Communists all too much leeway, with the result that both these age-long enemies are sabotaging the revolution right and left. This, comrades, is the greatest danger for the CNT-FAI. Being men of their words our comrades cannot well stop the pernicious counteractivities of their own allies. But in spite of this most discouraging situation, with the Fascists at the gates of Madrid, our comrades go about their constructive labor as though there were no Judases and armed enemies within and without their ranks. The great hope of the Fascists is not so much aid from other countries as it is the development of feud within the ranks of the United Front.

†*Goldman attempts to clarify her position in this 1/19/37 letter to close, but increasingly critical comrade Mollie Steimer.*

About the steps taken by the Spanish comrades I no more agree than you or Senia [Fleshin]. It is strange, however, that our positions should have changed. You and Senia resented my saying that our comrades should never have allied themselves with the Communists, or the government as far as that is concerned.[39a] You were even afraid of my going to Spain because I was critical of the CNT-FAI. Well, I still hold that the comrades made the blunder of their lives to go into the united front. But here is the difference between us now. You are now sitting in judgment on our people who are daily facing danger, and who are surrounded by enemies on every side, while I having been on the spot have come to realize that once they went into the so-called united front, they could do nothing else but go further. In other words, the one mistake, the one wrong step inevitably led to others as it always does. I am

[39a]Steimer's 1/14/37 letter to Goldman (AMS-F) refers to these earlier differences.

more than ever firmly convinced that if the comrades had remained firm on their own grounds they would have remained stronger than they are now. But I repeat, once they have made common cause for the period of the anti-Fascist war, they were driven by the logic of events to go further. Actually the comrades entered the ministry only after every other method they suggested for a Defense Council of the War had been refused by Caballero. They were up before the alternative to put Caballero to the wall and with him his Cabinet or go into the government if they were to have any voice in the direction of the war. Surely you and Senia and the others will not suggest that the anti-Fascist war is now not of the greatest and first importance, will you? Well, our comrades had no choice whatever. They could not afford to drive Caballero and his gang of politicians out of the government by force. For that would not only have strengthened the hand of Franco, . . . the whole international proletariat including some of our Anarchists would have turned against the CNT-FAI. Our comrades really did not choose, circumstances chose for them. If they had not submitted to the inevitable, Franco would now be in possession of Spain and there would have been no Anarchists left in Spain for the Anarchists of the rest of the world to find fault with or condemn . . . .This is the situation, my darling. Take it or leave it. But before you decide, go to Spain and see everything for yourself.

† *A month later (2/17/37), she tells her old American friend and comrade Harry Kelly that her dread about the effects of excessive Spanish anarchist tolerance is as great as ever, though now the comrades are beginning to take notice themselves.*

I quite agree with you that every nerve should be strained to keep the united front intact; certainly our people have shown tremendous patience and tolerance; but the other side is insidious. Not only the Communists—the "Left" Republicans[40] are also trying to get hold of the ship of state. Sometimes I fear that our people are making too many concessions: I dread the day when they might find themselves frozen out. Evidently they themselves are realizing it—because they have begun an intense campaign in the way of meetings, broadcasting and literature, before the Catalonian masses. They have neglected that for quite a number of months. When I spoke to them, pointing out that their allies are working day and night to spread their ideas, our comrades assured me that they did not need such mummery. Well, better late than never!

† *Within several days (2/23/37), she heatedly replies to comrade Alexander Schapiro's accusations against her tolerance of Spanish anarchist direction, her own*

---

40. "Left Republicans" included a variety of moderate conservative and liberal political groupings, with such prominent leaders as Luis Companys, head of the Catalan government, and Manuel

*compromise of basic anarchist principles. While agreeing with most of his cri-
tiques as to the disastrous implications of Spanish anarchist policy, she stresses that
all of these had their root in their mistakes before July 1936 and that then rather
than now, in crisis, was the time to be so critical. In her view, the crisis necessitated
some compromise; the issue was which form was the least detrimental to, the least
basic contradiction of anarchist principles.*

. . . Your letter brought back to me my first meeting with you in Moscow
when Sasha and I were there. How you explained the necessity of all the compromises, blunders and criminal mistakes the Bolsheviki made as inevitable
in the revolutionary struggle. And how you approved of your own position in
the Foreign Office as well as the cooperation Shatov[41] and others of our comrades were giving the Soviet regime. As late as Oct. 20 [1920] when we
returned from the Ukraine, you thought I was rash in finding fault with
Lenin's steps. In other words you made every possible allowance and excuse
for the machinery that was throttling the Revolution, oppressing the workers,
coercing the peasantry and crushing every breath of freedom because of
revolutionary inevitability. And how willing you are to condemn en bloc
every step taken by our Spanish comrades.[42] Is it that you have learned from
your Russian experience? Or that one is so often apt to be less understanding
of one's own and less tolerant?

Mark you, dear Sania, most of your charges against our people are only too
true and I agree with you. Where I differ is in the starting point of the
blunders. It was not only the declaration of lack of strength of the CNT-FAI to
carry the Revolution through.[43] The first dismal mistake was the lack of participation with the masses in the Asturias . . . in '34. It was again when the
CNT-FAI rallied to the elections to put the rotten Azaña and Caballero in
power. These wrong steps inevitably lead to all the other unfortunate ones like
a stone rolling down a precipice. Why have you not fought this then?[44] That
was the time and *not now*. With Franco at the throat of Spain, with all the so-
called allies against the CNT-FAI and the whole Socialist pack outside of
Spain deadly opposed to our people it seems cruel to condemn, as you are
doing, their wrong steps while saying nothing of the constructive work they
have done and are no doubt continuing even now. . . .

Now I said that I agree with much of what you have written. But I feel that

Azaña (President of the Republic) and José Giral (head of the first civil war republican government, before Largo Caballero) at the national level.
41. See footnote 41 at back of chapter.
42. She refers to Schapiro's indictment of the Spanish anarchists in his lengthy letter to Armando
    Borghi (an influential Italian anarcho-syndicalist then exiled in the U.S.) which he sent to
    Goldman for comments. Though fully supportive of the written critiques already being
    published in *L'Espagne Anti-Fasciste* (Paris), Schapiro waited several months more before
    publishing his own perspective in *Combat Syndicaliste* (Paris).
43. See footnote 43 at back of chapter.
44. See footnote 44 at back of chapter.

our people had but one of two things to choose, either dictatorship or their participation in the government. I think both reprehensible for Anarchists. But between the two, dictatorship is the greater evil. One can withdraw from ministries when they are proven useless and idiotic. But once a group of people begin with dictatorship, there is no halting on the way. The tolerance the CNT-FAI have and are showing to their allies may cost them much. But it will cost them less than having put everybody against the wall as they have in Russia and are doing to this day.

The one thing that certainly deserves the severest criticism and condemnation is the foolish overtures to the Stalin gang. The CNT-FAI seems to have realized that already. . . .

. . . . . . . . . . . . . . . . . . . . . . . . . . . . . . . . . . . . . . . . . . . . . . . . . . .

There is one point however I cannot let pass and that is your reference to my representing the Generalitat. My dear, you were premature. True, I did accept a credential from the Generalitat.[45] But I have so far represented it as much as you have. Fact is I have not been near the office [in London] nor have I even once spoken in the name of the Generalitat. And what is more I do not intend to. I have written the comrades to that effect. But even if I had actually spoken in the name of the Generalitat it would not have prevented me from criticism of the wrong steps of our comrades.

†*Concerning her own willingness to collaborate with potential allies in Britain, Goldman informs her friend Martin Gudell (3/6/37) of the circumstances and boundaries of that position.*

. . . Yes, I know the I.L.P.[46] is making desperate love to the CNT-FAI. . . . But I certainly do not intend to affiliate with the I.L.P. And it would be a great mistake for the CNT—FAI people to do so. The I.L.P., like the POUM,[47] are Marxians and like lepers they never change their character though they may change their skin.

*Given the absence of a significant anarchist movement in Britain, she is willing to work with the ILP to the extent of speaking from the same platform or organizing together a demonstration. But none of this in any way restricts her or the CNT-FAI for the future.*

45. See footnote 45 at back of chapter.
46. The Independent Labour Party was founded in 1893 and later helped to form the British Labour Party. Critical of the latter's increasing "moderation," it withdrew in 1931-32 to become again fully autonomous instead of simply a caucus within the larger organization. In the general spectrum of Left politics in the 1930's, many of its views tended roughly to coincide with, despite organizational hostilities, the Trotskyist Fourth International. For more details on the ILP generally, see G.D.H. Cole, *A History of the Labour Party from 1914* (1949; rpt. N.Y. Augustus M. Kelley, 1969) and Robert E. Dowse, *Left in the Centre* (London: Longmans, Green and Co., Ltd., 1966).
47. See footnote 47 at back of chapter.

†*In her lengthiest and most open expression in several months (3/9/37), her fears about Spanish collaboration re-emerge. Once again she trusts Milly and Rudolf Rocker to accept her self-questioning and to dialogue constructively with it.*

. . . Their insistence now on militarization, compulsory mobilization and the Single Command[48] are compromises that seem to augur badly for the future. It means losing ground inch by inch, only to find themselves trapped, when Caballero will have all power in his hands. Actually, our comrades are going through the same process as our comrades in Russia.

*As in that earlier context, she fears ultimately for the very safety of the Spanish anarchists. Their compromises with basic principles seem only to have endangered their position even more.*
　*The charges by Schapiro, Steimer and Fleshin against her own apparent inconsistency bother her a great deal. She wishes she could discuss these issues with Rudolf in person, to clarify her own position and relieve her tension.*

†*As this 4/5/37 letter to Harry Kelly illustrates, while tolerating Spanish anarchist efforts to choose the appropriate path in Spain, Goldman strongly resists their efforts to push her toward collaborationism in London.*

A couple of weeks ago, the 2nd International[49] met in this city [London]. There were Spanish delegates, members of the UGT. What they reported at that session there is no way of knowing, but I have it on very good authority that they denounced the CNT-FAI when they proclaimed that our people had no part whatever in the events of July 19th, '36. That the CNT is losing numbers; that it does not support Madrid; that it has begun to shoot peasants because they will not be collectivized—a network of lies from beginning to end. Yet our poor comrades have been trying (even before July 19th) to induce the UGT to join an alliance with them, to represent two powerful revolutionary trade union organizations. They have reiterated this offer in every one of their dailies, weeklies and bulletins. So far nothing has come of it. On the contrary, the Caballero comrades in the UGT are throwing mud on the CNT, and when they come out of Spain they villify them to the extent which I have already explained.

48. Under severe pressure from their "allies" in the government, and apparently from their own increasing conviction as well, the most prominent CNT-FAI leaders began in March 1937 calling for major military changes. These included restructuring and consolidating the politically-aligned militia groups (including those of the CNT-FAI, such as the Durruti Column) into regular units of the government army ("militarization"); re-instituting compulsory military conscription for males of military age ("compulsory mobilization'); and placing all military units under a single command accountable to the government. Such measures, of course, directly contradicted traditional anarchist positions. See Chapter VII for more discussion of these issues.
49. See footnote 49 at back of chapter.

It is tragic if it were not such a comedy that our people still continue to have faith in the UGT. Would you believe it, they sent me an express letter that I should attend the session of the Second International and take part in the demonstration held at Kingsway Hall after the private session of the delegates had been closed! It happens that the letter came too late and I was laid up with flu, but even if that had not been the drawback I should never have attempted such a grotesque measure as to beg the Second International, represented at this end by Sir Citrine, Bevin[50] and the rest of the gentry, [to] accept me as the delegate of the CNT-FAI. But our people are simply incurable children when it comes to the European Socialist movement. I am enclosing copies of letters recently written to Rocker and to Bell which will show you what inner struggle I am going through. I have to admit, unfortunately, that many steps taken by our comrades are contrary to everything they have stood for in the past, and certainly everything you and I have expounded. My grief is great because I know that these compromises will avail them not. On the contrary, they may be their undoing.

†*In a new (5/2/37) letter to Schapiro, replying to his response to her critical letter two months earlier, Goldman clarifies better than ever her own position within the spectrum of international anarchist perspectives on Spain: a middle-ground stance of tolerance, yet constructive criticism. It is precisely Schapiro's inconsistency with his earlier demand for tolerance in the Russian revolution which she finds so irritating now.*

Dear Sania, I am afraid I am like the poor little orphan who was damned when she did and damned when she didn't. You condemn me for not being critical of our comrades in Spain, and Nettlau condemns me for having dared in my statement published in the *Fr. Arb. St.*[51] and in *Spain and the World* to explain the mistakes and compromises of the CNT.

*She rejects both appeals and attempts once more to state her basic position; she agrees with his criticism of Spanish anarchist compromise, but she objects to the vicious, condemning nature of his attack. She reminds him again of his earlier defense of Bolshevik policy on the grounds of "revolutionary necessity," and asks that he not allow his emotional bitterness from that experience to be misdirected now toward the Spanish.*

*To his accusation that her failure to criticize publicly the Spanish anarchists repeats her unwillingness to do so against the Bolshevik regime while in Russia, she reminds him that in the latter context there was no significant public opportunity for such by the time she had solidified her opinion. In any case, it was certainly not*

50. See footnote 50 at back of chapter.
51. *Freie Arbeiter Stimme* (The Free Voice of Labor) was a Yiddish-language anarchist newspaper published in New York, 1890-1977.

*because she was afraid, as he may have implied.*[52] *In Spain, she reports that among those more influential anarchists who spoke French (including Montseny, Oliver and Santillán) she argued for hours against anarchists entering ministries and other government positions and against acceptance of militarization. Her failure to speak out in larger anarchist meetings was due only to her inadequacy with the language, not the fear of retaliation.*

*She also restates her resentment against his assumption that she herself compromised basic principles by accepting credentials to serve the Catalan government office in London. She originally accepted them merely to facilitate anarchist propaganda in Britain, not to serve the state. In any case, she found that it was impossible to use them in this way once she came to London, so she never did.*

*Finally, she urges him to state what third alternative he saw to anarchist participation in the government or dictatorship.*[53]

†*Now aware of the bloody Barcelona street fighting between anarchists and their supposed "allies," as well as the super-tolerant pacifying role at the time of leading figures in the anarchist movement, Goldman writes to Rudolf Rocker (5/14/37) that her "hope against hope" to avoid disaster from collaboration has now collapsed. Indeed she threatens to resign from her official role representing the Spanish anarchists in Britain.*

You will bear me out, dear Rudolf, that I tried and tried to explain and defend the CNT-FAI leaders for entering ministries as I have tried to explain their sudden love feast, now baptised in the blood of Berneri and Barbieri[54] and a number of other comrades, for the miserable contribution of [Soviet] arms. I have done so although I saw when I was in Spain what the . . . consequence will be. I had hoped against hope that the extermination of our comrades and the emasculation of the revolution would not come so soon. That they would be held back until Franco's hordes will be driven from the land. It is this fervent hope of mine which has given me the strength to carry on the work here against terrible odds, which made me argue with Sania, though I was willing to admit that his criticism was correct. But the death of Berneri and all the

---

52. Goldman did protest various Bolshevik repressive measures to several top-level leaders (including Lenin and Kollantai) in personal conversations. She also criticized the regime at the Red Trade Union International congress in July 1921 and signed a vehement written protest to Zinoviev against the imminent repression of Kronstadt several months before. She was one of the organizers of the Kropotkin funeral procession in Moscow in 1921 (the last public display by anarchists in the Soviet Union, aside from the increasingly-suppressed Makhnovista movement in the Ukraine) and in her last few months in Petrograd had a steady stream (under surveillance) of distraught Russian and foreign anarchists to her apartment for discussion. Commentary on these various activities is found in *LL*, II, and in *My Disillusionment in Russia*.
53. See her 7/1/37 letter to Tom Bell in this chapter below and footnote 20 above.
54. She refers here to the Barcelona assassination of Italian anarchists Camillo Berneri and Francisco Barbieri, described in Chapter V. Barbieri was a veteran anarchist with years of militant experience in Italy and Argentina before coming to Spain to fight with the anarchist militia. Goldman describes Berneri at length in Chapters V and X.

other comrades and the cowardly stand of Montseny and Oliver and the *Solidaridad Obrera* make it impossible for me to go on as the representative of the CNT-FAI. As you know I am not hasty in my decisions, nor do I ever come to definite conclusion unless I have fully looked into every side of the issue. I am more than ever determined to return to Spain and confront the National Committee of the CNT-FAI for their explanation of the worst betrayal of the revolution since Russia. If I fail to get that I shall certainly give up my mandate and retire from the field of action. Better silence than be a party to the slow bleeding to death of the Spanish Revolution.

Of course I may find that rank and file of the CNT-FAI have retained their revolutionary zeal and fervor. I will then work for them but in no official capacity.

†*In this letter three weeks later (6/8/37) to comrade Jeanne Levey, Goldman frankly expresses her despair at the rapid, tragic denouement in Barcelona, however strong her faith still in the revolutionary energy and courage of the grassroots anarchist movement.*

Unfortunately the entire blame [for the May events] cannot be laid at the feet of the Communists and their reactionary allies. The leaders in the CNT-FAI must carry part of the blame. They went into the net with open eyes, they foolishly believed that they can outwit the very institutions we have always fought, the crushing institutions of government; more childish was their belief that they would get the best of the modern Jesuits — Stalin and his aides — who are by far more skillful than the Jesuits of the past have ever been. Anyway, the situation in Spain is very grave; whether the government forces will win or Fascism, our comrades will be crushed and by either chariot wheel; and yet they had such golden opportunities if only they had stood their ground and had refused to bargain with people who were bent on their destruction. I have been in a frightful depressed state ever since the events in Barcelona. Spain had meant so much to me. It held out such hopes for the last years of my life. Now all that is gone by the board and I am left dangling in the air. . . . And I am left in uncertainty where to go or what to do. You must not think that I have lost faith in the Revolution itself or in the rank and file of the CNT-FAI. I know too much of their past, their inexhaustible revolutionary resources, their great courage to despair in the future of Spain. But it may take years to reach the heights of the Revolution as I saw it when I was in Spain. The odds are too great against our comrades. The European Powers and their colleagues in Spain will not easily permit anarchism to become a reality. Still, I will never cease to work for our comrades, no matter where I will be.

†*Nearly one month later (7/1/37), Goldman clarifies her dispute with Schapiro in*

*this letter to Tom Bell.*

. . . For the present I wish to say that my objection to Schapiro was not due to his criticism of our Spanish comrades. I agreed with him on that entirely. It was only his method that I couldn't agree with. As to Nettlau, I am afraid he has gone somewhat gaga; he simply can't stand the least opposition to the leaders of the CNT-FAI. He once used to speak out as you do in regard to absolute freedom anarchists must practice, and against every compromise on our part. Today he approves of every compromise. He has turned into a regular zealot who would burn every heretic at the stake. He hates us all because we do not accept 100% of everything done by Montseny and Oliver. I have actually stopped writing to him.

Now as to the various points raised in your letter. First, if you think that Schapiro's criticism of the leaders in Spain is due to their inconsistencies in re their anarchism you are mistaken. Schapiro believes in arbitrary measures. His objections are due to the fact that the CNT-FAI have not from the very beginning taken hold of power and . . . directed it to their own needs. I do not think that there need be any lengthy argument between you and myself regarding the practice of anarchist principles. I have maintained the same position all my life. Since the Russian experience I have repeatedly pointed out that a great aim cannot afford to use contemptible means. . . .

. . . . . . . . . . . . . . . . . . . . . . . . . . . . . . . . . . . . . . . . . . . . . . . . . . . . . . .

You express surprise that I should give as the alternatives confronting our comrades the entry into ministries or dictatorship. I hope that you do not think that I approve of either. I have considered them, and do at the present time, two great evils. But our comrades insisted that their part in the government is a much lesser evil than dictatorship. That they can at any time withdraw from their government position. But once dictatorship turns into a system it becomes a Frankenstein which ultimately pulls down the whole edifice. Anyway our comrades didn't seem to think and do not now that they had another alternative. That government means nothing to them has again been reiterated by García Oliver in his brilliant speech which he delivered in a very large meeting in Paris. There is not a single Spanish Anarchist who is deceived about the value of government during [a] revolutionary period. They participate in it because they think it is the nearest approach to making the anti-Fascist war successful. I am not arguing whether they are right or wrong. I know that there was a third alternative; the comrades could have refused alliance with all other parties and they would have attempted the revolutionary procedure by their own numbers and their own strength. This is really also Schapiro's point of view.[55] Evidently our people did not feel themselves

55. In his "Reflections on the Spanish Revolution," published in *Challenge* (N.Y.), June 25, July 2 and July 9, 1938, Schapiro maintained that the only proper course for Spanish anarchists in the inspiring atmosphere immediately following July 19, 1936 was to proclaim the social revolution

strong enough; in point of truth they admitted as such in their last congress at Saragossa. They said that they did not feel [able or] strong enough to carry out revolutionary measures by themselves. Added to this was also their apprehension that if they proceeded on their own Franco would conquer and they would stand exposed before the whole world as having brought about the anti-Fascist collapse. It is hardly necessary to emphasize that there is a good deal of truth in that; even now, though the CNT-FAI has been the greatest contributor in men, arms and provisions for the anti-Fascist struggle, their so-called allies have attacked them on all sides and have held them responsible for all the sins committed by themselves. Imagine what it would have been had they taken the final — consistent but desperate — step of standing alone in the attempt to defeat Fascism.

†*Having explained her own position to the international anarchist movement independently from that of the CNT-FAI,*[56] *Goldman now states (7/8/37) her determination to maintain her own course. She invites the CNT National Committee to withdraw her credentials if they disapprove of her stand.*

I do not have to tell you that the part played by the CNT-FAI [in] the last six or seven months has brought no end of confusion in our ranks in every country. I do not mean only among the young and careless comrades but even among the more serious, those who are with you in your struggle. I am one of them. I therefore felt impelled to state my position.

*She encloses a translated copy of her article and requests that they notify her immediately if they feel she should no longer represent them in Britain. For her it was essential to make her position known, since so many had requested her thoughts in order to clarify their own perspective on Spain.*

†*Her despair over the losses encouraged by collaboration only deepens as the weeks go on, as shown in a 7/13/37 letter to the Rockers.*
    *She reports that several days earlier a number of foreign anarchists were arrested in Spain and repression continues.*[57] *Compromises by the anarchist leader-*

everywhere and to defend with armed force its gains and momentum (at least in Catalonia, Aragón and the Levante) from attacks by fascists, moderates and anti-revolutionary "Leftists" alike. This was definitely a risk, since such an appeal might have been ignored in parts of loyalist Spain and such open division might have made Franco's path that much easier. Nevertheless, he felt that such a risk was well worth taking, compared to the gradual elimination of anarchist principles and revolutionary accomplishment through growing compromise with statist "allies."

56. In her "Where I Stand" article published in *Spain and the World*, I, no. 15 (July 2, 1937) and in *Freie Arbeiter Stimme*. The vast bulk of this statement appears in Chapter II.
57. According to CNT figures, by July some 800 members in Barcelona alone were imprisoned

*ship have now brought the movement to a sorry state of weakness, after earlier having everything in their favor.*

I feel completely shattered, without an idea what to do or where to turn. . . .
. . . Life is really too unbearable. I wish I knew why one goes on. . . . I cannot regret [Simion Koldofsky's[58]] death because I know he is done with the cruelty, suffering and meaninglessness of life. He is luckier than I am who keeps dragging it on, though I know not why.

† *Re-energized in her enthusiasm for the Spanish movement, Goldman shows here a totally different tone reminiscent of her first visit, in this 9/27/37 letter from Spain to her British friend Ethel Mannin.*

The situation here [in Spain] is overwhelming. So much greatness, so many confusing and agonizing sides. Above everything looms an optimism and faith in the triumph of the struggle, one is filled with awe. Having come close to the insurmountable difficulties confronting the CNT-FAI I can understand better the concessions my comrades have made and are making. I cannot reconcile myself to some of them but I realize that when one is in a burning house one does not consider one's possessions, one tries to jump to safety even if it means death. The possessions of my comrades have been their sterling quality, their staunch adherence to fundamentals. But they are surrounded by consuming flames and they feel if they hold on to every part of their past they would lose everything. Hence their compromises of which they are only too painfully aware.

† *In one of her rare written communications to Spanish anarchist leaders while in Spain itself, Goldman informs Vázquez (10/11/37) of her continued critique of anarchist collaboration and her continued sense of eroding CNT strength and integrity.*

. . . The conditions here [in Barcelona], wherever I have been and with most comrades I have spoken to, strengthen my conviction that the policy of the CNT is slowly but surely undermining the fundamental ideas and position of the CNT and will, if it continues, completely destroy its influence. Among many things is the renewed step of the CNT to satisfy the insatiable demands of the Soviet government. . . .

and another 60 murdered (Morrow, p. 192). A new Barcelona underground journal, *Anarquía*, spoke of a "blood bath" in the villages, where the Communist-led "Assault Guards" massacred and imprisoned many more anarchist militants (Bolloten, pp. 503-04). By mid-July, says Morrow, all the POUM's leaders and active cadres were in jail (p. 190).
58. Simion and Liza Koldofsky were London friends of Goldman with whom she resided in the winter of 1935-36.

*Last year was bad enough when the CNT went along with eulogies for the Stalin regime in order to gain arms for Spain, in the process betraying the comrades in Russia crushed by the Bolsheviks through murder and concentration camps. Yet now once again the Spanish anarchists plan to participate in official celebration of the anniversary of the Russian revolution. She cannot accept this policy without protest. She cannot justify such an action, though she does not intend publicly to denounce it.*

†*As after her first visit a year before, again in her letter now (11/11/37) to an anarchist comrade in the U.S. (published in part in* Spanish Revolution*), Goldman stresses how desperate Spanish anarchists feel in their struggle against Franco as their rationale for continued collaboration. And as before, she urges international anarchists, however critical, to view the Spanish position with tolerance.*

. . . When I tell you that our comrades have made every sacrifice, every possible concession and many deplorable compromises to maintain the anti-Fascist morale, you will realize how strong the hatred for these dreadful people is. You must understand, and so must all the comrades everywhere, that the anti-Fascist struggle has become a veritable obsession for the CNT – a religious passion! They were the first in the whole world to repulse Fascism,[59] and they feel that they will remain the last in the field of battle against it. In other words, our comrades will fight to the very last against the ogre that threatens the whole world. But at the same time, they have come to realize that the Moscow satraps are no less a menace. They know as well as we do that there will be a day of reckoning and they will be ready for it. What I mean to impress upon all our comrades is that while Stalin's henchmen are in power, politically speaking, [and] they are committing crime after crime without being held to account, the moral strength of the revolutionary struggle is not theirs and never will be theirs in Spain.

On the other hand, the CNT-FAI have gained moral prestige far beyond that which they held before the May events. Wherever I went, and I travelled more extensively on this visit, and with whomever I spoke I found the influence of the CNT-FAI growing. That gives me reason to believe that the power of the Communists is artificially created, hence doomed to perish, while the position of the CNT-FAI in the estimation of the Spanish workers and awakened peasants is stronger than ever.

. . . . . . . . . . . . . . . . . . . . . . . . . . . . . . . . . . . . . . . . . . . . .

We, outside of Spain, may not agree with these compromises and we may lament the concessions of the CNT-FAI. I certainly do not agree – but,

59. She refers here to the relatively bloodless takeovers of Italy by Mussolini in 1922 and Germany in 1933 by Hitler. It is true that in Austria the Left resisted with arms the right-wing authoritarian government of Engelbert Dollfuss in February 1934, a struggle Goldman publicly praised at the time while on a speaking tour in the United States.

having been in Spain twice within the year, I have learned to understand that our people were driven to the very brink of extinction by the advent of Fascism to accept help from a source no less a menace, yet not quite so immediate as the hordes of Franco, Hitler and Mussolini. After all, understanding should enable us to approach the mistakes and blunders made by our comrades more tolerantly than some of the critics of the CNT-FAI have so far shown.

†*In this important mid-December speech before the IWMA congress in Paris, Goldman again tries to articulate a middle stance of strong but non-dogmatic critique and to urge such a position on both sides of the international movement.*

I have seen from the moment of my first arrival in Spain in September 1936 that our comrades in Spain are plunging head-foremost into the abyss of compromise that will lead them far away from their revolutionary aim. Subsequent events have proven that those of us who saw the danger ahead were right. The participation of the CNT-FAI in the government, and concessions to the insatiable monster in Moscow, have certainly *not* benefited the Spanish Revolution, or even the anti-Fascist struggle. Yet closer contact with reality in Spain, with the almost insurmountable odds against the aspirations of the CNT-FAI, made me understand their tactics better, and helped me to guard against any dogmatic judgment of our comrades.

With the most fervent desire to aid the revolution in Spain, our comrades outside of it were neither numerically nor materially strong enough to turn the tide. Thus finding themselves up against a stone wall, the CNT-FAI was forced to descend from its lofty traditional heights to compromise right and left: participation in the government, all sorts of humiliating overtures to Stalin, superhuman tolerance for his henchmen who were openly plotting and conniving against the Spanish revolution.

Of all the unfortunate concessions our people have made, their entry into ministries seemed to me the least offensive. No, I have not changed my attitude toward government as an evil. As all through my life, I still hold that the State is a cold monster, and that it devours everyone within its reach. Did I not know that the Spanish people see in government a mere makeshift, to be kicked overboard at will, that they will never be deluded and corrupted by the parliamentary myth, I should perhaps be more alarmed for the future of the CNT-FAI. But with Franco at the gate of Madrid, I could hardly blame the CNT-FAI for choosing a lesser evil—participation in the government rather than dictatorship, the most deadly evil.

Their need to meet Franco's military equipment was a matter of life and

death. The Spanish people had not a moment to lose if they were not to be crushed. What wonder if they saw in Stalin the savior of the anti-Fascist war? They have since learned that Stalin helped to make Spain safe against the Fascists so as to make it safer for his own ends.

The critical comrades are not at all wrong when they say that it does not seem worthwhile to sacrifice one's ideal in the struggle against Fascism, if it only means to make room for Soviet Communism. I am entirely of their view – that there is no difference between them. My own consolation is that with all their concentrated criminal efforts, Soviet Communism has not taken root in Spain. . . .

†*In moving to create the British branch of the SIA, the Spanish anarchist relief organization, Goldman writes Ethel Mannin (12/21/37) of the relative difference between fascism and democracy and the need publicly to stress, as do the Spanish, an anti-fascist appeal.*

Dearest, I don't know whether Regie[60] is at your cottage or in town. Will you therefore tell him for me that while I am fully in agreement with his suggestion of a committee in defense of the Spanish Revolution[61] I do not think anti-Fascism should be left out from any appeal. True, anti-Fascism covers many sins, and its adherents are the very people who dread Revolution more than they dread Franco. Yet the fact remains that unless Franco is conquered not only the Revolution but all advanced thought will be crushed for many years to come. I do not believe I need to tell Regie or you that I am not deceived by the bombastic claims of democracy. I exposed it as a delusion and a snare in my magazine *Mother Earth* many years ago. But I have come to see that much in social affairs has relative value or harm. There is a vast difference between Fascism and Democracy. The one stifles everything, tortures and kills; under the other, one can still breathe, speak out and use one's pen. No doubt Regie will say that British so-called democracy is only for domestic use. In the colonies, it is as Fascist as Hitler, Mussolini or Stalin. I will grant him that. Still, there is some elbow space here, in France, in the Scandinavian countries and in the U.S. If only in a palliative way. I can therefore understand my comrades in Spain when they say "we must crush Franco first but also we must work for the Revolution." In other words whatever misconceptions the average anti-Fascist entertains, we know that the CNT-FAI and possibly also the POUM feel the menace of Fascism above everything else. Hence it is but

60. Writer Reginald Reynolds was the companion of Goldman's close English friend Ethel Mannin. The latter was a prolific author, including several books with sketches of Goldman herself with whom she worked during this period for the Spanish cause. See, for example, *Lover under Another Name* (London: Jarrolds, Ltd., 1953).
61. At the time they were drawing up plans for forming the British chapter of the SIA. For more on that organization, see Chapters III and VI.

right that we should approach people in the name of anti-Fascism. We may say INTERNATIONAL ANTI-FASCIST SOLIDARITY FOR THE DEFENSE OF THE SPANISH REVOLUTION. But we cannot discard the term anti-Fascism. At least I cannot.

† *Once again, Goldman declares her independence from the Spanish anarchist position by telling Martin Gudell (12/22/37) that she is unwilling to represent them if they seriously pursue collaboration with the Socialist and Communist Internationals abroad. Such a move obviously would directly affect Goldman's work in Britain.*

Believe me, my dear, it is anything but joy to have to carry stones up a high mountain. Don't think that I am not going to continue, unless the C.N.T. intends going on begging at the doors of Internationals that will only undermine and discredit our comrades. As you will probably have heard the report of the Spanish delegation to the conference of the A.I.T. [IWMA],[62] you will know what I am referring to.[63]

*She would give up her life if she thought that could help defeat the fascists and further the revolution. But despite others' criticism that she has compromised so much already, she does draw the line at these latest CNT steps.*

† *A week later (12/30/37), she informs Helmut Rüdiger that she is shocked that the Spanish movement intentionally neglects at least some of the imprisoned anarchists.[64] She finds this an embarrassing repetition of Lenin's claim that it was only "anti-social elements" in prison, not the idealists.[65] The illness of compromise and the subsequent decay of the anarchist position continues.*

*In the beginning, through the revolution, the Spanish masses and others internationally started to learn anarchist ideas and began to identify with them. Unfortunately, they have come to see anarchists compromising in revolution just like every other political group, so now they back away. Though many of their deeds are childish, the Spanish anarchists can be hardly explained to the world in such terms.*

† *Replying (1/1/38) to Harry Kelly's assertion that at best the struggle against Franco would lead only to a "liberal socialist" democracy, Goldman insists that all of the*

62. In Paris in December 1937.
63. See footnote 63 at back of chapter.
64. CNT leaders sought to continue their role as "responsible" non-disruptive members of the anti-fascist alliance. At the same time, they distrusted and disliked many of the more active anti-collaborationist, revolution-minded anarchists. Thus, they rationalized their inability significantly to assist or liberate such comrades imprisoned by the wave of repression since May 1937.
65. She refers here to Lenin's response to Berkman's and her concern for anarchist prisoners in their direct meeting with Lenin in early 1920 (*LL*, II, 765-66).

*compromises of the Spanish anarchists to date have social revolution as their goal, not a bourgeois state.*

I do not share your idea that all that can be expected in Spain is a Liberal Socialist government. In the first place there can be no such a thing as a Liberal Socialist government. Everywhere and every time the socialists got into power they became worse than the liberals. Besides, whatever government will follow the triumph over Franco will be short-lived. It is a great mistake for anyone to imagine that our people, after having fought and shed their blood will supinely submit to "democratic government." I know them well enough to insist that if the anti-Fascist war will be brought to a successful end, the actual determination to fight on for the Revolutionary cause will only begin. So please get rid of the notion that the CNT-FAI are fighting for democracy. If they did they would be taken to the bosom by the Negrín-Prieto government and by all the Marxists in the world.

No, they proclaim their adherence to the Revolution, and their opposition to any political institution that will return the old bourgeoisie and the church in Spain. Nothing doing, my dear, so let's not despair.

†*Agonized by Spanish anarchist efforts to impose collaborationist tactics on her own role, Goldman attempts a pained, yet diplomatic response (1/20/38) to CNT and FAI leaders Vázquez and Herrera. She declares emphatically both her unwillingness to conform to their approach and the futility of their position.*

Thank you heartily for your comradely letter of the 11th of the month, written in French, wherein you take objection to my article in the *Spanish Revolution* on political persecution in anti-Fascist Spain.[66] I appreciate deeply your solidarity that prompted your suggestion that we should "consider together the effects of my criticism of the Negrín-Communist government in the anti-Fascist struggle". It has always been my opinion that a kindly, warm feeling between comrades would lend to a better understanding of so many differences in our ranks.

Dear comrades, this is my third attempt to answer your letter. I wrote the first almost immediately on receipt of yours. I was terribly grieved at the suggestion that my articles might injure your struggle. I destroyed that letter because I feared it would convey the impression that I was hurt, therefore meant to forsake you in your crucial hour. I waited twenty-four hours, read and reread all the points in your letter, then made another attempt; but

66. Goldman published a brief report on her second visit to Spain in *Spanish Revolution* (N.Y.), II, no. 6 (December 6, 1937), including a strong denunciation of repression by the Communists. However, her much lengthier exposé, entitled "Political Persecution in Republican Spain," was published in the December 10, 1937 issue of *Spain and the World*. The entire article is reproduced in the next chapter.

I was no more successful than the first time – so I stopped the translation when more than half had been done, spent another tortuous day and night, and here I am trying for the third time to find the tone and the words that would help you to see that I have seriously examined your objections.

May I assure you, dear comrades, that in my work in your behalf I have considered every step I have taken; although often in total disagreement with your tactics, I have pleaded your cause because I knew the sinister force that made these actions imperative.

During my first visit in Spain, when Russian arms began to arrive, I knew that Stalin would add other blessings that will prove a curse to the Spanish Revolution and to you. But with Franco at the throat of Madrid I realised that you had no choice and I trembled for the price you will have to pay for Soviet help and Stalin's comradeship. Knowing that, I kept silent on the ruthlessness of Russian Communism which I had openly fought since I came out of Russia in 1922. I kept silent hoping that the Spanish people loved ideas too well to become an easy prey to Stalin's designs on them and your Revolution. I kept silent because of my passionate faith in the revolutionary spirit of the CNT-FAI, their dauntless courage, and their unimpeachable integrity. Then came the terrible May events, after which you yourselves, dear comrades, began to speak out against [the] villainy and perfidy of your Communist allies. Your voice was heard not only in Spain – it reached the ears of the workers in every land. It was only then that I felt released from the hateful task of making a falsehood appear as truth – something I had never done in all my active life. It will probably surprise you to learn that, though I began to call attention to the plots and conspiracies of Stalin's vassals and their clandestine and open crimes against your and my comrades, I did indeed use tact in my writing and speaking about them.

You will probably not guess why I treated them so mildly. Well, it was because I had been out of Spain six months and removed from the havoc I had read about. I felt therefore I should be careful in my indictment against the perpetrators of the May events. To learn about them at first hand was really the reason that made me strain every nerve to get back to Spain.

Well, dear comrades, a few weeks in your heroic country set all my doubts aside about the ruthless gang that had undermined much of your great achievements. Their savage march through some of the collectives – their terror they had let loose – the victims of this terror in prison and dead. And what seemed most tragic to me – the suppression of your freedom of speech, press and assembly. All that and more carried out by the Moscow gang.

Strange how history repeats itself. You will remember my saying at the congress of the I.W.M.A. that there is no comparison between the Spanish and Russian Revolutions.[67] I should have added no comparison in anything

67. See passages from her speech with this comparison in the second section of Chapter VI.

save one—the deadly Communist regime that had crushed the Russian Revolution and was using its power again on Spanish soil. I know, I know, it was the libertarian spirit of the Spanish people, it was the moral strength of the CNT-FAI that stemmed the tide from the East. But the harm they had succeeded in doing your revolution, your constructive work and the chance of a speedy reckoning with Franco were enough to make further silence a crime.

When I left Spain the second time I had quite decided to make known the facts of the counter-revolutionary atmosphere created by the Communists in power and certainly condoned by the Negrín Government. When I arrived in England I discovered that others had preceeded me who were publicly pointing out the evil effect of Communist activities on the anti-Fascist war. Such papers as the *Daily Herald,* the *News-Chronicle* and *Reynolds Weekly News,* who had always held up the Communists as the paragon of sweetness and light, were telling their readers that perhaps they had gone "too far". The *New Leader,*[68] once its party had emancipated itself from its amorous advances to the Communist Party for a United Front, has engaged in a systematic campaign to expose the wretched Stalin gang in Spain. Fenner Brockway, general secretary of the Independent Labour Party, and John McGovern, I.L.P. Member of Parliament, have both written scathing indictments of the Stalin plots and their detrimental effect on the anti-Fascist struggle. I am sending you John McGovern's pamphlet.[69] It fairly burns with indignation against the people who dare speak in the name of Socialism and Communism, and are yet in league with all the imperialists to crush the Spanish Revolution. I cannot believe, dear comrades, that you would have wanted me to either keep silent altogether, or to smooth over what had happened in Spain since May—surely not had you been aware of how widespread was the knowledge about the actual part the Communists have played in your country.

You write "one can say things sometimes; but one must use tact." Dear comrades, the most tactful comrade in the entire Anarchist movement is Rudolf Rocker. Yet no one could possibly be more forcible and outspoken in his exposure of Stalin's schemes in Spain and his cowardly acquiescence to France and England in regard to Non-Intervention.[70] I was told you were enthusiastic of the work of our brilliant and grand comrade, and justly so. Why then are you so perturbed with my article? Perhaps you will be even more so, when you read the report of my lecture on the betrayal of the Spanish people at a large and intensely interested audience last Friday.[71] I may not use enough "tact" but the restraint I have used has often violated all my sensibilities—and I have done so only for the sake of your struggle in which I believe implicitly and which I want to help.

68. The London publication of the ILP.
69. See footnote 69 at back of chapter.
70. No doubt she refers especially to Rocker's 47-page pamphlet, *The Tragedy of Spain* (N.Y.: Freie Arbeiter Stimme, 1937).
71. This ardent detailed attack on the Communist role in Spain is reported in *Spain and the World,* January 21, 1938. Passages from the speech appear in the next chapter.

You write that to speak abroad of the bad activities of the Communists and the Negrín Government is bound to do you harm. The workers in every country will ask "why should we help the anti-Fascist struggle if its Government persecutes our comrade workers even more than capitalist countries." The answer to this, dear comrades, seems to me *not* to be in the denial of the existence of the persecution—rather is it in the frank admission that it does exist due to intrigue and Communist interference since their putsch in May.

In 1922 when my comrade Alexander Berkman and I came out of Russia and began to show up the Bolshevik regime in its true light, we were told that we were injuring the Social Revolution and helping its enemies. Then our voices were crying in the wilderness; but time has proven them clear and sound. Now the whole world knows the effect in and out of Russia of the Soviet regime.

Isn't it strange, dear comrades, that you should make the same objections fifteen years later? True, mine is no longer a lone voice. The betrayal of the anti-Fascist struggle and the Spanish Revolution by Stalin and his emissaries in common with all the imperialists is becoming common knowledge; but the danger to the outcome of your struggle is still very acute—not as you think, because of my writing about your government or the Communists; but because there are still too many who believe in the lying propaganda of the Communists about you: the continued vilification in their own press and their influence on the so-called liberal papers. You may or may not know Stalin's scribe Louis Fischer who wrote last year that the "anarchists ran away from the Madrid front on November 6th and 16th 1936."[72] Or that the correspondent of the *New York Sunday Times* reported that the "anarchists preferred to go off to Valencia for the weekend instead of guarding the Front." Or the special correspondent of the *Manchester Guardian* in a recent report informing the readers of his paper that "in point of military morale at the front the Anarchists simply did not count." Added to this insult is the injury to the anti-Fascist struggle in the bombastic claims of Communist and liberal papers that Stalin has "saved Spain" —that the International Brigade[73] has saved Madrid— that he still sends arms and foodstuff—that the Communists alone are brave and daring—that they have taken Belchite—that the CNT-FAI are a negligible quantity, and alot more.

72. Louis Fischer was an American journalist, pro-Communist at the time. Apparently he even served temporarily as a quartermaster for the International Brigades (Thomas, p. 301). In later years, he became professor in international relations at Princeton University. The article Goldman refers to appeared in *The Nation*, December 12, 1936.

73. The Comintern-organized International Brigades served in Spain from early November 1936 to February 1939. They consisted primarily of foreign volunteers—for the first year at least probably numbering about 15,000 at any one time (Broué and Témime, p. 377). For more details, see footnote 17 in Chapter X. The Brigades helped Communist prestige internationally and served as a wedge, along with Soviet arms and advisors, through which the Soviet Union could gain increasing control of the overall Spanish military effort. Soviet arms were intentionally denied to the anarchist militia because they were outside of Communist influence. See also Goldman's brief comments on the Brigades on pp. 152, 167, and 206.

Really, dear Comrades, it is humanly impossible to keep silent in the face of such monstrous lies and malignity.

Don't you see that the injury you speak of comes from that source and not from my writing or speaking plainly?

You speak of the possibility of alienating the enthusiasm of the international proletariat. You are mistaken, my dears. The enthusiasm of the workers that flared up like huge flames in the beginning of your Revolution has been dampened by the very people you have been handling with kid gloves, and that you ask me to handle with "tact".

I do not think that I am mistaken when I say that the only way to rekindle the enthusiasm of the workers in every land for your struggle and your aims is to unmask the lying face of Stalin and his followers and to let the world see it in all its hideous nakedness. Whether you agree with it or not, it's being done by many people outside of our own ranks.

It is really impossible to escape the growing indignation in revolutionary ranks against the undermining effect of Soviet rule. One is confronted with it at every meeting. One must face the numerous questions about Communist activities in Spain—about political persecutions—about many other things. One must answer them freely and frankly, or make oneself ridiculous.

The significant side of it is that when the Communists try to interfere the whole audience becomes rebellious. That's what happened at our meeting Friday the 14th. With few exceptions the crowd came to our side.

Dear comrades, I would not injure your struggle for anything in the world. How could I who from the first moment of the 19th July decided to dedicate myself to your great cause?

Dear comrades, can you not trust my judgment of the best way to plead your interest in this country? You see, I know its people, its possibilities and the way to reach it. Continued hiding of stark facts is not the way.

I had not intended to write you at such length. But certain things had to be said which I never had a chance to do.

I hope fervently that you will understand that it is my passionate devotion to your gallant struggle for the Revolution and against Fascism which made me write as I did.

†*More personal in addressing her niece, Goldman refers to the above letter on 1/19/38. She speaks of the tremendous internal pressure she feels in trying to support the Spanish, while fundamentally opposing their endless sacrifice for the anti-fascist cause.*

I think I know the reason for my being unable to sleep. It is the wearing inner conflict between the growing realisation that our comrades in Spain are fast slipping down the precipice and the need of going on with the work for them.

They have become insane with the obsession that they . . . must hang on to the anti-Fascist front even if their so-called allies are doing everything in their power to smash it. . . .

*Already 95% of anarchist principles have been sacrificed, yet the Communist appetite remains unsatisfied. She never has been more agonized than in continually rationalizing to others the actions of the CNT-FAI. She simply will have to resign if they now insist on gagging her concerning the Communists.*

† *Five days later (1/24/38), she reiterates to Helmut Rüdiger her agony in responding to the criticism from Spain. Yet she is determined not to sacrifice her own basic principles despite ensuing problems.*

Ultimately one cannot spit in one's own face. However, it will be very difficult for me to break up my activity here. Not only because of the material loss for the CNT but also because the beginning of the Anarcho-Syndicalist Union here[74] will be ruined, not to mention the scandal which my resigning will cause.

† *Again expressing the agony and isolation of her stance, in this 2/10/38 letter to longtime U.S. friend and comrade Ben Capes, Goldman longs for that passionate dialogue with Alexander Berkman which was so crucial for clarifying her own positions in the past.*

I am thinking all the time what Sasha would have done. Would he have refused to work for the CNT-FAI? I admit that it is inconsistent on my part and I sometimes doubt our dead comrade, such a stickler to every iota of our ideas, would have joined me in my stand, and yet I rather think he would.[75]

† *In her letter to Rüdiger three weeks later (3/3/38), Goldman repeats her intention to proceed with an autonomous public critique,[76] all the more since the CNT seems unable to stop its ever-downward compromise of basic revolutionary principles.*

74. For more details on her involvement in organizing a local Anarcho-Syndicalist Union, see Chapter X below.
75. Another close friend of Berkman, Mollie Steimer, emphatically disagreed in a letter to Milly Rocker on 8/3/39 (AMS-F). In this attitude no doubt she also was supported by her companion Senia Fleshin and her close friend Schapiro. Precise positions to be taken several months later were often difficult to predict on the basis of pre-July 1936 perspectives. See Goldman's 1/19/37 letter to Steimer in this chapter above.
76. In the meantime Vázquez had replied to her agonized letter of 1/20/38 with more moderation of his own. She also felt support from Rudolf Rocker who was adamant in seeking to prevent further Communist entrapments.

. . . Take for instance the negotiations with the UGT which we received.[77] It makes my blood boil to see the concessions and compromises the CNT is prepared to make to satisfy the insatiable appetite of the Communists' gang that are now deciding the fate of the UGT. I consider it a calamity for Spain and our movement in the rest of the world that the CNT is willing to have the industries nationalised which the National Confederation of Labor had controlled for 18 months.

†*In an article appearing in* Spain and the World *one day later, Goldman demonstrates her continued diplomatic public stance toward CNT compromise, however angry her denunciation of the anarchists' allies.*

Shortly after July 1936, the National Confederation of Labor [CNT] began a campaign for unity between the CNT and the UGT. It considered it of the most imperative necessity to bring these two large syndicalist bodies together in order to strengthen the anti-Fascist front, without which the chances of victory over Fascism were rather precarious. The CNT has gone out of its way in its willingness to make all kinds of concessions to bring about this amalgamation. All through this time the disciples in Spain of Stalin have stooped to the most despicable methods to proclaim to the workers of Spain and of the rest of the world that it was the CNT which was undermining the united anti-Fascist front. Day after day there were scurrilous attacks on the CNT in the Communist press trying to make it appear that it was entirely the CNT which refused to cooperate with the UGT and that therefore it was not entirely sincere in its protestation against Fascism.

It was only after the Communist Party, together with other reactionary forces, had well-nigh brought about the collapse of the anti-Fascist forces that it finally realized the necessity which the CNT had propagated for eighteen months. Particularly was this the case after the C.P. had penetrated into the UGT, had bored from within and had filtered through this organization by its own Communistic venom against the CNT. Now it has come forward with a number of propositions as stated in the negotiations published in *Spain and the World*. The readers will be able to judge for themselves how far the present state of the UGT can be called revolutionary, communist or truly democratic. The demands they make are a negation of all the revolutionary achievements of the CNT in the workers' control of industrial and agrarian collectivization.

77. A copy of the CNT negotiation proposal for a united CNT-UGT alliance, a long-sought goal of the more syndicalist-inclined (as distinguished from the more anarchist-oriented) of the CNT, was reprinted in *Spain and the World*, March 4, 1938. (The negotiations and outcome are discussed in detail in Peirats, *La CNT . . .*, ch. 28 and Peirats, *Anarchists in the Spanish Revolution*, ch. 21.) Goldman's own public reaction was her article "Emma Goldman and the Alliance Proposals," in *Spain and the World* of the same issue. The most prominent passages form the next item immediately below.

It is therefore sad that the CNT should be willing to concede many of the demands of the UGT. There is only one explanation for this; it is the fact that the CNT has set its heart and has concentrated all its strength and power to crush Franco and his German and Italian hordes. It is for this reason and no other that the CNT is willing to comply with many of the reactionary demands made by the UGT.[78] There is, however, a gratifying aspect in the concessions and compromises of the CNT, and that is their insistence on workers' control[79] even in those industries nationalized by the Government. The CNT is by no means deceived in the good intentions of democracy as now presented by the Negrín government; but it is face to face with the open intent on the part of the so-called democratic governments outside of Spain to work in favor of Franco and to turn over anti-Fascist Spain to the tender mercies of Hitler and Mussolini.

· · · · · · · · · · · · · · · · · · · · · · · · · · · · · · · · · · · · · · · · · · · · · · · · ·

I therefore feel that, regrettable as [are] the concessions imposed on the CNT by the betrayal of the Spanish people by all governments, including the Spanish Republic, there is no reason to fear that the CNT will be lost in the meshes of concessions and compromises. Our faith in the CNT and the FAI continues to be as ardent as before.

† *Goldman reacts to the culmination of the "unity pact" negotiations discussed above, in a 4/5/38 letter to Rudolf Rocker. She finds the final CNT agreement with the UGT a tragic collapse of the CNT position.[80] As if to prove it, Luis Urteil Araquistáin[81] is gleeful about the CNT change. For Goldman, the pact is a nightmare and poisons her daily existence.*

† *One month later (5/6/38), she states to Rocker her continuing distress at maintaining a tactful public silence on the ever-more destructive compromises of the CNT-FAI. This is especially difficult when others on the Left who have no love for the anarchists correctly point out the futility of their stance.*

The letters I receive from Spain, and I have recently received four or five dated the same date, 21st April, do not give any idea what is going on there,

78. See footnote 78 at back of chapter.
79. See footnote 79 at back of chapter.
80. No doubt she refers especially to the March 18, 1938 pact's recognition of central State primacy (easy justification for *any* degree of intervention) in all aspects of the collectivized economy already developed by worker initiative, as well as the commitment to a *postwar governmental* political system. Beyond the critiques offered in Peirats' accounts, see also ch. 18 of Richards, *Lessons . . . .*
81. Luis Araquistáin was a leading figure in the Spanish Socialist Party, a very close associate of Largo Caballero. His comment is quoted by Peirats on p. 286 of *Anarchists in the Spanish Revolution.*

but from a letter of Helmut Rüdiger, and also M. Mascarell,[82] who recently returned from Barcelona, it looks terribly black to me. Helmut no doubt has written you about the demoralization that had taken place at the front some weeks ago.[83] I was shocked to hear that Vivancos, who was the hero of Belchite and who heroically helped to capture Teruel, should now be under arrest. Neither Helmut nor Mascarell have given the reasons for it. Another of the comrades, Yoldi, who was arrested was released. I dread to think of what is going on in the rear. I do not have to assure you that now less than ever do I sit in judgement of our comrades of the CNT-FAI; but there is no getting away from the fact that they have lost tremendous ground by the compromises[84] and that they either have nothing to say or keep silent at the present critical moment against the crimes that are being perpetrated b y the Negrín-Communist Government. I understand that young people are picked up on the street and forced into military clothes and driven by force to the front. Dear Rudolf, I cannot reconcile myself to this. It seems to me that nothing can justify such a price. Anyway I am torn into a thousand directions. I want to help our comrades and yet I feel that my silence is a sign of consent of all the dreadful and useless compromises our comrades are making.

The *Vanguard*[85] comrades have asked me for an article replying to the renewed scurrilous attack on the Kronstadt sailors, Makhno and the Anarchists in Spain by Leon Trotsky.[86] I have commenced a rough draft of my reply[87] which I hope to get into perfect shape by next Tuesday. While it is true that Leon Trotsky is the last man in the world to condemn the actions of the Spanish Anarchists, I nevertheless feel that what he says is not far from the truth. It is very hard and painful not to be able to demonstrate that our comrades have remained consistent, or at least [that] what they have done has brought beneficial results to the CNT-FAI and to the struggle. To point out that two wrongs do not make one right, that the compromises and concessions do not justify him to condemn the compromises of the CNT is not very

82. See footnote 82 at back of chapter.
83. See footnote 83 at back of chapter.
84. During the same crisis atmosphere promoted by the Nationalists' Aragón offensive, the CNT signed the pact with the UGT, authorized once again a CNT representative in the national government (Segundo Blanco as Minister of Health and Education) and successfully pressed into existence an "Executive Committee of the Libertarian Movement" (uniting the CNT, FAI and Libertarian Youth), thus significantly legitimizing centralist organization of the anarchist movement more than ever.
85. *Vanguard* was an anarcho-syndicalist publication in New York from 1932 to 1939. The full set of issues has been reproduced by Greenwood Reprint Corporation (Westport, Ct., 1970). One of the editors of that periodical was Sam Dolgoff, recent editor of *The Anarchist Collectives: Workers' Self-Management in the Spanish Revolution, 1936-1939*, and present co-editor of *Anarchist News* (formerly *News From Libertarian Spain*).
86. Published in *The New International* (N.Y.), February 1938, April 1938.
87. Published in *Vanguard,* July 1938, as "Trotsky Protests Too Much." A more complete version was issued as a pamphlet by that title in 1938 (Glasgow: The Anarchist-Communist Federation). Parts of this text appear in Ch. IX below.

satisfactory. But what is one to do with the actual facts staring me in the face? Like you I did not expect super-human results for our people from the anti-Fascist struggle. I know that whichever side wins our people will pay the price. If Franco should be defeated, the Negrín-Stalin government will certainly be on top and will use every method to prevent the CNT from reviving the Spanish revolution. If Franco should be the winner, our people will be condemned for all times and will be torn into shreds by the pack of hounds in and outside of Spain. Still, if the CNT had not given up so much of its strategic position at least it could have strengthened the constructive work in the industrial and land collectives; but what is the use of talking about what might have been? The future looks black enough to me to speak of nothing that has happened in the past.

†*Almost seven months later (11/29/38), Goldman tells Rudolf Rocker that she is encouraged, even at this late stage, to see the FAI finally criticizing CNT collaborationism strongly, at least at anarchist gatherings.* [88] *Nevertheless she still disciplines herself in public denunciations of the Communist role in Spain. Though she is miserable from doing so, it is not due to any submission to the CNT national committee. This she would not accept.*

It is because I realise that a real exposure of the treacherous part played by the Communists at this time would in the first place not be believed even by the anarchist critics and would probably work into the hands of Franco and his backers: but you may believe me that it cost me no amount of effort to control myself.

†*As the civil war draws to a close, Goldman writes Rudolf Rocker (3/17/39) of the heavy evidence now gathering* [89] *on the disastrous results of collaboration — in practical, not simply ideological terms. She also clarifies her own belief that May 1937 was a decisive point at which the descending evolution of compromise could and should have been stopped. Stalin's "solidarity" ended by late 1937.* [90] *In fact, after May 1937, there was no need for the CNT-FAI to continue appeasing the Communists when thousands of the comrades were being murdered in the army or arbitrarily arrested and tortured by the Communist secret police.* [91]

*She admits that she and Rocker should have shown the Spanish more forcefully the inevitable disaster their compromises with Stalin would bring about. Unfortunately,*

88. See Chapter II for other Goldman comments on this change of position by the FAI.
89. In this letter she mentions receiving on her last visit to Spain detailed material from those FAI leaders now openly opposing the CNT National Committee. She also received further evidence in letters from Spain after her return to England.
90. Despite the worsening military and international situation for the Spanish anti-fascists, Russian aid already was being reduced by this date.
91. See footnote 91 at back of chapter.

*despite her warnings on many occasions, she "did not have the heart to be too critical" in the face of the tremendous courage, suffering and sacrifice of the comrades.*

*She is shocked that even now Vázquez argues that they didn't compromise enough. But rather than argue with them at this time of great pain, she prefers to wait awhile for them to revive themselves.*

*She has yet to hear details on the current Madrid struggle with the Communists.[92] As she understands it, the comrades forced out the Communists because the latter sought to take dictatorial power and exterminate the anarchists to gain Franco's favor. In fact, the anarchists should have forced out the Communists two years earlier in Catalonia. If the comrades had taken a stand against Negrín even six months ago, Barcelona and the anti-fascist struggle still could have been saved.*

†*Continuing her analysis of the Spanish struggle, Goldman writes Rocker (5/10/39) again that she is certain fundamental compromises should not have been made, despite the risks of an earlier fascist victory.*

I realize as well as you do, my dear Rudolf, that life is more intricate, more contradictory and more compelling than any theory or philosophy about life. I also realize that we have no assurance whatsoever of the success of our people in Spain had they not entered the government or submitted to the dreadful iron hold of Stalin. We can merely speculate what might have been.

*In fact, they could not have had a worse result than they did. Their constant fear was that maintaining their own independent position might have allowed Franco's forces to take over Spain much sooner. This possibility they would not permit, as was shown in their retreat before the Barcelona provocations of May 1937.*

*Yet nothing but disaster could come from the anarchists' complete submission to Stalin's conditions. And Stalin would have sent arms even without anarchist compliance, such as the revolting praise of the Soviet Union that was printed in the CNT's Barcelona paper every day for over a year.*

92. See footnote 92 at back of chapter.

## Further Footnotes for Chapter Four

1. For reasons suggested in part III of Chapter I, many anarchists, including Goldman and Berkman for a time, willingly offered support in various capacities to the new Bolshevik regime in Russia. The majority of these no doubt subsequently turned away in disillusionment, as did Goldman herself. Nevertheless, during the period of this assistance to the state, they were strongly criticized by those who remained aloof. For descriptions of this debate in the Russian case, see Avrich, *The Russian Anarchists* and H.J. Goldberg, "The Anarchists View the Bolshevik Regime" (unpublished Doctoral dissertation, University of Wisconsin, 1973).

On a more reduced scale, the same conflict developed in Germany in the revolutionary upheavals following its defeat in World War I. See the discussion of this issue in Chapters 7 and 8 of Charles B. Maurer, *Call to Revolution: The Mystical Anarchism of Gustav Landauer* (Detroit: Wayne State University Press, 1971) and Ch. 6 of Eugene Lunn, *Prophet of Community: The Romantic Socialism of Gustav Landauer* (Berkeley: University of California Press, 1973). The full implications of such collaboration are explored in the material of this chapter.

5. For an example of this perspective in the North American context, see Rudy Perkins, "Breaking with Libertarian Dogma: Lessons from the Anti-Nuclear Struggle," *Black Rose* (Boston), no. 3 (Fall 1979); also, Leonard Krimerman, "Anarchism Reconsidered: Past Fallacies and Unorthodox Remedies," *Social Anarchism* (Baltimore), I, no. 2 (October 1980).

10. This was made clear in her 1924-25 efforts to organize support for Russian political prisoners among British Labour Party intellectuals such as Harold Laski and Bertrand Russell. For her part, though she thought the Labour Party "perhaps a little bit more advanced than the other politicians" because "it stands, in theory at least, for progressive ideas," she also felt "it will do no more than any other political organization" and in fact "if they will ever be in the position of the Russian rulers they will set up a dictatorship as surely as Russia has" (Goldman 11/6/24 and 4/20/25 letters to Roger Baldwin, NYPL).

15. All four of these individuals had contact with each other and were connected with a variety of publications at the time: *L'Espagne Anti-Fasciste* (Barcelona and Paris) (Voline, Prudhommeaux and Schapiro); *Combat Syndicaliste* (Paris) (Voline and Schapiro); *Guerra di Classe* (Barcelona) (Berneri); *Terre Libre* (Paris and Nimes) (Voline and Prudhommeaux); and *L'Espagne Nouvelle* (Nimes) (Prudhommeaux). The first of these should not be confused with a Paris newspaper of the same name, fully supporting the official line of CNT-FAI leaders from late in 1937.

After participating as a student in the 1905 Russian Revolution in St. Petersburg, Voline (V.M. Eichenbaum) (1882-1945) was sentenced to Siberian exile. Shortly after, he escaped to France, there coming in touch with new political circles and by 1911 becoming an anarchist. To escape a French concentration camp for his anti-war activities, in 1915 he came to New York where he was active in the large anarcho-syndicalist Union of Russian Workers. With many others, he returned to Russia in 1917 at the outbreak of the revolution. In Petrograd and later in the Ukraine, Voline resumed his activity as a leading anarchist propagandist. By 1919, he joined the massive Ukrainian revolutionary movement led by anarchist Nestor Makhno, again in a leading intellectual role. Arrested by the Red Army in 1920, he was ordered shot by Trotsky. He escaped that fate due to anarchist protest. Released, then returned again to prison, he was finally freed only through protests mounted at the 1921 Red Trade Union International congress by foreign anarcho-syndicalist delegations (coordinated by Goldman and Berkman). For the next fifteen years, first in Berlin, then in Paris, he worked diligently to publicize the plight of Russian political prisoners, to make known the experience of the Makhnovista movement and to further the cause of anarchist propaganda generally. He died at the close of World War II after living a marginal underground existence during the Nazi occupation of France.

A brief sketch of Schapiro appears already in Chapter I, footnote 32 above.

In protest against the Socialist Party's indecision about World War I, Camillo Berneri (1897-1937) joined the anarchist movement in 1917 while still a student but already a conscript in the Italian army. Struggling then against the rising tide of Italian fascism, this young philosophy teacher and anarchist propagandist was forced into exile in the early 1920's. Despite constant moves and imprisonment in many different European countries, he still produced numerous thoughtful and provocative anarchist and anti-fascist essays and was regarded as one of the most brilliant minds in the movement. In the early weeks of the Spanish civil war, Berneri helped to organize and himself participated in a military column of Italian volunteers, predominantly anarchist in composition. Shortly thereafter, he began publishing his newspaper from Barcelona. Publicly criticizing increasing collaborationist turns by CNT-FAI leaders and denouncing Communist manipulations and sabotage, he was assassinated by Communist gunmen in early May 1937. Extensive remarks by Goldman on Berneri appear in Chapter X. His daughter, Marie Louise Berneri, shortly thereafter moved to London and actively involved herself in the work of *Spain and the World* at the same time as Goldman.

André Prudhommeaux (1902-1968) was heavily involved in the cooperative and anarchist

movements of France from his early years. Though trained as an agronomist with a university degree, he refused to accept any official position which would compromise his ability to think, write and be active clearly and consistently with his ideals. From his printing cooperative in Nimes, he and others (with the collaboration of Voline) produced an anarchist journal *Terre Libre*, the periodical of the French Anarchist Federation from 1937 to 1939. From mid-1936 to early 1937, he spent five months in Barcelona before beginning *L'Espagne Nouvelle* – an effort undertaken at least partly in response to the CNT-FAI withdrawal of support from the critical Paris-based *L'Espagne Anti-Fasciste*. (He had published the first number of the latter from Barcelona.) He continued to be active in the French anarchist movement after World War II.

18. Indeed one of the decisions of the December 1937 congress of the IWMA, the anarcho-syndicalist International, was to suspend all criticism of CNT-FAI policies in publicly-circulated publications of the movement. This decision was adopted despite the very sharp criticisms of the CNT position made by various delegates to that meeting (*L'Espagne Nouvelle*, no. 62 [February 15, 1939]). As a result, such previously-critical journals as *Combat Syndicaliste* and *L'Espagne Nouvelle* drastically modified their tone. In effect, out of the same principle of solidarity felt and articulated by Goldman, critics such as Voline, Schapiro and Prudhommeaux now for the next year silenced their tongues in public, as Goldman had chosen to do earlier.

20. It is quite possible, perhaps even likely, that in the existing particular context of international alignment, social consciousness within Spain and the relative paucity of material resources available, *no* alternative political formula would have succeeded in defeating the fascists while simultaneously accomplishing social revolution. Nevertheless, certain alternatives perhaps had a greater chance of doing so and in any case represented greater moral consistency – thus greater strength in the short and long range both. Books by Peirats (*Anarchists in the Spanish Revolution*) and Vernon Richards (*Lessons of the Spanish Revolution* [London: Freedom Press, 2nd ed., 1972]) mention and explore briefly several of these possibilities without necessarily endorsing any single one of them, despite their clear anti-collaborationist critique. Among such potentials was development of massive guerrilla war efforts behind fascist lines (where roughly half of the organizational strength of the anarchist movement was caught within a few weeks after the outbreak of war). An alternative was to create and defend solidly revolutionary organs of social coordination in Catalonia and Aragón alone, with no statist pretenses or links. Likewise, anarchists throughout republican Spain might have withdrawn completely from all government positions while participating in tactical coordination against fascist attacks or in genuine popular community councils, subject to the same federalist principles as the anarchist movement itself. Above all, they could have emphasized positive creative social and economic transformation at the grass-roots level (an option indeed chosen in practice by thousands of Spanish anarchists). Given the slim possibility of anti-fascist victory and sustained revolutionary society while pursuing any of these more morally consistent alternatives, Peirats indeed speculates whether any genuine revolution as presently conceived is possible in the contemporary era (p. 188). Goldman herself develops a similar line of questioning in Chapters IX and X. However, neither questions the personal and social significance of carrying on the struggle toward that goal.

21. In search of potential allies against the rise of aggressive Nazi power in Germany, Stalin presented a public change of policy at the Communist International's Seventh Congress in 1935. Subsequently the Soviet Union and Communist parties in the West "became the most ardent and even vociferous supporters of national defense in the democratic countries. So earnestly did the Comintern enforce this new 'line' that from this point onward it perceived residual anti-militarism and pacifism in the ranks of the left as a dangerous heresy and it welcomed, as its virtual allies, the men of the traditionalist anti-German right," such as Winston Churchill (Isaac Deutscher, *Stalin: A Political Biography* [N.Y.: Vintage Books, 1960], pp. 419-20). China's late 1970's and early 1980's encouragement of Western military strength and the echo of this line by followers of China in the West is an obvious parallel.

22. This questionnaire was sent out just days after the February 1936 elections and just a month after a CNT regional meeting in Catalonia discussed these same critical issues of voting and collaboration. (See Peirats, *La CNT . . .*, I, 106-11 for details about this meeting and debate.) Actually, it was sent to Goldman's close comrade Alexander Berkman, no doubt one of a few respected foreign comrades to receive a copy.

28. See details about Malatesta in Chapter I, footnote 10. Francisco Saviero Merlino was a leading anarchist thinker and activist in Italy in the last decades of the 19th century. He worked in close association with Malatesta until the massive state repression of 1894. Imprisoned then until 1896, Merlino after his release began advocating the tactical use of parliamentary elections to combat the increasingly reactionary state machinery. Though remaining friends with Merlino personally, Malatesta was among the first to attack this new revisionism. This debate is discussed in more detail in Nunzio Pernicone, "The Italian Anarchist Movement: The Years of Crisis, Decline and Transformation (1879-1894)" (unpublished Doctoral dissertation, University of Rochester, 1971), pp. 376-77, and is reproduced in Merlino and Malatesta, *Anarchismo e democrazia* (Rome: Centro Editore, 1949).

31. By mid-1936, the Socialists and their UGT labor organization were indeed a significant force in Spain as a whole. The recent elections made the Socialists the largest bloc in the parliament (the Cortes). The UGT apparently had about 1.5 million members. In Catalonia, the heartland of anarchist strength, however, which Goldman may have been referring to here, neither the Socialists (the PSUC) nor the UGT played a significant role at that date. The Communists in turn were insignificant regionally and in the country as a whole. (Apparently the party membership numbered no more than several thousand in early 1936 and no more than 30,000 in July.) Relying on small- and middle-bourgeois followings whose right-wing parties effectively had dissolved in the republican zone after the outbreak of civil war, the Communists moved to a membership of some 200,000 in Spain generally, with the PSUC (rapidly coming under their control) having some 50,000 by early 1937. (Figures based on estimates in Bolloten, *La révolution espagnole*; Broué and Témime, *The Revolution and the Civil War in Spain*; Brenan, *The Spanish Labyrinth*; and Thomas, *The Spanish Civil War*.) Their overall strength is estimated at one million by June 1937, a figure no doubt heavily influenced by the prestige of Soviet aid and the "protection" and patronage offered by the Party in the bureaucracy, military and private sector.

34. Arthur Müller-Lehning was a German anarcho-syndicalist militant with whom Goldman had contact in earlier years. A scholarly writer, he produced already in 1929 a lengthy analysis of the Russian revolution. This was translated and re-issued in France as *Anarchisme et marxisme dans la révolution russe* (Paris: Spartacus, 1971). In recent years, Lehning has compiled and edited several massive volumes from the archives of Michael Bakunin, under the auspices of the International Institute of Social History at Amsterdam.

41. Bill Shatov was a Russian-born anarcho-syndicalist militant in the U.S. who worked with the IWW, helped organize the large Union of Russian Workers (U.S.) and was for a time manager of the Ferrer Center in New York. He returned eagerly to Russia with Voline and others in July 1917. Within a month he was elected to the Petrograd Conference of Factory Committees. From this base he became a delegate on the Military Revolutionary Committee during the October Revolution and soon was entrusted by the Bolsheviks themselves with critical military and organizational responsibilities. Goldman refers to his role and her meetings with him in Russia in more detail in *LL*, II, 728-35, and in *My Disillusionment in Russia*, pp. 5-6.

43. She refers here to statements by various CNT-FAI leaders, at the May 1936 CNT congress and in the first weeks after July 19, 1936, that the anarchist movement was not strong enough to sustain the revolutionary momentum against *both* fascist and anti-revolutionary statist "allies" throughout Spain. Perhaps such an effort could have been made at least in regions of greatest anarchist strength (and not under Franco's control: Catalonia, Aragón and much of the Levante) by declaring and defending their own autonomy. The standard retort to such a proposal was that even if the various antagonistic Spanish republican forces themselves would be unable to combat such strong anarchist societies, foreign hostility (France and Britain especially) would greatly surpass that shown already to the republic itself and would lead to direct military intervention.

44. As Schapiro pointed out in his reply to this letter on March 20, 1937 (AMS-G), he indeed had warned strongly against CNT collaborationist tendencies (when they compromised basic anarchist principles) as early as several years before – in the first weeks of the Second Republic. His critiques were presented directly to the CNT as well as to the IWMA, the anarcho-syndicalist International, whose representative he served as at early CNT congresses in Spain. He told Goldman that he had sent critiques to her by mail, such as the IWMA report he and Eusebio Carbó wrote in 1933 ("Rapport sur l'activité de la Confédération National du Travail

d'Espagne, 16 décembre 1932-26 février 1933," a copy of which exists in the IWMA collection in Amsterdam), but Goldman noted in the margin of his letter that these items were never received. Similar critiques in the early 1930's appeared in the French syndicalist periodical *Révolution Prolétarienne.* Several of these appear in L. Nicolas, *A travers les révolutions espagnoles* (Paris: Editions Pierre Belfond, 1972).

45. Her accreditation letter stated that she was the official CNT-FAI representative to the Catalan government office in London – loosely equivalent, though at a *much* reduced scale, to being one of the anarchist participants in the regional government in Barcelona. In addition to letters from the CNT and FAI, Goldman herself originally suggested credentials from the joint Antifascist Militia Committee of Catalonia (8/21/36 letter to Augustin Souchy, AMS-G), as a means for her to gain propaganda access to non-anarchist organizations in England. In a letter four months later (12/8/36 letter to Stella Ballantine, NYPL), she sees her credentials as implying participation in the planning and production of joint *anti-fascist* propaganda, while at the same time not preventing separate publicity activity for the CNT-FAI. There is no indication she ever meant it to imply participating in or influencing governmental decision-making, as anarchists were doing in Barcelona and Madrid. In fact, she regarded that interpretation and role with disgust, one that would only leave her "hands tied." Apparently she went by the Catalan government office in London only briefly on two occasions by mid-1937. Not only was she repulsed by Communist domination ("a beehive of Communists"), she also resolved to stay clear of it since it seemed in serious debt, since she was too preoccupied with CNT-FAI propaganda, and because she had never been sent promised instructions as to the precise nature of her mandate (2/24/37, 3/11/37, 5/3/37 letters to the National Committee of the CNT; 3/9/37 letter to Augustin Souchy; 3/6/37 letter to Martin Gudell; all in AMS-G).

47. The Partido Obrero de Unificación Marxista (the Workers' Party of Marxist Unity) was formed in 1935 from two earlier dissident Communist groups in Spain, the Workers and Peasants Bloc and the Communist Left of Andrés Nin and others. Internationally it was linked with the London Bureau of Revolutionary Socialist Parties of which the ILP's Fenner Brockway was general secretary. To outsiders, it seemed associated with the general critique and approach of Leon Trotsky and his international allies, with whom indeed its leaders were connected in the past. However Trotsky himself was critical of the POUM (and the London Bureau) from its start (Trotsky, *The Spanish Revolution (1931-39)* [N.Y.: Pathfinder Press, 1973], pp. 206-21). With its main strength (about 3000 members in mid-1936) in Catalonia, the POUM joined the Catalan militia committee and the government alongside anarchists, republicans, Socialists and the Soviet-aligned Communist Party (the latter through the PSUC). A much more detailed critical description of the POUM can be found in American Trotskyist Felix Morrow's *Revolution and Counter-Revolution in Spain* (1938; rev. ed., N.Y.: Pathfinder Press, 1974). Another work by Victor Alba is also useful, *Historia del P.O.U.M.* (Barcelona: Editorial Pórtic, 1974).

49. The Second International loosely associated various social democratic parties from 1889 on, as one of several heirs to the First International. The latter brought together the whole spectrum of socialism from cooperative leagues and labor unions to Marxists, aspiring Leftist parliamentarians and anarchists until its split in the 1870's because of these basic conflicts of orientation. Inspired by the Russian revolution, the Bolsheviks and their followers abroad in turn broke away to form a Third International (the Comintern) in March 1919. The Second International still exists today, loosely uniting through financial support, conferences and other communication a number of parties around the world and such figures as Helmut Schmidt and Willy Brandt (Germany), François Mitterand (France), Mario Soares (Portugal), Abba Ebban (Israel), Felipe González (Spain) and Michael Harrington (USA). George McGovern and Ted Kennedy from the U.S. chose to attend the Spring 1981 International meeting as observers.

50. From 1925 to 1946, Sir Walter Citrine was secretary-general of the Trades Union Council (TUC), the overall federation of British labor unions. Ernest Bevin was a longtime British Labour Party leader who became Labor Minister in Churchill's wartime coalition government and Foreign Minister in the Labour government (1945-51) of Clement Attlee. At the time of Goldman's remarks, he was secretary of the powerful Transport and General Worker's Union.

63. The CNT proposed establishing a broad international propaganda and organizational alliance of the various anti-fascist political forces (including the Second and Third Internationals), similar to the united front in Spain itself. By late 1937, the unquenchable power thirst of the Communists had frightened and alienated some of their past political allies in Socialist and

Left Republican ranks, most notably Negrín's Minister of Defense Indalecio Prieto. In response to this threat to their position and desiring to further augment the splits in the anarcho-syndicalist movement, Communists in Spain once again showed friendly signs toward and negotiated with certain anarchist leaders, especially the National Committee of the CNT (Bolloten, pp. 508-11). Goldman speculates in this letter that perhaps this factor explains in part the new CNT proposal.

69. McGovern visited Spain in November 1937. Passages from his pamphlet, *Terror in Spain* (London: ILP, 1937?), were translated into French and published in *Révolution Prolétarienne*, no. 263 (January 25, 1938). These passages are also reproduced in L. Nicholas, pp. 178-88.

A. Fenner Brockway was a pacifist imprisoned for his activity during World War I. After the war he helped found and became chairman of the War Resisters International, a worldwide pacifist organization still active today. Within the ILP in this same period, he was a leading enthusiast of G.D.H. Cole's "Guild Socialism" and the ILP's organizing secretary. In 1929 he was elected to parliament and in 1931 became chairman of the ILP. Within several more years he became general secretary of the party and editor of its periodical, *The New Leader*. In 1946 he left the ILP and rejoined the Labour Party. His autobiography, *Inside the Left*, was written in 1938-39 (London: George Allen & Unwin, Ltd., 1942) and includes relatively complementary images of both Goldman and the Spanish anarchists in general.

78. Anarchists favoring this pact for so many months argued originally at least that a genuine workers' alliance could substitute for a governmental regime by political parties — thus supposedly being less of a compromise with traditional anarchist principles. Certain elements of the CNT had proposed this alliance in the early 1920's (such as Salvador Seguí) and early 1930's (such as Angel Pestaña).

79. It is important to distinguish between the different meanings of "workers' control," since confusing connotations still inhibit meaningful discussion today. Those who believe in the traditional state socialist position argue that a "workers' government" (under Labour Party or Communist, etc., domination) by itself automatically means effective "workers' control" when key economic sectors are nationalized. By now, many years of experience with East, West and Third World "socialist" regimes have shown the fallacy of this argument, though indeed it was well recognized by Anarchists, Socialist Revolutionaries, and Left Communists in the Russian Revolution itself. A recent emphatic articulation of this understanding appeared in demands by "Solidarity" workers in the nationalized industries of Communist Poland from August 1980 on. A second meaning of "workers' control," a compromise position accepted here by the CNT, assumes that workers somehow can control the significant decisions concerning their own productive units, even though all units are under the formal control of the state. The limitations of this approach are well-illustrated in probably the furthest experiment in this direction — Yugoslavia since 1948. The restraints there on genuine workers' control come from three contradictory sources: tendencies toward capitalist-style "free market" competition (as opposed to coordination); continued restraints by the hierarchical state, Party and Party-controlled trade union; and hierarchy in the structures of workers' control themselves. The third and more traditional anarchist understanding of "workers' control" implies a total absence of hierarchical state, Party and union structures, with decision-making (and coordination between units) by local workers' assemblies, community assemblies, and when necessary federated bodies of coordination. Clarity on these distinctions is crucial for understanding much of the antagonism between different orientations on the Left and indeed much of the manipulative mystification of terms consciously used by many "Leftist" leaders (beginning with Marx, Lenin and Trotsky) for their own bids to power.

82. Manuel Mascarell was a member of the National Committee of the CNT, as well as one of its representatives in Paris during 1937. Following a compromise accord at the December 1937 IWMA meeting in Paris, he replaced Pierre Besnard as secretary-general of that organization in February 1938. He remained in that post until the IWMA meeting later that year chose to remove the headquarters to Stockholm. In his Paris CNT position, he was one of Goldman's regular correspondents since most often the Paris office was in far better direct contact with Spain than Goldman was.

83. The massive motorized Aragón offensive by the Nationalists, beginning in March 1938, caught the republican army in the midst of reorganization and made unprecedented sweeping advances toward the Mediterranean. By April 15, these forces reached the sea, dividing republican Spain

henceforth into two separate zones – the center (including Madrid and Valencia) and Catalonia. Goldman's 5/20/38 response to one letter about the disaster appears in Chapter VII below.

91. Along with arms, military advisors and political commissars, the Soviet Union also exported to Spain another essential part of the Communist state apparatus, the secret police (the NKVD, earlier known as the Cheka). The latter, with Spanish accomplices, set up their own private network of "safe" prisons, totally separate from the already substantial and increasingly Communist-controlled jails of the Spanish government. There, political opponents disappeared without trace. The most notable example, because it involved a high-ranking critic of the Communists, was Andrés Nin, one of the two co-founding leaders of the POUM. For more on his case in particular, see Broué and Témime, pp. 302-04, and Semprun-Maura, *Révolution et contre-révolution* . . . , pp. 275-76.

92. She refers here to the last-minute coup d'état on March 5-12, 1939, against the Madrid remnants of the Negrín regime, with Franco's army preparing itself for a final assault on the city and defeat of the republic. The military coup and establishment of a new Defense Council was led by Colonel Casado, the commander of the army of the Center, with very substantial, active support from anarchist military units and civilians, among others. (Also in on the plan approvingly was a close Socialist friend of Largo Caballero, Wenceslao Carrillo, father of the recent leader of the Spanish Communist Party.) This followed a March 2nd *de facto* coup by Negrín, who had reshuffled his government, placing the most critical military, police and evacuation commands openly in the hands of the Communists. Apparently a similar coup against the Communists and the Negrín government then in Barcelona was being prepared in November and December 1938 in the face of their refusal to plan a serious defense of Catalonia (3/16/39 letter to Goldman from a comrade who was at the front for two years, RAD).

# Chapter Five

# Communist Sabotage of the Spanish Revolution

*Goldman's discussion of collaboration relates closely to her critique of Stalinism in Spain. While concerned with how anarchists damaged their own cause, here Goldman describes how the revolution and anti-fascist struggle were subverted by their "allies"—especially the Communists. As in earlier writings on the Soviet Union, her tone here is anguished, of course, yet also fatalistic, given her sense that such destruction derives from the very nature of Marxism-Leninism itself.*

*The manipulatory, destructive side of Soviet Communist politics (internally and abroad) by now is commonplace knowledge, even among Communists themselves. In fact, much evidence was admitted at the highest level of power in the Soviet Union itself.[1] Yet behind such critiques is a wide spectrum of perspectives. Leaving aside explicitly anti-revolutionary conservatives and liberals, this range begins with those (such as Khrushchev) who attribute errors solely or primarily to Stalin himself. Beyond this position are those (such as the various brands of Trotskyists) who criticize Stalin and his successors but not the original Leninist movement and regime. Still others (including Maoists, Titoists, and various independent communist movements) view "capitalist restoration" as inherent in the Soviet Union's bureaucratic approach to development. Though often detailed and interesting, such critiques fall short of understanding that revolutions are inevitably corrupted when organized or channelled by a hierarchically-structured, self-proclaimed vanguard movement.*

*The downfall of an oppressive regime is obviously a liberatory development of great significance. So also is creation of new social opportunities through assuring adequate food, medical care, education, and other basic requirements for decent existence. Yet, as Chapter Three suggests, hierarchical social organization is not the only, let alone the most humane and efficient way to bring these about.[2] In what*

---

1. By Khrushchev at the 20th Party Congress in February 1956.
2. A blatant example is the reliance of both the West and the Soviet Union on nuclear power, in each case chosen by hierarchical governing structures.

*overall sense is a society truly progressive when any challenge to the wisdom of the governing elite may be interpreted as "a threat to the revolution itself," thus justifying new restrictions or outright repression?[3] Despite their progressive rhetoric[4] and no doubt the best intentions of large numbers of their followers, for Marxist-Leninist leaders to see themselves as carriers of the scientific world-view and the very embodiment of the revolution inevitably forces them to model originally popular liberation movements to their own design, thus to narrow the channels of potential development once the old regime is overthrown. "To save the revolution" becomes the "Newspeak" rationale for even the severest anti-revolutionary measures. The November revolution and its imitations lead to forced-labor camps and the bland "consumer society" alike.*

*In this sense, Goldman's description of Stalinist treachery in Spain portrays a logic inherent in vanguard movements and regimes themselves—now and in the future, as well as in the 1930's. Today, many in good faith seek inspiration and guidance from the accomplishments and proclaimed goals of China, Cuba, Vietnam, Yugoslavia or a variety of independent "revolutionary communist" or "revolutionary nationalist" movements in power and out. In doing so, in accepting revolutionary elites in their own society and abroad, such admirers expose their own honest and legitimate radical aspirations to potentially the same corruption, contradictory behavior, cynicism and disillusionment experienced in Spain.[5] The contemporary proliferation of rival Marxist-Leninist regimes and movements provides a healthy source of mutual criticism, sometimes in the most vigorous terms. While this is a welcome improvement over the stifling monolithic Comintern atmosphere of the 1930's, it should not mask the fundamental contradictory logic behind them all. Self-defined vanguards, by their very nature, must attempt to sabotage any potential revolutionary transformation of soceity occurring beyond their own leadership and control. It is this lesson, timely as ever in the present, that Emma Goldman portrays so clearly from the context of the Spanish revolution.*

*In Spain today, the Communist Party attempts to prove its own social respectability by cooperating with the monarchy in designing a new framework for labor relations, by presenting a new gradualist ideological program of "Eurocommunism," and by rejecting even the Leninist label itself. The transparency of such efforts, plus the documented Stalinist role of certain of the party's present leaders in the 1930's,[6] surely should raise questions among progressives in Spain and abroad. However, to the left of the Communist Party have appeared other potentially more credible pretenders to revolutionary leadership. These include various radical regional separatist groups and Marxist-Leninist offsprings from the New Left wave*

---

3.  On the part of a Communist regime, the greatest openness to criticism yet permitted was during the Chinese Cultural Revolution of the late 1960's. Even in this case, however, the "wisdom of Mao" (the highest level of the Party) was untouchable, a sacred realm thus providing leverage for later purges of the sort seen after his death in the "Gang of Four" campaigns.

4.  It should be remembered that the *ultimate* Marxist goal is indeed synonymous with the general vision of anarcho-communism.

5.  Recent examples in Chinese foreign policy are its backing of the Shah in Iran, South Africa's allies in Angola and the fascist regime of Chile; similarly, the open warfare between China, Vietnam and Kampuchea, three hierarchical "socialist" states, in early 1979.

6.  See footnote 6 at back of chapter.

*of the 1960's. Yet the same criteria articulated by Emma Goldman forty-five years ago should be applied here to judge the genuineness of their commitment to true liberation. From this perspective, once more in Spain only the anarchists or nonparty anti-authoritarians pose a serious challenge to hierarchical exploitative society.*

# II

*Emma Goldman's autobiography and her book,* My Disillusionment In Russia, *well portray how her views toward the Bolshevik party and the Soviet regime evolved during her two years in that country, 1920-21. Later published essays and letters from the 1920's and 1930's[7] address this same theme as well.*

*In brief, Goldman consistently and enthusiastically admired the spontaneous upsurge in Russia during the Spring, Summer and Fall of 1917. From the distance of another continent and in the isolation of federal prison until late 1919, Goldman was unable to acquaint herself with the detailed maneuvering and confrontations there among the several political groupings on the Left.[8] To her, the tremendous spirited mass support for the uprising and the Bolshevik promises to pursue many of the immediate revolutionary social, economic and political goals long advocated by anarchists precluded any open attacks on the regime, especially with the latter under the armed siege of reactionary forces. Once Goldman and Berkman were forcibly deported to Russia from the United States, they continued for months to interpret the obviously contradictory behavior of the Bolsheviks in the most benevolent light one was able to from an anarchist perspective. Eventually, they simply saw too much. Painfully reconstructing a new interpretive framework, they concluded that what had happened was indeed no matter of mere circumstance (personality, pressure from outside or internal reactionary forces, etc.) but was inherent in the very Bolshevik conception of vanguardism and revolution.*

*Bolshevik cooptation of an immensely vigorous popular social explosion was tragic enough within Russia. In Goldman's view even more disastrous were its international implications.[9] For many years to come, the image of "revolution" would be equated with the particular events, policies and regime of Russia – all interpreted for the outside world to the specific advantage of Soviet leaders themselves. Added to this understandable magnetic allure of revolution from a distance was the power base of the Soviet state itself. Diplomatic maneuverings, trade missions, a significant budget for international cadre training and propaganda and a centralized international organization based in Moscow, all were significant resources. Through these and the inspiring image of Russian revolution, the Soviet regime could and did attract millions of followers throughout the world to a movement whose foremost concern was not revolution wherever possible but the protection of*

---

7.  See Part II – "Communism and the Intellectuals," in Drinnon and Drinnon, eds., *Nowhere at Home,* as well as Goldman's essay, "There Is No Communism in Russia," *American Mercury,* vol. 34, April 1935 (reproduced in Shulman, ed., *Red Emma Speaks*).
8.  See footnote 8 at back of chapter.
9.  Goldman 11/6/24 letter to Roger Baldwin, NYPL.

*the Soviet state.*

*As Goldman states below, the same ultimate motivation which led Bolshevik leaders from the beginning to repress existing or potential internal dissent became equally, then, their ultimate guideline internationally as well.*

# III

*In the first few weeks of armed struggle against the insurgent Right, the Communists in Spain were an insignificant factor. Yet by September, as Emma Goldman prepared to enter that revolutionary scene for the first time, she already was concerned enough with their manipulatory intrigues that she considered preparing a "political will" to be released upon her possible death.*[10]

*As the statements below indicate, very quickly from the time of her arrival, she discovered Soviet influence to be spreading rapidly in the anti-fascist camp. Understandably, to her there was little distinction between the different instruments of Communism—Soviet diplomats, agents of the NKVD secret police, Soviet military advisors, and the Spanish Communist Party. Essentially, in their aims and allegiances, there was none. In addition, leading Spanish socialists and republicans themselves were so enticed by Soviet flattery, material assistance, supposed proficiency in centralized organizational skills, and the moderate, explicitly anti-revolutionary goals of the Communists that they also became for many months Communist apologists and bold co-conspirators in betraying anarchists and the revolution in general.*[11] *In this role, they also are denounced by Goldman. Nevertheless, she directs her greatest wrath at the Communists, since they had the most international influence and became increasingly the dominant force in the reactionary policies of the republican government.*

*Having seen it all before in Russia itself, Goldman was scarcely surprised at the Communists' deadly maneuvers against social revolution. But this did not lessen her frustration when her Spanish comrades appeared naively to minimize the seriousness of this threat. In addition, as one forever hopeful in the midst of revolution, Goldman inevitably was pained from its wounds. It was an agony she would hardly have chosen were it not for the brilliant courage and spirit of the Spanish anarchists, a movement of large-scale determination and constructive energy unprecedented in her entire life.*

*For contemporary readers unaware of the struggles against elites within the process of revolution, or unfamiliar with the nature of this clash within Spain itself, Goldman's impassioned account is a healthy introduction, factually and emotionally both.*

10. Goldman 8/26/36 letter to Milly and Rudolf Rocker, AMS-R; Goldman 9/11/36 letter to Stella Ballantine, NYPL. By one year later, Communists had engaged in so much political repression, including the murder of internationally known Italian anarchist Camillo Berneri in May 1937, she did prepare a "political will" for potential publication in case she was murdered or tortured into making a false "confession" (Goldman 9/12/37 letter to Roger Baldwin, NYPL; Goldman 9/12/37 letter to Ethel Mannin, NYPL). The statement itself (Goldman's 9/10/37 letter to Mollie Steimer, NYPL) appears in Chapters IX and X.

11. See footnote 11 at back of chapter.

136   Vision On Fire

*†Within only a few days of her arrival in Spain (9/29/36), Goldman writes to comrade Alexander Schapiro of her fears about the anarchists' "allies."*

Our comrades have a more colossal task than the workers in Russia. Spain is so near European reaction and the Socialist breed in Europe too powerful. Also there is Russia in league with the reactionary forces only too ready to make common cause with Fascism if need be rather than to permit the CNT-FAI to survive. So many enemies and so many odds. It will be miraculous if the Spanish Revolution will triumph in spite of all that. But whether it does or not it is the first example of how revolution should be made. And I glory in this beginning.

*†Two days later (10/1/36), she repeats her same concerns to Rudolf Rocker.*

It is already apparent that once our comrades will succeed in crushing Fascism they will have a more bitter enemy, a life-long enemy to overcome. For the Socialists and no less the Communists are already throwing stones between the feet of the CNT-FAI, they are already lying in ambush to destroy all our people are doing. Perhaps that explains some of the negative sides of the struggle the CNT-FAI is making. I feel very puzzled and grieved at moments when I see certain decisions and resolutions that seem contrary to the marvelous spirit of the comrades and their Libertarian determination. Oh, I wish you were here to help me see as I want to see this tremendous upheaval and how it can be safeguarded against pitfalls.

*†Three months later (1/4/37), now out of Spain and beyond the reach of mail censors, Goldman writes her longtime friend Michael Cohn about the true motives and dangers of Soviet aid to the Spanish republic.*

You probably think it nothing at all that Stalin waited four months before he sent anything. And that since he began sending arms it was never anything for Catalonia. True it went to Madrid. But remember Catalonia has a number of important fronts. But the CNT-FAI being the strongest there, Stalin would rather see it taken by Franco than our comrades.

*While acclaimed internationally for "coming to the rescue" of republican Spain, in fact Stalin had his own hidden designs. The vast majority of men sent by Stalin to Spain are being armed to establish a Communist dictatorship, not to fight at the front lines. Once successful, they would put all anarchists up against the wall.[12]*

12. By this date, various Soviet sources—including the newspaper *Pravda*—had indicated explicitly their desire to treat "Trotskyites" and uncooperative anarchists in Spain just as they had

*While such plans will be difficult to accomplish, each new repressive action should be cause for great concern. Already in Madrid, where they are more powerful, they have closed down the CNT newspaper. The immediate excuse for this step was an important Communist official shot for refusing to show his papers to CNT sentries in Madrid.*[13] *While such a drastic anarchist response was foolish and unnecessary, one must understand the emotional climate in which it occurred. Knowing the plans of the Communists, Spanish anarchists have shown amazing patience. Yet even with the strongest will to maintain the united front, this patience might well come to an end.*

*Concerning Stalin's overall support for Spain, if the European powers decide to insist on banning outside "volunteers," surely Russia will go along, just as it joined in Blum's non-intervention policy for the first three months.*[14]

†*In a letter one day later to two New York anarchist newspapers (*Freie Arbeiter Stimme *and* Spanish Revolution*), Goldman clarifies the relationship of Spanish anarchists with the Marxist-Leninist Spanish POUM.*

Imagine, I actually found willingness on the part of members of the Independent Labour Party [in England] to cooperate with me in behalf of the CNT-FAI. Thus, Fenner Brockway, the General Secretary, has consented to speak at our mass meeting Jan. 18th. And he and other members have shown eagerness for a joint exhibition of the material I brought from Spain. This is indeed an event. Ten years ago when I tried desperately to make the plight of the political prisoners in Russia known, not a single person in British Labour ranks would help.[15] Not even Fenner Brockway who is among the most revolutionary in the I.L.P. This time he and others are willing to be of help. But then, the CNT-FAI are not to be sneezed at. They are a great force, in fact the most dominant force in Catalonia. One cannot afford to ignore them especially when one's comrades, the POUM in Catalonia, have had a change of heart towards the Anarchists.[16] It is ironic that Anarchists should be the defenders of Marxists against their own family. For after all the Trotskyists and the honest-to-god Stalinites are the offsprings of the same holy trinity: Marx, Engels and Lenin. But family feuds are always the most bitter and relentless. How very relentless Stalin himself has proven when he dispatched

been in the Soviet Union—executed or imprisoned. In fact they never gained enough control in Spain to carry out this goal, at least with the anarchists who were too numerous to discard in the face of Franco. Nevertheless, POUMistas and anarchists were persecuted severely, as much of the Goldman commentary in this chapter makes clear. The arbitrary arrests, imprisonments and tortures already had begun by September 1936.

13. The incident she refers to here most likely is the one described in Peirats, *La CNT* . . ., II, 64.
14. See footnote 14 at back of chapter.
15. Details about that effort, including the refusals of Harold Laski and Bertrand Russell, are found in *LL*, II, ch. 55.
16. See footnote 16 at back of chapter.

his erstwhile comrades to their death.[17] His satraps in Spain would do the same with the POUM members if they only had the power. As to the CNT-FAI, they would long before this have been put against the wall. There is a German saying to the effect that the Lord takes care the trees should not grow into sky. Fortunately the comrades of Stalin have not the power, and if the CNT-FAI can help it they never will. They and the POUM are therefore safe for the present. Not that the CNT-FAI is in love with the POUM. But that our comrades believe in freedom for their allies as they do for themselves. Anyhow, the I.L.P. seems to realize that. Hence the readiness of some of its members to cooperate with anything done for the CNT-FAI. Whether this or any other motivation, the I.L.P. is the most revolutionary in England and perhaps also the most interested in the revolutionary outcome in Spain. I am therefore quite content to have whatever support some party members will give me. It's not an official support, thank goodness. For the rest, we will see.

. . . . . . . . . . . . . . . . . . . . . . . . . . . . . . . . . . . . . . . . . . . . . . . . . .

Dear comrades, bear in mind Catalonia is carrying the whole brunt. Thousands of dollars and pounds have been raised for anti-Fascist Spain. But not a cent went to Catalonia.[18] Yet Catalonia is feeding Madrid, and it is feeding thirty thousand women and children from other parts of Spain. Last but not least, Catalonia is the spearhead of the Revolution, the one part of Spain that is doing constructive work amidst the horrors of war, cold and hunger. And in all this the CNT-FAI plays the leading and dominant part. Strength to the CNT-FAI.

† *The same day Goldman explains to longtime friend and comrade Ben Capes that it was the very sabotage of the Madrid front by the Caballero regime which forced the anarchists to join the government.*

[The CNT-FAI] consented to enter four Ministries which have been forced upon them. Forced by the criminal sabotage of Caballero and his comrades. . . . Caballero sabotaged the defense of Madrid until it was almost too late. His hatred for the C.N.T.-F.A.I. is perhaps deeper than the hatred of Franco, therefore he did everything possible to undermine the

17. She refers here to results of the August 1936 and January 1937 Moscow purge trials of former top Bolshevik leaders such as Zinoviev, Kamenev, Smirnov, Radek and Sokolnikov. A crucial charge against all of these was that they were serving Stalin's arch-enemy Leon Trotsky in attempting to assassinate Stalin and others of the Politburo. Their alleged plan was then to restore capitalism and to turn over the country to fascist Germany and Japan. Further trials of top-level officials occurred in June 1937 and March 1938.
18. As with the case of Soviet arms shipments, Communist-sponsored relief funds raised abroad were directed to Valencia and Madrid, where the Communists dominated the government and military, while avoiding Catalonia with its heavy anarchist presence and revolutionary accomplishment.

influences of the C.N.T.-F.A.I.[19] All this will come out in due time.

*† To Milly Rocker, Goldman writes (2/9/37) of her concern over the central government's dangerous neglect of Catalan defense.*

Now, I realize that concentration on the defense of Madrid is imperative, but, on the other hand, Catalonia is in equal measure in danger—especially from the sea. It is therefore nothing short of a crime to leave Catalonia bare of everything it needs to protect itself against the possible attack of the Franco-German-Italian forces. Actually, the latter have already bombarded Port Bou;[20] they have proved therefore what their plans are as far as Barcelona is concerned. Fortunately our people in Barcelona are realizing that they cannot go on indefinitely pouring men, arms and provisions into Madrid—not only because they must prepare themselves to meet the dreadful enemy, but also because of the Communistic force.

Thanks to the generosity of our people, they have become stronger and are now dominating Madrid. Thus they have stopped the CNT-FAI paper (not for long, to be sure), and they have now suppressed the paper of the POUM, which merely goes to show what they are likely to put forward should they be unable to do so by the CNT-FAI.

*† In a letter to the* New Statesman *one month later (3/2/37), Goldman defends the Spanish POUM against Communist labels of "fascism."*

I am not a Marxian and not in accord with the POUM. But in justice to this party whose men are fighting heroically at every front, I cannot but point out that it is scandalous on the part of the Communists to charge them with Fascism. That is just the trouble with the Communists. In their Jesuitical belief that "the end justifies the means," they will stoop to every method, no matter how reprehensible, in their dealings with their opponents. However, that is an old and painful story which those who flirt with Communism have yet to learn.

*† In a 4/1/37 letter to Chicago anarchist Boris Yelensky, Goldman states that Soviet aid was delivered to Spain only on condition that criticism of the Communists be curtailed.*

---

19. See footnote 19 at back of chapter.
20. Port Bou is about 75 miles northeast of Barcelona, along the Mediterranean coast and very near the French border.

It is of course stupid to call the POUM "Trotskyists." Trotsky himself has repudiated them. They are in point of fact in the opposition to the Stalin regime. But that is all.

However, that is quite enough to be hounded into the grave by the modern Torquemada,[21] Stalin, and his satraps all over the world. . . .

. . . . . . . . . . . . . . . . . . . . . . . . . . . . . . . . . . . . . . . . . . . . . . . . . . . .

As regards the unfortunate stand taken by our Spanish comrades in relation to Russia, I quite agree with you that it is a terrible thing—not only because it is in a measure a betrayal of our comrades in Russian prisons, but also because it is reacting very badly on the Spanish comrades themselves. From whatever angle one considers it, and of course their step was due to the imminent danger of Fascism, the fact that Franco was and still is at the throats of the Spanish people does not minimize the unfortunate step taken by our comrades. I can only tell you that I have protested against it. I didn't know the full details when I was in Spain. I have since learned that the damnable gang in Russia offered assistance in the way of arms and food supplies to the Spanish anti-Fascist forces, only on condition of a complete stoppage of anti-[Soviet] propaganda.[22] If the CNT-FAI had been the only organization engaged in the struggle, I don't believe our comrades would ever have made that concession, but you must not forget that they are but one fraction of the parties allied in the anti-Fascist struggle. Had our comrades refused and Russia would have abstained from sending arms, it is reasonably certain that Franco would already now be in possession of Spain—which would have meant the extermination not only of the CNT-FAI, but of half of the Spanish people. I imagine that the CNT-FAI felt that it could not take such a responsibility on its shoulders.

It goes without saying that they would have been held responsible for the triumph of Franco but I do not believe that even that was the deciding factor with the CNT-FAI. It was more the feeling that if they will refuse they will jeopardize the lives of millions of people and the marvelous constructive effort they have made. Mind you, I am not excusing the concessions; I am only explaining the possible motivations which induced our comrades to go back on our imprisoned comrades in Russia and on their own traditions.

†*Just after the armed confrontation between anarchists and their "allies" in Barcelona (5/9/37), Goldman shares with Max Nettlau her analysis of Soviet aims*

21. Tomás de Torquemada (1420-98) was the priest for King Ferdinand and Queen Isabella of Spain. In 1492 he led the move to expel the Jews and the next year founded the Spanish Inquisition—the terroristic effort to weed out "heretics" from among the faithful through the use of mock trials and torture.
22. Within a few months, even the "anti-*fascist*" mobilization drives of Communist parties internationally began to be moderated. Stalin desperately sought to appear respectable enough to France and Britain to gain their support against Hitler, or, eventually, even to open the door to an accord with Hitler himself, as indeed happened in 1939.

*in Spain and their use of the "democratic" label to help accomplish them.*

Granted that to save the anti-Fascist situation arms from Russia were needed, but why was it necessary to make it more than a business deal, for which Spain paid heavily in gold and the CNT paid in loss of much of its position and its strength? Surely no one with any clear vision could be blinded to the motive of Russia's sudden "interest," after three and a half months of the anti-Fascist struggle in Spain. Now the real motive is beginning to be recognized by the very people who sang hosannah to comrade Stalin; it was for no other reason than to get possession of Madrid and, if possible, to increase the armed Communist forces in the rest of Spain, in anticipation of the "happy" moment when the Anarchists can be exterminated as they have been in Russia. By right I should have given this to the public. I should have written about all this. My silence was, in a measure, consent of the betrayal of the comrades in Russia. I readily admit that. I did not do it because I did not have the heart to expose Federica and the others in our press outside of Spain. Yet you come along and throw brimstone and fire on my head[23] because I dared, if you please, to explain some of the blunders of the leading members of the CNT-FAI in my statement. I consider it very unkind, to say the least of it.

. . . . . . . . . . . . . . . . . . . . . . . . . . . . . . . . . . . . . . . . . . . . . . . . . . . . . . .

. . . What is of the utmost importance is that our comrades in Spain have had their eyes opened; that they now see the danger lurking in every corner from the Marxists, and that they are coming out openly in their papers and bulletins calling the necessary alarm. The Jesuits of the Stalin brand are hard at work preparing all kinds of pitfalls for the comrades; they are hard at work in every country. In England they spread the rumor that Catalonia is sabotaging Madrid. They even succeeded in influencing the *Manchester Guardian*, as you will see by my letter of protest published in the *M. G.* of April 24th. In fact, their sudden discovery of Democracy as a beautiful bride is nothing else but the deliberate intention of the Soviet Government to destroy the Revolution in Spain, and they are losing no time to achieve this. I would not be surprised if Caballero and the Communists were to make a separate peace with Franco, provided the latter would assure them of safety of their own miserable hides. All that should never have been given a chance to raise its head. It was done, unfortunately, through the compromise of the comrades of the CNT-FAI.

† *The May events in Barcelona aroused Goldman to present her first scathing*

23. In Nettlau's 3/8/37 letter to Goldman (AMS-G). There he criticizes her reference to errors by CNT-FAI leaders, in her letter of 1/25/37 reproduced in *Spain and the World*, February 5, 1937. The letter repeats themes found in other statements of hers at the time, such as seen in Chapter IV above.

*published critique of the Communist role in Spain, in the 6/4/37 issue of* Spain and the World.

The events in Spain this month eloquently . . . demonstrate that the Soviet political grinding machine does not only do its deadly work in Russia, but in all other countries as well.

The events in Barcelona [of] the last two weeks have demonstrated how foolish were some of our comrades of the CNT-FAI to believe that Stalin had begun to send arms to Spain out of revolutionary solidarity, or that there ever can be a unity between fire and water. Apart from the fact that Stalin waited 3½ months, the most critical period of the Spanish revolution and the anti-Fascist war, before he began sending arms, [which] should have proven to our comrades and to all thinking people that the man was waiting for the decision of his allies — France — and that he cared little for the sacrifices daily made in Spain in the anti-Fascist struggle. It also should have proven to them that Stalin sent arms in return for good gold and that he imposed conditions on the CNT-FAI which have unfortunately fettered both organizations to a very large extent. One of the conditions was that no anti-Soviet criticism or propaganda should be continued in the anarchist press. The other that Soviet emissaries should have full control of the procedure of the defense of Madrid. Of course they never would have succeeded had it not been for the fact that Durruti was foully murdered. I did not believe the rumors while I was in Barcelona that he was put out of the way by a Communist. But from the events of the last two weeks I am beginning to think that there was more truth than fiction in this rumor.[24] Durruti was too astute a strategist and absolutely consistent with his ideas and he would never have submitted to any political deal with the Communists. The Communists were not slow in taking advantage of these conditions. They not only increased in numbers, sometimes 2000 a week who arrived in Spain, but a great deal of the arms sent for the defense of Madrid went to the headquarters of the Communists for the arming of their comrades. The next step dictated by Stalin was to change the slogan of the defense of the revolution to the defense of democracy, the kind of democracy which the old reactionary police officials and the reactionary middle class wanted to bring back in order to destroy the constructive work of the CNT-FAI and to crush the revolution. There is no doubt that this "great dream" of Stalin was shared by the other powers who are all in favor of some kind of a deal with Franco in order to establish "peace." Otherwise it is difficult to explain how it happened that British and French warships should be rushed to Spanish waters almost at the identical moment when this well-prepared plot in Spain was brought to a head, namely the attack on the telephone building — the

24. Abel Paz, the biographer of Durruti, discusses this and other hypotheses in detail (part IV in the French edition of his book, *Durruti: Le Peuple en armes* [Paris: Editions de la Tête de Feuilles, 1972]).

most strategic point of Barcelona—by armed force. Incidentally, at the same moment the same attack took place in Tarragona and Lérida, 250 kilometers from Barcelona. Naturally our comrades defended their position. They could not be expected to do anything else. They realized that they had already given way far beyond what they should have done. In other words the anarchists were not the originators of the attack. To have done otherwise than defend the position would emasculate the revolution.

The originators of the plot did more than an open attack. They raided the rooms of a very distinguished Italian anarchist who shared them with a comrade; they confiscated all their documents and material, they put them under arrest and supposedly were to take them to police headquarters. The next day both were found dead, shot in the back, exactly as the many victims of Mussolini and Hitler were found. One of these comrades, Camillo Berneri, was one of the most distinguished anarchists in Italian ranks. Before Mussolini, he was Professor of Philosophy in the Florence University. He had been victimized by Mussolini while he was still in the country and then pursued . . . to France where the life of Berneri was made impossible. From the very first moment of the Spanish revolution, July 19th, Berneri rushed to Spain and put himself and his abilities at the disposition of the CNT-FAI. He organized the first Italian column. He fought at many fronts and he was the spirit of all the Italians in the rear. I had occasion to meet and know Berneri and I found him one of the kindest and sweetest personalities, besides being one of the most brilliant. The Communists, together with the Fascist forces, have murdered Berneri because, like Durruti, he was in their way. He was too outspoken, too consistent and his vision was clear. He saw what was coming and he warned the leading comrades against it.

It is certain, however, that Stalin and his new bed-fellows have made their calculations without taking into account that the Spanish workers, with their background of an incessant struggle for a century for Libertarian Communism and a federalist basis of a new economic and cultural society, cannot be subdued to dictatorship and Fascism as has been done in other countries. Times without end the Spanish feudal lord, the Church, the Monarchy have tried to crush the glowing spirit of freedom of the Spanish masses. Their success was ever short-lived. For the Spanish workers love liberty more than their lives and no power on earth will ever eradicate that love.

True, reaction is again on top in Spain, our comrades foully murdered in the dead of night, the CNT-FAI betrayed once more, as in the past. But no one who has been in Spain, who has come close to the Spanish masses in country and towns will believe for a single moment that the old masters in new disguise will be able to impose their will on the workers for long.

†*In a June 1937 letter to American lawyer Arthur Ross, Goldman expresses*

*continued anguish at the success of Soviet propaganda and the tremendous shock she felt from the events of May.*

It is terrifying to find how a myth will perpetuate itself. Even the so-called intellectuals are not exempt from its mesmerizing effect. Never before has the Bolshevik myth demonstrated its far-reaching devastating ramifications as it has in Barcelona the first week in May. Twenty years ago Lenin and his comrades held up democracy, as represented by Kerensky,[25] to scorn and condemnation as the vilest political institution in the world. Nor would they rest until they had exterminated everyone who dared to speak in behalf of democracy. Today, the followers of Lenin with Stalin at the helm are celebrating the love feast of democracy and are trying to exterminate all those who have come to see that bourgeois democracy is a perpetuation of the capitalistic class. Though sworn to a United Front with the anarchists and other political bodies for the purpose of exterminating Fascism, the Communists in Barcelona have joined a deliberate conspiracy to destroy the anarchists and crush their constructive revolutionary efforts. They are guided in this by the iron hand of Stalin whose imperial designs had chosen democracy as their beloved bedfellow. Yet the so-called radical world goes on in the [perpetuation] of the myth, shouting from the housetops the revolutionary character of Stalin and his regime, misrepresenting and lying about everyone who will no longer be blinded by them.

I need not tell you what a shock the recent events in Barcelona have been to me. Actually it left me in the same depleted condition as did the untimely death of A.B. [Berkman]. Then, too, I felt the ground pulled from under me, life robbed of its meaning.

† *Goldman pursues the same theme again, seeing a* de facto *accord between fascism and "revolutionary" dictatorship, in a new published article of 7/2/37.*

The advent of dictatorship and Fascism has resulted in appalling indifference to the most harrowing crimes. Time was when political abuses in any country were met with immediate response from all liberals and revolutionaries. Especially was this the case with the victims of Czarism: more than one heroic fighter in Russia was saved from death or banishment by the concerted action and protest undertaken everywhere outside of Russia. All this wonderful spirit of solidarity and fellowship has gone by the board since dictatorship and Fascism have infested all ranks. No matter how heinous the crime committed in their names, hardly a voice is being raised in indignation against

25. Alexander Kerensky was a right-wing Socialist Revolutionary Party leader at the time of the revolution. He was a minister in several provisional governments following the February 1917 revolution, then headed his own from July 21 to the Bolshevik-led coup several months later.

them. Indeed they are accepted as a matter of course and quite in keeping with dictatorship as a redeemer of the human race.

The astounding accord between Fascism and dictatorship has again been demonstrated in two flagrant recent crimes. I mean the murder of Professor Camillo Berneri and his comrade Barbieri, anarchists, by Communist police in Barcelona, and the equally foul murder of Prof. Carlo Rosselli[26] and his brother by Fascist thugs. They all use the identical methods in destroying their political dissenters. They not only take their lives, they also defame their characters. Thus Stalin perpetuates the infamous story that Russia has become a cesspool of self-confessed "spies, traitors, Trotskyists" and crooks of every sort. Mussolini on the other hand proclaims the conversion of anti-Fascists to his creed.[27] He paints them as miserable weaklings and renegades who have come to see the error of their ways.

† *One month later (8/10/37), Goldman informs Milly Rocker of the continuing deadly repression of Spanish anarchists.*

The murderous Communists and the blackest reaction are in power now and our people have lost all of their position. . . . It is heartbreaking to learn every day of the arrests of hundreds of comrades, of the foreign comrades who came to help being kicked out of Spain, and of our people being killed in broad daylight. I agree it is taking one's life in one's hands to go to Spain now.

† *Fully aware of the personal dangers she may face in her new visit to Spain as an outspoken critic of the Communists, Goldman assures her friend Roger Baldwin (9/12/37) of her advance preparations.*

Yes, dear Roger, I am going to Spain. I will fly from Marseilles this Wednesday. . . . I am well aware of the danger and the risk awaiting me. Yet I must go. . . .
. . . . . . . . . . . . . . . . . . . . . . . . . . . . . . . . . . . . . . . . . . . . . . . . .
Well, dear Roger, I am going into the cage of mad dogs. Whatever they will do to me I want you and my other friends to know that I hope to die as I live. True one never knows what one will do under duress. I can only hope

26. Rosselli was a liberal anti-fascist Italian intellectual and journalist in French exile since his escape from Italian prison in 1929. He was very active, along with Berneri, in helping to organize Italian exiles into a fighting unit against the fascists in Spain in the Fall of 1936. He viewed such fighters as the core of a future armed struggle against Mussolini. Rosselli was assassinated in June 1937 by French fascists sympathetic to Mussolini's regime.
27. To confuse those who assumed his own role in crdering Rosselli's death, Mussolini claimed that Rosselli had recently converted to supporting fascism and therefore was murdered by his own ex-associates.

that I will be strong enough neither to "confess" nor to "recant" nor to grovel in the dust for my life. I have prepared a statement which has gone to Stella and others of my comrades to give to the public if anything should happen to me.[28] I have done that because I do not want the same miserable lies hurled against me by the Spanish Communists as those sent out broadcast against the unfortunate victims of the Moscow regime. They will try, I know, to besmirch my revolutionary integrity. But they will not succeed with my last statement to call their bluff.

Don't imagine I take my going to Spain tragically. I only like to be prepared and my friends to be prepared. That is all.

†*Just returned from the repressive atmosphere in republican Spain (11/18/37), Goldman informs Ethel Mannin of her heartfelt intent to expose the Communist role.*

Dearest, I wish you were here and I could talk to you about the tragedy of Spain, the treachery of the Communists and the Negrín outfit. Both are too overwhelming to write in a letter, especially now when I have to get ready for our group meeting where I am to make a report about the situation. Perhaps next week I will get time to write you at length. For the present I only want you to know that the prisons are filled with political CNT-FAI [and] POUM men and women without any charge against them except the most despicable inventions, that Barcelona is slowly starved into submission and that the Revolution lies gagged and fettered though the revolutionary spirit is still alive. I do not know what will become of it all. I only know I must cry out against the murderous gang directed from Moscow that is not only trying to squeeze the life out of the Revolution and the CNT-FAI. It has and is deliberately sabotaging the anti-Fascist front. I do not know of any other such instance of betrayal. Judas betrayed only Christ, the Communists have betrayed a whole people. They have done no less than the European powers that have been sitting back while the Spanish masses were being delivered to Franco's knife. And what about the international proletariat? Have they not played false to all their protestations of workers' solidarity? All, all have acted the Judas Iscariot to Spain. But none so brazenly, deliberately than Stalin's henchmen. Oh my dearest, my heart is full to overflowing. I must, I must cry out against the whole pack. I know I will have the greatest difficulty to be heard. But I will try to the uttermost.

†*A day later, writing to the Rockers, Goldman deplores the imprisonment of anarchist militants and calls for some form of effective response. Though the CNT*

28. This is her so-called "political will." See footnote 10 above.

*National Committee writes protest letters to the Negrín regime, it does no good. Prisons remain filled with so-called "Trotskyists,"[29] while many victims are simply picked off the street and vanish. Goldman also denounces the withholding of arms from anarchist trenches on the military front:*

The Aragón front had been criminally sabotaged from the moment arms from Russia arrived. But what few people know is that our divisions in the trenches of Madrid are forced to beg for every piece of ammunition.[30] I know whereof I speak, I was in the trenches in Madrid, our sectors consisting of 56,000 CNT-FAI members, and I saw the correspondence between the man in charge of our divisions and that mountebank Miaja.[31] . . .

*At the same time, she admires the accomplishments of the International Brigades, though deplores their worldwide publicity to the neglect of the anarchists. Indeed, though anarchists have shown tremendous battlefront courage, they intentionally were denied entrance into the republic's air force, exclusively controlled by the Communists. The only way some CNT members were admitted was by denying their own beliefs.*

†*This detailed article on political repression in republican Spain, published in* Spain and the World *just several weeks after her return to England (12/10/37), finally gives Goldman a public release for her enormous anguish on this issue.*

On my first visit to Spain in September 1936, nothing surprised me so much as the amount of political freedom I found everywhere. True it did not extend to Fascists; but outside of these deliberate enemies of the Revolution and the emancipation of the workers in Spain, everyone of the anti-Fascist front enjoyed political freedom which hardly existed in any of the so-called European democracies. The one party that made the utmost use of this was the PSUC, the Stalinist party in revolutionary Spain. Their radio and loud speakers filled the air. Their daily marches in military formation with their flags waving were flaunted in everybody's face. They seemed to take a special pleasure in marching past the House of the Regional Committee as if they wanted to make the CNT-FAI aware of their determination to strike the blow when they will attain . . . complete power. This was obvious to anyone among the foreign delegates and comrades who had come to help in the anti-

29. See footnote 17 above.
30. Further details concerning Communist intentional murderous sabotage of anarchist soldiers and units are found in ch. 23 of Peirats, *Anarchists in the Spanish Revolution*, and chs. 34-35, vol. III of his *La CNT* . . . .
31. General José Miaja, a career army officer of moderate Republican orientation, was named by Caballero to head the defense of Madrid in November 1936. Relying heavily on Communist arms and staff, Miaja himself joined the party for personal protection within several weeks and acted at its behest in commanding the military operations for this front.

Fascist struggle. Not so our Spanish comrades. They made light of the Communist brazenness. They insisted that this circus claptrap could not decide the revolutionary struggle, and that they themselves had more important things to do than waste their time in idle display. It seemed to me then that the Spanish comrades had little understanding of mass psychology which needs flag-wagging, speeches, music and demonstrations – that while the CNT-FAI, however, were concentrated on their constructive tasks, and fighting on the various fronts, their Communist allies made hay while the sun shone. They have since proved that they knew what they were about.

During my stay of three months I visited many of the collectivized estates and factories, maternities and hospitals in Barcelona, and last but not least, also the "Modelo" prison. This is the place that had harbored some of the most distinguished revolutionaries and anarchists in Catalonia. Our own heroic comrades Durruti and Ascaso, García Oliver and many others had been cell neighbors of Companys,[32] the new President of the Generalitat. I visited this institution in the presence of a comrade,[33] a physician who had made a special study of criminal psychology. The director gave me free access to every part of the prison and the right to speak to any of the Fascists without the presence of guards. Among the few hundred admirers of Franco were officers and priests. They assured me in one voice of the decent and just treatment they were receiving from the management in charge of the place, most of whom were CNT-FAI men.

The possibility that Fascists would soon be replaced by revolutionists and anarchists was far removed from my mind. If anything, the high water mark of the revolution in the Autumn of 1936 held out hopes that the stain of prison would be wiped out once Franco and his hordes were defeated.

The report of the foul murder of the most gentle of anarchists, Camillo Berneri and his roommate, the anarchist Barbieri, was followed by wholesale arrests, mutilation and death. They seemed too fantastic, the change in the internal political situation too incredible to be true. I decided to go back to Spain to see for myself how far the new-found freedom of the Spanish masses had been annihilated by Stalin's henchmen.

Once again I arrived on the 16th September this year. I went straight to Valencia and there discovered that 1500 CNT members, comrades of the FAI and the Libertarian Youth, hundreds of the POUM and even members of the International Brigade were filling the prisons of Valencia. During my short stay there, I left no stone unturned to get permission to visit some of our comrades, among them Gustel Dorster whom I had known in Germany as most active in the Anarcho-Syndicalist movement before Hitler ascended to

32. Luis Companys was imprisoned from 1934 to 1936 for his attempt to lead a Catalan secessionist rebellion from the right-wing government in Madrid.
33. The visit by Goldman and H.E. Kaminski is described in the latter's book, *Ceux de Barcelone.*

power. I was assured that I would be given permission; but at the last moment, before my return to Barcelona, I was informed that foreigners were not allowed to see the prison. I soon discovered the same situation repeated in every town and village I visited. Thousands of comrades and other genuine revolutionaries were filling the prisons under the Negrín-Prieto and Stalinist regime.

When I came back to Barcelona in the early part of October, I immediately sought to see our comrades in the Modelo prison. After many difficulties, comrade Augustin Souchy succeeded in obtaining permission to have an interview with a few of the German comrades. Much to my surprise I found on my arrival there that the same director was still in charge. He too recognized me and he again gave me full entry to the prison. I did not need to speak to the comrades through the hideous bars. I was in the hall where they foregather, surrounded by German, Italian, Bulgarian, Russian and Spanish comrades, all trying to speak at once and tell me of their conditions. I discovered that no charge whatever that would stand in any court, even under capitalism, had been preferred against them, except the idiotic charge of "Trotskyism."

These men from every part of the globe had flocked to Spain, often begging their way across, to help the Spanish Revolution, to join the ranks of the anti-Fascists and to lay down their lives in the struggle against Franco [and now] were held captive. Others again had been picked up on the street and had vanished without leaving any trace behind. Among the many was Rein, son of the internationally-known Russian Menshevik Abramowitch.[34]

The most recent victim is Kurt Landau, a former member of the Executive Committee of the Austrian Communist Party, and before his arrest, on the Executive Committee of the POUM.[35] Every effort to find him has met with failure. In view of the disappearance of Andrés Nin[36] of the POUM and scores of others it is reasonable to conclude that Kurt Landau met with the same fate.

But to return to the Modelo prison. It is impossible to give all the names because there are so many incarcerated there. The most outstanding is a comrade who, in a high responsible position before the May events, had turned over millions of pesetas to the Generalitat found in churches and palaces. He is held under the ludicrous charge of having embezzled 100,000 pesetas.

Comrade Helmut Klaus, a member of the CNT-FAI. He was arrested on the 2nd July. No charge has been made up to this date, neither was he brought

34. She refers here to Marc Rein, a correspondent at the time for a Swedish Social Democrat journal, arrested in early April 1937. Rafail A. Abramovich, a leading Menshevik emigré figure after the Bolshevik consolidation of power in Russia, still actively writing and with contacts among the anti-Bolshevik underground in that country, was one of the principal targets in the Stalinist purge trials of the 1930's.
35. See footnote 35 at back of chapter.
36. See footnote 36 at back of chapter.

before a judge. Comrade Klaus was a member of the FAUD in Germany (German Anarcho-Syndicalist Organization). After having been arrested several times, he emigrated to Yugoslavia in the summer of 1933. Expelled from there in February 1937 because of anti-Fascist activity, he came to Spain in March. He joined the frontier service of the FAI, in the "De la Costa" Battalion. After the dissolution of this battalion, in June he took his discharge, and entered the service of the Agricultural Collective of San Andres. In compliance with the request of his group he later undertook the reorganization of the Tailors' Collective of the Emigrants' Committee. The charge made by the Cheka of his having disarmed officers while in the frontier service at Figueras is entirely without foundation.

Comrade Albert Kille. He was arrested on September 7th. No reason was given. In Germany he had belonged since 1919 to the Productive Supply Union. Besides this he was a member of the Communist Party. In 1933 he emigrated to Austria. After the February events he fled to Prague but later returned to Austria, where he was expelled and left for France. Here he joined the German Anarcho-Syndicalist Group. In August 1936, he went to Spain where he at once proceeded to the front. He was wounded once. He belonged to the Durruti column right up to the time of the militarization. In June he took his discharge.

I also visited the POUM Section. Many of these prisoners are Spaniards, but among them there are also a large number of foreigners, Italian, French, Russian and German. Two members of the POUM approached me personally. They said little of their own suffering, but begged me to take a message to their own wives in Paris. They were Nicolas Sundelwitch—the son of the famous Menshevik who had spent the longest part of his life in Siberia. Nicolas Sundelwitch certainly didn't give me the impression of being guilty of the serious charges . . . of "having given the Fascists information" among the many other charges against him. It takes the perverted Communist mind to hold a man in prison because in 1922 he had illegally left Russia.

Richard Tietz was arrested as he came out of the Argentine Consulate in Barcelona where he had gone on behalf of his wife, previously arrested. When he demanded to know the grounds of his arrest the Commissar nonchalantly said "I consider it just." That was evidently enough to keep Richard Tietz in the Modelo since July.

As far as prison conditions can be humane, the Modelo is certainly superior to the Cheka prisons introduced in Spain by the Stalinists according to the best party examples of Soviet Russia. The Modelo still maintains its traditional political privileges such as the right of the inmates to freely mingle together, organize their committees to represent them with the director, receiving parcels, tobacco, etc., in addition to the scanty prison fare. They can also write and receive letters and reading material. Besides, the prisoners issue little prison papers and bulletins which they can paste in the corridors where

they all foregather. Both in the section of our comrades and the POUM, I found such prison papers, posters and photographs of the heroes of the two parties. The POUM had even a very fine drawing of Andrés Nin and a picture of Rosa Luxemburg,[37] while the anarchists' side had Ascaso and Durruti on their wall.

Most interesting was the Durruti cell which he had occupied in Barcelona until released by the 1936 elections. It was left intact as it had been while Durruti was its involuntary lodger. Several large posters of our gallant comrade made the cell very much alive. The strangest part, however, is that the Durruti cell is in the Fascist section. In answer to my question as to how Durruti's cell comes to be in there, [I] was told by the guard "as an example of the living spirit of Durruti that will destroy Fascism." I wanted very much to have the Durruti cell photographed; but permission had to be obtained from the Minister of Justice. I gave up the idea. I had never in my life asked favors of Ministers of Justice, much less would I ask for anything from the counterrevolutionary government, the Spanish Cheka.

My next visit was to the women's prison, which I found better kept and more cheerful than the Modelo. Only six women politicals were there at the time. Among them Katia Landau, the wife of Kurt Landau, who had been arrested several months before him. She was like the old time Russian revolutionists, utterly devoted to her ideas. I already knew of her husband's disappearance and possible end; but I did not have the heart to disclose this fact to her. This was in October. In November I was informed by some of her comrades in Paris that Mrs. Landau had begun a hunger strike on the 11th November. I have just received word that as a result of two hunger strikes Katia Landau has been released.[38]

A few days before my departure from Spain I was informed on good authority that the old dreadful Bastille, Montjuich, was again being used to house political prisoners. The infamous Montjuich, whose every stone could tell of man's inhumanity to man, of the thousands put to death by the most savage methods of torture, or driven mad or to suicide. Montjuich, where in 1897 the Spanish Inquisition had been reintroduced by Cánovas del Castillo, then Premier of Spain. It was at his behest that 300 workers, among them distinguished Spanish anarchists, had been kept for months in underground damp and dirty cells—repeatedly tortured and denied counsel. It was in

---

37. Luxemburg was a revolutionary socialist leader, then co-founder of the Communist Party in Germany. She was murdered in 1919 for her role in the Spartakist uprising in Berlin against the moderate bourgeois Socialist regime established at the end of World War I. Similar in temperament and perspectives to Trotsky, she indeed was denounced posthumously as a "Trotskyite" by Stalin in 1932.

38. Her description of her own arrest and imprisonment is found in her publication cited in footnote 35 above. Actually, the release Goldman speaks of here lasted only one week. Re-arrested, she was imprisoned again and subsequently expelled from Spain.

Montjuich that Francisco Ferrer[39] was murdered by the Spanish Government and the Catholic Church. Last year I visited this terrifying fortress. Then it held no prisoners. The cells were empty. We descended into black depths with torches guiding our way. I almost seemed to hear the agonized cries of the thousands of victims who had breathed their last in the ghastly holes. It was a relief to get to the light again.

History does repeat itself after all. Montjuich again serves its old ghastly purpose. It is overcrowded with ardent revolutionaries who had been among the first to rush to the various fronts. Militias of the Durruti column freely giving their health and strength but unwilling to be turned into military automatons; members of the International Brigade who had come to Spain from every land to fight Fascism, only to discover the harsh differentiation [between] them, their officers and the political commissars, and the criminal waste of human lives due to the military ignorance and for party purpose and glory. All these and more are incarcerated in the fortress of Montjuich.

Since the world slaughter and the continued horror under dictatorship, red and black, human sensibilities have been atrophied; but there must be a few left who still have a sense of justice. True, Anatole France, George Brandes and so many great souls whose protests saved twenty-two victims of the Soviet state in 1922 are no longer with us. Still there are the Gides, the Silones, Aldous Huxley, Havelock Ellis, John Cowper Powys, Rebecca West, Ethel Mannin and others,[40] who would surely protest if made aware of the political persecutions rampant under the Negrín, Prieto and Communist regime.

At any rate I cannot be silent in the face of such barbarous political persecutions. In justice to the thousands of our comrades in prison I have left behind, I will and must speak out.

† *Goldman's mid-December 1937 address to the IWMA Paris congress includes this stinging attack on and assessment of the Communist position in Spain.*

Russia has more than proven the nature of this beast [dictatorship]. After twenty years it still thrives on the blood of its makers. Nor is its crushing weight felt in Russia alone. Since Stalin began his invasion of Spain, the march of his henchmen has been leaving death and ruin behind them. Destruction of numerous collectives, the introduction of the Cheka with its "gentle" methods of treating political opponents, the arrest of thousands of revolutionaries, and the murder in broad daylight of others. All this and more

39. See Chapter I, section II above.
40. Of this list of prominent European writers, Goldman had very positive direct contact with all, to my knowledge, but Gide and Silone.

has Stalin's dictatorship given Spain when he sold arms to the Spanish people in return for good gold. Innocent of the jesuitical trick of "our beloved comrade" Stalin, the CNT-FAI could not imagine in their wildest dreams the unscrupulous designs hidden behind the seeming solidarity in the offer of arms from Russia.

. . . . . . . . . . . . . . . . . . . . . . . . . . . . . . . . . . . . . . . . . . . . . . . . . . . .

. . . My own consolation is that with all their concentrated criminal efforts, Soviet Communism has not taken root in Spain. I know whereof I speak. On my recent visit to Spain I had ample opportunity to convince myself that the Communists had failed utterly to win the sympathies of the masses: quite the contrary. They have never been so hated by the workers and peasants as now.

It is true that the Communists are in the government and have political power — that they use their power to the detriment of the revolution, the anti-Fascist struggle, and the prestige of the CNT-FAI. But strange as it may seem, it is nevertheless no exaggeration when I say that in a moral sense the CNT has gained immeasurably. I give a few proofs.

Since the May events the Madrid circulation of the *CNT* [paper] has almost doubled, while the two Communist papers in that city have only 26,000. The *CNT* alone has 100,000 throughout Castile. The same has happened with our paper, *Castilla Libre*. In addition, there is the *Frente Libertario*, with a circulation of 100,000 copies.

A more significant fact is that when the Communists call a meeting it is poorly attended. When the CNT-FAI hold meetings the halls are packed to overflowing. I had one occasion to convince myself of this truth. I went to Alicante with Comrade Federica Montseny and although the meeting was held in the forenoon and rain came down in a downpour, the hall was nevertheless packed to capacity. It is the more surprising that the Communists can lord it over everybody; but it is one of the many contradictions of the situation in Spain.


† *To Harry Weinberger, her attorney at the time of her U.S. anti-conscription trial, Goldman insists (1/4/38) that the Communists would sell out to the fascists rather than see anarchism triumph in Spain.*

. . . If the Negrín-Prieto Government [and Communists] had not sabotaged the Aragón front Franco would have been driven from it long ago. It may seem preposterous but [it] is yet true [that] Negrín, Prieto and the Communists would rather consent to any armistice than see the CNT-FAI victorious. It is the filthiest treachery the world has ever seen. So you see why I continue crying even if it is in the wilderness.


† *On the same date, Goldman reminds her friend and associate Ethel*

*Mannin (a member of the ILP) of the crucial distinction between the approaches of anarchists and Marxists (including the ILP and the Spanish POUM).*

Don't you see, dearest, Marxists simply cannot get away from the idea of "political" as government power. They will not admit the difference between political and social forces. That's the gulf between the Marxists and Anarchists which will probably never be bridged. That is already very plainly expressed in the Manifesto of the POUM reprinted in the Bulletin of the ILP.

You know how I feel about the persecution of the POUM, and how I have tried to help them; but that does not blind me to the fact that the POUM is hanging to the skirts of the CNT (not the FAI however), because the CNT is a formidable social force which the POUM never was. The part of the POUM in the May events was really to use the CNT in order to seize power, government power. Had they succeeded and had they created the dictatorship they would, I am sure, have done the same with the CNT-FAI as Trotsky did with the Russian Anarchists and with the Kronstadt sailors, they would have exterminated the Anarchists in Spain. In relation to us the POUM does not differ from the rest of the Communists, whatever their opposition to Stalin. . . .

. . . . . . . . . . . . . . . . . . . . . . . . . . . . . . . . . . . . . . . . . . . . . . . . . . . .

. . . The trouble is that what Padmore,[41] Conze and the others in their position mean by "revolutionary" is really their Party brand, which is quite another matter. I have already stated that their meaning of "revolutionary" is the conquest of power. I know it is to be labour power, the capture of the political machinery. That is precisely what it meant to Lenin and the early Bolshevik idealists. See what it has come to. After all, the Trotskyists and the ILP groups are also vulnerable. They speak of a "Labour Government Now" and I am sure they mean it. The trouble will only begin when they are caught by the machine. They will not be able to check the march of events of becoming the dictatorship, surely just as Lenin, Trotsky and the rest became. Stalin is merely the exaggerated form of the dictatorship.

†*Several days later (1/10/38), Goldman informs American philosopher John Dewey that Stalin overestimates his potential influence in Spain.*

The irony of all the Bolshevik tactics is that though they are dictated by Stalin, the unfortunate devils who carry out his orders are sooner or later held to account. Thus, the Soviet Consul Antonov-Ovseenko, who negotiated the sale of arms to Spain, has now been recalled to Moscow and imprisoned, if

41. George Padmore, from Trinidad, was a key intellectual figure in the early drive for African independence and pan-African unity. Before joining the ILP he was an important Comintern leader on African affairs.

not already shot.[42] Stalin simply over-reached himself in his megalomania to think that his methods would be accepted by the Spanish people as cringingly as they have been accepted by the Russian people. Actually, the Communists with all the demoralizing bribes have taken no root in the Spanish people.

†*This excerpt from a 1/14/38 public speech in London analyzes the broad forces affecting Stalin's policy toward Spain.*

More heinous than this crime [the betrayal of Spain by the Western democracies] is the despicable part played by the man at the helm of the socialist republic. His treachery against the Spanish people and against the Revolution far outsweeps the crime of all the other countries. . . . No amount of talk will do away with the fact that Stalin has sabotaged the Spanish Revolution.

During the first 3½ months of the anti-Fascist struggle and the Revolution, the Soviet press paid scant attention to the world-stirring Spanish events. But even their colorless reports were enough to rouse the Russian masses on behalf of their comrades in Spain. There were mass demonstrations and collections in factories, mines and shops poured forth in aid of the Spanish Revolution. For some unknown reason this all came to a sudden stop. Yet the reason was not far to seek. Stalin was too busy liquidating the old Bolshevik guard and impressing the Russian workers with the infamy of these old revolutionaries to permit any reawakening of the Russian Revolution inspired in the Russian masses by the Revolution in Spain.

When Soviet Russia finally made up its mind to send arms to the anti-Fascists it was by no means out of class-conscious solidarity. It was because it had awakened to the importance of a strong foothold in Spain for its foreign policy.[43] And not less important, to lay its hands on the gold which the central government in Valencia offered to pay in return for Russian arms.[43a] . . .

The young and ardent, but hopelessly blind Communists in the world could not be expected to know all the crooked back-stage acrobatic stunts of world diplomacy. . . . Stalin's international propaganda machine worked day and night to make known that their master had saved the Spanish anti-Fascists. The world was yet to learn that in addition to the arms, though never quite profuse, Stalin sent his Communist "blessing": his GPU and Cheka methods

42. A close assistant to Trotsky and leader of the assault on the St. Petersburg Winter Palace in the November 1917 Bolshevik-led coup, Vladimir Antonov-Ovseenko was part of Lenin's first government. In 1923 he sided with Trotsky against Stalin, then several years later reconciled with the latter. Ironically, though no doubt very consciously, Stalin sent the ex-Trotskyist to Barcelona as Soviet consul in the Fall of 1936 to undermine the "Trotskyites," anarchists and other anti-Stalinist "heretic" Leftists. He was recalled to Russia later and shot, as Goldman expected, at Stalin's orders.
43. See footnote 43 at back of chapter.
43aSee footnote 43a at back of chapter.

to extort confessions.


†*In this 4/28/38 letter to Italian-American veteran anarchist Carlo Tresca, Goldman compares Stalin's policy in Spain to his betrayal of Chinese Communists ten years earlier.*

The notion that the end justifies the means has induced Stalin not only to betray the Russian Revolution and the Russian people, but also the people in Spain and those in China. You probably do not know that for many years millions of roubles were thrown over to China to build a formidable Chinese Communist army. Tens of thousands of young Chinese enthusiasts lost their lives unscrupulously butchered by Chiang Kai-shek.[44] Since Stalin, for reasons of his foreign policy, has decided to hobnob with the imperialist governments, the gallant Chinese Communist army was ordered to dissolve and to submit to the authority of the very man who has covered China's soil with the blood of Stalin's victims,[45] and he has done the same in Spain. Only future historians will bring out the fact that in sending arms to Spain after the most critical 3½ months were lost, Stalin also sent his emissaries to destroy root-and-crop all the magnificent constructive achievements of the CNT and the FAI. That they did not succeed to the extent they had hoped is due to the fact that they had never gained a footing among the Spanish people, but they have done enough harm to make the advance of Franco easier than it would otherwise have been. More than that even—their power in the government made it possible for them to corrupt the militias, to give the usual preference to their comrades, to give them advantages merely because they were members of the Communist Party, though they were worthless as officers or leaders of the war. Believe me, it is not an exaggeration when I tell you that it is entirely due to the Communists that so many important places like Belchite, Teruel and other places were lost to Franco's German and Italian hordes.[46] Unfortunately the situation in Spain is so grave and so disastrous that it is impossible now to put the damnable Communists and their master Stalin in the pillory where they belong. But history has its own way of making the truth known, even if it takes long.

†*In a new letter to John Dewey (5/3/38), chairperson of an international commis-*

---

44. See footnote 44 at back of chapter.
45. To fight growing Japanese belligerence in the Far East (including attacks against Russia itself) and to assure respect for Western economic-political interests in China (again with a view toward an anti-fascist alliance), Stalin in 1935 ordered the Chinese Communist Party, with its own independent Red Army, to link up with its Civil War enemy Chiang Kai-shek in a second political-military United Front against the Japanese. Nevertheless, Red Army subordination to the Nationalists was far more nominal than real.
46. See footnote 30 above.

*sion the previous year to investigate Stalin's charges against Trotsky, Goldman
again clarifies that the Soviet dictatorship originated with Lenin and Trotsky, not
later with Stalin. Trotsky's continued attack on the Kronstadt sailors along with the
Spanish anarchists demonstrates that his essential dictatorial objectives are
unchanged.*

I was very glad to get your letter and to read what you have to say about the
changes that have taken place in the minds of many of the intelligentsia in the
United States regarding the Soviet regime and the activities of the C.P. in
America. The trouble with most of these good people is that they have emancipated themselves from one superstition and are again in the throes of
another. They are now blaming everything on Stalin, as if he had come to the
fore out of nothing, as if he were not merely the dispenser of the legacy left
him by Lenin, Trotsky and the unfortunate group that have been savagely
murdered in the last two years. Nothing amuses me so much as the contention
that all was well in Russia while Lenin, Zinoviev and Trotsky were at the
helm of state. Actually the same process of elimination or, to use the C.P.
term, "liquidation," begun by Lenin and his group, took place from the very
beginning of the Communist ascendency to power. Already in the early part
of 1918, it was Trotsky who liquidated the Anarchist headquarters in Moscow
by means of machine guns, and it was during that same year that the peasant
Soviet, consisting of 500 delegates with Maria Spiridonova, had been liquidated by sending many of them, including Maria, to the Cheka. Also it
was under the regime of Lenin and Trotsky that thousands of people of the intelligentsia, workers and peasants were liquidated by fire and sword.[47] In
other words, it is the Communist ideology which has spread the poisonous
ideas in the world: first, that the Communist Party has been called upon by
history to guide "the social revolution," and secondly that the end justifies the
means. These notions have created all the evils, including Stalin, that have
followed Lenin's death.

As regards Trotsky, I do not know whether you have seen the *New International* of February, March and April, especially of this month. If you have,
you will see that the saying about the leopard changing his spots, but not his
nature, applies forcibly to Leon Trotsky. He has learned nothing and forgotten nothing. The usual Bolshevik calumny, falsehoods and misrepresentation
have again been dug out from the family closet and hurled at the memory of
the Kronstadt sailors. More than that, neither the dead nor the living are exempt from their venomous and scurrilous attacks. The new *bête-noir* for
Trotsky are the Spanish Anarchists of the CNT and the FAI. Just think of it, at
a time when they are fighting with their backs to the wall, when they have

47. Beyond Goldman's own *LL* (Vol. II) and *My Disillusionment . . .*, for more details on this
repression see Maximoff, *The Guillotine at Work* (1940; rpt., Sanday, Orkney Islands,
Scotland: Cienfuegos Press, 1979); Avrich, *The Russian Anarchists*; and Voline, *The
Unknown Revolution.*

been betrayed by the Blum Popular Front government, by the National government[48] and by Stalin's regime, Leon Trotsky, who has roused the whole world in his defense, is attacking the heroic people in Spain. This more than anything else merely proves that Trotsky is woven from the same cloth as his arch-enemy Stalin, and that he hardly deserves the compassion in his present plight which most people entertain for him. Yes, the C.P. in and out of Russia have done so much harm to the labor and revolutionary movement in the world that it may well take a hundred years to undo. As to the harm they have done in Spain, it is simply incalculable. One thing is already too apparent – Stalin's satraps in Spain, by their methods of undermining the revolutionary achievements of the Spanish people and of keeping up a system of Communist favoritism among officers and other military authorities, have worked right into the hands of Franco. I am not exaggerating when I say that the thousands of lives and the rivers of blood shed by Franco's German and Italian hordes must be laid at the feet of Soviet Russia. I realize that the truth will out some day, but the last twenty-odd years have proved that it takes longer to slay a lie.

† *Referring to the British context in a 5/24/38 letter to Margaret de Silver, the companion of Carlo Tresca and a veteran activist herself, Goldman explains the organizational success of the Communists and their supporters in developing public campaigns. Beyond rigid party discipline is the unlimited resource base and prestige of the Soviet Union for international propaganda. The result is an obedient mentality which would accept even an unthinkable alliance with the Communists' arch-enemy.*

The average Communist is like the average Catholic. You might give him facts a thousand times over. He will still believe that his Communist church can do no wrong. I am certain that if Russia should decide to ally herself with Hitler, which is not at all unlikely,[49] the Stalinites will justify and approve that as they are justifying the betrayal of China and of Spain.

† *In a 6/2/38 letter to comrade Helmut Rüdiger, Goldman denounces the new promises of "respectable" moderation proposed in his 13-Point program by the Communist-supported prime minister of Spain, Juan Negrín. The rotten intent of Negrín was no doubt to appease the British. For this, he clearly plans to bring back the Church, private property and everything else from the old status quo. She finds it hard to imagine how the Spanish comrades will be able to counter Negrín once the war is over, after such erosion of their physical and ethical position.*[50]

48. She refers here to the government of Britain.
49. As happened indeed in August 1939. See more on this in the next chapter.
50. See footnote 50 at back of chapter.

†*Just after her final visit to Spain (11/11/38), Goldman presents to Rudolf Rocker additional charges against the Communists.*

When I tell you that hundreds of our people in the first ranks at the front have been done away with by the Communists—that they are invading the industries, eliminating CNT committees,[51] and that they are insidiously undermining the strength of the CNT and FAI, you will have an idea of some of the actions of Stalin's henchmen.

*The arms sent by Russia are mostly ineffective, dating back to World War I.*[52] *Its specialists in the arms industry were so inept they were recalled. Worse yet, successful Communist infilitration in this sector actually reduced its output by one-third. Beyond this, they invaded the headquarters of the workers' self-managed transport sector, destroying furniture, breaking open the safe and threatening its militant anarchist leaders. They also discriminate in hospital treatment between Party members and others and have taken over the higher positions in the military, forcing anarchists to submit to their dictates.*

*Despite all of this, Goldman finds that the Communists have not succeeded in taking root in Spain and in fact no longer can act as brazenly as a year before. But the CNT National Committee still has taken no clear stand against the continuing destructive role of the Communists and the Negrín government. On the other hand, the FAI now favors an open and frank exposure and has already gone back to revitalize the grass-roots level of the syndicates for the approaching direct confrontation.*

†*In this brief passage of a letter to Ben (Capes?) several days later (11/15/38), Goldman extracts from the Spanish experience the clear lesson that the state and economic freedom cannot coexist.*

You say that once economic freedom is gained by the masses the state as an instrument of oppression and upholder of privilege would be dissolved. The trouble is that economic freedom cannot be gained by the masses unless the state is undermined in the process, for the state will never permit economic freedom. This has been demonstrated a thousand times over and is again being demonstrated in Spain. The Negrín government, reactionary to the core, is doing its utmost to undermine the revolutionary economic

---

51. Concerning the first charge, see footnote 30 above; the second is discussed in detail in Peirats, *La CNT* . . ., ch. 33. Further discussion of governmental and Communist interference with the workers' self-managed industrial sector is found in Leval, *Espagne Libertaire*, pp. 247-49, 367-72, 376; Semprun-Maura, *Révolution et contre-révolution* . . ., ch. 4; and Richards, *Lessons* . . ., ch. 10.

52. As already noted, the best war material went to the Communist units, with troops of other political orientation receiving the rest—including some 1886 Swiss rifles as well as ammunition and guns from the 1904 Russo-Japanese War (Mintz, p. 352; Paz, p. 418).

gains of the Spanish masses. . . .

*† Within a month of her exit from Spain (late November 1938), Goldman produced this detailed article (most of which was published later) on the Spanish state's October frame-up trial of POUM leaders, an outgrowth of the vicious repression against that party in early 1937.*

Shortly after the State Attorney had completed his summing up of the indictment against the POUM prisoners, *L'Humanité*[53] made this comment: "Emma Goldman, the international and famous anarchist, gave her impression of the POUM spy trial as being the fairest she had ever witnessed." I do not know what I have done to "deserve" being quoted in a Communist paper which did not know enough of my standing in the revolutionary movement even to spell my name correctly. I want, however, to assure the readers of *Vanguard* and all our comrades that I never referred to the POUM men on trial as spies. Far from considering them as such I was convinced even before I returned to Barcelona and the opening of the trial that the charges against them prepared by Stalin's satraps in Spain were on par with the same kind of doctored evidence repeatedly used in Russia against everyone whom Stalin wishes to dispose of. If ever I had doubted the innocence of the POUM members brought to trial, the proceedings in court during eleven days, the witnesses against and for the defense would have convinced me of the utter baselessness of the evidence used by the State Attorney. In fact I never witnessed such a crude and deliberate falsification of facts and the truth as contained in the material used against the prisoners.

Here I wish to give you one of the many methods to incriminate Gorkin, Andrade, Bonet, Gironella, Arquer, Escuder and Rebull. "Joaquín Roca Mir (on trial for espionage, his case is still pending) states that he entered the espionage service of Dalmau-Riera[54] of Perpignan. He sent all military information to Riera. *One day they took him a letter for Riera and left him a valise to be picked up the following day. Three hours later the police appeared. He said that they kept him without food for forty-eight hours, that he was coerced by the police to confess what they wanted.*" He retracted this confession by his DECLARATION before the Judge and in a *letter rectifying the false testimony* that he had any relations with the POUM and added that he did not know any POUM people.

This witness went on to state that in the valise were found documents with plans for manufacturing a bomb. On them was written "Central Committee of

---

53. The Paris newspaper of the French Communist Party.
54. A Spanish fascist.

the POUM." There were other ciphered documents which revealed that secret groups of the POUM were preparing to attempt an attempt against Prieto's life. He said that he did not know the man that took him the letter and the valise.

It is clear that, knowing the man was suspected of being a spy, Stalin's agents planted the valise in order to connect the indicted men with the Fascist spy. This as well as the largest part of the prepared evidence was thrown out of court, since even a child could see the crudeness of the attempt to destroy the men on trial. There was other such so-called evidence; but it is hardly necessary to go into it because the court itself, in imposing sentences on five and a verdict of not guilty on two, had completely rejected the charge of espionage and connection with either Fascism or the Gestapo.[55]

The prosecuting attorney tried his utmost to make this witness admit that they had received support from Hitler and Mussolini for their extensive POUM propaganda in Spain and abroad; but that too failed utterly. In other words, the whole concocted conspiracy and outrageous propaganda carried on since the May events against the POUM, as a party and its members, did not survive the light turned on it during the trial.

I admit that similar "evidence" in Russia would have sent the enemies of Stalin to their death, but though I hold no brief for the liberality of the Negrín government, I must say that Spain has not yet reached the brutal dictatorial condition of Russia. Perhaps this is not the virtue of the Negrín Government so much as the numerical and moral strength of the CNT-FAI and the socialist syndicate UGT that has still kept its skirt clean from the Communist scourge. It is still impossible for such heinous crimes to take place in the anti-Fascist part [of] Spain as those staged in Stalin's dominion.

I have been in courts a great many times in my life. I therefore expected to find the same harshness, vindictiveness, and lack of fairness at the trial of the POUM as I have known in America in the past. I was therefore considerably surprised with the tone maintained during the eleven days. Although it was a military court, there was not the least military demonstration, no one in military uniform or military rigidity used with the public which attended the trial freely, or [with] the prisoners. Two guards brought the seven into court and two other guards were at the back of the courtroom, never making themselves conspicuous in any way. The prosecuting attorney was obviously either a Communist or strongly in sympathy with the Stalin followers. He was vindictive, hard, and did his utmost to incriminate the prisoners. At the close of his summing up, he demanded no less than fifteen and thirty years imprisonment for them. The very fact that he did not dare to call for the death penalty was in itself a proof that the whole fabricated [set of] charges had collapsed.

55. The secret police of Nazi Germany.

I was particularly struck by the objectivity of the superior judge. At no time did he permit the prosecuting attorney to drag in ulterior motives that had no bearing whatever on the guilt or innocence of the indicted men. When they were cross-examined and the prosecuting attorney attempted to bully them, or rush them into a statement derogatory to their party or to their ideas, the judge immediately objected. On the other hand he patiently listened to a five-hour speech of the defending attorney. It was a masterly analysis of the various political parties that represent the anti-Fascist front. He spoke in the highest terms of the CNT-FAI, he made it very clear that the ideology of the POUM and the personalities on trial precluded every possibility of any connection with spying or Fascism. He also related the frightfulness imposed upon the workers of Barcelona during the May events by the henchmen of Stalin which resulted in the killing of our comrades, Camillo Berneri and Barbieri, as well as a number of other victims whose names were not even known. In other words, the whole proceedings in the court during eleven days impressed me as being absolutely free from partisanship, political trickery or Communist venom against the men on trial. I have to admit therefore what I stated before the Minister of Justice when together with other correspondents I was asked for my impression of the trial: that the court was extremely objective and that it was the fairest trial I had ever witnessed.

The readers of *Vanguard* may well ask how it comes that five of the indicted members of the POUM were given eleven and fifteen years imprisonment respectively. Is that not a sign of unfairness? In reply I must say that such a sentence in any other country would be harrowing indeed. In Spain it is not anything so grave because nothing in Spain with the exception of the spirit of the people to conquer Fascism is lasting. Any change in the government or other event is likely to bring about a political amnesty. There is no reason whatever therefore to assume that the men will have to serve their full time. The reason for the sentence is twofold. First the judges had to do something to appease the insatiable appetite on the part of Stalin's representatives. The second, to prevent the disappearance of Gorkin and his comrades as Nin and others disappeared. This is not only my impression, but also the impression of a number of people who attended the trial.

It is hardly necessary for me to impress on the readers of *Vanguard* that I do not agree with the ideology of the POUM. It is a Marxist party and I have been and am absolutely opposed to Marxism, but that cannot prevent me from paying respects to the mentality and courage of Gorkin, Andrade, and their comrades. *Their stand in court was magnificent.* Their exposition of their ideas was clear cut. There were no evasions or apologies. In point of fact the seven men in the dock demonstrated, for the first time since the demoralization of all idealists in Russia, how revolutionists should face their accusers. At the end, after the prosecuting attorney had tried their patience to the breaking point, Gorkin, Andrade, Bonet, Gironella, Arquer, Escuder and Rebull rose

to their full stature with their clenched fists held high in the air, sure of themselves and defiant against their enemies. That was indeed a splendid demonstration in the court which the people who unscrupulously prepared their undoing will not so easily forget.

In view of the fact that much was rumored abroad of the indifference of the CNT to the fate of the POUM prisoners and to their trial, it is not out of place to say that the defending attorney is a member of the CNT and that the testimony of Federica Montseny was among the most laudatory of the character of the men on trial. Perhaps I had better quote from my notes about her statement:

"She says she knows some of the accused through their trade union work and through their literary production, and also as proven anti-Fascist militants. She states that she was sent by the government to mediate the May events and that when full light can be thrown on this disturbance many things now obscure will be understood. *That neither the POUM nor the CNT-FAI were responsible for the May events.*

She adds that this affair had all the earmarks *of being hatched in an underground and secretive manner to overthrow the Largo Caballero government and thus do away with the proletarian influence in the government. This naturally hurt the workers' cause.*

In answer to the questions of the prosecuting attorney she says that upon arrival from Valencia they held a meeting in the Generalitat to appease the excited spirits and to keep the situation in hand so that events would not follow the course mapped out by its provocateurs. They were convinced that *these events were a maneuver against the interests of the popular masses."*

I cannot emphasize enough that it was the quiet and determined stand of the CNT-FAI to secure a fair trial for the POUM members and to give them every comradely assistance which has no doubt prevented a more severe sentence than the one imposed; but as I have already said I feel certain that an amnesty will be granted in not too distant a future. I know for a fact that the CNT-FAI are already working for it. But it is but right that workers in every country should send a protest to Negrín against the sentences and demand an amnesty.

† *Brief comments beyond the above text are presented by Goldman in this follow-up manuscript of December 1938.*

I have already written a report for *Vanguard* and *Freie Arbeiter Stimme*. I need not repeat what I recorded of the amazing fabrication of so-called evidence on which the seven POUMists were to be sent to their death. Its most striking point to me was its identity with the kind of evidence used in nearly every trial in Russia, just as villainous and completely barren of originality or fact.

There are, however, a few sides that need some elucidation which I did not give in the report. . . .

. . . . . . . . . . . . . . . . . . . . . . . . . . . . . . . . . . . . . . . . . . . . . . . . . . . . . . . .

The sentence imposed on the five POUM leaders is atrocious, but I must point out that it would have been much graver and fatal had not the united Libertarian Movement stood back of the prisoners. As long ago as June 1937, the CNT addressed a vigorous protest to the President of the Republic, the President of the Cortes and all the other members of the government, against the persecution of the POUM party and its leaders, and it also sent a warning against any attempt to railroad the men on perjured testimony. It soon became known that the force of the CNT-FAI and the Libertarian Youth would be brought to bear to safeguard the rights of the defendants. It was also the CNT who had secured counsel for their defense. After the man had been threatened by Stalin's worshippers he was forced to flee for his life. Thereupon it was again the CNT who engaged another attorney, a member of the CNT, because no other attorney dared to take the case. In fact, our comrades Santillán and Herrera were the ones to negotiate with Vicente Rodriguez Revilla, a brilliant young criminal lawyer, to take charge of the case. His plaideur in court which lasted five hours impressed everybody as one of the most scholarly and profound analyses of the conspiracy against the defendants, the aims of their party, the significance of the May events and the position and importance of the CNT-FAI in the life of the Spanish workers and peasants. There is no doubt that his defense speech knocked the bottom from under the prosecution. Added to this, as I have already said, was the moral backing of the CNT-FAI that completely spoiled the game of the Spanish Cheka. These people kept up a violent attack in their press, trying their utmost to influence the court. It was left to the press of the CNT, the evening paper by this name and the *Solidaridad Obrera,* to keep silent during the trial and then to come out in a dignified article condemning in unmistakable terms the miserable campaign carried on by the Communist press.

I should not have written all this were it not for the fact that I have recently come across an attack against the CNT in the *Independent News* published in Paris by the POUMists. I consider this outburst uncalled for, ungracious and unjust. I cannot imagine that the men now serving time would approve of such cheap tactics, only used to discredit the CNT. I am sure the outburst in the *Independent News* is doing their comrades and party irreparable harm, while in no way detracting from the moral strength of the CNT-FAI. I see that some papers who call themselves Anarchist have reprinted the contention that the CNT, because of its member in the government as Minister of Culture, Segundo Blanco, is responsible for the heavy sentence imposed on the men on trial. All I can say is that these Anarchists are pulling the chestnuts out of the fire for the 150 varieties of Marxists now afloat in their world. They will only burn their own fingers, as Anarchists have done before.

In conclusion, I want to emphasize once more that far from being responsible for the sentence imposed on the POUMists, the strong support given them by the CNT-FAI has prevented a repetition in Spain of the terrible methods used in Russia against the old Bolsheviks.

†*Shortly after the fall of Barcelona, Goldman writes to Rudolf Rocker (2/10/39) about reports she received on the sabotage of its defense.*

You will see that actually the people who are responsible for the surrender of Barcelona and the collapse of Catalonia are the Carabineros, Negrín's counter-revolutionary police force. Their cowardly withdrawal from the Ebro front[56] made it possible for Franco's forces to march into Catalonia and to take possession of it.

*Among other reasons were the lack of arms and other assistance, but also the weakness of the Negrín government and manipulations by the Communists. However it is clear that the CNT National Committee itself is to blame for being too lenient and too trusting in its allies.*
   *All of the organizations in Britain currently raising money for Spanish refugees are Communist-led. As a result, no assistance from them has ever reached anarchists. This she finds despicable since Spanish refugees should never be denied help on the basis of political affiliation.*

†*In a letter to a "comrade" during the final weeks of the civil war (3/21/39), Goldman offers her bitterest attack yet against the legacy of Karl Marx.*

. . . I am sure you cannot know the things Marx permitted his followers to do during the Paris Commune, and his methods, as well as those of Engels, in dealing with every great issue in their time. Marx always insisted on having "his finger in every pie." In other words, in directing the fate of every revolutionary uprising from his safe vantage point—either England or Switzerland or some other country far removed from the scene of action. But even if Marx had used more humane methods in dealing with the revolutionary events of his time, the very fact that he stood for dictatorship, for the centralized power of the State, inevitably led in the past and led in the Spanish issue to disaster. They are like those who surround the Pope, far worse than the Pope himself, but the fact remains that the introduction of Marxist theories into the world has done no less harm, indeed I would say more, than the introduction of Christianity—at any rate in Spain it has helped to assassinate the Spanish revolution and the anti-Fascist struggle.

56. On December 23, 1938 (Thomas, *The Spanish Civil War*, p. 570).

*† As part of her final public speech in London (3/24/39), Goldman provides details on the betrayal of Catalan defense and the demoralization of the Communist-organized Lister Division in the same zone.*

Naturally I wanted to know how it happened that the very cradle of revolutionary ideas, Catalonia, and the stronghold of the Spanish National Confederation of Labor . . . was lost. I have before me a document[57] that shows that eight months ago, eight months before Barcelona was given up, the members of the Anarchist Federation of Iberia had gone to the government after they had consulted some of the highest men in the army, and had told the government of Negrín, or the government of the Negrín Communist agency, that the enemy would destroy Catalonia unless steps were taken immediately to reorganise the army and to reorganise the means of defense. They proved that a voluntary army, better trained, better equipped for war than it was on the 19th of July, 1936, could be created of the members of the F.A.I., that every one of the Youth and the Anarchist Federation of Iberia were ready to volunteer to defend Catalonia and defend Barcelona, provided the Communist command was done away with. They knew from personal experience that to fight under the Communist command means to lose their lives. What did Negrín do? Negrín and his Communist friends arranged a banquet and invited some of our comrades to attend, to discuss like comrades the best way of defending Catalonia and Barcelona. It was a banquet equal to the banquet in the Russian Embassy which Mr. Chamberlain attended. There was plenty to eat and champagne in a country where people were starving, where the civil population had been underfed for a year, because Negrín and his Communist friends thought that they could bribe the representatives of the FAI. But neither Negrín nor Companys, who was the President of Catalonia, nor the Communists, accepted the plan. To accept the plan meant to put the defense of Catalonia and Barcelona into the hands of the Anarchists, and Negrín and the Communists would rather have Franco than the Anarchists. It is a mistake to say that Catalonia was surrendered or that Barcelona was defeated. There was no struggle. Catalonia and Barcelona were betrayed. They were betrayed by Russia, by Stalin, by his methods, by his purges, by everything he has done in Russia to destroy the revolutionary element and the revolutionary fire, and the very same thing which he carried on in Spain.

I have before me a letter by a man, a German, a scientist, an anti-Fascist, who rushed to Spain right after the 19th of July and who fought at every front. I met him, I know the man, and I know that everything he writes is absolutely reliable. He gives a description of when he came to the Lister Division. . . . This man came to the Lister Divison and found absolute demoralisation and disintegration in that Division, because the people, the

---

57. Presumably Santillán's 3/14/39 letter to Goldman (RAD) in which these details are presented.

workers who came from the rank and file and who enlisted or were recruited in the army, were held by terror, by *terror*, not by the interest in the war any more, for they said, "It is not our war any more; it is not our struggle any more. It is the war of Negrín, it is the war of the Spanish government. It is the war of Stalin; it is the war by which he hopes so to blindfold the democracies that the democracies will not come to the rescue of the republican government." He found appalling disintegration and demoralisation and graft and partiality in Lister's Division. That, friends, was the reason for the collapse of Catalonia and Barcelona.

† *Writing to Helmut Rüdiger months after the collapse in Spain (8/4/39), Goldman praises a letter she received from a disillusioned ex-member of the International Brigades. He claimed that if the dead Brigadists could be revived their indictment of treachery would brand Stalin and the Communists with "letters of fire." For her it is important to see that those who were ardent followers could come to such awareness.*

† *In her continuing effort to publicize lessons from Spain and the persisting discrimination against anarchist refugees, Goldman offers new details in this 9/19/39 public speech in Toronto.*

I remember very well stating here some months ago that the arms sent to Spain by Russia were arms which were produced in Czechoslovakia by the munition factory of Skoda, and that the arms which were sent to Spain proved to be manufactured for the use of the last war – absolutely inadequate to help the Spanish people to defend themselves against Franco, and my statement was challenged by Communists in the hall. I have since received letters from four members of the International Brigade who bore out my contention, who said that from their personal experience they can testify that the arms were absolutely useless in the Spanish struggle.[58]

. . . . . . . . . . . . . . . . . . . . . . . . . . . . . . . . . . . . . . . . . . .
But not only did Russia sabotage the anti-Fascist struggle in Spain. It has been doing the same thing every since. There are nearly 500,000 refugees in French concentration camps. They have been treated worse than criminals by the French government and it was again Stalin's power over his adherents who are practicing the crassest discrimination against the unfortunate Spanish refugees in those dreadful camps. When I tell you that some of the ships that took refugees to Mexico – 1,800, and 2,000, and 5,000 – had only the smallest percentage of the most militant people among the Spanish refugees, you will realize the criminal discrimination, the criminal partiality which is going on in the camps by the Communists, at the order and the command of Stalin.

58. See footnote 58 at back of chapter.

Only today I received a letter from Mexico, from one of the Spanish militants who told me that even in Mexico the long arm of Stalin crushes everything in its way, that even in Mexico the same partiality, the same discrimination, the same brutal differentiation between the party sectors of the former anti-Fascist Front in Spain is going on.

† *In this 10/18/39 letter to London friend Liza Koldofsky, Goldman sees the recent Soviet-Nazi pact as consistent with Stalin's overall policies, though a welcome revelation for those on the outside still mesmerized by the Soviet myth.*

I do not think, my dearest, that I was so prophetic in re Russia.[59] I had simply followed Stalin's actions since he ascended to power. I saw what he was doing at home to crush every breath of life. I knew that no one can do that at home without having it in him to use similar policies outside of his own country. More than that I knew that Stalin had but one consuming ambition: that was to turn revolutionary Russia into a powerful empire with him as the reigning power. It was simply inevitable for him to use the most despicable means to realize that dream. In this respect and in many others there is no difference between him and Hitler. The pact [between Germany and the Soviet Union] and all that Stalin has already done or will do are mere links in the chain of events he had forged on the Russian people, their hopes and that of the rest of the proletariat. It is for this reason that I welcome that the mask from the man's lying face is off and that all can see it in its hideousness. Unfortunately there are still fools and knaves in the world. His blind boot lickers still find excuses. But it is in vain. Stalin's black treachery cannot be washed away or forgotten by history.

† *One day later, she writes to Rudolf Rocker that the policies of Stalin, Lenin and the other Bolsheviks merely reflect the same negative traits of Marx in his own time.*

. . . Stalin is after all carrying out the legacy of Marxism. If I needed proofs for that, a recent biography of Marx by Carr[60] which I am now reading convinces the most credulous that the Moscow gang from Lenin to Stalin were repeating parrot-like the dicta of their master. What a narrow, jealous, vainglorious and dictatorial creature Marx was and how barren of all feeling [except toward his family and possibly Engels].[61]

---

59. She refers here to her earlier predictions that Stalin eventually would sign a pact with Hitler.
60. E.H. Carr, *Karl Marx: A Study in Fanaticism* (London: J.M. Dent and Sons, Ltd., 1934).
61. Concerning Marx' personal behavior, see also the recent book by Jerrold Seigel, *Marx's Fate: The Shape of A Life* (Princeton: Princeton University Press, 1978).

*She is convinced that Marx would have been guilty of the same crimes as Stalin, had he himself come to power. This is shown by the nature of his dealings with Proudhon,*[62] *Bakunin and others who dared oppose his views.*

62. See footnote 62 at back of chapter.

## Further Footnotes for Chapter Five

6.  Concerning Santiago Carrillo, the party secretary-general until November 1982, his dictatorial manipulations as head of the JSU (Unified Socialist Youth), his facilitation of the Cheka police takeover in Madrid and his strongly counter-revolutionary line in Spain from 1937 on (helping to justify the persecution and arrest of all elements to the left of the Communist Party, among other things) are well-documented. See, for example, the books by Bolloten and Broué and Témime. Felix Morrow, in his *Revolution and Counter-Revolution in Spain,* p. 168, mentions that Carrillo even recommended that the Communist Party recruit "fascist sympathizers" among the youth in its opportunistic effort to broaden its base. True to form, Carrillo himself resorts to continued slanders, falsehoods and distortions in his own presentday recollection of that period (see Fernando Gomez Pelaez, "Santiago Carrillo or History Falsified," in *Cienfuegos Press Anarchist Review,* no. 4, pp. 29-39, a translation of the same article originally in Spanish in *Interrogations: International Review of Anarchist Research,* no. 2 [March 1975]; Carrillo's remarks are set forth in an interview-format book, *Tomorrow Spain,* in 1974).
8.  The difficulty in obtaining accurate long-distance information on the confusing events in Russia was enormous. Even the well-known veteran and strongly anti-collaborationist Italian anarchist Malatesta, despite strong suspicions as to the authoritarian turn of the new regime, still by July 1919 was unwilling definitively to judge the Bolsheviks. In a letter to Italian militant Luigi Fabbri, Malatesta still saw the possibility that "the things which seem bad to us are the fruit of this situation [defending the revolution against reactionary forces] and that in the particular circumstances of Russia, there was no way to act differently than they have done" (Daniel Guérin, ed., *Ni dieu ni maître: anthologie de l'anarchisme,* III, 55).
11. No doubt the leading example of such a politician was Indalecio Prieto. As leader of the "moderate Socialists," he was an arch-enemy of Francisco Largo Caballero and collaborated with the Communists in the latter's downfall as Prime Minister in May 1937. A few months later he himself was ousted from power as Minister of Defense when eventually regarded as an expendable, excessively independent obstacle by the Communists. Such persons were no less treacherous "allies" *before* 1936 or *after* themselves being burned by the Communists in the course of the civil war. They were just less bold.
14. Léon Blum, the Socialist party leader in France and head of its Popular Front government (June 1936-June 1937, March-April 1938) proposed for the major European powers a "non-intervention policy" toward Spain in early August 1936. Large numbers of the majority Popular Front electorate favored direct armed support or at least maintaining an open arms, food and supplies market for the Spanish republic in the face of large-scale German and Italian support to the fascists. But Blum refused to endorse any action which might risk breaking the alliance with Britain, the keystone of French foreign policy at the time. France took its lead from Britain and the latter preferred not to involve itself in any foreign entanglement, such as risking additional provocation of Germany and Italy by favoring their opponent in Spain. Besides, a conservative military dictatorship in Spain was seemingly far preferable for British economic interests than a moderately socialist government, let alone an experiment in revolution. The non-intervention policy therefore provided an idealistic sounding rationale for French and British refusal to allow any support for the Spanish republic, even on the open market. At the same time, through the lack of any enforcement mechanism, they allowed German and Italian intervention to continue as before. In addition, they permitted the Soviet Union to become virtually the total (with the minor exception of Mexico) foreign source of support for the republic – thus giving it a position to exercise moderating control. (This latter calculation

hardly differs from the 1977 statement by President Carter's foreign policy aide Andrew Young that it was to the United States' advantage to let Communist Cuban troops become the military prop for the new radical regime in Angola, thereby keeping the latter from engaging in adventurous involvements elsewhere in Africa disruptive of American interests.) See further discussion of the international context and the non-intervention policy specifically in the next chapter.

16. Having taken a traditional Marxist-Leninist (and Trotskyist) stance against "naive, nihilistic and petty-bourgeois" anarchism in Spain up to 1936, the POUM quickly changed its line with the struggle against fascism and the commencement of the revolution. Although seeking a revolutionary *government* as opposed to the traditional anarchist anti-state position, POUMistas saw the CNT-FAI in *practice* also endorsing the former approach. (Soon, though, even many POUMistas expressed concern over the CNT-FAI's endless ability to compromise away revolutionary gains to the other elements in the governing coalition.) If there was any hope in maintaining revolutionary momentum, let alone holding on to those revolutionary accomplishments to date, POUMistas saw CNT-FAI mass strength and militancy as essential. And as Goldman points out, the support of anarchists also was essential for the very survival of the POUMistas in the face of their sworn enemies, the Communist party and its Soviet masters.

19. In the face of the Nationalist troops' drive to Madrid, the capture of which they assumed would achieve their victory, the Caballero government did relatively little to mobilize the population to defend the city until the last desperate moment in early November (while itself fleeing to Valencia). Not only did it neglect organizing necessary defense measures, such as constructing fortifications. It also failed to commit itself actively to social revolution, as through socialization of capitalist landholding and industry and recognition of full workers' control. Through such measures it could have encouraged that much more mass revolutionary enthusiasm (and demoralization of the peasantry in Franco's army as well). Instead, Caballero's government wanted primarily to gain positive support and intervention from Britain and France by demonstrating its bourgeois liberal respectability – a strategy insisted upon by the Soviet agents and supporters whom Caballero depended upon for Soviet assistance itself. In a negative sense, Caballero obviously *feared* relying on the revolutionary capacities and enthusiasm of the anarchist and socialist working-class and peasant base which had aspirations far more radical than his own. He also feared French and British direct intervention *against* a committed revolutionary society. In any case, at the top level of political decision-making, originally anarchists thus were excluded. Collaboration with the government on its own terms or the alternative of totally autonomous decision making – the latter open to charges of dividing the anti-Fascist struggle – seemed the double-bind plight for anarchist leaders.

35. Landau became a leader of the pro-Trotsky German Left Opposition Communists in 1923 and secretary of the loose international organization of such tendencies. In 1931 he formed his own political group, then fled the Nazi regime two years later. He came to Spain in November 1936 to assist the POUM – though apparently he was not, as Goldman suggests here, on the Executive Committee. Nevertheless Soviet agents and the Communists generally portrayed him as a major link in the "fascist-Trotskyite international conspiracy." He was kidnapped on September 23, 1937 and subsequently killed by the Stalinist police. For more details, see the account by his wife Katia Landau, "Le Stalinisme: Bourreau de la révolution espagnole, 1937-1938," *Spartacus* (Paris), no. 40 (May 1971).

36. Andrés Nin was earlier a leader of the CNT and represented it at the Comintern founding conference in Russia. After his own conversion to Communist allegiance, with others he formed the Spanish Communist Party and personally served as secretary of the Red Trade Union International. In this capacity, he sided with Trotsky against Stalin and returned to Spain in 1931 to form the oppositional Communist Left. In 1934 this group merged with another to form the POUM, with Nin as one of its two top leaders. Arrested on June 16, 1937 along with other POUM leaders in a Communist attempt to break the party, prove its "responsibility" for the May Days and worse yet its role as Gestapo agents, Nin never appeared again with the others and in fact totally disappeared. Given his world contacts and prestige, his disappearance and presumed Stalinist murder was an international scandal.

43. See the next chapter for more comment on how the Soviet Union rationalized involvement in Spain from its broad international perspective. Basically, Stalin wished to preserve Soviet prestige and power through a strong world Communist movement. Yet he also realized the need to ally with the West against Nazi aggressive designs. Soviet policy in Spain thus

was designed to show "anti-fascist" progressive international solidarity and hopefully to keep Germany involved in Western Europe. At the same time it sought to pressure the Spanish Republic to be moderate enough and in relatively equal balance with Franco, so as not to frighten Britain and France. Hopefully, the latter could be lured into an anti-fascist alliance there which inevitably would bind them with Russia against Nazi Germany on a broader scale as well. Other objectives were, as Frank Mintz suggests, to gain military experience and train Soviet military officers and to discredit any alternative model of revolution which might weaken Russia's monopoly in that realm (*L'Autogestion dans l'espagne révolutionnaire* [Paris: François Maspero, 1976]).

43a In October 1936, Soviet agents arranged with Juan Negrín to send almost ⅔ of the Spanish treasury (nearly $600 million) to the Soviet Union for "safekeeping" and to assure credit for continuous Soviet supplies. But this secret transfer in fact left republican Spain without negotiating power; indeed, Stalin told his Politburo that Spain would never again see its gold. (Bolloten, pp. 164-70.)

44. In the Shanghai massacre of 1927, Nationalist leader Chiang Kai-shek, himself trained militarily in Russia two years before, authorized the murder of his Communist urban working-class "allies" who had revolted against the supposed common enemy, a right-wing local war-lord. In doing so, Chiang assumed that he had eliminated his main threat within the overall nationalist movement. Indeed this was true temporarily. From that point on, the urban-based Chinese Communists played a secondary role, superceded within their own movement by the unorthodox efforts of Mao Tse-tung and others, organizing liberated zones in the countryside.

50. On May 1, 1938, Prime Minister Negrín issued a 13-Point list of republican war goals designed by their moderate nature to appease France and Britain in an effort to gain their potential mediation for a truce with Franco. The program encouraged capitalist property (without large trusts) and basically promised to return to the condition of republican Spain before the Civil War. This document indeed encouraged a significant and widening split between an increasingly critical FAI and a CNT leadership willing to follow Negrín to the end. The debate precipitated by the 13 Points is discussed in detail by Peirats in *La CNT* . . . , III, 89-99, and to a lesser extent in his *Anarchists in the Spanish Revolution*, pp. 291-94.

58. Accounts on Stalin's betrayal in Spain already had appeared the previous Spring in *The American Mercury*. "Escape from Loyalist Spain" (April 1939) was a brief personal description by a veteran of the International Brigades, Bill Ryan (see also footnote 42 in the next chapter). The more detailed critique, closely paralleling much of Goldman's analysis, was "Russia's Role in Spain" (May 1939) by Irving Pflaum, a United Press reporter there until mid-1938. Important revelations from the Communist side which themselves validate Goldman's critique in this chapter include General Walter Krivitsky, *I Was Stalin's Agent* (London: Hamish Hamilton, 1940) and Jesús Hernández, *Yo, ministro de Stalin en España* (2nd ed., Madrid: NOS, 1954). Krivitsky was chief of Soviet military intelligence in Western Europe until seeking asylum in late 1937; Hernández was a top leader of the Spanish Communist Party until his break after World War II.

62. Pierre-Joseph Proudhon (1809-1865) was the most prominent early anarchist writer in nineteenth century Europe. Along with strong anti-authoritarian critiques of existing society ("property is theft" is a well-known phrase with which he begins one of his books), he also formulated a utopian vision of a decentralized mutualistic society based on federated producer cooperatives and communes and the absence of the state. His writings and personal initiative inspired the first significant development of an anarchist movement in Europe, which itself was much responsible for creation of the First International and the later prominence of Bakunin. More on Proudhon's struggle with Marx can be found in Marx, *The Poverty of Philosophy;* George Woodcock, *Pierre-Joseph Proudhon: His Life and Work* (New York: Schocken Books, 1972); Carr, *Karl Marx* . . . ; and an interesting new study by Paul Thomas, *Karl Marx and the Anarchists* (London: Routledge and Kegan Paul, 1980).

# Chapter Six

# The International Context

*During the last century, billions of individuals experienced the immense pain of war and poverty produced by power politics on the international scale.*[1] *Anarchists are among many who described and attacked these barbarous conditions at great length. Yet anarchists seldom analyzed in detail the particular relationships involved — the bases of national power, the conditions of shifting coalitions, or the strategies and tactics of international "statecraft." One reason for such neglect is obvious. Anarchists abhor anything concerning the state and its own self-interested calculations. If it is the existence of the state itself which is the problem, why bother to analyze distinctions among and interactions between its several varieties? Anarchists always emphasized an internationalist perspective, thus discouraging detailed critiques of the narrow vision of national foreign policies.*

*But this area of relative analytical neglect obviously weakens anarchist clarity on other issues, such as the detailed economic dynamics of international capitalism. In turn, the tendency toward basic principles or fundamental critiques encourages many anarchists to rely upon more available liberal and Marxist analyses of the more intricate workings of "mainstream political reality."*[2] *Compared with these ideological rivals, this relative weakness discourages potential recruits to the movement as well. Many who sympathize with the anarchist program and basic critique still dismiss the whole as unrealistic simply because anarchists apparently have no clear strategic or tactical sense of how anarchist society itself could survive in a hostile statist world.*[3] *Worse yet, in situations of social crisis and potential revolution — as during both world wars and the upheavals in Russia and Spain — this analytical neglect forces anarchists themselves into hasty and paralyz-*

---

1. See footnote 1 at back of chapter.
2. This is not to deny the usefulness of certain aspects of liberal and Marxist analyses. It is only to stress the potential dangers from *depending* upon products of intellectual frameworks contradicting that of anarchism.
3. See footnote 3 at back of chapter.

172

*ing internal debate, leaving the movement searching for makeshift formulas of action in contradictory settings it did not foresee.[4] At a time when strength and clarity are most needed, such floundering immobility tragically undermines anarchist possibilities at the national and international levels both.[5]*

*It is ironic that anarchists tend to neglect the context of international power, given their considerable concern with governments they confront locally.[6] Of course in the latter context, it is obvious how state repression threatens survival, let alone the spread of anarchist consciousness. Anarchist activists everywhere confront harassment or persecution by the police. Accordingly, the movement frequently shifts tactics as liberals and conservatives exchange power. Programmatic priorities evolve, a sense of which authoritarian institutions deserve greatest confrontation at any particular time. Yet each of these local concerns has its parallel in the international arena as well. Anarchists consistently do stress the need for internationalist solidarity with other oppressed peoples. Yet even here, a distinguished record of international protest campaigns and varying degrees of underground personal support rarely have been matched by effective forms of broader direct action (such as strikes and boycotts) when the need arose.*

*In the anti-authoritarian movement, these weaknesses are today just as glaring as they were in the 1930's and before. It is just as important now, in Europe, the Americas and elsewhere, to find appropriate solutions with an informed internationalist perspective. In this sense. Emma Goldman's analysis of Spanish anarchist vulnerability in the international realm appropriately reminds us of the danger of ignoring this dimension for too long. It remains an impassioned plea for anti-authoritarians everywhere to be more knowledgeable and sophisticated in their trans-national analysis and more effective in their solidarity, all the more in our era when national boundaries mean so much less than at anytime in history.*

## II

*In the period before and including World War I, Emma Goldman's thoughts on the international context typified those expressed in the anarchist movement generally. While steadfastly against war and firmly internationalist, her own writings on international issues do not compare in depth with those on either the domestic scene or broad universal topics. Nevertheless, her international travels and her impassioned writings and speeches against persecution and war in Spain, Russia, Cuba, South Africa, Japan and elsewhere[7] gave her greater background than most for serious analysis in this realm.*

*Having witnessed Western intervention against the Russian revolution*

4.  See footnote 4 at back of chapter.
5.  This is not an objection to continuing anarchist *debate* on this issue, not at all. It is meant to criticize the last-minute pressured context in which such a debate finally originates. The previous two chapters illustrate the problem very well.
6.  The *psychology* of this neglect is understandable to the extent that anarchist activism focuses more on direct immediate targets of daily oppression than on those at a more abstract distance.
7.  See accounts of these international concerns and involvements in her autobiography and in the issues of *Mother Earth*.

*as well as the rise of an equally machiavellian world power center in the Soviet regime,[8] Goldman was forced to concern herself further with the international level of politics. Her own personal experience of wandering exile and lecture tours among a variety of states in east, central, and western Europe in the 1920's and 1930's added that much more sophistication to her perspective. Although especially concerned with the power structure and manipulations of international Communism, she also devoted much thought and writing to British foreign policy generally, the rise of fascism in Italy and Germany, British and French appeasement, and even the issue of China's struggle against Japan.[9] Already by the mid-1920's, she was appalled by the apparent numbness of the world to the butchery and oppression all around. In her view, this resulted from both the mass brutality and exhaustion of World War I and the subsequent Comintern desensitization and regimentation of progressive mass sentiment in general. The Soviet Union began courting Nazi favor as early as 1933.[10] This was followed by British and French acquiescence to German rearmament, to Italian aggression against Ethiopia and to the March 1936 German invasion of the Rhineland buffer zone. Goldman was surprised neither by the cynical power calculations behind such policies nor by the apparent public disinterest which permitted them. Nevertheless, despite widespread public lethargy, she thought it essential that those with clear vision persist in attempting to rouse others to the vast, growing dangers of the worst authoritarianism—fascism on the right and Soviet Communism on the left.[11]*

III

*Emma Goldman thus brought to Spain in late 1936 a heavy sense of realism about the international context. From the beginning, she defined the Spanish situation in global terms. At stake there were both the offensive of social revolution, hopefully international in scope, and the defensive stance of holding the line against international fascism. As indicated in the third and seventh chapters, she felt it was only the former aspect which permitted her support of the military war involved in the latter. Yet it was precisely this linkage of anti-fascist war and social revolution which complicated immensely the international issue.*

*In the then current "popular front" period in Britain, France and the United States, many liberals, socialists and communists defined their progressiveness in terms of how strongly they denounced fascism. On the other hand, especially given the pressures from the Right in their own countries, the same forces (politicians and organized movements alike) seemed paralyzed to go beyond words, to take*

8. For Goldman's personal experience with and impressions of the Comintern (Third International) and Red Trade Union International while in Russia, see especially ch. 29 of *My Disillusionment in Russia.*

9. See footnote 9 at back of chapter.

10. See the account of Stalin's policy toward Hitler and the rise of German fascism in chs. 10 and 11 of Isaac Deutscher, *Stalin: A Political Biography.* Soviet courting of the German military dates back to the Rapallo Pact of 1922.

11. See footnote 11 at back of chapter.

*genuinely effective action. Immobility was all the more obvious when anti-fascism potentially implied supporting the cause of revolution, even if in a foreign country. Behind the virtuous cloak of neutrality and despite bursts of strong rhetoric, for all practical purposes these same "progressives" were content to sit on their hands. Along with local Communist parties, the Soviet regime had its own complementary stance in this game. Feeling threatened by growing German strength on the west and openly hostile or leery toward revolutionary movements beyond its own control (including anarchists and Trotskyists, but also loyal Communist movements with strong national bases, as in China), the Soviet Union was only too willing to play the limited role of well-publicized but effectively constraining assistance described in the last chapter. All of these phenomena Emma Goldman anticipated, understood and of course criticized.*

*Yet despite her clear awareness, Goldman still expressed hope. Or perhaps more accurately, during most of this period, she continued struggling even beyond hope simply because her Spanish comrades—however naive their own perceptions internationally—so courageously fought their own desperate battles and asked for her assistance abroad. Beyond description and critique, therefore, her supportive commentary below also appeals for massive international solidarity—to outflank the immobility or open hostility of the united front of foreign governments. To this end, she advocates direct action in the form of strikes, boycotts, and collections of relief funds and supplies. (Also, to this end, she desperately urges the international anarchist movement to spend less energy criticizing their Spanish comrades and more in constructive direct solidarity.) Though with increasingly less conviction, she even portrays the more militant of these steps as the beginning of social revolution outside of Spain as well. Also against her own experience and better judgement, she appeals for mass pressure to force the "liberal democratic regimes" of the West to see the anti-fascist struggle in Spain as essential for their own survival as well.[12] Needless to say, she is hardly surprised, though ever more bitter, when these governments consistently refused any supportive intervention. Increasingly Goldman describes all the governments (including France, Britain and the United States, as well as the Soviet Union) as essentially gliding toward fascism themselves, thus eliminating any prior significant distinctions. It is this perspective, in turn, which leaves her unwilling to support the Western Allies in World War II.*

## International Significance of the Spanish Anti-Fascist Civil War and the Politics of "Neutrality"

†*Less than two weeks after the civil war begins, to writer John Cowper Powys (7/31/36) Goldman emphasizes Spanish determination to halt the spread of fascist dictatorship.*

12. Of course, Goldman doubted that liberal democratic regimes ever were very responsive to public pressure. Worse yet, she also perceived them as ready to permit the rise of fascism abroad and then, when it grew to a clearly dangerous level, to use it as an excuse for launching massive war—thus conveniently escaping the impossible political and economic plight of the Great Depression.

Yes, the dictatorships, they are like a frightful epidemic, they infest the whole world. Now it is Spain. If it should succeed in spreading its poison, France will be next and so will England. No wonder the Left elements are making such an heroic struggle in Spain. True many of them fight Fascism only to put another form of dictatorship in its place. . . . [The Spanish anarchists] alone still believe Liberty worth fighting and dying for and they alone have the passionate faith in its ultimate triumph. But for the present the world has been made bleak by dictatorship whatever its color or claims.

† *In her second radio speech from Barcelona aimed at English-speaking audiences abroad (9/30/36), Goldman denounces the tragic farce of politicians proclaiming neutrality in the struggle against fascism — and a most unbalanced neutrality at that. Already she foresees the disastrous broader war which will result from such appeasement.*

This old proverb ["whom the gods would destroy they must first strike mad"] has proved true in more than one instance in human history. It also applies most forcibly to the political leaders of today. They maintain that neutrality to the heroic struggle of the Spanish masses will stave off a new world conflagration. Now it is only too true that political leaders and statesmen have seldom demonstrated clear thinking when confronted with calamitous issues. But, in their attitude towards the struggle in Spain, the gods seem to have done their job more deliberately than before.

Were it only a question of a score of politicians one would have no cause for alarm. Unfortunately they are at the helm of state. And their decisions motivated by utter mental confusion as well as criminal willfulness will not only not prevent a new world carnage. They actually are hastening the new holocaust whose flames are likely to be more devastating than the last.

One might grant the politicians some modicum of reason had they taken a neutral stand against both contending forces in the civil war in Spain. It is the one-sidedness of their attitude which makes one question both the sanity and the integrity of the neutrality sponsors. Their stand is the more reprehensible because the Spanish masses are the first to have risen against the Fascist foe who has already taken root in a large part of Europe and, if not stopped, will do so in the rest of the world. Verily the Gods grind slowly but surely.

Hitler and his savage gang found their inning in the utter madness of the so-called [Versailles] peace treaty and their best support in the criminal indifference on the part of all governments to his reign of terror. This and this alone gave National-Socialism time and impetus to perfect the deadly military machine. Not only the swastika but also Hitler's heavy boot is to be planted on the neck of Europe and Asia, as it has been planted on the neck of the entire hapless German people.

Also, politicians never forget or learn anything. Else they would realize that by their neutrality to the Spanish defenders of liberty they are rendering [to] Spanish Fascism precisely the same service they have given to other Fascist powers. They are doing more, they are helping to create a formidable Fascist alliance that, if successful, would fetter the spirit of freedom for many decades.

Curiously enough the loudest sponsors of neutrality proclaim that democracy must be maintained at all costs. Yet they fail to see that democracy never was in graver danger and that neutrality, if maintained much longer, will stab democracy in the back.

Does any intelligent man or woman imagine that the two star Fascist lords are giving Franco and Mola[13] such generous supports in armaments and money out of love for them? Certainly they have been promised lucrative returns for their cooperation which is to enable Spanish adventurers to drown the Spanish people in a sea of blood. Hitler and Mussolini, whose ambitions are so modest, want a mere bagatelle. Just the largest part of the Mediterranean and the Pyrenees as their bulwark and with their cannons directed on France. This would of course put Hitler and Mussolini in a world key position.

Will France go back on her glorious revolutionary past by her tacit consent to such designs? Will England, with centuries of liberal tradition, acquiesce to such a degrading position? And if not, will that not mean a new world carnage?

In other words, the very thing the proclaimers of neutrality are hoping to prevent will occur. And only lack of clear perception can remain blind to its danger. Quite another thing would happen, if the anti-Fascists were helped to cope with the Fascist epidemic in Spain that is poisoning all the springs of life and health. Fascism exterminated in Spain would also mean the purified waters in the rest of Europe and the end of Fascism in Europe would do away with the causes of war. The workers of the rest of the world and other liberty loving groups inspired by the new social experiment of their brothers in Spain would be enabled to begin a new transformation of their own life.

It is about neutrality as it is about people who can stand by a burning building with women and children calling for help, without moving a muscle to come to their aid. Or to see a drowning man desperately trying to reach shore. No words of condemnation could possibly express the universal contempt for such cowardly indifference. Fortunately there are not many such creatures. In time of fire, floods, storms at sea or the sight of any fellow-creatures in distress, human nature usually is at its best. Men in danger to their

---

13. General Emilio Mola (1887-1937) was one of the top Spanish military officers involved in plotting, organizing and leading the Nationalist rebellion of July 1936. He later died in a plane crash in the North, thereby eliminating Franco's one major rival.

own lives and limbs rush into burning houses, throw themselves into the foaming sea and bravely carry their brothers to safety.

Spain is in flames, the Fascist conflagration is spreading. Is it possible that the world outside will stand by and see the country laid in ashes by the Fascist hordes? Or will thinking and justice-loving people muster up enough courage to break through the ban of neutrality and come to the rescue of the Spanish people who are fighting Fascism to the bitter end?

I have faith in humanity. I have infinite faith. I know the governments come and go. But the intrinsic quality of human feeling and the sense of justice remains forever.

It is to these that the heroic people of Spain appeal for help, for the means to bring Fascism to its knees and save the world from the new impending holocaust neutrality is certain to bring in its wake.

*† Goldman offers reasons for the delay in Soviet intervention in this 11/14/36 letter to her niece.*

Apropos of Russia, darling, I hate to disappoint you. Russia never does anything "handsomely." If she really had any sympathy with the struggle of the anti-Fascist forces here she would have acted four months ago. That was the time when the war against Fascism would have been successful and thousands of lives would have been saved. She waited because she did not dare go against the Powers.[14] And if she finally acted it is to pose as truly sympathetic to the Spanish. Actually, however, it was again to throw sand in the eyes of the dissatisfied and disgruntled elements within. Since the murder of the sixteen cowardly men,[15] Stalin has lost prestige among his own comrades all over the world and most of all in Russia itself. Something was needed to counteract that opposition, hence the sudden love of Spain. Rather late I fear.

*† In this 12/1/36 article written for the CNT-FAI information bulletin, Goldman points out how the foreign press distorts the nature of the Spanish struggle, thus discouraging international support.*

The bourgeois press, always the mouthpiece of capitalism, is rejoicing openly over the mere thought of a Fascist victory in Spain. Franco, the butcher of thousands of innocent men, women and children in every city and hamlet seized by his savage hordes, is their hero. His march on Madrid and the blood drunken orgy he will inaugurate should he succeed in entering the Spanish capital are already being brazenly hailed in nearly every newspaper in the world. One expects such glee from the capitalist scribes in Fascist countries,

14. See footnote 14 at back of chapter.
15. She refers here to the sixteen former top-level Bolshevik leaders who "confessed" to treason at the purge trials of August 1936 and were executed. See footnote 17 of Chapter V.

or even the reactionary press in democracies. But to find the same sadistic glee in the loud proclaimers of high democratic principles merely proves that they are more Fascist than the Fascists. They hate with an implacable hatred the least change of the old order. Indeed, so black is their hatred of social and human progress and consequently so stark their fear that the most intelligent among them become incapable to distinguish facts from fiction.

A case in point is the London *Observer*. Its editor, by no means a fool, seems to have lost all his critical judgment of the real issue involved in the struggle between the anti-Fascist forces and the group of adventurers led by Franco. In an editorial of the *Observer* of October 25th, entitled: "Which Flag? Madrid and Moscow," he makes it appear that the popular uprising in Spain was staged by Soviet Russia. And that its aims are nothing else but the dictatorship of the Third International. Had this man but taken the trouble to send one of his intelligent correspondents (if there is such a breed among newspaper men) to investigate the real situation in Spain, he would soon have had all the data needed to prove the utter stupidity of his perverted notion about [the] origin and purpose of the Spanish Revolution.

In point of truth, the adherents of the Soviet regime in the anti-Fascist united front represent the smallest group. The rest of the political alignments of the Spanish struggle for social and economic freedom are not only *not* backed by Moscow. They are damned with faint praise.

The superior value of the Spanish Revolution over nearly all other such uprooting historical events consists in the fact that it sprung from the loins of the people themselves, and by their inner urge and will to freedom from the crushing yoke they had endured so long. The Revolution is a mass avalanche and not the device of one or more leaders who have planned its sweep. The hope and the security of the Spanish Revolution lies in the villages with their awakened peasantry and in every factory and workshop where Spanish toilers produce the wealth of the country. No one outstanding personality is at the helm of the gigantic social and political transformation that has been conditioned by the heroic July battle. It is therefore the height of folly and deliberate falsification to say, as the editor of the *Observer* does, that "the red regime under Largo Caballero represents nothing but the desperate minority of Communists, Anarchists and Extremists of other stripes." Or that "Franco is already sure of three quarters of the country, backed by a growing majority of the population." One must indeed be stricken blind, deaf and dumb to thus pervert the actual state of affairs in Spain.

Of course, the editor of the *Observer* knows as well as we do that there is not a scintilla of truth in his whole editorial. He is not stupid. He is merely a good servant of capitalism and Fascist interests. Hence his hatred of the Spanish Revolution and his love for Franco. It is said: "Birds of one feather, flock together."

For the heroic people of Spain, engaged in a life and death struggle against

these black vultures, it is important to know their enemies. And they are not only the Spanish Fascists aided by their worthy colleagues in the profession of wholesale butchery. Our enemies are also in democratic countries and their satraps who poison public opinion by daily outpourings of their venom against the Spanish masses and their magnificent revolutionary struggle.

† *Back in London, Goldman finds it difficult to reach large numbers of the British to convince them of their government's* de facto *alliance with the fascists (2/8/37 letter to Mark Mratchny).*

All in all, the situation in Spain is not very bright. True, the Spanish people have almost superhuman courage; their power of endurance is like nothing that was demonstrated before, but how can they possibly hold out against a numerical force such as Franco represents — not to speak of his superior arms? The talk of non-intervention and of "volunteers" is certainly among the most outrageous hypocrisy.

Still, the democratic countries are jabboring about these things, while Germany and Italy continue to pour in tens of thousands of trained soldiers.[16] It should be obvious to the blind that not only Hitler and Mussolini but Mr. Blum and Mr. Baldwin[17] are in league in their intentions to crush the anti-Fascist struggle and to drown in the blood of the Spanish people the magnificent beginnings of a new social structure. It is like crying in the wilderness to make the masses in this country [England] see the frightful treachery against the Spanish people. . . . On the other hand, I realize how necessary it is to be heard about Spain — if only by a negligible minority.

† *Two weeks later (2/26/37), Goldman bitterly reiterates her view of British and French complicity, contrasting it with the outrage expressed two decades earlier at the violation of neutral Belgium (letter to Robert [?]).*

I wonder, dear Robert, whether you still cling to your agreement with non-intervention. Surely your intelligence and your fair-mindedness must by this time have realized the outrageous treachery of the Blum government. The treachery to his own conception of socialism and to the Spanish as well as to the French workers. If the man were a fool or an ignoramus, one might explain the denial of the right of the Spanish government to purchase armaments and to enlist the cooperation of real volunteers, and not those driven like sheep by Hitler's and Mussolini's whips; but for a man of Blum's intelligence, it is downright treachery to sponsor non-intervention. The man

16. See footnote 39 in Chapter IV.
17. British Prime Minister Stanley Baldwin.

must know that a political move which condones one side of the struggle to a fight with bare hands, while it permits the other side to be supplied with men in their tens of thousands and modern machinery of warfare, is nothing but a fake, a delusion and a snare.

Many people have realized that already. Alas, they are still a small minority compared with the dense masses that never see through the machinations of politicians. But it is certain the conspiracy of France and Great Britain against the supreme effort of the Spanish people to exterminate Fascism will stand out in history as one of the greatest crimes ever committed.

Forgive me, dear friend, if I seem too harsh, but the outrageous invasion of Spain by Germany and Italy, now joined by all the Powers, cries to the very heavens to revenge a cruel attitude. Talk about the injustice of the invasion of Belgium![18] It falls into insignificance compared with the invasion of Spain on land and sea and air; and yet the invasion of Belgium rouses millions of people to sacrifice the very flower of its country; to wound and mutilate 20,000,000 who escaped death in that so-called "War to end War," the war for Democracy, while the invasion of Spain leaves some of the most intelligent and generous people, like yourselves, coldly indifferent. I cannot understand that, dear Robert. I can only hope that the injustice of the latest move of the Powers has helped you to change your mind and your attitude.

Surely you must see by this time that the present embargo is not going to end in the tacit acceptance of the Spanish people on one side, nor the avaricious designs of Germany and Italy of planting their heavy heels on the possessions of Spain, as well as England and France. And what else but a new world-conflagration can possibly result out of it? That the Spanish united [anti-] Fascist forces have no intention to yield easily, they have demonstrated by their defense of Madrid. Think of a people, poorly equipped with arms, and with very little experience in warfare, driving back an enemy so formidable in numbers and arms!

Can it be possible that the democratic countries will not only stand by, but actually participate in the slaughter of millions? For that is actually what is going to happen if the invaders are to conquer Spain: it will mean the slaughter of millions—bear that in mind.

† *In this public commentary on the role of the Left press (5/19/37), Goldman finds it as fearful of, thus actively malicious toward the Spanish struggle as the Tory press itself.*

To find falsifications in the Tory press of the position and activities of the CNT-FAI is by no means surprising. To them the anti-Fascist struggle is

18. By Germany in World War I.

anathema enough. But the National Confederation of Labour and the Anarchist Federation of Iberia are worse than the red cloth to the bull. Tories and their mouthpiece, the press, have been known to adjust themselves to republics or so-called democratic governments. But the possibility of a society that will have none of a deadly state machine is too far removed from the cramped and warped Tory mind. And as all fear is motivated by ignorance, the Tory papers and their scribes must needs be terrified by the CNT-FAI whose supreme effort is directed towards the creation of a non-governmental social life.

Unfortunately one finds the same inhibitions in the so-called Left papers. They, too, fear the CNT-FAI and their dominant influence on the Catalan people. They try desperately to silence the achievement of the Spanish Revolution and its socialized work. From time to time the Left papers grudgingly say something about the CNT-FAI. Mostly it is garbled and misleading. Believing this to be the case rather than intentional lying I have written to these newspapers to correct their statements. But as they studiously refused to publish my protests I have come to the conclusion that the Left press is as dishonest as the Right and that the CNT-FAI is as much a thorn in their flesh as they are in the Franco confreres. This attitude on the part of the British Leftists is proof positive that the CNT-FAI represent the only champions of the Revolution in Spain and that they are the only organizations that have done with the farce of capitalist democracies. The CNT-FAI is in action on two fronts, the anti-Fascist war and the defense of the Revolution. That is why they are hated by all sides and loved by the masses whose ideal is COMUNISMO LIBERTARIO, Libertarian Communism.

† *Western "non-intervention" permitted Franco's forces to keep their lifeblood of Italian and Nazi support. In Goldman's view it also forced Spanish anti-Fascists to depend on Soviet aid, thus assuring constant attacks on the social revolution within the Loyalist camp itself (11/11/37 letter to "Comrade").*

As to the masses at large, they were, of course, carried away by the "solidarity" of comrade Stalin. But they too have learned that his "generous" help to the Spanish people was that of the usurer who makes capital out of the dire needs of his clients and, once in his clutches, the struggle and strangle hold continues far beyond the value of the aid rendered the victim of the money lender. And if that strangle hold continues it is entirely due to the criminal alliance of the so-called democratic countries and the non-intervention agreement, for it is certain that if the anti-Fascist forces could have freely purchased arms for Spain, Stalin could never have laid his crushing hand on the Spanish Revolution, nor could his satraps have infested the whole political life of Spain. Even at this late hour, Stalin's rule in Spain would collapse

like a house of cards if the still-born child of Blum were buried at last. It was non-intervention, now exposed to the world in all its farcical and lying hypocrisy, and nothing else that forced our comrades to make the compromises that they have made.

†*Energized again by her second visit to revolutionary Spain, Goldman informs comrade Helmut Rüdiger (11/24/37) that after a few days in London she is reminded once more of the difficulties there for organizing effective solidarity.*

I came back with all sorts of plans to help our Spanish comrades, but a few days in London have already paralyzed my energies. The longer I live and work here, the more convinced I am that England is sterile ground for our ideas. The self-sufficiency of the average English person is beyond belief. What is more to the point: I find the workers even more indifferent than many members of the middle class.

*It is true that there are many discontented elements among the workers. But contrary to experience in the United States, they do not attend independently-organized meetings. However she plans one last effort to reach them, by sending a letter on the Spanish cause to some 15,000 local branches of the various trade unions.*

†*One month later (12/30/37), Goldman complains to Rudolf Rocker that the British Labour Party's supposed new support for republican Spain fails to include support for the revolution. The Labour Party and the trade unions hate the anarchists. They would probably rather have reactionaries in Spain than even to mention the CNT-FAI. At their large public gathering in London on the 19th, they enthusiastically praised the "liberal government" in Spain but said nothing about the anarchists or their role.*
*Even ILP locals are sabotaging efforts to publicize the CNT-FAI, despite the positive individual contributions by members like Fenner Brockway, Reginald Reynolds and Ethel Mannin.*

†*Writing to Spanish anarchist leaders Mariano Vázquez and Pedro Herrera on 2/14/38, Goldman describes the encouragement she felt from a huge London meeting organized by the Communists the night before in support of China and the boycott of Japan.*[19]

. . . It was very gratifying to me to see the response and enthusiasm whenever the anti-Fascist struggle was mentioned. This leads me to believe

19. She refers to the response against the Japanese invasion and occupation of China, beginning in 1931 and greatly expanded in 1937.

that there is a tremendous feeling for Spain; but how to organize that feeling into direct action—that is the problem. I am as certain as I can be that it will continue to be a problem until we have created some kind of Anarcho-Syndicalist or anti-Fascist movement here.

*†A sobering letter to Martin Gudell a month later (3/24/38) informs him of other factors behind continued difficulty in gaining significant British support.*

The reason for our poor results [in Britain] are two-fold. First, the numerous Spain aid organisations and groups under different names, yet exclusively Communists, have worn the people out in giving. Secondly is the fact that Spain is no longer of such insistent news as it was months ago, especially since the invasion of Austria and the frightful results of it there.[20] Lastly is the reactionary tendency of the Labour Party and the Trade Unions.

*The British government has decided that it needs Labour Party support for a new arms program and she fully expects Labour leaders to go along.*

*† In this May 1938 published article, Goldman places British and French appeasement in Spain within a broader framework of capitalist plans to restore economic prosperity by forcing new worldwide military conflict.*

Again the European sky is black and sinister with impending war. The powers that breathe war and their allies who grow rich on the implements of death and destruction are again competing with each other. The cry for armaments, more deadly machines, more devastating explosives, greater manpower, a mightier navy, again rent the air. The shibboleths used in the last world conflagration to deceive the masses are again to serve the warmongers of the day in their conspiracy to lead the masses to slaughter. "The War to end War," "the war for Democracy." What a lying face was hidden under the hideous mask of democracy.

. . . . . . . . . . . . . . . . . . . . . . . . . . . . . . . . . . . . . . . . . . . . . . . . . .

[Among many in Europe the] clamour for peace is only bringing nearer and nearer the black spectre of war which will again engulf the world in a new sea of blood and tears.

One of these perfectly senseless ideas of peace entertained by many well-meaning people outside the charlatans at the helm of the state is non-intervention in Spain. Today, even the most weak mentally are beginning to

20. On March 12-13, 1938, Germany invaded Austria and annexed it to the Reich. Immediately, all Jews, freemasons, liberals and radicals who did not flee or kill themselves were forced to concentration camps or murdered.

grasp the fact that non-intervention in anti-Fascist Spain has been the greatest loan to the Fascist side and has already prepared the stakes of the coming conflagration. The villains in this world drama are the democratic countries, England and France. They have, and are still, playing the most despicable role.

It can at least be said of the Fascist megalomaniacs, Mussolini and Hitler, they have openly and brazenly boasted of their alliance with Franco. Nor have they minced matters in the support they have given him in arms and men to better enable their hireling to crush the Spanish people. The hypocritical measures were left to the British and French democracies. The National government, originally supported in the non-intervention policy by the British Labour Party, and the old Socialist Blum supported by the Popular Front, under cover of their love of peace, have worked right into the hands of Franco and incidentally have paved the way for a new war, more devastating than the last. In other words the democratic countries and the workers' "fatherland" have outdone Judas in their black treachery of the heroic Spanish people. No, not for the pitiable biblical 30 pieces of silver are they helping to crucify the Spanish workers and peasants; their stakes are higher, much higher. Nothing less than the rehabilitation of their imperialist power and wealth will satisfy these pseudo-democrats.[21] It is for this and this alone that Spain is permitted to bleed to death, and the rest of the world brought closer to the nightmare of another world holocaust.

†*Writing to longtime friend and comrade Rose Pesotta (5/3/38), Goldman views the Labour Party and Tories as equally treacherous. Harold Laski,[22] Herbert Morrison,[23] Attlee and the rest are all social climbers. Their concern with their own careers and their general complacency have left the Labour Party in a basically reactionary position. In power this party, like the Conservatives, would be merely servants of the capitalists.*

*She finds one encouraging sign in publication of a new book.*

. . . George Orwell, one of the young writers, has just had his book [*Homage to Catalonia*] published on his experience in Spain. He was at the front eight months. His book, aside of being of great dramatic and literary value, exposes

---

21. See footnote 21 at back of chapter.
22. Harold Laski was a well-known political science professor at the London School of Economics from 1920 on and a prominent intellectual figure in the Labour Party's developing interpretation of "democratic socialism."
23. Herbert Morrison was active in the Labour Party from 1914 and first elected to parliament in 1923. Quickly moving to a very influential role in the party, he competed with Clement Attlee for its leadership and strongly pushed it in a pragmatic reformist direction. He held important Cabinet posts in Churchill's wartime coalition government and was the Deputy Prime Minister under Attlee and Labour leader in the House of Commons following that party's victory in 1945.

the conspiracy against our people and the dreadful sabotage carried on by the Communists last May. I wish that book could circulate in tens of thousands of copies.

†*Two days later, she reports to Vázquez on problems of large conferences organized by others for their own purposes. But also she finds a rising grassroots enthusiasm for direct-action solidarity. The immediate occasion for these comments was an emergency London conference on the Spanish civil war (4/23/38) which she attended despite serious misgivings.*[24]

It did not take me long to realize that the conference was to a large extent packed by the Communists (*bona fide* delegates) or by those whom they sent and who did not represent anyone, and that the main purpose of the conference was to use Spain as the peg on which to hang the call for a popular front. True, there were a number of trade union delegates and some from the co-operatives. All honor to them.

*It was only the latter elements who showed interest in direct action, such as a general strike. The others spoke only of replacing Chamberlain's Conservative government[25] and were completely silent on the role of the CNT. Though Goldman submitted her name as a delegate with proposals, she was completely ignored. Nevertheless, she finds encouragement in the apparent awakening of the working class, especially certain of the rank-and-file engineers, miners and workers in the aircraft industry and transportation.*

†*Goldman tells Harry Kelly (6/17/38) that she is not surprised at Roosevelt's unwillingness to lift the U.S. ban on sales to Spain. But she is much more indignant when representatives of the mass British labor movement bridle the militancy of the base.*

Yes, it is sad that a man like Roosevelt should be the one to block the move to lift the embargo,[26] but it seems that he has done many things contradictory to his starting point. Surely you and I need not be surprised at that. There never has been a man in power who can stand out for long against the power of reaction.[27] Besides, why expect the impossible from Roosevelt who is, after all,

24. Ethel Mannin, a delegate alongside Goldman at this "Save Spain" conference, describes it in more detail in *Spain and the World,* April 29, 1938.
25. Neville Chamberlain first was elected to parliament in 1918. He participated in Conservative government cabinets and emerged as a major party figure from 1922 to 1929. From 1931 to 1935 he was Chancellor of the Exchequer, then in 1937 succeeded Baldwin as Prime Minister. Following the 1940 German invasion of Norway, his appeasement-oriented government collapsed.
26. See footnote 26 at back of chapter.
27. See footnote 27 at back of chapter.

born and bred in the most conservative traditions? What is the suffering of the Spanish people to him? In point of truth, I am no longer so indignant over anything Roosevelt and his class does. I am much more outraged at the cowardice of people who call themselves Labour: the Citrines, the Attlees and the rest. They have risen on the shoulders of Labour, they have gained tradition and renown at the expense of the working class, and all they do is to jabber in the House of Commons. Even when the masses are willing to break loose, to strike the necessary blow on behalf of their heroic comrades in Spain, they are kept in check. It is a sorry picture indeed. Imagine, in the Oslo International Trade Union Conference,[28] Citrine boasted that 20 million workers were represented there. Yet these 20 million workers remain inert and do nothing to come to the rescue of their Spanish brothers. A boycott, an embargo, not for Spain: against Japan, yes. The reason for the difference is only too obvious. The British Government is interested in the Sino-Japanese war. Therefore a boycott against Japan may be introduced; but not against Franco. The whole situation would be the worst farce if it were not so tragic.


†*Five days later (6/22/38), Goldman expresses to Rüdiger her anger at the new international farce of "non-intervention" and the British effort to bring a truce in Spain.*

Yes, it again looks desperate in Spain. And now the agreement of the government gangsters including Russia, all agreed on choking off the life stream of Spain. We know what their so-called agreement means, their control of only some ports with the land route free [for] Italian and German supplies to continue. And the suggested truce?[29] How can there be such a thing with Franco?

*She feels sick at the prospects of hypocritical Britain posing as a peaceful mediator, one which will probably succeed in convincing the Negrín regime and selling out the anarchists.*


†*As Goldman points out in this 1/30/39 letter to Mark Mratchny, at his liberal best in foreign policy, Roosevelt is still a man of words, not action.*

Yes, perhaps it is our growing age that we are so easily satisfied with the very

---

28. The Oslo International Trade Union Conference was a gathering of those national trade union bodies, like the TUC in Britain headed by Citrine, committed to the general perspective of the Second International. In 1938, the TUC voted to boycott all handling of trade for Japan.
29. In June 1938, the international Non-Intervention Committee in London, including the Soviet delegate, agreed to follow a British plan for neutral observers in Spanish ports who would supervise and enumerate the withdrawal of foreigners from both sides of the Civil War. At the same time, Britain worked to attempt to establish a truce between both sides, a move encouraged by Negrín himself.

things we once repudiated – so I am not so surprised that you rejoice over the stand of the State Department protecting Ickes against the demands of Hitler that he should be held responsible for daring to attack the unholy man.[30] It may also be that we see so much horror and injustice about that we are thankful to the fates if we see even the smallest sign of justice and decency. I too am very glad indeed that my erstwhile country has shown greater pride in dealing with the Nazis than Great Britain has;[31] but on the other hand reaction seems to be rampant in America and it is by no means changed by the high sounding phrases made by the President and his cabinet. More immediate action for Spain and less words and sympathy would still save the harrowing situation there.

†*Feeling bitter defeat from the fall of Barcelona to Franco, Goldman expresses (2/9/39 letter to an anonymous friend) her outrage at those who appeased their consciences through sending supplies to Spain yet who did nothing to prevent the British government from maintaining its* de facto *alliance with fascism.*

It was impossible to hold out [in Barcelona] against the overwhelming physical force of Franco, in addition to starvation which ended the last four days in actual famine. All that only intensifies the deep tragedy of the tens of thousands of heroic people literally forsaken by the whole world. O yes, many of the ladies and gentlemen in this country who have been sending food and medical supplies to Spain, thereby soothing their own guilty conscience, because they permitted Mr. Chamberlain and the National government to work directly into the hands of Franco, Germany and Italy. They all talked in Parliament while sitting in their comfortable seats and knowing full well that their wives and children will be safe, and that no one of their own will go hungry. Sympathy is the cheapest thing in the world.

†*In this 2/17/39 letter to American friend Lillian Nedelsohn (Mendelsohn), Goldman reports that anti-fascist Spanish still face international manipulations, only now as refugees. She also assesses French Prime Minister Daladier, Roosevelt and others, in the context of rising European tensions.*

As to the horrible condition of the refugees, for myself I should have preferred death at Franco's hand rather than to be exposed to the horrors of tramping the road from Barcelona to the French border, cold, starved and under constant bombardment, and then to be placed in a perfect hellhole of concentra-

---

30. See footnote 30 at back of chapter.
31. See footnote 31 at back of chapter.

tion camps and treated like criminals[32] — that is the hardest thing to bear for me, and I know for many of the comrades the insult and the humiliation they are subjected to must be greater agony than even the hunger and the cold.

. . . . . . . . . . . . . . . . . . . . . . . . . . . . . . . . . . . . . . . . . . . . . . . . . . .

Tens of thousands of refugees, while granted "asylum" by the French authorities, are being kept as prisoners under the most appalling conditions. What will become of them when England and France recognize Franco's rule I cannot contemplate, and what country will let them in if they should want to settle anywhere? Already some of the French papers write "that the Anarchists and undesirables will have to be disposed of." The same writers are good enough to say that for the rest of the refugees they should be put in the French Army, "surely they will want to show their gratitude for the hospitality given them by our Government." It is all so tragic and one is so terribly helpless to do anything really vital.

. . . I can see that Lore again believes very much in the state if he can be sympathetic to Daladier because of what he learned from Bullitt and Kennedy.[33] I do not know what it can possibly be that should induce anyone who is clear-headed about the function of the state to believe in Daladier. He is not only a rank reactionary, but the coward to boot. It was he who was responsible for the wanton slaughter of the men during the demonstration in 1936[34] and it is he who is entirely the tool of the large industrialists in France, particularly the Comité des Forges[35] and all the munition manufacturers. True, he fears nothing so much as to hurt the feelings of Mr. Chamberlain and the National government, but that is not the only reason for having broken the general strike and for being determined to serve only his master class. While I should never charge Bullitt with being a coward, I do charge him with being a careerist. True, he was once in sympathy with the Russian Revolution and for a long time after served Stalin as he served Lenin before, but the moment he

---

32. The French government admitted hundreds of thousands of Spanish refugees after the collapse of Catalonia only on condition that they submit to the full control of French authorities — which meant concentration camps in southern France for the overwhelming majority. These were "simply open spaces of sand dunes near the sea, enclosed by barbed wire. Men dug holes for themselves like animals, to find some shelter" (Thomas, *The Spanish Civil War*, p. 576). Neglect of the wounded and the lack of food, water, sanitation and shelter was appalling. As Thomas states, "it is certain that the French Government hoped, by neglect, to force as many as possible of the refugees to throw themselves on General Franco's mercy" (p. 576).
33. See footnote 33 at back of chapter.
34. She perhaps refers here to the March 1937 Clichy affair, where police fired into a crowd of Popular Front demonstrators against a meeting of the French fascist organization, the PSF. At least 5 were killed and 150 wounded. The Blum government was attacked by the Left as a repetition of the Noske Socialist regime in late 1918 and early 1919 Germany, which cooperated with right-wing police and the military to suppress the rising left-wing revolutionary momentum.
35. The trade association of the French iron and steel industry, a major behind-the-scenes political force in the French Third Republic and publisher of Paris' leading afternoon newpaper, *Le Temps*.

saw the greater advantages of serving the United States he acquiesced without much compunction. You can therefore see that there is no reliance on Bullitt's having changed not only his skin but also his character. As for Kennedy I do not know him and therefore do not feel justified in writing about him. I do know, however, that he is an official and undoubtedly carries out the orders of the State Department. How then can any clear-headed man, which Lore is supposed to be, believe anything he gets from those quarters? . . .

As regards Roosevelt I think the man began with good intentions, but soon proved that he lacks the stamina to hold out against Wall Street and against the military clique who want war for the sake of war. That of course also includes the Du Ponts, the Westinghouses and all the other merchants of death. Not for a moment do I believe in Roosevelt's real desire to avert war. On the contrary his latest [statement], even if he were not properly quoted, that the American frontier is in France proves that he is in no way different from the Chamberlains, Daladiers and the dictators of the Fascist countries. They are all obsessed by competing with each other in unheard of rearmaments, although they must be conscious that this is the very thing which will unavoidably lead to a new world conflagration. On the other hand are the isolationists. They also know where their bread is buttered. They know that to strengthen American imperialism they must keep America out of any European entanglement, for it will be easier to gather the spoils while Europe is wading in blood.

† *Ten days later (2/27/39), Goldman admonishes Mariano Vázquez for suggesting that to win support from Western democracies Spanish anarchists should have de-emphasized the social revolution even more.*

I was not only shocked but I was amazed at the amount of shortsightedness on your part this implies. It seems to me, dear comrade, that if this is the main lesson you have gathered from your struggle and the awful amount of sacrifice you have made, then you should discard your belief in revolution altogether and never again call yourselves libertarians.

*The only way to appease capitalism is to abandon the essence of revolution, as the Russian example shows well. Not only has it brought capitalism—Fascist and democratic—to seek favors from Stalin, it also paralyzed the potentially decisive role of the international working class. When Stalin proclaimed the Spanish struggle as merely an effort to assure democracy, why should the workers have been interested? That was the slogan of World War I which succeeded in killing or wounding 30 million and only tightened their chains.*

*Essentially democracy and Fascism are the same. Of course, she prefers the slight political liberties under the former to none at all. But this is little compared to the great revolutionary constructive beginning in Spain. However this inspiring*

*example was hidden from the international proletariat by the Communists' reform-
ist appeals and by their slander of the anarchists.*

*It is probably true that no revolution in a single country can succeed without the
active support of workers internationally. However, to seek to appease world
capitalism instead is gradually and inevitably to compromise one's revolutionary
vitality and vision, a result sure to alienate workers abroad.*


† *One day later she repeats to Milly Rocker her outrage at French and British treatment of the Spanish.*

It's all too terrible to bear this tragic defeat of so glowing a beginning. How
rotten France has proven itself, how unspeakably inhuman in the treatment of
the refugees and in the brazen hurry to recognise Franco.[36] As to England, I
have no words to express my loathing of Chamberlain, the Labour and trade
union leaders, and the people themselves.


† *In a final public speech in London (3/24/39), Goldman summarizes her indictment of the roles of Britain, France, Russia and the United States in opening the
door to fascism in Spain and thus to the rest of the world.*

. . . Certainly I am indignant against the invasion of Austria or
Czechoslovakia, but I cannot be more indignant than I have been all this time
against the deliberate betrayal, the deliberate assassination of the Spanish
struggle and the Spanish people. I go further, I insist that it was the assassination of the Spanish Revolution and the Spanish struggle against Fascism
which increased the sadistic lust of Hitler to invade Austria and
Czechoslovakia; for it was the example given by the democracies, by Britain,
by France and by my own erstwhile country, the United States, which made
Hitler realise that he could get away with murder and nobody would stop him.
It was the defeat of Spain, it was the attitude of Great Britain and of France
against Spain which made the German Nazis realise that there would be no
protest except when it injures the pockets of the British Empire or the French
Government or of any government. It is for this reason that Hitler can now
march through Europe and leave death and destruction behind. So why this
hypocrisy? Why do Labour papers like the *Daily Herald* and the *Chronicle*
and the others fight now and insist on the necessity of resisting the invasion of
Hitler even by means of arms? In other words, the British government with all
its hangers-on and the French government are now willing to turn the whole

36. Following the Munich Pact with Germany in September 1938, France was ready to abandon
   any remaining entangling ambiguities in Spain as well. In early 1939, it sought to establish
   recognition of Franco's government, a step accomplished simultaneously with Britain on
   February 27.

world into a vale of tears and blood, to destroy once more millions of men on the battlefield or to maim them for life; they are willing to have war now in order to stop Hitler. Had they been willing to help the Spanish people in their struggle, there would have been no necessity for a world war, which we are going to have whether we like it or not.

Why was this done? It is perfectly plain to anyone who can think. Don't you see, friends, in Spain there was a social revolution on the 19th of July 1936. The people had risen spontaneously, as you were told, to fight back not only Fascism – that of course was the first incentive – but also to fight back capitalism, to attempt in Spain to fulfill that which the Russian Revolution had not fulfilled, because the Russian Revolution was slain, was murdered by those in power in Russia today. Because the Spanish people dared to rise against the whole world, dared to rise against all the empires of the world, the empires of the world have sworn not to rest until the Spanish Revolution will be stifled in the blood of the Spanish people, and they work day and night to achieve it. I need not tell you what your own Empire did, what the Chamberlains did, and the present government, in supporting the Non-Intervention Pact which meant the most outrageous intervention in the struggle of the Spanish people. . . .

. . . [Russian agents in Spain] changed their slogan from "Workers of the world, unite," into "Democracies of the world, unite." "Democracy and Peace" became the slogan of Russia, and she imposed it upon the Spanish people in Spain.

I do not suppose that you have realised, some of you, that in the last analysis democracy means Fascism in disguise. You do not have Fascism in this country. You are supposed to have democracy in England: better consult India and Africa and the Arabs and all the other people, and they will tell you that your Empire and your democracy are covering the same kind of crimes and sins and horrors that exist in Germany or anywhere else. That of course does not excuse Germany, but it is necessary to open the eyes of people to realise that what is called democracy and peace today is nothing but an illusion and a snare.

So the Russian government began its work, its sinister work, its insidious work in Spain against the militant workers, against the Confederation of Labour, against the Anarchist Federation of Iberia. Everything had to be done in order to make it impossible for the Anarchists to conquer the situation. So there were sabotage, imprisonment, brutal methods of people vanishing off the earth without ever being found, and all the other methods so successfully practised by Stalin in Russia.

. . . . . . . . . . . . . . . . . . . . . . . . . . . . . . . . . . . . . . . . . . . . . . . . .

I said that the democracies and Russia were more afraid of the Revolution, more afraid of the workers of Spain than they were even of Franco, and that is why they supported Franco right and left, and it is precisely for the same

reason that the Spanish refugees are treated worse than criminals, like wild beasts. . . . Don't you see that the French government is hounding, persecuting and torturing the Spanish refugees in order to force them to go back to Franco, and that it is indifferent to the suffering of the Spanish refugees because the mass of the Spanish refugees are still Anarchists, are still revolutionists.

. . . The people in the camps who are known to be Anarchists, who are known to be Anarcho-Syndicalists, receive no help from the money collected in this country for Spanish relief. I am glad that anybody receives relief. I do not want people to be discriminated against. I do not care whether anyone is a Catholic or a Communist or a working man or a middle class man, if he is in distress, hounded, persecuted, his liberty fettered, his freedom encroached upon – I stand for him. It does not make any difference to me, but I only want to point out that the same discrimination practised by Russia in Spain against the Anarchists and against the Anarcho-Syndicalists is being practised by the same organizations outside of Spain. In England, in America, in France thousands and thousands of pounds and dollars have been raised, but never a penny goes to the National Confederation of Labour with a membership of two million people.

. . . . . . . . . . . . . . . . . . . . . . . . . . . . . . . . . . . . . . . . . . . . . . .

About the concentration camps so much has been written, even in Tory papers, that it is hardly necessary to add anything. Nevertheless I have a number of letters and descriptions from eyewitnesses, men who are certainly not Anarchists, not even Socialists or liberals, but who have this sense of horror in seeing how these men and these women are treated in the concentration camps, and they all give the same description. One man wrote that nothing he had seen even on Franco's side was so appalling and so horrible and so inhuman as the treatment in some of the camps in the country that has a tremendous history and a tremendous background of revolutions, and that is in France.

†*In a speech one month later (4/27/39), Goldman attempts to educate her new Canadian audience to similar themes.*

The democracies knew that Franco might be bought off and would recognize the holdings of England and France in Spain. Representatives of labor and trade unions in England supported the policy of non-intervention at the start but when they found out its vicious workings they asked questions of Mr. Chamberlain. But that's all they did – ask questions. The leaders of the labor groups knew how to hold their masses in check.

Mr. Attlee and Mr. Greenwood[37] knew how to put a damper on the ardor

37. Arthur Greenwood became a leading figure in the British Labour Party following his first election to parliament in 1922 and post as undersecretary in the first Labour government (1924). He served as

of the labor people so far as Spain was concerned. . . . From Stalin's point of view he knew that if he could establish a Communist stronghold in Spain he would be able to force France and England to his terms.[38]

†*Interviewed in Windsor, Ontario on 5/19/39, Goldman discusses both foreign policy toward Spain and the rise of fascism as a product of overall capitalist appetite.*

Hitler and Mussolini had it easy compared to Franco. Franco would never have been able to win the Spanish war like he did had it not been for the help of the democracies because Franco was definitely assisted by means of the Non-Intervention Pact. England and France held off and in so doing they showed both poor statesmanship and a selfish interest in their own country. Certainly Germany and Italy are waiting to collect their spoils in Spain. And when they do[39] it will bring England and France to war. All this business of Chamberlain's appeasement has been a farce. The appeasement was merely because England was not prepared for war.

. . . . . . . . . . . . . . . . . . . . . . . . . . . . . . . . . . . . . . . . . . . . . . . . . . . . . . . .

In Fascism, I see the last attempt to bolster the capitalistic system. International finance, all manufacturers of arms, all large industrial interests have backed Fascism in Italy, Germany and other countries where it is a force. Representatives of the capitalistic system believe that Fascism will bolster the debris of the system — foolishly, because it won't. In putting labor in a straight-jacket and throttling culture, Fascism cannot hope to continue. Temporarily? Yes. But in no way permanently.

†*In this 9/2/39 letter to Milly Rocker she offers a first reaction to the new Nazi-Soviet pact.[40].*

Yes, darling, Stalin's pact has vindicated us beyond our own imagination.

Deputy Leader of the Labour Party in parliament under Attlee in the late 1930's, was in Churchill's original coalition war cabinet, and then Lord Privy Seal in the Attlee government of 1945.
38. His "terms" were for Britain and France to become clearly involved in a war against Hitler, thus distracting the latter from his primary appetite in the East.
39. With Italy and Germany soon preoccupied on other fronts following the outbreak of World War II, they were not in a position to enforce their claims. Thus Franco very early sought a loan from Britain and maintained "official" neutrality during the war. Nevertheless, Germany received submarine, air and monitoring bases in Spain as well as war material and a military division of 47,000 "volunteers" to assist in the attack on Russia.
40. On August 23, 1939, the Soviet Union and Nazi Germany signed a ten-year non-aggression pact in which both secretly divided eastern Europe into their own spheres of influence. On September 1, Poland was invaded by Germany. By the 17th, Soviet troops began moving into their share of the defeated country, with partition established down the middle.

What a spectacle, Stalin pressing Hitler to his loving Socialist breast in an orgiastic dance. It must make the gods howl with laughter. Of course, the lickspittles of Stalin's boots are now proclaiming the latest treachery of their idol as the greatest wisdom. That was to be foreseen.

† *Five days later she tells the same correspondent of the Spanish refugees' increasing vulnerability and of her sense of the imminent outbreak of war.*

What will become of our refugees? A letter from Martin Gudell informs me that some have already been forced back to Franco. They were given the choice of that or digging trenches in France. Most of our people have refused both. How long will the French government permit them to stand firm? . . . The camps are still in the open; they will, therefore, be the first targets in case of bombardment.

*In this context, she ominously recalls the large anti-war campaign that she and Berkman began three decades earlier. Lasting only a few weeks, both it and their life work in the U.S. were suddenly swept away.*

† *To British writer and anarchist Herbert Read (10/7/39), Goldman expands on the significance of Stalin's pact with the Nazis and its roots in the policy of Lenin.*

I am not surprised that Stalin's "latest move has given you a certain *Schadenfreude* [malicious pleasure]." Why shouldn't it? It has vindicated us in our attitude to Soviet Russia far beyond my expectation. You probably know the saying "give a man rope enough and he will hang himself." Certainly not the worst enemy of Stalin could have undermined his prestige and the position of his adherents as the pact with Hitler and his invasion of Poland. I do not know how much you were aware that Stalin's latest treachery was on the way. I know you will think it an exaggeration on my part when I tell you that I foretold it six years ago. I had quite forgotten that I had stated in an interview with the *Toronto Evening Telegram* in 1933 that Stalin would make overtures to Germany and would eventually come to terms with it. A year ago, however, I already had any amount of indications that this was going to take place. After all the beginning of the pact dates back to the time when not Stalin but Lenin was still at the helm of Soviet Russia. It was the treachery of Brest-Litovsk[41] which laid the foundation for all the other treacheries committed by the Bolshevik regime. True, Stalin continued in a more drastic measure, but he was reaping what was sown by Lenin and his Jesuitic tactics. Stalin's treachery in Spain and his pact with Hitler are merely links in the chain of

41. See footnote 42 in Chapter II above.

events introduced by the ascendency of Bolshevism in the world. Nor is this the end. Stalin's lust for imperialist power is as insatiable as Hitler's and it will not be appeased in any more humane manner than that of his German colleague. I am therefore right in saying that we Anarchists are vindicated in our stand against the hydra-headed monster, the dictatorship whether red, brown or black. And this is the line of reasoning I am taking in my lecture on the pact.

While I have witnessed the bungling of the British statesmen in the attempt to soften the heart of Stalin, I am yet constrained to say that they must have been utterly dumb not to know that Stalin has long ere this taken root in Nazi soil. But of course the western powers have much to account for before the world and history. Certain it is that Hitler was made by the spineless tactics of the democracies, their betrayal of Spain, their appeasement. It is nevertheless necessary to emphasize that it was Stalin's pact which strengthened the guts of Hitler immeasurably and without which he would not have started his military avalanche on Poland.

† *Writing to Rudolf Rocker on the same day, she admonishes especially those Western intellectuals who for years defended Russia and who now, with the Nazi-Soviet pact, are in desperate disarray. She understands the problem when reactionary forces now attempt to use the anti-Soviet critiques of herself and others to their own advantage. It is important to distinguish oneself from these longtime enemies. But it is also crucial to speak out, now more than ever, since Stalin's latest action presents his general orientation in such bold relief. She views with envy Rocker's ability to write so well in the midst of such a dire world context.*

† *In a 12/19/39 letter to American comrade Bill Ryan,[42] Goldman compares the West's hypocritical concern with Finland and Poland to its neglect of Spain for three years. She also clarifies her own position toward reactionaries who try to make use of her anti-Communist stand.*

I don't know who is more contemptible, the Communists who keep up the stupid defense of the criminal actions of their hero or their fellow-travellers. It is sickening to read the apologies in the *New Republic* and in the *Nation*. These two papers have known for years what is going on in Russia, yet they have continued to cover up all the horrors because they haven't the courage to go out against the Communists. Since the pact, these two miserable sheets have tried their utmost to explain and to excuse the indefensible treachery of their hero, at the same time showing utter indifference to injustice

42. Ryan was one of the International Brigade members who became disillusioned with the Communists in Spain, subsequently writing to Goldman about his experience. A brief account also appeared in the *American Mercury* article mentioned in footnote 58 of Chapter V. In 1942, Ryan was sentenced to two years in prison for refusing to register for the U.S. military draft.

close to home. Thus, neither the *New Republic* nor the *Nation* have found it convenient to bring [out] the articles I wrote them about the suppression of civil liberties in Canada.[43] They are a sour lot. As to their frantic efforts to defend the Kremlin, they are in vain. The world is no longer deceived in what the Kremlin covers and what treachery Stalin is capable of. Mark you, I am not deceived by the crocodile tears that are being shed in the world for the Finns.[44] In point of fact, the Finnish, like the Polish, [were] Fascist to the extreme and guilty of the same crimes in their own country as their arch-enemy Stalin. I have by no means forgotten the White terror in Finland[45] and the barbarous and brutal treatment of the Jews in Poland and the minorities. Not that these justify Stalin's invasion. On the other hand, it is precisely the Fascist nature of Poland and Finland which has aroused the sympathies of the imperialists and their generous help. It is to weep when one thinks what the same governments and the same world opinion have done for Spain. No Hoover relief[46] for the heroic Spaniards. Of course not. The powers that be knew only too well the personnel that constituted the Spanish workers and peasants. Why then should they have rushed relief to suffering Spain? Finland is, of course, another matter. It is a *bona fide* Fascist government in league with the other Fascists and, therefore, the best colleagues of all other governments. All this is terribly tragic. Still, as I said, it does not excuse or minimize Stalin's treachery, nor does it take away from the admirable defense the [Finnish] masses are putting up. But the hypocritical sympathy is loathsome.

Dear Comrade, each one must decide for himself whether to go before the Dies Commission[47] or not. I could not do it, even though hopes were held out that I might be permitted to stay in America for some time.[48] I couldn't do it because I should hate to buy my entrance to the States by any connection with the people who back the Dies Commission. Not because all that has been discovered in the investigation is not absolutely true, but because the Commission itself is reekingly reactionary, because it is intensely ignorant in mixing all isms together, and because it is done for show and aggrandizement. Then, too, there is an old revolutionary, ethical conception not to

43. See footnote 43 at back of chapter.
44. See footnote 44 at back of chapter.
45. See footnote 45 at back of chapter.
46. See footnote 46 at back of chapter.
47. The Dies Committee was the late 1930's equivalent to and basis for the "Un-American Activities" investigations by Joseph McCarthy and others in Congress in the early 1950's. It was established by the House of Representatives in 1938 and was very active in this initial period, among other targets attacking those who supported Republican Spain.
48. For years, Goldman deeply desired to return to the United States from exile because of her family and friends still there, as well as her certainty that this was the context of her greatest political effectiveness. Nevertheless, apart from her 90-days speaking tour permitted in 1934, the Roosevelt administration steadfastly refused a visa. The only glimmer of possibility came when she was informed by one of her American contacts that in exchange for testimony before the Dies Committee, the government might well look favorably on a new application.

recognize government investigators in the actions of workers even if they are duped by Stalin. For myself, I can say without boast that if my life were attempted I would never consent to expose the one who wanted to kill me. Altogether, the Dies Commission has been an odorous gang and the ex-Communists who have now confessed are also a very sad lot. It was a self-gone conclusion that the Dies Commission would not publish what you were most interested to disclose. All that the Dies Commission is doing is to use everyone who is coming before it for its own black hundred[49] purposes. In your case, you could, of course, not help yourself because you were summoned, which is tantamount with compulsion. I quite understand that you "cannot find it in my heart to be forgiving." . . . I, too, have nothing but the deepest contempt for the miserable Communist satraps and for their power-seeking maniac, Stalin. Still, I would never voluntarily go before the Dies Commission.

## Appeals for International Support

†*In this first direct appeal for international support of the Spanish struggle, a 9/23/36 radio speech from Barcelona, Goldman suggests concrete issues and actions of solidarity.*

Men and Women, are you aware of the fact that the supporters of Fascism are supplying Franco with tremendous amounts of weapons of modern warfare while the defenders of liberty have to battle almost with bare hands? True, the Spanish people are invincible and overwhelming in their fortitude, courage and will to consecration, whereas the enemy's war is being waged with hirelings. But the most inspired men cannot conquer without weapons. Will you sit by supinely while your brothers and sisters are being murdered and Fascism placed in power? I appeal to you, men and women of English-speaking countries, to come to the assistance of the gallant fighters in Spain. Every hour lost strengthens the position of the enemy. Raise yourselves, men and women, protest against the hypocrisy of neutrality towards the Spanish anti-Fascists while the other side has active help from all reactionary governments and their worthy colleagues in human slaughter.

Protest against the vilification of the CNT-FAI. Make known that they are back of the heroic struggle against Fascism as well as the reconstructive work in Catalonia. The CNT-FAI is the last to deny credit to the other political groups bravely fighting at the front. But as a matter of historic fact the

49. The "Black Hundreds" were the early 20th century czarist Russian equivalent of the Ku Klux Klan in the United States: reactionary local organizations, supported by and containing many government officials themselves, dedicated to violent attacks on any scapegoat ethnic community (as the Jews and Armenians) or politically progressive individuals and groups.

CNT-FAI is the most formidable active and moral force in Barcelona and all of Catalonia. This must be proclaimed from the very housetops in England, the United States and Canada. And it is up to you, liberty and justice loving people, to do so. Organise relief! Raise funds to equip the valiant voluntary militia ready to lay down their young lives fighting to the bitter end!

Men and Women! You have the grandest historic opportunity to help crush the hydra-headed monster that lies like a hideous nightmare on the hearts of Europe. Only then will the peoples of this earth be able to breathe freely once more. Only then will they be able to undertake the task of social transformation.

† *Writing to Rose Pesotta (4/2/37), Goldman expresses her frustration and anger with the propaganda machine of the Communists and Leftist intellectuals.*

Oh yes, the Communists are active. Their bitterest enemies cannot deny them their propaganda genius. They know how to penetrate through every crevice and to get under the skin of all kinds of people and all kinds of parties. You have no idea how many parties there are in England going by all kinds of names, who are out-and-out Communists; but they get away with it. In the last analysis this is not difficult to explain. If you are willing to run with the hounds, to compromise on every step, to damn democracy one day and shout for democracy the next, if you are willing to barter your ideas for the faiths of every government, then it is not difficult to reach everybody. Besides that, the intellectuals in this country are like those in America – they are nothing but climbers; they would be the first to sabotage a Revolution were it to take place here. They are drunk with the power of the Soviet Union, because they can still remain in England free from the tender mercies of Stalin, well fed and well housed. You bet their Communism would go quickly if a Revolution in England or the U.S. would deprive them of their comforts. I respect the average Communist of the rank and file but I have utter contempt for these pseudo-intellectuals.[49a]

† *This direct call to British and Irish workers, written by Goldman and several others (published on 4/2/37), attempts to unmask the pretenses of official governmental policy and appeals for direct action to support the struggle in Spain.*

49a. A similar indictment, more recent but also grounded in the experience of Spain in the late 1930's, is Noam Chomsky's excellent "Objectivity and Liberal Scholarship," one among various essays of similar argument in his *American Power and the New Mandarins* (N.Y.: Pantheon Books, 1969).

## An Appeal To The Workers

1. The struggle in Spain is at its climax and the workers of the world have failed up to now to answer the lying farce of non-intervention by positive intervention in their own cause.

2. The Spanish workers await the action of the workers everywhere, but especially that of the British workers, realizing that the action of Britain is the key to the international position.[50]

3. If there is any excuse for the shameful inaction of the British workers, it is that they have been grossly deceived. They have been deliberately deceived by the false hope of their government's adherence to a United Front of the democratic nations against international Fascism.

4. That hope has proved a delusion, encouraged by some ignorance of the realities, encouraged by the National government with deliberate intention to deceive.

5. Britain's continuous surrender to international Fascism, in apparent defiance of her own imperial strategic interests, has not been dictated by impotence or incompetence; but by the requirements of a positive policy, which has consistently underlain all her actions.

6. Under the cloak of democracy she has schemed to emasculate and destroy democracy everywhere, fearing that the real economic democracy, which in parts of Spain has already been achieved, would undermine the power and prestige of the financiers and industrialists, of which the National government is the creation.

7. Thus every Fascist aggression has received British support: diplomatic support for the Japanese aggression in Manchuria,[51] financial support for the Nazi militarization in Germany,[52] a mere pretense of resistance to Mussolini's rape of Abyssinia with no purpose of sincerity beyond the convenience of an electioneering ramp, followed by a betrayal, which began the destruction of the League of Nations;[53] even an Anglo-German naval agreement to enable Germany to re-establish control of the Baltic Sea;[54] and finally the pressure on France to betray the ideals

---

50. See footnote 50 at back of chapter.
51. Actually sympathetic to Japanese problems in pursuing its "legitimate economic interests" in Manchuria, the British government refused to condemn Japan's September 1931 invasion, content with its promise to maintain an "open door" in Manchuria for other countries as well. Unquestionably, this attitude of the British encouraged Japan to pursue each of its later stages of attack against China throughout the 1930s.
52. Indeed, the head of the Bank of England helped arrange British bank loans for the new Nazi regime in its first few months, regarding it as a welcome "stabilizing" influence in Germany and a solid bulwark against Bolshevism. (See details on this and other forms of British financial support in James and Suzanne Pool, *Who Financed Hitler: The Secret Funding of Hitler's Rise to Power, 1919-1933* [New York: The Dial Press, 1978].)
53. See footnote 53 at back of chapter.
54. In June 1935.

of the Popular Front by proposing the infamous non-intervention policy in Spain, which preceded open and organized invasion by the Fascist powers.

8. In face of such a record, the belief in the National government's good will to democracy, or good faith to a democratic front against Fascism, becomes insane superstition.

9. We must support the Spanish workers and peasants, fully recognizing that their fight against Fascism is not a fight for the maintenance of existing parliamentary institutions; but a revolutionary struggle for the overthrow of the class system of society.

10. We call upon the working class in Great Britain and also in Ireland to show the same unity and international solidarity with their comrades in Spain that the Fascist and other capitalist governments have exhibited in their armed or financial support of the Spanish reactionaries.

11. We note with strong approval the action of seamen and dockers in the Scandinavian countries and of British seamen in America in organizing refusal to handle munitions or supplies for the Spanish Fascists, and we urge that this example be followed without delay by the organized workers in this country.

12. We know that the mutual jealousies of the great Powers are of secondary importance when compared with their common fear of social revolution.

13. We urge the workers to beware of any schemes which depend for their fulfillment on the British government, or any other capitalist government, and call for direct action in every sphere to place an embargo on supplies to the Spanish Fascists and their allies, and to ensure a continued supply of all they require to the Spanish workers and peasants.

14. They are the vanguard of the world revolution, and the front line of defense against International Fascism for us as well as for themselves.

† *In this mid-December 1937 speech to the IWMA Paris congress, Goldman contrasts the crucially distinct international contexts in which the Russian and Spanish revolutions occurred.*

The CNT-FAI are not so wrong when they insist that the conditioning in Spain is quite different from that which actuated the struggle in Russia. In point of fact the two social upheavals are separate and distinct from each other.

The Russian Revolution came on top of a war-exhausted people, with all the social fabric in Russia disintegrated, the country far removed from outside influences. Whatever dangers it encountered during the civil war came entirely from within the country itself. Even the help

given to the interventionists by England, Poland, and France were contributed sparingly. Not that these countries were not ready to crush the Revolution by means of well-equipped armies; but Europe was too sapped. There were neither men nor arms enough to enable the Russian counter-revolutionists to destroy the Revolution and its people.

The revolution in Spain was the result of a military and Fascist conspiracy. The first imperative need that presented itself to the CNT-FAI was to drive out the conspiratorial gang. The Fascist danger had to be met with almost bare hands. In this process the Spanish workers and peasants soon came to see that their enemies were not only Franco and his Moorish hordes.[55] They soon found themselves beseiged by formidable armies and an array of modern arms furnished to Franco by Hitler and Mussolini, with all the imperialist pack playing their sinister underhanded game. In other words, while the Russian Revolution and the civil war were being fought out on Russian soil and by Russians, the Spanish revolution and anti-Fascist war involve all the powers of Europe. It is no exaggeration to say that the Spanish Civil War has spread out far beyond its own confines.

As if that were not enough to force the CNT-FAI to hold themselves up by *any* means, rather than to see the revolution and the masses drowned in the bloodbath prepared for them by Franco and his allies—our comrades had also to contend with the inertia of the international proletariat. Herein lies another tragic difference between the Russian and Spanish revolutions.

The Russian Revolution had met with almost instantaneous response and unstinted support from the workers in every land. This was soon followed by the revolution in Germany, Austria, and Hungary;[56] and the general strike of the British workers who refused to load arms intended for the counter-revolutionists and interventionists.[57] It brought about the mutiny in the Black Sea,[58] and raised the workers everywhere to the highest pitch of enthusiasm and sacrifice.

The Spanish revolution, on the other hand, just because its leaders are Anarchists, immediately became a sore in the eyes not only of the bourgeoisie

55. See footnote 55 at back of chapter.
56. Germany saw a widespread revolutionary upsurge from November 1918 through the Spring of 1919, especially prominent in Kiel, Berlin and Munich. The Hungarian revolution produced a "Soviet Republic" under the leadership of Béla Kun from March to August 1919. Revolutionary upheavals also occurred in late 1918 and early 1919 in Austria, with workers' and soldiers' councils playing a significant role. By mid-1919, the Social Democrats in power defeated this radical upsurge through cooptation and armed force.
57. For information on the successful general strike against British intervention in the Russian revolution, see John Quail, *The Slow Burning Fuse: The Lost History of the British Anarchists* (London: Granada Publishing Ltd., 1978), pp. 296-303, and G.D.H. Cole, *A History of the Labour Party from 1914* (New York: Augustus M. Kelley, Publishers, 1969), pp. 104-07.
58. French sailors brought to Odessa to support counter-revolutionary armies in the Russian civil war mutinied in April 1919 and forced the French commander to withdraw rapidly in the face of an impending Bolshevik attack.

and the democratic governments, but also of the entire school of Marxists and liberals. In point of truth the Spanish revolution was betrayed by the whole world.

. . . . . . . . . . . . . . . . . . . . . . . . . . . . . . . . . . . . . . . . . . . . . . . . . .

Dear comrades, it is not a question of justification of everything the CNT-FAI have been doing. It is merely trying to understand the forces that drove and drive them on. Whether to triumph or defeat will depend a great deal on how much we can awaken the international proletariat to come to the rescue of the struggle in Spain; and unless we can create unity among ourselves [the international Anarchist movement],[59] I do not see how we can call upon the workers of the world to unite in their efforts to conquer Fascism and to rescue the Spanish revolution.

† *In this brief passage of a 12/21/37 letter to associate Ethel Mannin, Goldman suggests specific types of solidarity measures to help the cause in Spain.*

. . . What positive suggestions can such a committee make? Well, the boycott, sympathetic strikes, direct action of every form, material help.[60] All such measures were done for the Russian Revolution in its early stages. Why cannot it be done for Spain?

† *Eight days later to the same individual Goldman admits the anesthetizing of public sensitivity and yet the importance of continuing to protest, if only for one's own relief.*

Nothing is so awful to me as the atrophy of human sensibilities since the World War and the horrors going on in Russia. No one cares a damn anymore, no matter how frightful the crimes committed in the name of an ideal. Still, the few of us who still feel deeply must go on protesting, if only to bring some relief for our own pent-up indignation.

† *In a 3/4/38 published article, Goldman sees the international proletariat as partly responsible for new anarchist concessions in Spain and urges specific direct action to change British policy.*

English workers will probably be surprised to read of the concessions the CNT is making to the UGT.[61] It is therefore necessary to point out that

59. See footnote 59 at back of chapter.
60. She apparently refers here to the planned London SIA committee which, however, never took on more than the last of these tasks.
61. She refers here to the CNT position in its negotiations for a united front with the UGT. See part of the same article and additional comments on this issue in Chapter IV above.

people in a burning house cannot stop to consider theories. They must use the best methods at hand to save themselves from being burned alive. It is therefore the bounden duty of the English workers to come to the rescue of their comrades in Spain who have so gallantly fought Fascism for eighteen months. It is their duty not merely to talk or listen to the fine speeches of their leaders and M.P.'s, but to act directly to force their government to discontinue its Fascist methods to destroy Spain and to rush England into a war of extermination. Certainly the last events in the National government prove its Fascist tendencies. Not that Mr. Eden[62] has not contributed considerably to involve the situation. If he resigned, it is only because the intention and methods of his Premier have gone even beyond his political leanings. In the last analysis it is of no importance what either Mr. Chamberlain or Mr. Eden decide. The battle is on the economic field and the soldiers in that field are the working class. It is therefore essential for the workers of England to wake up from their lethargy and their acquiescence to the reactionary methods of their leaders and misleaders. It is imperative that they should begin to see that the Spanish anti-Fascist struggle is not only to save Spain from Fascism. It is to save the whole world from the spread of the blackest scourge of modern times. Surely the workers who in '21 came to the rescue of the Russian Revolution and have recently acted deliberately against Japan and on behalf of China, will not continue to content themselves with a few large meetings in Albert Hall or some tins of milk for the Spanish children, necessary as the latter may be.

The time has come, even if it is the eleventh hour, to organize direct action: demonstrations before the House of Commons, the determined refusal to load ships with anything going to Franco. In other words with an organized, concerted direct movement to break the conspiracy of the British government against the anti-Fascist struggle. This and the lesson which the stand of the National Confederation of Labour is giving, might prepare the workers of England for the coming battle between capital and labour which is bound to come much sooner than anyone comfortably fixed is willing to admit.

† In this published statement of 3/18/38, Goldman explains the creation and nature of the new International Anti-Fascist Solidarity organization (Solidaridad Internacional Antifascista) and the activities of its new British section.

You will be interested to know that the English section of the SIA (International Anti-Fascist Solidarity) was organized in London. Among the sponsors

62. Anthony Eden, a later British Prime Minister (1955-57), was Foreign Minister in Chamberlain's Conservative government at the time. He resigned on February 20, 1938 over differences with Chamberlain on whether to press Italy for the withdrawal of troops in Spain.

are some of the most outstanding men and women in letters.[63] We have already started a fund for the purpose. At our meeting on January 14th we collected £75. Since then we have received many contributions. We have organized an Exhibition which is held at the office of the SIA at 21 Frith Street, London, W.1, and we are organizing a literary and musical affair at the Friends House, on April 1st for the same purpose.

The SIA, organized in Spain only six months ago, has already met with remarkable results. In Spain itself it has a membership of 100,000. The French section has members in every part of the country. Its members contribute a certain amount a month to the SIA, voluntarily of course. Speakers canvass France from one end to another on behalf of International Solidarity.

In the United States the American section also meets with great success. The same in Holland and Sweden. We hope that we will soon be able to say the same thing about England. We are certainly trying the utmost to make the English section as successful as in other countries. That it may not be a mere boast we need your help, cooperation and generous contribution. We want membership and anything you can give out of the fullness of your heart to the SIA.

If you do not yet know we wish to inform you that the SIA is covering tremendous ramification in the way of succour and support to the thousands of thousands of refugee women and children, and to the care of our heroic fighters at the front and to the wounded at the rear. Surely a commendable undertaking. Will you respond?

† *Writing to Vázquez and Herrera on 4/14/38, Goldman indicates willingness to try more desperate tactics if necessary to gain British interest in the Spanish cause.*

We leave nothing undone to rouse interest. But the response is small. Our meeting yesterday was disappointing although it was not badly attended. We decided that it is highest time to make a straight appeal for money for arms. It is supposed to be "illegal" but it is no use [to wait] until the Fascist government of this country will give us permission to call for money for arms or arms as such.

*Perhaps by breaking the law and some, including herself, going to prison, more attention could be gained for the Spanish anarchists.*

† *This 7/19/38 letter to Roger Baldwin states that even direct relief aid for Spain proves not to be the solidarity effort many intended.*

63. Initial sponsors were W.H. Auden, Thomas Burke, Stella Churchill, Nancy Cunard, Havelock Ellis, Louis Golding, Sidonie Goosens, Lawrence Housman, Brian Howard, C.E.M. Joad, Miles Malleson, George Orwell, C.V. Pearson, John Cowper Powys, Llewelyn Powys, Herbert Read, Reginald Reynolds, Rebecca West and Rev. James Whittle.

What interests me is whether you know how much of that tremendous amount of money collected for foodstuffs and medical supplies have gone to Catalonia or Aragon. Up to last November, when I was in Spain, very little was sent by way of Barcelona. Most of the aid went through Communists' hands. It certainly does not require much proof to convince one that the CNT-FAI, though representing millions of members, has benefited nothing at all by all the monies and aid raised in America or in this country – yet these are the people who fight on every front, and who fall by the thousands.

†*A brief passage from her 5/19/39 speech in Windsor, Ontario shows Goldman's respect for sincere solidarity with the anti-fascist cause from whatever quarter.*

I think many of the Communists in the International Brigade were sincere idealists who fought heroically at the front. Many were wounded, some mortally, and so were the Anarchists. I do not think the bullets of Franco were any respecters of individuals or political creeds.

## Further Footnotes for Chapter Six

1. Meant here by "international power politics" is the entire political structure of the capitalist world economy, its internal divisions and rivalries, its efforts to incorporate increasing numbers (social groups and entire societies) into its system and its combat with the major rival bloc of "socialist" state capitalism led by the Soviet Union.
3. To the extent anarchist literature to the present deals with this issue (for the most part the question is ignored), it is usually with one or both of two alternatives in mind. On the one hand, it is assumed, justifiably I think, that a truly anarchist revolution and emerging large-scale anarchist society would greatly inspire others elsewhere to attempt the same. The powerful myth of the necessity for hierarchy would evaporate if indeed an accurate description of the new revolutionary society could be communciated abroad. (Of course, this is a difficult achievement itself, as Goldman's comments in this chapter make clear.) Thus, especially if the new society were a former super-power like the United States, potential interventionists would be too preoccupied at home and the old Western capitalist alliance too disrupted from within to launch major attacks. (See Murray Bookchin, *Post-Scarcity Anarchism*, pp. 23-24, 239, for one expression of this view.) If indeed there were invasions from abroad, the new society would have to be ready to defend itself – not as national patriots, but as social libertarians (see Alexander Berkman, *What is Communist Anarchism?*, ch. 21). Unwilling to wait or struggle for a large-scale anarchist revolution in their own lifetimes, many anti-authoritarians in the past and present have tried to establish autonomous small-scale "free societies" on the margins of the authoritarian world. Yet inevitably they too are infiltrated by destructive attitudes and behavior acquired in the old contexts and rarely achieve genuine economic self-sufficiency. Even then, the state and capitalism abhor a power vacuum and will not allow such experiments to persist, certainly not if they seem to impress others outside. Most writers on anarchist utopias, in turn, have been unwilling or unable to cope with this general issue of survival in the midst of hostility. Imaginary contexts are created where such problems don't exist. A leading example of this is Ursula Le Guin's very interesting *The Dispossessed* (N.Y.: Harper and Row, 1974) where the anarchist society of Anarres is at such a distance (another planet!) that the home society no longer perceives it to be a threat, thus a target for attack.
4. Apparently there was little or no discussion of the international context and revolutionary defense even at the May 1936 national congress of the CNT (only two months before the

beginning of the civil war), despite the knowledge of ongoing military-fascist plots! (Richards, *Lessons* . . . , p. 24.)

9. Among her unpublished writings on such developments from the late 1920s and early 1930s are a 5-page manuscript on Hitler, a 35-page manuscript on Mussolini, and notes on books and issues concerning the Chinese revolution — including a very interesting and in many ways accurately prophetic manuscript entitled "China: The Unfettered Spirit Unbound." These are found in the New York Public Library manuscript collection. Detailed notes on her Brooklyn speech of February 15, 1934 concerning Germany and Austria are found in the N.Y.U. Tamiment collection. No doubt local newspaper coverage of her 1934 three-month U.S. tour also could be consulted to gain a sense of her international perspectives at the time. She apparently felt that newspaper articles and editorials about her visit were generally fair and accurate (Goldman 5/11/34 letter to William Jong, NYU).

11. The term "worst authoritarianism" is used here purposefully. While anarchists see *any* form of hierarchical politics as "authoritarian" — thus to be struggled against — the intensity of exploitation characterizing Soviet and fascist regimes was unprecedented historically. It is this fact which caused Goldman and many other anarchists — including the bulk of the Spanish movement — eventually to give priority attention to *those* particular statist enemies more than others. As Chapter IV describes, where the Spanish movement went *further* than Goldman was in emphasizing the fascist menace above all, to the point even of accepting temporary collaboration with (and sabotage by) the Communists. For Goldman, the fascist and Communist movements were equally deadly enemies (though she did acknowledge the progressive motivations of many *individuals* in the Communist rank and file). Furthermore, she refused to accept the principle of alliances with the state. By 1939, she returned to her prior and more traditional anarchist perspective, a position held by the strong anti-collaborationists all along: that is, that *all* hierarchical political movements and regimes, including those of the "liberal democratic" or parliamentary variety, are essentially the same.

14. Preoccupied with its own relative international isolation against an increasingly belligerent Nazi German regime, the Soviet Union wished to form an anti-fascist alliance with the West — meaning primarily France and Britain. Even more deeply, Stalin feared presenting the Soviet Union again — through immediate support of the republican government (and, implicitly, of the anarchist-led social revolution already underway) — as the leader and instigator of a world revolutionary effort. Such an image might motivate British and French attacks against it directly, as during the Russian Civil War. For both reasons, the Soviet regime waited until early October before making public its decision to intervene. By then, German and Italian intervention was so significant and obvious that the Soviet move could be better justified as defensive aid, not an offensive move into an area of British and French major interest.

21. Already, in the first weeks of the civil war, the British gave important support to the Nationalist rebellion through naval action in the Strait of Gibralter. On November 16, 1937, the British gave *de facto* recognition to Franco's government by exchanging official representatives. This followed the Nationalist conquest in previous months of northern Spain, a region with extensive British economic interests. Several weeks later, Britain concluded an agreement (not signed until 4/16/38) with fascist Italy, accepting the status quo power distribution in the Mediterranean, including the thousands of Italian troops assisting Franco in Spain. In effect, Prime Minister Chamberlain had agreed to accept fascist control over at least a large part of and potentially (as came to pass in 1939) the whole country. Indeed, in May 1938, the British ambassador to Spain expressed his belief that a fascist victory there was necessary for peace and for the protection of British interests (Dante Puzzo, *Spain and the Great Powers, 1936-1941* [N.Y.: Columbia University Press, 1962], p. 100). (The Puzzo book is an excellent source for u n d e r -

standing the international context generally.)

26. In response to the European Non-Intervention Pact of August 1936, the United States government promised to apply an embargo on arms shipments to either side in Spain. Despite significant initial support for this policy in 1936, public opinion polls showed increasing support for the Loyalists by 1938. Yet Roosevelt refused to alter his policy, even in the face of a large-scale public campaign. Crucial factors were the strong influence of the Catholic church and U.S. reluctance to take any initiative of its own in Europe, independently from France and especially Britain. (An important exponent of both of these factors was Joseph Kennedy, the new U.S. ambassador to Britain, and father of John F., Robert and Edward.)

27. This comment should not be read to imply that Goldman was impressed with even Roosevelt's initial policies. In her 1934 speaking tour of the U.S., she characterized his NRA and AAA policies as nothing more than "pink tea and bridge party"! (*St. Louis Post-Dispatch*, 4/3/34). On the other hand, it's interesting that Roosevelt himself was reported to have read Goldman's autobiography with great admiration (Roger Baldwin 12/27/33 letter to Goldman, NYPL), ironically indicating again the distinction between words and action.

30. In the mid- and late-1930's, Harold Ickes increasingly was viewed by the Nazi regime as its worst enemy in the Roosevelt government. He was attacked by name in official diplomatic protests, press statements and even directly in a speech by Hitler at the time of Goldman's letter. (James V. Compton, *The Swastika and the Eagle* [Boston: Houghton Mifflin Co., 1967], p. 73.)

31. Through the Munich Pact of September 1938 the British and French governments, supposed allies of the moderate liberal government of Czechoslovakia, agreed with Hitler to allow Germany to occupy the Sudetanland region of that country without military retaliation by the West. Chamberlain described this as an effort "to preserve peace in our time." Six months later, Hitler proceeded to occupy the rest of the country, in defiance of the Munich Pact, but again without military response from Britain and France.

33. She refers here to Ludwig Lore, leftist editor of the *New York Post* at the time. (Lore last saw Goldman in London in 1937 and wrote a very praising article after her death [*New York Post*, May 16, 1940].) Edouard Daladier, a moderate Radical Party leader and the War Minister under Blum, replaced the latter as Prime Minister of the French government in April 1938. His government lasted until March 1940. William Bullitt became U.S. ambassador to France in October 1936 after serving 2½ years as the first U.S. ambassador to Moscow. Earlier he had been Wilson's special envoy for top-level talks with Lenin and other new Soviet leaders. After this contact, he had recommended to Wilson that the new regime be recognized officially. When Wilson refused, he resigned. See the reference to Joseph Kennedy in footnote 26 above.

43. Having moved to Canada in April 1939, by a few months later Goldman became intensely involved in trying to prevent the imprisonment of four active Italian anti-fascist comrades in Toronto. Anarchist militant Arthur Bortolotti and one other were threatened also with deportation to Italy, and likely death at the hands of Mussolini's police. To gain publicity and support for the defendants, Goldman wrote numerous letters to contacts in the States as well as potential articles for the U.S. press, as she indicates here. That the suppression of civil liberties easily could extend beyond the particular four defendants in this case was obvious from the wording of the War Measures Act under which they were prosecuted. Among other things, it prohibited making any statements "intended or likely to cause dissatisfaction to His Majesty."

44. Leery of potential German advances through the "buffer zone" of independent Baltic countries north and northeast of Poland, Stalin sent troops into Estonia, Latvia and Lithuania in September and October of 1939 to occupy strategic bases. Finland, however, refused permission and on November 30 faced a Russian invasion. Showing surprisingly strong resistance, the Finns gained much sympathy in Britain and France which promised military aid and permitted the recruitment of volunteers. By March 1940, however, Finland was finally defeated.

45. Encouraged by the revolution in neighboring Russia, Finnish Left socialists in early 1918 attempted to establish a revolutionary regime of their own. This soon led to a bloody civil war, as in Russia itself. In contrast to the latter, the Whites in Finland defeated the Red forces, thereafter engaging in savage reprisals and offering the country as a launching base for Western and White Russian troops against the Soviet regime. The anti-Communists retained their control during the subsequent two decades.

46. With approval from the U.S. State Department, ex-President Herbert Hoover led a nationwide drive to raise private money, beyond the $30 million in loans granted by the government. Hoover's Finnish Relief Fund raised about $3.5 million by October 1940. A detailed discussion of U.S. involvement in this area is found in Andrew J. Schwartz, *America and the Russo-Finnish War* (1960; rpt. Westport, Ct.: Greenwood Press, Publisher, 1975).

50. The Soviet Union, France and Britain were the crucial European powers potentially able to repulse fascism in Spain and elsewhere, before the momentum became too strong. Her attitude about the unreliability, indeed treachery, of the Soviet Union in this struggle is clear. France, in turn, took its lead from Britain, not daring to antagonize Germany and Italy on its

own. The United States was in no way willing to take initiatives in Europe before Britain and France took action themselves. Indeed, highly-placed U.S. officials argued that the Soviet Union ought to be forced into becoming Germany's main target, thereby producing a struggle that would diminish the power of each, relative to the United States. Senator (later President) Harry Truman even argued that the United States should come to the aid of *either* party which happened to be losing the struggle (William Williams, *The Tragedy of American Diplomacy* [New York: Dell Publishing Co., Inc., 1972, rev. ed.], p. 198).

53. In October 1935, Italy launched a military attack on Ethiopia (Abyssinia) in an effort to conquer this last remaining independent country in East Africa. The League of Nations quickly declared for economic sanctions against Italy. The British government, under the Conservatives, now moved a fleet to the Mediterranean supposedly to help in enforcement. After this show of toughness and the Conservative victory again in November elections, the government planned with France to offer Italy a "concession" of ⅔ of the territory of Ethiopia. At the same time, oil exports to Italy continued. In May 1936, Italy completed the conquest of Ethiopia. Two months later, acknowledging its own failure, the League abandoned its policy of sanctions, thereby demonstrating its own discredit.

55. For the right-wing conspiracy of Nationalist generals, the "Army of Africa," the military units occupying the colony of Spanish Morocco in the mid-1930's, was a far more reliable force (tested already in brutally suppressing the Asturian revolt of 1934) than the mainland army filled with peasant recruits. The army in Morocco was composed primarily of an elite corps of mercenary soldiers, the Legion, and mountain troops from the native Moroccan population. The critical importance of the latter for Nationalist military strength was also a significant potential vulnerability. Yet once again, a longtime anarchist principle – in this case, abolition of Spanish colonies – was abandoned as a serious demand by the anarchist movement to appease other forces in the anti-fascist coalition as well as France and Britain internationally.

59. This was a plea on several levels: for unity at the anarcho-syndicalist IWMA meeting itself; for unity in defense of the Spanish comrades between all anarchists of whatever persuasion (anarcho-syndicalist, anarcho-communist or anarcho-individualist) and whatever their view toward CNT errors; and for an end to all the traditional petty bickering between groups and individuals within the movement as a whole. More on this theme appears in Chapter X.

# Chapter Seven

# Anarchists, Violence and War

*Every movement activist eventually must define what circumstances, if any, justify violent strategies and tactics as part of progressive social change. The decision depends on prior assumptions and impulses concerning the appropriate balance of emotions and rationality, of destructive vs. constructive emphases, and of defense vs. offense as priorities. One also must define social revolution itself. All of these questions are debated as sharply in movement circles now as they were decades ago.*

*Based largely on* a priori *assumptions derived in great part from intensely personal experience, each movement position has its jealous and often dogmatic defenders. All the more so with such potentially drastic social conflicts at stake. Yet it is crucial for activists to examine periodically both the rational and emotional sources for their positions and to evolve appropriate revisions. As we expect or hope for constant individual growth, likewise we would wish for a movement wisdom to accrue from the increasing intellectual clarity and emotional sensitivity of each individual. And, of course, this wisdom must include the possibility that present positions may be wrong. Especially when it comes to the crucial issue of violence, honest re-appraisals are essential in one's own internal dialogue as well as in the debate of the broader movement. If the axe of clear self-awareness and self-criticism chops cleanly, confusing and often paralyzing dogmatism over the issue of violence must fall finally to the side.*

## II

*Emma Goldman's statements here on violence and war reflect a lifetime of gut-level emotionality, experiential testing, rational reflection and a willingness to change. Given the depth of her political involvement and her commitment to herself as a constantly growing individual, her life action and words clearly articulate the type*

*of accumulating movement wisdom on these issues which deserves our attention even now. As with other issues discussed in earlier chapters, her perspective on violence evolved considerably during her fifty years of movement involvement and culminates with the Spanish upheaval. To be sure, informed as they are, Emma Goldman's thoughts here must be tested also by the perceptions each of us has toward our own experience.*

*At the crucial moments, Emma Goldman above all never feared to express her own emotional intensity. As with all of us, her own politics overlapped greatly with her personal life, her emotions with her political analysis. She, far more than most, however, willingly admitted these connections. Beyond not fearing them, she also never denied the* validity *of her emotions. This is a constant in her personal and political life, from childhood to the end. For her, rational analysis seemed consciously a tool of her more basic emotional instincts.*[1] *Indeed because of the very strength of her emotional experience and the social conflicts this forced upon her, she naturally felt attracted to that rational framework — anarchism — which for her best resolved and explained their roots. Anarchism provided a clear emotional and rational vision that allowed her to link her own daily turmoil with an ideal future.*

*Given this nature of her own personality, Emma Goldman was thus thoroughly sensitive to the emotional roots of violence among oppressed peoples. Never would she condemn the human impulses behind a desperate act of social revenge by an individual or a group embittered by years of oppression and misery. In this particular sense, acts of violence, however terrible their immediate consequence, always were justified.*

*Beginning in her twenties, however, Goldman became increasingly critical of such actions — including, retrospectively, the assassination plot against Frick in which she herself participated.*[2] *In her view, there were two fundamental problems. First, such actions were hopelessly insensitive to the predictable negative public response.*[3] *And whatever shock and outrage emerged initially were inflamed inevitably all the more by mass media and "responsible community leaders." Second, such violence also often implied a burning-out of the activist's own human sensitivity, as shown when no precautions were taken to protect innocent potential victims nearby.*[4] *Beyond these arguments, and here was the cutting-edge of her attitudes toward violence in later years, Goldman was critical or at least skeptical even when violence was aimed solely toward a clear lifelong personal or institutional oppressor. In her view, the violent radical — by denying to some degree the deep-down understandable human and therefore common roots with the*

1.  In this priority, she of course is a precursor and inspiration for current feminist activists.
2.  See footnote 2 at back of chapter.
3.  However, she did make exceptions in the case of obvious tyrants, such as the Russian czar and Prime Minister Cánovas of Spain (*LL*, I, 189, 207).
4.  She was especially critical on this point in referring to the Manhattan bomb explosion of 1914. Several activists were preparing the device as part of an anti-Rockefeller campaign, following the Ludlow, Colorado mining camp massacres. It exploded prematurely in a tenement house on Lexington Avenue, causing the death of four. (*LL*, II, 535-36.) Goldman saw those willing to engage in activity endangering the lives of innocents, as she herself had done two decades earlier, as allowing the ends to justify the means (*LL*, I, 88). As to the "burning-out" problem generally and Goldman's perception that it sometimes led one more easily to die than to continue the struggle, see her comments in *LL*, I, 329.

*oppressor—lost some of his or her* own *humanness in the act. By justifying such actions, the breadth of liberatory vision was to that extent compromised. Some humans were by definition excluded from the race. The first critique judges the* effectiveness *of violent tactics and strategy.*[5] *The second two are* moral *concerns and* psychological *observations both. They also complement the debate on collaborationism since they suggest that to some extent, consciously or not, we easily may absorb the traits of our enemies while waging the struggle against them.*

*The latter issue, in turn, leads logically to considering the violence in revolution itself. Like the great majority in the international anarchist movement, Emma Goldman always opposed war between nation-states as the most vicious and destructive result of capitalist greed and rivalry.*[6] *Social revolution, by contrast, aimed to bring socially-caused suffering to an end. As at the individual level, violent action by large numbers of the oppressed was always understandable as a reaction to the lifelong violent conditions they had endured. But not only that. Because it emerged as a large-scale* group *effort instead of an easily cooptable or repressible individual response* and *because it aimed to overthrow the entire* framework *of social violence, in fact it was to be welcomed. This remained Goldman's attitude during her whole fifty years of activism.*[7]

*As mentioned before, Goldman personally avoided close formal ties with larger movement organizations because these would both restrict her own creative energy and help legitimize others' "empire-building" designs. For similar reasons she rejected the idea of a movement organization as such attempting to* precipitate *and* lead *a revolution. In this view, she was again thoroughly consistent with anarchist tradition. Nevertheless, anarchists do see themselves as hopefully* influencing *society toward and during revolution in deeply significant ways. The desired nature and extent of such influence may vary. Some anarchists attempt to provide cultural or political* examples *of successful micro-communities, living by the guidelines of the group's libertarian ideals. Others concentrate on active propaganda efforts through publishing, speaking, and demonstrations. Another main focus (not necessarily exclusive of the others) is to develop and recruit for massive organizations openly committed to revolutionary change. Among such alternatives, Goldman from the beginning would commit herself only to affinity-group propaganda efforts or inspirational violent activity in the context of seemingly imminent revolution.*[8] *By the time she left Russia in 1921 she doubted more than ever that large-scale leadership or organizational roles could precipitate, let alone direct, a massive social revolution. Her analysis of the Russian situation in fact saw the most organized revolutionary force, the Bolsheviks, as only at best* following *and then eventually* braking *the transformational momentum of the masses.*

---

5. *LL*, I, 322-23.
6. See footnote 6 at back of chapter.
7. As a result of her Russian experience, however, she no longer lived in that "romantic revolutionary haze" which assumed a "revolutionary instinct" of the masses. In this, she was critical of historical anarchist tradition, including Bakunin and Kropotkin, as well as her own past beliefs (Goldman 3/9/29 letter to Max Nettlau ["Comrade"], AMS-G).
8. The latter path was exemplified especially by the assassination plot against Frick after his bloody attempt to suppress the steelworkers' strike, a worker rebellion paralleled in other parts of the country at the same time.

*Goldman viewed social revolution as a volcanic explosion, a wild hurricane, an overwhelming tidal wave of simultaneous and essentially spontaneous human revolt. Like these other natural phenomena, social revolutions had roots in concrete reality, they could not emerge from a void. As in nature, the interrelated factors eventually producing at one moment such a tremendous sudden redirection of energy were simply too complicated to predict in advance.[9] Hence, any claim of revolutionaries to be* leading *a society toward that event was largely pretention — self-serving and false rhetoric.*

*Nevertheless, Goldman did assume that such explosions would occur periodically and that these heroic historical experiences held tremendous potential for advancing societies in positive directions. She therefore strongly believed, especially after seeing the limits of the Russian experience, that committed revolutionaries should prepare an atmosphere of consciousness as widespread as possible that both would make such an explosion easier to occur and would encourage the greatest* constructive *activity once underway. Especially through the revolution's constructive efforts, remaining archaic social consciousness would be best and most rapidly transformed. By demonstrating concretely that the utopian vision could become an immediately rewarding reality, past inhibitions would be overcome.*

*However important strategically and as a psychological release, to dwell solely or primarily on the destructive tasks led to those dangers she already described in individual violence. Nevertheless, Goldman also recognized that social revolution usually implies war — at the domestic level, internationally, or both. (Retrospectively, though, she felt she had over-stressed the determining significance of this factor in the Russian situation.) Those who lost privilege and power will do everything possible to gather allies (domestic and foreign) from the deposed, threatened and insecure and will use physical force if necessary to regain their position. In Goldman's view, effective defense against guns requires guns of your own. Powerful social propaganda, especially through efforts to construct the new society, may weaken the enemy's potential base of social allies. But at some point guns will have to be used. And in a situation of social revolution, a situation of potential qualitative leap forward for human society, armed defense is absolutely justified and essential. Indeed, to be unwilling to defend this opportunity would be to demonstrate one's lack of commitment to the ideal, to the validity of one's own basic emotions. This Emma Goldman could never do, despite her awareness that the very process of shooting one's enemies inherently implied limits to how far one's ideals had advanced.[10]*

9. The similarities here with the process of mental "breakdown" and positive reintegration are striking, a comparison brought out especially well, for example, in Marge Piercy's *Woman on the Edge of Time* (N.Y.: Alfred A. Knopf, 1976).
10. Concerning the armed Makhnovista insurrectionary movement in the Ukraine, Goldman refused to believe that "anarchism had anything to gain from military activity or that our propaganda should depend on military or political spoils" (*LL*, II, 813).

## III

*Goldman's Spring 1936 comments cited in Chapter IV defined the situation in Spain as revolutionary—that is, justifying, demanding open defiance and reversal of the old order. In her view, Spain had been at the same revolutionary take-off point for at least several years. Apparently she was misinformed and therefore unaware of anarchist participation in the Asturian uprising of late 1934. Nor did she seem to understand the political context at that time simultaneously inhibiting anarchists in Catalonia and elsewhere from taking similar action.*[11] *She strongly denounced what therefore appeared to be sheer unwillingness of anarchists to join a major revolutionary wave. Though more ambiguously before then, by at least 1934, she felt the revolutionary momentum in Spain was already underway and that Spanish anarchists should be very active within it.*[12]

*It is important to remember that Emma Goldman and others saw the issue of revolution in Spain as part of a broader international context of drastic political change. In response to the obvious deterioration of their economies and thus the rising political credibility and strength of critical forces on the Left, capitalist strategists embraced fascist alternatives in Italy, Germany, and Austria.*[13] *Their purpose was to preserve basic structures of profit and privilege which parliamentary democracy could no longer guarantee. In Goldman's view, for countries such as Spain, fascism became both a dangerous political model and a threatening armed base of international aggression. In this context, revolutionary effort in Spain was simultaneously a struggle against a mounting domestic and international tide of reaction and an attempt to transform society in qualitatively new and progressive directions.*

*The linkage of both struggles from July 1936 on was by no means accepted by the anarchists' "allies" in Republican Spain. Domestically, the latter (except for the POUM) wanted to preserve a moderate reformist political context which, in their view, offered political power with the least disruptive cost.*[14] *Internationally, they wished to avoid hostile intervention in Spain from France and England and at best even to gain Western and Soviet arms and support against the forces of fascism. Thus, the liberal Republican, Socialist, and Communist forces preferred not only to* avoid *revolutionary transformation but to actually* sabotage, *when they could, efforts in that direction from below.*

*For Emma Goldman, supporting the armed conflict with fascism in Spain was possible only if the social revolution was vigorous as well. However ugly, fascism was actually no more than a stark banalization of usual capitalist logic. Goldman of course supported the general struggle against capitalism, whatever its veneer. Yet*

11. A clear portrayal of anarchist participation in the massive Asturian workers' insurrection as well as a description of the farcical opportunistic "Catalan nationalist" uprising by explicit opponents of the CNT-FAI appears in Bookchin, *The Spanish Anarchists*, pp. 260-71; Peirats, *Anarchists in the Spanish Revolution*, pp. 93-100; and Paz, *Durruti . . .* , ch. 10.
12. See footnote 12 at back of chapter.
13. Such an alternative also was partially attempted in Spain itself in the 1920s with the Primo de Rivera dictatorship.
14. This was their hope before and after the outbreak of civil war—in the latter case, through an arranged mutual truce.

*to use armed violence in such a struggle was justified only in the context of a popular wave of revolutionary activity, a people's assertion of their own right to free space and their commitment to protect that space when under attack. If opposition to fascism was merely part of a national or international struggle between competing capitalist political forces, she wanted no part of it. Whatever gains would be accomplished by defeating fascism would be outweighed by the losses of war itself and a further entrenched capitalist system.*

*Goldman emphatically asserts this crucial distinction in various of the writings below. Because of this position, she was attacked by and was herself critical of pacifist anarchists (as in Holland) who found anarchist participation in the Spanish civil war an abandonment of traditional beliefs. Goldman needed little reminder of her own longtime principled opposition to war.[15] While painfully insisting that revolutionary war makes certain compromises inevitable, she thus promised to abandon support of the anarchist armed conflict if the demands of war took precedence over continuing the revolution (as occurred in Russia). While logically clear, this cutting-edge was difficult to apply in practice. As with other issues during this period, it caused her endless uncertainty and agony. Ultimately, she opposed (though understood) the CNT-FAI leadership's collaboration in the government and their acceptance of militarization of the militia, since both positions seriously compromised the revolution. At the same time, she continuously insisted that the constructive will and achievements among the anarchist base were strong enough to justify viewing the armed conflict as still revolutionary in nature, not primarily or solely a civil war against fascism.*

*Franco's victory ended whatever remained of the revolution. Increasingly, antifascism became primarily a broad alliance of threatened capitalist states, soon leading to World War II.[16] With this development, Goldman's position was clear. It was impossible for her to support armed anti-fascist struggle defined and carried out in traditional statist terms.[17]*

*This return to an emphatic antiwar position completed her 1930s cycle of personal involvement in, then withdrawal from, the maelstrom of violence and its justification. Her various efforts through this period to define consistency and boundaries for her position can be useful to all of us in the present. Especially they help to clarify the nature of non-pacifist anarchist opposition to violence, an opposition which regards true social revolution as an attempt to end the terror of hierarchically-employed violence once and for all.*

15. Such opposition brought her the two-year federal prison sentence during World War I.
16. At this point, the Spanish anarchist movement split on the issue of appropriate strategy, but it was a division already present (though largely patched over) during the crisis of the civil war. Some insisted on continuing collaboration with statist forces – as part of Allied armies, as well as with the Spanish Republican government-in-exile. Such anarchists hoped that Allied victory in World War II would force restoration of the legitimate Spanish republican government, including also a major political role (or room for political activity) for the anarchists. Others in the movement chose independent guerrilla struggle against Nazi and Spanish fascism as their own path toward a new revolutionary context, a path free from the corrupting effects of collaboration. For details on the very significant participation of Spanish anarchist exiles in the armed struggle against the Nazis, see David Schoenbrun, *Soldiers of the Night: The Story of the French Resistance* (N.Y.: E.P. Dutton, 1980) and Louis Stein, *Beyond Death and Exile: The Spanish Republicans in France, 1939-1955* (Cambridge, Mass.: Harvard University Press, 1979).
17. See footnote 17 at back of chapter.

*† To Montreal friend Marjorie Goldstein over one year before (5/19/35) the out-
break of the Spanish conflict, Goldman critiques the belief that social revolution
emerges only through the suffering of major disaster.*

Of course a world conflagration may knock all . . . our plans on the head.
But one cannot just wait until the calamity will overtake humanity. One has to
go right on. If only the world were not full of fools who insist that people
never learn except through some cataclysm. They forget that only the very
sensitized learn through sorrow. The majority only grows bitter through suffering. The idea of having to suffer in order to become purified is the old
theologic concept. It is cruel and silly at the same time. For if the world could
learn from great tragedies surely the war now so close at hand could not be.
For far from having brought anything worthwhile to man, the last war has
brought more evils than it was supposed to destroy. And the next war will only add to the frightful results of the last. War is a vicious circle and must be
fought to the bitter end. Surely someday humanity will realize the crime and
futility of the monster and will have none of it anymore.

*† Goldman's first radio talk from Barcelona (9/23/36) shows her enthusiasm for the
fact that constructive effort far outweighed destruction in the social revolution
underway.*

During the week since my arrival in Barcelona I had ample opportunity to
verify the changed conditions, and I was amazed to find everything in perfect
order. Nothing destroyed or demolished, not a nail moved in factories,
workshops or the former luxurious houses now occupied by the numerous
departments of the CNT-FAI. I made it my business to talk to some of the
workers and to express to them my astonishment that they had been able to
prevent wholesale damage to the property now in their possession. In a direct
and simple manner I was told that the workers felt they had produced the
wealth and that it would have been nothing short of stupidity to destroy
anything that can now be made accessible to all who labor. This marks a new
departure in revolutionary consciousness of the value and sanctity of human
effort and set a convincing example for the quality, intelligence and practical
judgment of the CNT-FAI.

True, a number of churches were burnt. But those who know the sinister
influence of the church on the Spanish masses, the superstitions fostered, the
toll exacted and the alliance of the church with the monarchists and military as
well as the capitalist interests will not blame the masses for having vent their
wrath on these structures. In addition it is a fact, as I have been able to ascer-
tain, that in a number of cases the workers set fire to the churches only after
they had been attacked by the priests. These men, though sworn to live up to

the admonition "Thou Shalt Not Kill," yet sent volley after volley from the high church windows into the mass below. It is also significant that very few churches of historic or artistic importance have been touched.

However, it is the spirit of the people, their great courage and their high aims that should be considered and not a few demolished stone buildings. This sublime spirit is giving birth to a new conception of the dignity and value of every man, woman and child in the new Spain the CNT-FAI is working for.

†*In a 10/4/36 letter to comrade Tom Bell, she specifically addresses the issue of "revolutionary reprisals" against long-standing social oppressors.*

Dear Tom, your references to reprisals by our comrades surprises me. Where did you get this from? Is it possible that a weather-worn rebel like you and versed in the atrocity-mongering of the daily papers should take such accounts for granted without first finding out? Now the facts are these: the comrades here would be the last to deny some excesses that have taken place. With the best of will they could not prevent this in the first weeks of the upheaval because of the accumulated wrath in the masses against their exploiters and tormentors. You know yourself the devastating hold the Spanish Church had on the people, the black superstitions fostered, the toll of sweat and blood exacted from generations of the Spanish masses. How do you of all people expect that these victims of the Church, of the military caste, of the large landowners who had held the peasantry in a feudal state should have treated the whole parasitic class with kid gloves? And yet frightful as the provocation has been, the workers showed remarkable restraint.[18] In point of fact most of the "reprisals" took place against priests who first opened fire against the people and such representatives of the aristocracy, military clique and leaders of industry and finance who had openly boasted of their Fascist allegiance and their support of the Fascist conspiracy. I feel sure that you never have believed that revolution can be fought with kid gloves, I certainly did not. I am as ever opposed to the suppression of opinion. But I have and do maintain that an armed counter-revolutionary and Fascist attack can be met in no way except by an armed defense. Believe me, my dear, your old comrade is no fool to judge merely by superficial impressions. That's why I insisted on coming here first to see and study the situation. It would be denying my entire past, were I to say all is well. It is far from that. But the constructive achievements of the CNT-FAI are already so formidable, they put all else in the shade. It seems to be the unfortunate fate of all revolutions to spring from the loins of war.

18. A detailed discussion of this issue and the attitude of Spanish anarchists at the time is found in Broué and Témime, *The Revolution* . . . , pp. 123-27; Bolloten, *La Révolution espagnole*, pp. 66-71; and Peirats, *La CNT* . . . , I, 173-81.

†*Three days later (10/7/36), she admits to her English friend "Auntie" Crotch that the destructive, violent aspects of defending the revolution are hard for her to bear.*

The constructive achievements are truly extraordinary. But of course all is not brilliant color. How can it be amidst a devastating war with such uneven stakes? The Fascist side has everything, the anti-Fascist nothing at all. The butcher Franco is reported to have said, "I have all the armaments I need and more. But no men." Meaning Spaniards who are moved by any real fervor. "And the other side has all the men flocking to their colors but nothing else." That is only too true. Fervor, enthusiasm, courage go a long way. But what can they do against bombs and machine guns? . . .

. . . . . . . . . . . . . . . . . . . . . . . . . . . . . . . . . . . . . . . . . . . . . . . . . . . . . . . .

It is a tragic fact that all revolutions have sprung from the loins of war. Instead of translating the revolution into social gains the people have usually been forced to defend themselves against warring parties. Spain makes no exception. . . . Individual life seems very insignificant indeed when a whole people have risen and are struggling for the right to free themselves from their drab and meaningless existence. A people surrounded by enemies within and without can hardly be expected to worry about the health or comforts of one. I feel this more and more every day and am often sick at heart over some of the crude sides of the Revolution. And yet I know it is for the generation of the individual as well as the mass that my people are fighting for so valiantly and at a frightful cost. It seems nothing great is born without pain and travail. There is so much here. But no one complains, they go on indefatigably 18 hours out of 24. It is their selflessness, their truly sublime abandon to their great task which so stirs my heart and which has renewed my faith in humanity.

†*To Irish rebel activist Mrs. Sheehy-Skeffington, Goldman writes (11/12/36) that the international implications of the fascist threat in Spain are crucial for her defense of the anarchists' military struggle. She even states her willingness to go to the front if only she were younger.*

All my life I have stood out against war and now that the defenders of freedom are besieged not only by the Fascist hordes, but also by international capitalism, I feel I must stand by my comrades to the bitter end. Were it only a question of liquidating the civil war in Spain, I might not have set aside my lifelong stand against war. But the question here that is being fought out is a question for the whole world, for it is certain if Fascism should conquer, it would mark the beginning of black reaction that probably would take half a century or longer to exterminate.

I feel therefore that I must set aside my inner abhorrence of the cruelty of war. It is after all a struggle of life and death between two world conceptions,

between slavery and freedom, between dictatorship and liberty.

. . . . . . . . . . . . . . . . . . . . . . . . . . . . . . . . . . . . . . . . . . . . . . . . .

If only I were younger, I should most assuredly go to the front and share with my comrades and the other brave militias at their fate. One cannot do so at the age of 67. Since that is impossible I try to do what I can to add my might, little as it is, to the gallant fight my people are making.

†*In a published article of 1/8/37, Goldman favors voluntary over coercive discipline as the organizing bond between soldiers on the front line.*

[Concerning the Spanish government's move toward traditional forms of discipline of anti-fascist soldiers[19]] I am against all coercive discipline, because so much more can be achieved by reasoning. I believe that one should feel the necessary discipline in one's self.

. . . Discipline can be given in the form of example. Take the Durruti column, of some eight to ten thousand men. While Durruti was alive there existed no discipline[20] in his ranks, and I believe this still holds good. He was always with his men and inspired them by his courage and faith in them. For instance, one of his men during a moment of military inactivity asked Durruti for a permit to visit his parents, poor and ill. "So you want to go home," asked Durruti, "and leave the fighting line. But don't you understand that we are fighting just because your parents, and so many other men and women, are living under conditions that cause so much illness? By our victory everybody will be able to live decently and in comfort. Of course if you insist on going, leave your rifle and go home on foot. But your village will soon learn that you broke faith with the Revolution." I need hardly add that the soldier begged to remain at the front! You see, Liberty is so much stronger than military discipline!

†*Writing to old American friend and comrade Cassius Cook (2/8/37), Goldman states emphatically that passive resistance would have accomplished nothing against the armed rebellion of the right-wing military in Spain.*

You are quite right, my dear, I am not made to sit by supinely in the face of overwhelming dangers. Passive resistance is all right for some people and no doubt it has its value, but I cannot see for the life of me how it would work in the face of armed resistance! Bear in mind that the revolutionaries in Spain were not the ones to attack. They took to arms only when they were face to face with an armed force, officers directed by generals who were known to be

19. See footnote 19 at back of chapter.
20. She means here the *traditional* form of discipline, imposed from above.

in military and Fascist conspiracy. Had our people not armed themselves, Spain would now be in the position of Germany and Italy, where hardly any resistance was offered to the invasion of the Fascists' power.

In offering active resistance, the Spanish workers gave a shining example to the rest of the Fascist world, that they still love Liberty well enough to struggle and die for it.

†*On the same day, Goldman tells Mark Mratchny of her concern over arbitrary shootings on the part of anti-fascist forces, including anarchists.*

[In his recent critical speech] Santillán expressed the very ideas I tried to convey to the comrades while I was in Spain – the idea that while an armed attack on the Revolution calls for an armed defense, it doesn't also, to my mind, necessitate the shooting of people whose only crime is their difference of opinion.

†*Two days later, Goldman presents Dutch anarchist William Jong with an elaborate critique of pacifism, in the Spanish context and more broadly.*

Now as to the problem of pacifism and the armed resistance which our people in Spain are offering: it is quite true, dear comrade, that I opposed war and went to prison for it.[21] I would do so again, for I hold now (as I ever have) that war does not solve any problem. On the contrary, it usually brings more evils in its wreck than the evil it supposedly comes to fight. The trouble is that our Dutch pacifist comrades do not seem to be able to distinguish between imperialistic wars (always engaged in loot and conquest) and the defense of revolution. Unable to distinguish between the two, they naturally now feel at sea over the Spanish situation.[22] For myself, I have always maintained that armed counter-revolutionary attack cannot be met in any other way except by an armed revolutionary defense. Passive resistance is no doubt of value at times; in most cases it depends on a number of factors – economic as well as psychological. Thus the Hindus practice passive resistance, because passivity is preeminently an Eastern characteristic – and even they have proven that it does not go very far. In Western Europe, passive resistance has proven a failure: whenever and wherever it was tried.[23] In the case of the Spanish people, who have struggled against oppression and subjugation by feudal

21. In 1917. (See Chapter I.)
22. Most likely, she refers here to articles in the monthly *Bevrijding (Liberation)* of Bart de Ligt, the author of an influential manual of passive resistance at the time, *The Conquest of Violence: An Essay on War and Revolution* (London: G. Routledge and Sons, 1937).
23. See footnote 23 at back of chapter.

lords and the Catholic Church, it would be nothing short of suicide. The success numerically and morally of the CNT-FAI is due entirely to the heroic struggle these organizations made for their emancipation.

But, granted that passive resistance were preferred, it could only be so if the workers and peasants had been first to rise in revolution. Then perhaps their economic power might have decided the issue. What the Dutch comrades seem to overlook is that the Revolution, as well as the anti-Fascist War, were imposed on the masses by the military and Fascist conspiracy hatched and perfected over a period of 2 years, in Germany and in Italy.[24] In other words, our people found themselves face to face with an armed military force which could not possibly have been met lying down. It was therefore a question either of offering armed resistance, or of complete annihilation.

That the CNT-FAI are not overlooking the importance of the economic factor in their struggle is demonstrated by their procedure, immediately after July 19th, to collectivize both factories and the land. This in itself is the greatest achievement in the history of the revolutionary struggle. At no other time was any attempt made to construct in the very teeth of the danger of war and the bitter difficulties of Revolution. Yet our people have gone ahead and have shown the whole world that Bakunin was right after all when he insisted that "the spirit of destruction is also the spirit of construction."

Now, it is all very well, dear comrade, to remain consistent and to be tied by theories when one is far away from a battlefield, but REALITY imposes many things not provided in one's ideology nor in theoretic hair-splitting of this or that idea. Confronted with facts, such as the military and Fascist conspiracy in Spain, supported by the feudal lords and even more so by the Church, our comrades were forced by circumstances either to fight back or be destroyed. It is really expecting too much to expect our gallant comrades to abide by the kind of pacifism entertained by comrades in Holland. I am quite certain that our comrade Domela N.[25] (were he alive now, and aware of the facts in the Spanish struggle) would have been with our comrades with all his generous nature; for he realized as I do and many others that there is a vast difference between capitalist wars and the defense of Revolution. True, a great many well-meaning people have lost sight of the Revolution; they are stressing the anti-Fascist war. To be sure, that is very necessary, because the

24. For details on such plotting, see Ivone Kirkpatrick, *Mussolini: A Study in Power* (New York: Hawthorne Books, Inc., Publishers, 1964); Heinz Höhne, *Canaris* (Garden City, N.Y.: Doubleday and Co., 1979); and Brian Crozier, *Franco: A Biographical History* (London: Eyre and Spottiswoode, 1967).
25. Domela Nieuwenhuis (1846-1909) was a leader of the Dutch Social-Democratic Union until he turned toward anarchist beliefs during a term in parliament in the late 1880's, gradually also bringing most of the movement with him in the early 1890's. Goldman met him personally at the time of the Amsterdam international anarchist conference in 1907. He was a very influential figure in strong anti-militarist campaigns throughout his career. (See Goldman's sketch of Nieuwenhuis in *LL*, I, 404-05.)

victory of Fascism would not only destroy all the constructive achievements of our Spanish comrades, but it would throw the whole world back into savagery—as it has already done in Germany and Italy. But while the anti-Fascist struggle is important, our people have never lost sight for one minute of the more vital issue—which is the social revolution in Spain; and that cannot be [protected] by any [passive] resistance or well-meaning Christian pacifism.

This is my position, dear comrade, which I hope you will place before comrades in Holland. I feel deeply and intensely the struggle which Spanish comrades are making. I am not uncritical but am ready and willing to go with them to the bitter end, and want nothing better than to stand with them in the battle towards victory; or if the dread thing should happen (their defeat) to go down with them.

†*In a new 3/8/37 letter to Tom Bell, Goldman again addresses his concern with the issue of "reprisals." She also reveals her emotional unwillingness to sit in life-and-death judgement against fascists on trial.*

I see only too clearly the compromises our comrades have made and are making. Certainly, "militarization," "single command," and all other such fancy steps, very close to dictatorship, are only too true. Not only do I see that, but while in Spain I have tried desperately to make our comrades aware of the danger of their acquiescence to governmental methods; but also I know that they themselves realize the untenability of some of their concessions. . . .

. . . . . . . . . . . . . . . . . . . . . . . . . . . . . . . . . . . . . . . . . . . . . . . . .

To revert to my letter in regard to your charge of reprisals—I assure you that I have made it my business to investigate every place I visited to find out whether reprisals had taken place. Nor have I been "shown" these places. There was no such a thing during my three months in Catalonia as "being shown and taken round." I had complete liberty to go by myself or take anyone with me I desired. That is precisely the difference between the situation in Spain and Russia. I don't deny that there were shootings. I mean that Fascists were condemned to death. I attended such a trial, and while all the evidence was against the men tried, I went away ill and heartbroken that such a thing should have to take place during a revolutionary period.

For myself, I have never denied that Revolutions cannot be fought with kid gloves. I have always insisted that an armed attack on the Revolution must be met with armed force. Nevertheless, I could act neither the judge nor the executioner, no matter what was at stake. Perhaps I am a bad revolutionist, but that does not blind me to the imperative necessity of defending the Revolution, and that is what the CNT-FAI is doing.

† *In a published 4/28/37 letter to the* Manchester Guardian, *Goldman attacks their misinformed criticism of the role of Catalonia and anarchists in the anti-fascist struggle.*

. . . I was therefore not a little surprised to find that even the *Manchester Guardian* is sadly misinformed as to the actual place of the C.N.T.-F.A.I. in the anti-Fascist struggle. In your leader of April 3 you say: "It is remarkable, for example, (although not perhaps without an historical explanation), how little military assistance has been given by the Catalonians to Madrid during the war. The Anarchist leader Durruti was sent with 15,000 men to fight on the Madrid front, but the bulk of the valuable Catalan resources seem to have been frittered away on ill-managed and fruitless skirmishes in Aragón." I do not know where you got this information. I can only say that completely misstates the facts of the situation in Catalonia. Will you permit me therefore to place before your readers several incidents which occurred while I was yet in Barcelona?

First, as late as September, 1936, the C.N.T.-F.A.I. submitted to the Madrid government a plan for the immediate organisation of a Council of Defence.[26] That was rejected. Secondly the C.N.T.-F.A.I. offered to reorganise an old depleted munition factory in Madrid and to proceed at once with the intensive manufacture of arms. That was also refused, although it was known to the central government that the C.N.T.-F.A.I. had succeeded in turning a famous automobile plant into a munition factory within forty-eight hours of July 19 and that it was working day and night in producing the largest amount of arms for the anti-Fascist struggle.[27] Thirdly, Durruti went to Madrid to offer his services and the services of the International Column he had organised to begin the fortification of Madrid. He begged to be permitted to appeal to the people directly to defend themselves, their city, and the revolution. That was also refused.[28]

One month later, when the danger to Madrid became acute, it was again Durruti, with 15,000 of his column, who undertook the defense of Madrid. Actually it was Durruti who repulsed the first attack of Franco's Italians and Germans.[29] Durruti had set his heart on conquering the Aragón front. He

26. A CNT national plenum in Madrid on September 15 called for replacing the government by a "National Council of Defense." Despite the label, this was meant to be a quasi-governmental body capable of directing military affairs and coordinating matters in economic and political realms – no doubt modelled on the original bodies formed in Catalonia and Aragón immediately after July 19. Ministries would become "departments," while those who led them would be "delegates." In such a body anarchists were willing to participate.

27. For further details on the conversion of this factory and the construction of a war industry in Barcelona, see the passage by Souchy quoted in Dolgoff, ed., *The Anarchist Collectives* . . ., p. 96, and Peirats, *La CNT* . . ., II, 97-98, 100-07.

28. See Durruti's interview in the Madrid publication *CNT* of October 6, 1936, as quoted in Paz, pp. 389-93.

29. Though popular accounts of the day mentioned the figure of 15,000, actually the number of anarchist militiamen accompanying Durruti was no more than 1800, according to Paz (p. 422). A detailed account of Durruti's role in the defense of Madrid is found in Paz, chapter 14. It was

worked for that day and night and he perfected his column to that end, but when the call came to go to Madrid he did so without a moment's hesitation. The heroic battle was short-lived, for, as you know, he was killed on November 20.

From the earliest beginning of Franco's rebellion, the C.N.T.-F.A.I. and Catalonia have contributed arms, man-power, and foodstuffs to Madrid, depriving their own city of the necessaries of life and of arms to defend itself. It is also Catalonia that is saddled with the main burden of the evacuated women and children, already numerous before I left at the end of December and since numbering hundreds of thousands as a result of the exodus from Málaga. (Incidentally, it is an open secret that, while large sums are being raised in England for all sorts of purposes for Spain, Catalonia as such has received very little help in any shape or form.) I cannot emphasise enough that Catalonia has strained every nerve and muscle for the needs of Madrid.

You state that "valuable Catalan resources seem to have been frittered away on ill-managed and fruitless skirmishes in Aragón." Actually Catalonia remained without "valuable resources" because everything it could muster went to Madrid. As a result the column on the Aragón front was condemned to inactivity against the enemy, for even burning faith and enthusiasm cannot make up for the lack of munitions.[30] It seems, therefore, unjust to charge Catalonia with having "frittered away resources on ill-managed and fruitless skirmishes in Aragón."

The charge against Catalonia of having in any way sabotaged the defence of Madrid is pure invention on the part of the people who, though claiming to belong to the United Front in Spain, have left nothing undone to stab their allies, the C.N.T.-F.A.I., in the back. They simply cannot forgive these organisations, who have been steeped in libertarian ideas for three generations, for having been the first to go on the streets of Barcelona [on July 19] to fight the military and Fascist conspiracy and who have since endeared themselves to the Catalan people by their magnificent constructive work and their valour. But the truth has a way of making itself heard sooner or later. I am certain that the time is not far distant when the whole world will know the sacrifice, the consecration, and the fortitude of the Catalan people and of [the] C.N.T.-F.A.I. in the anti-Fascist struggle and in the attempt to build a new social order amidst danger and death.

† *Reacting against Spanish anarchist leaders calling off an armed confrontation between Barcelona anarchists and their statist "allies" in May, Goldman informs*

in the sector defended by his unit, opposite the University City, that the main attack actually began on November 15th.
30. Paz, p. 384.

*comrade Max Nettlau (6/1/37) that she is unwilling to go on supporting the anti-fascist war if the social revolution is to be sacrificed in its pursuit.*

I have received a manuscript giving a detailed account of the day by day fight in May.[31] The conspiracy of the Communists and their reactionary allies stands out in bold relief. It aimed for nothing less than the crushing of the Revolution and the extermination of the CNT-FAI. I cannot imagine what induced Oliver and Montseny to call for a retreat of the fight unless it be that they knew that the CNT is after all not so strong as it had pretended to be and that it would go down in a bloodbath. As I cannot go to Spain to get the necessary impressions I am not able to form a definite opinion. I can see the irony however of the anarchists, who stood foremost in the world for direct revolutionary action, suddenly turning pacifist in calling to the comrades to maintain peace and order when their enemies were in the process of destroying both. Gandhi could not have done better. That part of the manuscript made me want to weep and try as I may I cannot explain it.

Is the war now to continue only to bring back the old regime? If so I see no reason to support it. I have gone to prison for my stand on the war and if I changed my position on behalf of the anti-Fascist [war] it was only because I believed passionately that it was for the defense of the social Revolution. I am not in the least interested in a national war, which I consider always on behalf of conquest and loot. I know too much of democratic liberties to be deceived by them.

†*In a new letter to the* Manchester Guardian *(6/37), Goldman again denounces journalistic images of anarchist "terrorism."*

There is, however, one fact of more than usual significance. It is the change of the leaders of the National Confederation of Labor and the Anarchist Federation of Iberia from their tradition of direct revolutionary action to passive resistance.

These Anarchists ever reviled, repeatedly charged with fostering confusion, terror and destruction, these men and women all through the four days' armed attacks cautioned peace and patience and did their utmost to hold back the pent-up wrath of the rank and file of their organizations. And that, if you please, in the very sight of the mowing down of their comrades by Communist and other reactionary forces. That is passive resistance with a vengeance. Verily, Mahatma Gandhi could have done no more.

Nevertheless, the misrepresentation goes merrily on. Thus, a gentleman writing from Spain for a London liberal weekly does not hesitate to speak of

31. The May Days of Barcelona. See footnote 16 in Ch. II above.

"gun-men" in Anarchist ranks. True, he pays tribute to the CNT — I suppose because they were willing to be killed rather than to kill. "If only the gun-men were eliminated from the Anarchist organization, all would be well," the author assures us. It is obvious that the writer obtained his information from his Communist friends. They are past masters in putting facts on their heads. They are the loudest to cry "hold the thief" while they make their own getaway.

While I myself believe that situations in the social struggle may arise that would call for passive resistance rather than direct action, I am not at all sure that the wanton assault on the CNT-FAI by the enemies of the Spanish Revolution presented such an emergency. But whether it did or not the fact remains that the Anarchists and syndicalist leaders and no other party urged loyalty (too much so, I fear) to the anti-Fascist unity, and that they called a halt to fratricide, and not their assailants.

The outstanding phase of Catalan life that so impressed me during my visit was the amount of political freedom everybody enjoyed. Certainly as far as it is possible to enjoy such rights under any government and in the face of war and revolution, the freedom all the parties of the anti-Fascist front had was truly extraordinary. This was entirely due to the CNT-FAI, numerically and morally the most important part. Steadfastly they refused to have any truck with dictatorship. When their attention was called to the abuse of freedom on the part of their allies, to the open and secret preparation to undermine their position and destroy their magnificent constructive efforts, their reply used to be "we will be ready when such [a] moment arrives. Better abuses of liberty than dictatorship. The value of liberty only comes with the exercise [thereof]. Dictatorship turns everybody into abject slaves, barren of feeling for, or appreciation of physical, mental and spiritual freedom."

The present reaction in Spain denotes the danger of dictatorship once more. But also it demonstrates that my comrades were babes in the political woods. That they naively underestimated the perfidy of their enemies. What effect can peaceful methods and the call to retreat mean to people who have for years waded in rivers of blood and have heaped up mountains of human lives for the sake of their power? It is childish to expect anything but reaction from such methods.

---

† *Within a few days (6/10/37), Goldman indicates to Milly and Rudolf Rocker that she now questions her critique of the May Days, allowing that passive resistance might be preferable to potential bloody repression or the alternative of anarchist dictatorship. In her view, British and French naval ships were positioned near Barcelona to assist the central government in crushing the anarchists had the latter fought to the end. She acknowledges that some anarchists argued that a massacre*

*could have been prevented had the CNT-FAI seized power,[32] and not simply through passive resistance.*

I consider dictatorship, even by Anarchists, yes, more so by Anarchists, as the greatest menace to the Revolution. And I cannot get myself to believe that Anarchist dictators would be more amicable than Communist or Fascist dictators. I would like to think that it was this consideration which motivated the stand of the leading comrades in the CNT-FAI. And I will not be sure of it until I get back to Spain as I am absolutely set on doing.

†*In this 7/1/37 letter Goldman continues her discussion with Tom Bell on how violence in war and revolution affects long-standing anarchist principles.*

. . . Do I mean to suggest that Anarchists should not carry out in practice what they have preached? That they should limit anyone's freedom? Not at all. I only mean to say that life is stronger than theory and that the Anarchists have not given enough thought to the emergencies arising out of a Revolution and even more so of a civil war. For myself I would rather have my liberties taken away than be guilty of depriving others thereof. But I cannot expect large groups of comrades to submit to a similar course. It is therefore extremely difficult and has so far been impossible to live up to the fullest to our Anarchist ideals.

It seems to me that the reason for the difference between Anarchist principles and tactics lies much deeper than the inconsistency of our comrades. It lies in the fact that Anarchism and Revolution are of themselves separate and distinct. Revolution is always coercive and violent—it is always the culminating expression of the accumulated wrong and injustice as well as brutalities caused by our system; to expect therefore that people who have for centuries known every physical and mental torture should during the Revolution deal with their enemies with kid gloves and gentleness, this is expecting the superhuman of the individual and the most impossible of the mass. Now while we realize that fundamental changes have never taken place without a revolutionary upheaval we must face the fact that we cannot expect Anarchism [to be] expressed to the fullest during the revolutionary period. All we can expect is that Anarchists should avoid organized dictatorship and organized terror; that is precisely what the Spanish Anarchists have done and for which they deserve the highest credit.

I hope you know me well enough to know that I do not glory in violence. If ever I believed in taking a human life, no matter how dangerous that life and

32. Anarchists associated with the "Friends of Durruti" affinity group did propose such an approach during the May Days, along with certain elements from the POUM. Passages from their manifesto appear in Semprun-Maura, and Chazé, *Chronique* . . ..

how evil, I was entirely cured from it after Sasha's act.[33] I am certain that if the introduction of Anarchism and its success of the revolution would depend on my killing people or ordering them to be killed, I should prove a bad revolutionist. But I have always tried to understand the individual act and the collective act of the oppressed and the disinherited. And I feel that they are justified in breaking the bounds in which they have been held from generation to generation. I can therefore not wax indignantly over the death of a few priests when I know that thousands of workers, innocent women and children, have been enslaved and degraded in the past and have been and are daily slaughtered in Spain. After all, is there any comparison between the loss of lives of the priests and the terrible bombardment of Guernica, of Madrid, of Bilbao? That is not to say that the worst evils . . . make one right or that any retaliation is compatible with Anarchist principles. I admit all that, but I insist again and again that life is stronger than theory, and that we cannot expect the bulk of humanity to act as consistently as now we have the right to expect from an individual. You seem to lose sight of the fact that the CNT-FAI, though numerically the largest organization in Spain, are still a handful of people compared with the rest of the so-called allies, and with the rest of the Spanish population. It is the first time in revolutionary history that the Anarchists were able to take some initiative, that they have made the first halting steps towards the beginning of a new social structure. I cannot see therefore how we can personally hold them to account because they did not and do not live up 100% to Anarchist thought. I am sorry, dear Tom, but I cannot agree with you in your demand, which doesn't mean that I deny you the right of criticism of our Spanish comrades. I have criticized them myself and as you will see by my statement as to my position,[34] I will continue to criticize them. But at the same time I cannot be blinded as to their position and to their possibilities and I consider it childish to expect the CNT-FAI to include Fascists and all other forces engaged in their destruction in the extension of complete political freedom. The comrades are paying dearly for the unlimited liberties extended to the Communists, and they would pay a double price had they also included the Fascists. They would have no longer been in existence had they done so.

I have to revert to your demand of freedom for the Catholic Church and its spokesmen and religious exercise. My dear, can you explain why the Protestant churches have not been touched and why they continue religious exercises without . . . hindrance? You may not believe it but that is a fact. Perhaps you think that I am partial to the comrades who have not interfered with them. In that case I call your attention to a similar report by such people as Lady Atholl;[34a] aside of everything else it would have involved the danger of

---

33. Berkman's assassination attempt against Henry Clay Frick.
34. Presumably her "Where I Stand" article published in *Spain and the World*, July 2, 1937.
34aThe Dutchess of Atholl, a Conservative MP, wrote and spoke in favor of the Spanish republic.

complete extermination of the CNT-FAI, the Revolution and whatever constructive efforts our comrades had made. Here again I can only repeat that it is
very well to decide such actions for oneself, but it is quite another matter to
make such a decision when it involves the lives and liberties of millions of
people. I confess I find it difficult to judge our comrades [when they] have not
and do not live up to Anarchist principles in toto. I fear that it will take more
than one revolution before it will be possible for Anarchism to emerge in all
its beauty and all its humanity.

To come back to your demand that Anarchists should give absolute
freedom to everybody including the Catholic Church. You ridicule the idea
that the Churches were arsenals and that many of the priests were armed; permit me to say that you are wrong. Nobody of our comrades insisted that all
churches were arsenals and all priests armed, but that there were many guilty
of this Fascist position no one has been able to disprove. Actually many
leading Catholics in Spain who are opposed to Fascism have admitted this
fact, but why go for surer proof than the position of the Basque churches and
the Basque Catholics? The very fact that no churches were burned in that part
of Spain and no priests killed by the anti-Fascist forces (Franco was not so
particular when his German and Italian planes threw bombs on churches,
monasteries and cloisters) should be proof to the most incredulous that the
Anarchists and Revolutionists in other parts of Spain have [not] burned
churches and killed priests out of the love for it. It certainly proves that the
Basque Catholics joined forces with the anti-Fascists whereas the rest of
[Catholic] Spain joined forces with Franco.[35] I can only repeat what I have
written you at the beginning of my stay in Barcelona, that there is in-
contestable proof that the Catholic church was aligned with the military and
Fascist conspiracy, that large fortunes were found hidden in the palaces of the
Bishops in a number of cities, and that priests fired on crowds from the high
church windows. Besides, you who know Spanish history surely know that
the church has always been on the side of Feudalism and against the people,
and that always the people show their loathing and their hatred of their
enemies in the church by burning churches. So why be surprised if this was
done once more in the beginning of the struggle last year. Incidentally it is
nonsense to say that the churches were burned by irresponsible bands of
Anarchists, or that acts of violence were committed on priests and nuns or the
owners of large estates by criminal gangs. The element which differentiates
the Spanish revolution from any other revolution consists in the fact [that] the
masses themselves, the peasants and the workers, had risen from the very
bowels of the earth. There is actually no outstanding leader who would

35. From July 1936, most Spanish priests sided with the rebellion against the republic. One year
later, an official "Collective Letter from the Spanish Bishops" (7/1/37) gave a detailed ra-
tionalization of this position. Three months later, the Pope's official representative presented
himself to Franco, thereby indicating the approval of Rome.

compare with Lenin or with Trotsky in the Spanish struggle. It is certainly a mass uprising and it is the mass itself which vent its wrath and its hatred against those who have exploited and ill-treated them for centuries. I firmly believe that our people would have been swept aside by the mass avalanche had they attempted to stem it.

†*In her mid-December 1937 address to the IWMA Paris conference, Goldman attempts to explain the Spanish anarchist decision to accept certain aspects of traditional military organization.*

. . . The tacit consent to militarization on the part of our Spanish comrades was a violent break with their Anarchist past. But grave as this was, it must also be considered in the light of their utter military inexperience. Not only theirs but ours as well. All of us have talked rather glibly about antimilitarism. In our zeal and loathing of war we have lost sight of modern warfare, of the utter helplessness of untrained and unequipped men face to face with mechanized armies, and armed to their teeth for the battle on land, sea and air. I still feel the same abhorrence of militarism, its dehumanization, its brutality and its power to turn men into automatons. But my contact with our comrades at the various fronts during my first visit in 1936 convinced me that some training was certainly needed if our militias were not to be sacrificed like newborn children on the altar of war.

While it is true that after July 19 tens of thousands of old and young men volunteered to go to the front — they went with flying colors and the determination to conquer Franco in a short time — they had no previous military training or experience. I saw a great many of the militia when I visited the Durruti and Huesca fronts. They were all inspired by their ideal — by the hatred of Fascism and passionate love of freedom. No doubt that would have carried them a long way if they had only the Spanish Fascists to face; but when Germany and Italy began pouring in hundreds of thousands of men[36] and masses of war material, our militias proved very inadequate indeed. If it was inconsistent on the part of the CNT-FAI to consent to militarization, it was also inconsistent for us to change our attitude toward war, which some of us had held all our lives. We had always condemned war as serving capitalism and no other purpose; but when we realized that our heroic comrades in Barcelona had to continue the anti-Fascist struggle, we immediately rallied to their support, which was undoubtedly a departure from our previous stand on war. Once we realized that it would be impossible to meet hordes of Fascists armed to the very teeth, we could not escape the next step, which was

36. Though this figure seems excessive, it was in part due to the difficulty of estimating at the time. Nevertheless, it is clear that the large numbers of German and Italian military were of decisive significance for Nationalist success.

militarization. Like so many of the actions of the CNT-FAI undoubtedly contrary to our philosophy, they were not of their making or choosing. They were imposed upon them by the development of the struggle which, if not brought to a successful end, would exterminate the CNT-FAI, destroy their constructive achievements, and set back Anarchist thought and ideas not only in Spain but in the rest of the world.

. . . . . . . . . . . . . . . . . . . . . . . . . . . . . . . . . . . . . . . . . . . . . . . . . . . . .

Our comrades have a sublime ideal to inspire them; they have great courage and the iron will to conquer Fascism. All that goes a long way to hold up their morale. Airplanes bombarding towns and villages and all the other monster mechanisms cannot be stopped by spiritual values. The greater the pity that our side was not prepared, nor had the physical means to match the inexhaustible supplies streaming into Franco's side.

It is a miracle of miracles that our people are still on deck, more than ever determined to win. I cannot but think that the training our comrades are getting in the military schools will make them fitter to strike, and with greater force. I have been strengthened in this belief by my talks with young comrades in the military schools—with some of them at the Madrid front and with CNT-FAI members occupying high military positions. They all assured me that they had gained much through the military training, and that they feel more competent and surer of themselves to meet the enemy forces. I am not forgetting the danger of militarization in a prolonged war. If such a calamity should happen, there will not be many of our gallant militias to return as military ultimatums. I fervently hope that Fascism will be conquered quickly, and that our comrades can return from the front in triumph to where they came from—the collectives, land and industries. For the present there is no danger that they will become cogs in the military wheel.

†In a 1/24/38 letter to comrade Helmut Rüdiger, Goldman elaborates on distinctions between anarchism, war and revolution and places that discussion within the broader context of an assessment of mass anarchist consciousness.

To conduct war, even in defense of revolution, is different from anarchism. Indeed, the Spanish experience convinces her that there can be no anarchist revolution, since the violence involved is the opposite of what anarchism stands for. Acknowledging this, however, does not make her a pacifist. She recognizes that revolution cannot depend on words to defend itself. Yet in Spain it is clear that using force has set back anarchism, rather than bringing it closer.

She admits that she and others perhaps were too hopeful about the prospects of achieving anarchism. It is impossible to accomplish without mass anarchist consciousness and such a level of awareness may be still a century in the future.

It is also important to re-think the significance of the general strike. To attempt such a tactic in the republican zone would have absolutely no effect for the sector under Franco. Though, of course, a world general strike would be a totally different phenomenon, indeed it would be a world revolution.

†*In a 3/4/38 article prepared for publication, Goldman describes certain of her direct impressions of anarchists in the military struggle gathered during her Fall 1937 visit.*

[In Valencia in September 1937] we had a long interview with Comrade Avelino Entrialgo[37] of the Council of Defense. We learned that the number of fighters in the Popular Army who belong to the CNT amount to 35 percent of its total strength. A distinction must be made between the brigades entirely composed of members of our organization and the mixed brigades. We have 100,000 men in our own brigades and 250,000 who are serving in the mixed brigades. From the military schools more than 5000 officers have been trained who belong to the movement, the said schools also belonging to the CNT. The Lister Brigade also has CNT members in its ranks. From these figures the reader will be better able to appreciate the outrageous charges of cowardice against our comrades made by the wretched capitalist and Communist press.

Last, but not least, I had occasion to talk to comrades of the FAI, young militia boys who were in the Military Training College. They told me much of the attempt on the part of the Communist allies of the anti-Fascist front to impose their dictatorship on them. The CNT-FAI press was forbidden in the training school, but after a hard struggle and many threats of strikes, our young military students succeeded in establishing their right to be themselves and to read whatever publications appealed to them most.

I was passionately anxious to know the reaction of these young comrades to militarization. They were of course opposed to it, but explained that, Spain being attacked not only by the Fascists but also by the imperialist countries calling themselves democracies, they felt that the voluntary militias were neither numerous enough nor sufficiently trained and equipped to offer successful fight against that formidable international array against anti-Fascism. These young people assured me that our comrades at the front have in no way changed through militarization and that they were determined to gain whatever knowledge and experience they could, not merely to conquer Franco and his hordes, but for the purpose of defending their revolutionary gains in the rear. It was very refreshing indeed, and encouraging, to see these young comrades, their enthusiasm and their faith in the ultimate triumph of their ideal.

We left Valencia in the afternoon for Madrid, but had to go very very slowly and carefully owing to the fact that one road leading to the Fascist front, the other to Madrid, were so intertwined that we might just as well have made the wrong turn and paid an unexpected visit to Franco's German and

---

37. Avelino González Entrialgo (1898-1977) was a member of the National Committee of the CNT, from Asturias, tending to concentrate on military affairs.

Italian friends. It does not require much imagination to know just the kind of reception we would have been given. . . .

The following day we went to visit Comrade Val,[38] the Secretary of the Centre Committee of Regional Defense, one of the live wires among the active comrades in Spain. He at once offered to take us all through Madrid to let us see the havoc left by constant bombardment from Fascist planes. No one who has not seen the terrific destruction wrought by the constant bombardment can possibly realize the fortitude of the Madrid people who have withstood the frightfulness of Franco for eighteen months.

We saw the Lydia Palace, University City, the National Palace, and also the Palace of the Duke of Alba which, by the way, was destroyed to the very ground by his friend, Franco, and the aeroplanes so kindly supplied by his backers. But more overwhelming even than the destruction was the proof of the resourcefulness and the determination of the Madrid people to defend their city to the very bitter end.

I have described my impressions before, which appeared in nearly our entire press, so I will not repeat the story. I can only say that never in my wildest fancy did I imagine such a miracle possible as the one that met me in Madrid at every step.

Franco heralded to the whole world that he would take Madrid within a month. Since that time eighteen months have passed, eighteen months of superhuman courage, of a stoicism unheard of before, of a determination of the people to fight to the last man and the last drop of blood in defense of Madrid. I found this spirit prevailing everywhere, at the front, in the rear, among the ordinary people, men and women, in the various departments occupied with the perfection of the work of the revolutionary efforts begun on the 19th of July, 1936. I met all sorts of people in the trenches, from the commanding officer to the militias, among whom I met a boy of fifteen who assured me with pride that he had enlisted voluntarily and that he wanted to fight side by side with his comrades much older than he to conquer Fascism.

We met Commandant Palacios, a striking figure, and a man of iron will. He had been an army physician under the Monarchy and the dictatorship. On the 19th of July he made common cause with the CNT in whose ranks he is serving to this present moment.

I learned the amazing fact that the CNT-FAI have 56,000 men at the Madrid front besides the large numbers in the mixed divisions. The capitalistic and Marxist press have fed the world on lies and misrepresentations of the CNT and FAI. They have dared to charge them with running away from the front. The correspondent of the New York *Nation*, Mr. Louis Fischer, stands out as the most dishonest of his profession, for it was he who

38. Eduardo Val, one of the key CNT organizers of Madrid defense from the Fall of 1936 until March 1939.

wrote in the New York *Nation* last year that on the "6th and 16th of November, 1936, the Anarchists took fright and ran away from the Madrid front." This was the more reprehensible because he must have known that Buenaventura Durruti was then still alive and in charge of the column which stood its ground in repulsing the first attack of Franco and his hordes. But that is beside the point. It is impossible to meet all the malignity sent out to the world by the various war correspondents. We have more important work to do.

It was a memorable experience, that day in the trenches, one hundred yards from the Fascist front and with the sniping going on without let up.

† *In a separate letter to Mark Mratchny on the same day, Goldman again indicates how the Spanish experience forces her to distinguish between anarchism and revolution.*

More and more I come to the conclusion that there can be no Anarchist Revolution. By its very violent nature Revolution denies everything Anarchism stands for. The individual ceases to exist, all his rights and liberties go under. In fact life itself becomes cheap and dehumanized. Perhaps it is due to the fact that Anarchism is too far ahead of its time. Whatever the reason it is certain, as Spain has again proven, that nothing remains of Anarchism when one is forced to make concessions that undermine the ideal one has struggled for all one's life. You see, my dear, I do not feel very happy in my shoes.

† *In a published article two months later (5/38), Goldman portrays fascism itself as simply a continuation of the brutalized mentality produced by World War I.*

We who had fought the Great War[39] had never for a moment been deceived in the din and tinsel that loudly proclaimed the alluring motives stressed by the war apologists. We knew too well that the aftermath of the war may prove more terrible than the ghastly thing itself, yet even we did not imagine the monstrosities that will arise out of the four years' horrors.

Yet here we are in the throes of Fascism and National Socialism. The most frightful world menace came quick enough on the heels of the war. Gaunt and hideous, it has infested a large part of Europe, devastating all social and human values, and savagely exterminating those in their way.

Fascism and National Socialism and all the frightfulness they imply are the direct legacy of the last war. Their thirst for blood, their will to murder, their sadistic trend to the vilest deeds have found their innings in the world carnage.

39. Meaning "we who had fought against World War I."

And so have their dupes whom the trenches and the battlefield have twisted out of human semblance. Brutalized and degraded they have been caught in the blood-drunk obscene orgy of Fascism and National Socialism. For in these ranks alone, millions of war derelicts are finding an outlet for their accumulated hatred and vengeance for the forces that had driven them to the battlefield.

†*To Spanish comrade Manuel Mascarell, Goldman expresses (5/20/38) her understanding of and faith in those anarchist soldiers who fled the front in northeastern Spain a month previously.*[40]

. . . The bravest and most heroic that our militia has been till now cannot stand for long the frightful continuous attack from the air and land – so I really do not blame our militias if they preferred to tramp their weary and painful way to France. The very fact that the majority of them quickly offered to go back to Barcelona to join the ranks at the front proves that it was not weakness or cowardliness or even loss of "faith and enthusiasm."

†*To comrade Hall, a young U.S. anarchist, Goldman expounds (5/27/38) in detail on the relationship of anarchism to revolution, pacifism and violence.*

Your letter of the 10th instant reached me some days ago. As I happen to have a moment free I want to answer it at once. First of all let me thank you for your confidence in me and your belief that I might be able to help you in your struggle regarding the question of "violence to achieve Anarchism."

I understand perfectly your distressed state of mind. With so much organized violence in the world, in fact with violence raised to the very pinnacle by the dictatorships, it is indeed very harrassing to find one's bearings in relation to one's ideal. You are of course right when you say that violence is contradictory to Anarchism. As a social philosophy, as a theory of the rights of the individual and the freedom of the collectivity, Anarchism is the only philosophy which does not propagate violence. But in coming to a correct understanding of the relation between Anarchism and violence it is necessary to face the fact that the present system in all its ramifications rests on organized violence, and that neither individual nor even group passive resistance can possibly change the course of the system.

In order to understand the inevitability of resistance to organized or legalized violence it is necessary to understand the real nature and meaning of

40. During the Aragón offensive by the Nationalists which brought the geographical split of republican Spain. (See footnote 84 in Chapter IV above.)

revolution. So few people realize that it is not anything willed. Revolution is, as a matter of fact, the expression of the preceding accumulated evolutionary forces come to a breaking point. Revolution in society is exactly what a cloudburst, an earthquake or a tornado is in the atmospheric realm. Nature breaks loose as a result of the elemental forces that have accumulated to the breaking point. I therefore maintain and have maintained that revolutions are inevitable, whether we are in favor of violence or against it.

Now what are the accumulated evolutionary elements that inevitably lead to revolution? On one side are the abuses maintained and perpetuated by our very system of violence. On the other side is the awakening of the masses to the need of some fundamental change. These two are bound to clash and do clash whether we like it or not. If we do not resist or resist only passively, the revolution will sweep over us just as the tornado will sweep over us if we are in its way. In other words, if any fundamental change is to take place the awakened masses must needs put themselves in harmonious rapport with the revolution instead of standing passively in its way or using what you call "militant non-resistance." (I do not see how non-resistance can ever be militant.) The function of Anarchism in a revolutionary period is to minimize the violence of revolution and replace it by constructive efforts. This has been done in Spain.

You say the Spanish comrades should be given every help because they began with violence and nothing else can be done now. In point of fact the Spanish people did not begin the use of violence. The violence was used against them by the military clique and the Spanish Fascists. The generals attacked the masses with arms. There was only one of two things that the workers could choose. One was to be exterminated and the other to resist. Fortunately our own comrades chose the latter. Otherwise Spain would have been saddled by Fascism just as Italy, Germany and Austria. For you must bear in mind that in Germany and Austria not a single hand was raised in any form of resistance against Hitler. The only reply the poor Austrians can give is that many of them are committing suicide. You see, it saves Hitler the task to kill them off. The workers in Spain were traditionally and temperamentally unable to permit the Fascist generals to impose the black scourge on Spain and the Spanish people. That is why it was a question of life and death for them to resist Fascism.

It is a mistake to assume that our Spanish comrades believed that they could establish Anarchism on top of feudalism and the power of the Church and that they could do so by means of arms. The arms they used were merely a means of clearing Spain from Fascism. The Anarchist part consists entirely of the marvelous constructive work which our Spanish comrades began almost immediately after the Fascists had been driven out of Catalonia and Aragón.

I will grant you that an individual may free himself from his manacles by "militant non-resistance," though the frightful odds to do so may so break him

that he will have no strength left to make use of his freedom. But the mass, as such, cannot gain its freedom by non-resistance; for whatever step it takes, even the simplest strike, organized violence will drive it to resist with more drastic measures than folded hands. Every stay-in or sit-down strike has proved that. Surely these were peaceful methods. The whole machinery of government was brought down with a bang on strikers, and there was nothing else to do but to resist.

Your supposition that were the Anarchists in the United States to attempt a violent struggle, their efforts would be drowned in rivers of blood, is only too true. But that would, however, depend on the numerical, intelligent and determined strength of the Anarchist movement. Suppose the Anarchists had reached the position of the CNT-FAI, could they not play such a constructive part as our Spanish comrades?

I note your examples, such as Gandhi and his followers, the Dukhobors and the others you mention in favor of non-resistance. Unfortunately the actual facts in these cases disprove your point. It is quite true that Gandhi is a great moral force, although even he finally compromised by urging his followers to take part in Congress, by himself taking part, thus actually recognizing the very government that is holding India in bondage.[41] On the other hand, the organized violence used against the followers of Gandhi has finally forced them to use violence, much to the distress of Gandhi. Whatever concessions Great Britain has made have been wrung from her by the determined stand and determined action of many of the followers of Gandhi and the other revolutionists. As to the Dukhobors,[42] their non-resistance had no effect whatever on their social surroundings. True, they carried out their scheme by passive methods, but they had to do so by withdrawing within themselves. They had no effect on the rest of the community. Nor were they able to establish communal relations. In other words, all those who have in the past engaged in passive resistance or non-resistance, while they may in rare instances have been able to live their lives in their own way, they have remained a group apart, and they have not advanced any social changes that had any bearing on society at large.

Most important of all is the fact that mechanized warfare and violence used by the State make non-resistance utterly futile. What do you think non-violence could do during bombardment from the air—a daily occurrence in Spanish cities and towns? I can see no other method than planes that could bring down the German and Italian monsters that have already destroyed tens of thousands of lives.

41. See footnote 41 at back of chapter.
42. A persecuted Russian religious sect for which anarchists Leo Tolstoy and Peter Kropotkin assisted in finding refuge at the turn of this century in western Canada. There they continued their practice of non-resistance, in opposition to obligatory government taxes, schools and military service.

In former times individual non-resistance was possible, though it rarely accomplished its objective. But our mechanized age makes it utterly futile, it seems to me; and therefore as a method of combating the complex social injustices and inequalities non-resistance cannot be a decisive factor. If fundamental social changes are to take place, it will only be through the uprooting of the old regime and that only the social revolution can do. Yes, I realize that it means alot of confusion, loss of lives, a great deal of suffering, but it would mean the same if it were possible for large masses of people to practice non-resistance. You admit yourself that it probably would mean even more suffering.

I agree with you, dear comrade, that education, especially from an Anarchist point of view, will go a long way, but it is not enough. People must also intensely love their freedom, be willing to die for it if need be, and to die for it in the consciousness that they have contributed to the clearing of the ground for the new social structure that is to replace the old.

Certainly, if one judges revolution by the frightfulness in Russia, one has reason to be discouraged, but when one considers that the Russian Revolution was not given a chance to assert itself, that it was almost immediately tied to the coat-tails of the Communist State,[43] then one will understand the abyss which exists between the Russian Revolution and the Soviet regime. No, it was not the Revolution that failed; it was the Soviet regime, the dictatorship. In point of truth, we Anarchists and our ideal have been vindicated by the results of the dictatorship.

Spain, on the other hand, has demonstrated the superior value of the free initiative of the workers. For it was that which has made possible collectivization and socialization by the workers and under their management. I go so far as to say that this beginning which the CNT-FAI have made has taken root in Spanish soil and in the Spanish people so deeply, whatever the outcome it will continue to bear fruit. So you see, dear comrade, that wherever a Revolution lays greater stress on construction rather than destruction, it is bound to express itself less in violence than in real living and building of the new life on the part of the people.

I know, I know, the frightful price our comrades have paid, the odds still against them, the danger and death staring them in the face. All the greater the miracle the CNT-FAI have brought about by their collectives and their emphasis on the need of building the new edifice immediately, and not to wait until all else will be equal.

To sum up, I wish to say that while it is true that violence and Anarchism

43. For Goldman, the spontaneous February 1917 overthrow of the czar and the subsequent massive upheavals constituted the genuine Russian revolution. This should not be confused with the various measures of state power consolidation by the Bolsheviks after November 1917 which occurred alongside and increasingly domineeringly over initiatives by the people themselves.

seem contradictory, it is nonetheless a fact that every revolution brings humanity nearer to the libertarian ideal. Think what the French Revolution has given to the world in thought, social ideas and ideals, in culture and in the conception of the rights of man. And the Russian Revolution, regardless of all the horrors of the Communist State, has struck deeply into the mind and the hearts of the Russian people. That will assert itself in the next social upheaval that is bound to take place in Russia. And now the Spanish Revolution — nothing has advanced the conception as conceived by Anarchism as all these great historic events. You may think that I am seeing through roseate glasses in the face of all the violence of Fascism, Nazism and Bolshevism. I will grant you that they make it almost impossible to believe that underneath it all the restless spirit of man for freedom, for harmony, goes on nonetheless.

† *To* Spain and the World *editor Vernon Richards (9/10/38), Goldman writes that Spanish anarchists hope to extend their own anti-fascist struggle into the coming world conflict, though she herself cannot go along.*

I have a hunch that the Spanish comrades will support the war against Germany and Italy. They probably will have no choice, for as one Spanish comrade here told me, "We are condemned to death anyway, a world war might help us." It is reasonably certain that the moment war will be declared both France and England will rush supplies to Spain to help get the Germans and Italians out of the country, which would of course mean the end of Franco. In consequence the anti-Fascist forces will feel duty bound to come to the side of France, England, and Russia. But I will not be deceived by that. I know already that all the high sounding slogans of war to crush Fascism and Nazism will only be used to blind the masses and to strengthen imperialism as well as Bolshevism. With my most ardent desire to be of help to our people I could not join them in support of the new world war. I am inclined to think I will stand pretty much alone in my protest against the coming conflagration.

† *With fresh impressions from her final visit, to Rudolf Rocker two months later (11/11/38) Goldman reveals that the FAI plans to sabotage a Munich-type international plot to carve up Spain. Even now they seek to carry out guerrilla struggle in the zones held by Franco*[44] *and to convince many workers on Franco's side to join them in later effective blows.*

† *By the time of her 11/15/38 letter to Ben (Capes?), Goldman reiterates more than ever her commitment to oppose the coming world war.*

44. See footnote 1 of Chapter II for sources detailing anarchist guerrilla resistance against Franco following the end of the Civil War.

. . . Another war may or may not destroy Fascism but it will also destroy our entire civilization. I grant you there may not be much in it worth keeping, but it has taken thousands of years and the powerful efforts of millions of people to make it what it is. It would be a great pity if it were to all go up in wreck and ruin. It would only leave hatred, discontent and a depleted humanity behind who will be lucky enough to survive the actual battle or the horrors awaiting the civil population. . . .

. . . I realize that my position and that of those who agree with me will be infinitely more difficult than in the World War. The issue will be so involved. The glamour to defend Russia and to save the world from Fascism will be so blinding that very few will be able to see through them; but I hope that I shall retain a clear head and sufficient energy to bury myself somewhere if it should be impossible to engage in anti-war work.

† *To her British writer friend Evelyn Scott, Goldman states on 11/22/38 her belief in the inevitability of revolution, yet also its shortcomings rooted in immature mass consciousness.*

. . . All my life I have insisted that the only test of real freedom is whether people have the right to disagree, because it is very easy indeed to agree. It is much more difficult for friends to disagree and yet cherish their friendship, their mutual regard and respect. . . .

What you say about the attempt to grant to the underdog the highest and purest motives is only too true. It is nothing but the cheapest kind of demagoguery and used as a means of attracting masses of people without any regard to their real understanding of what they are opposing. This, too, I have maintained all my life—that the economic motive for the rebelliousness of the workers is not enough. Time on end it has been proven to me that no sooner do the masses fill their empty stomach than their idealism and revolutionary spirit flies out through the window. I have had sufficient proofs of men and women beginning at the bottom who reached economic security and safety and then denied their whole past, or the men who have risen on the shoulders of the masses to power as their leaders or M.P.'s in England. With very few exceptions they have all gone back on their past and have become more reactionary than the reactionaries they have fought. . . . Besides that, there is also the fact that the masses in the last twenty years have demonstrated one of my contentions, that, while they are capable of bringing about deep revolutionary changes, they have not the sustaining power to carry them along in their great revolutionary task. Proof for that is Russia, Germany and Italy. It is all very well to lay all the blame at the feet of Stalin, Hitler and Mussolini. True, they are drunk with power, and they have not and will not shirk the most despicable as well as sadistic acts to maintain that power. But it is

nothing but the rankest hypocrisy to overlook the fact that these dictators could not maintain themselves in power if they did not have the active and silent support of the people in these countries. The masses unfortunately are swayed hither and thither by the man who can bully them, and appeal to their lowest instincts. So you see, my dear, I have always maintained what you say regarding the halo placed on the brow of the "underdog." It is, however, nevertheless true that the individual, whether artist or worker, can never hope to assert himself to the fullest unless the mass is emancipated, unless all the evils of our present system are eradicated root and all, and that can only be done by means of fundamental upheavals, not because we want it so, but because those in power and owning the wealth of the world will fight back as has been proved over and over against even the most pacific attempt on the part of the workers to better their condition. It is from this angle that I believe in the inevitability of revolution.

. . . . . . . . . . . . . . . . . . . . . . . . . . . . . . . . . . . . . . . . . . . . . . . . . . . . .

You say that "Anarchist philosophy is handicapped where the struggle is between brutes because its standards are so much beyond what is average acceptance." On the whole you are right. Our struggle is desperate and our ideas and ideals handicapped by the world-wide ignorance, studiously maintained, as to what Anarchism really stands for. Nevertheless Spain is a living example that the principles of what the Spanish people call Comunismo Libertario is not a thing of the distant future but can be made a living force today.

†*Replying to Mark Mratchny, Goldman writes (1/30/39) on the nature and origins of Spanish anarchist beliefs in a "national revolution." She comments as well on the impossible contradictions of a struggle for a Jewish national state.*

Dear Mark, not believing in the efficacy of nationalism does not mean that we remain "objective and cool" about the plight of the Jewish people. For myself I can say that I feel it very deeply; but I insist that it was the bounden duty of the Jews to fight for their rights and freedom and in every country where they were born and raised to help to create its culture and its civilization. I fail to see the benefit that it will get by establishing a new State in Palestine with the same old feelings of nationalism and a State. I see no great gain in the possibility of the Jewish masses being put in concentration camps or exploited by Jewish capitalists.[45] That is the only difference between you and me, I

45. Unenthusiastic about nationalist independence struggles leading only to new capitalist regimes (she pointed with disgust to the new fascist states of Poland, the Baltic region and most of the Balkans), in the case of Palestine she also felt that Jews had as much right to participate in such a struggle as Arabs. While opposed to Zionism as "the dream of capitalist Jewry the world over," she recognized the desperate need for an asylum for Jewish political refugees. (Goldman, "Palestine and Socialist Policy," *Spain and the World*, August 26, 1938.)

suppose. As to the Spanish libertarians, they were driven to the statement "our revolution is a Spanish revolution" only because they were forsaken by the international proletariat and betrayed by the democracies. Prior to that disgraceful and criminal treatment the Spanish libertarians have received from the rest of the world, there was never a talk of "our revolution is a Spanish revolution." On the contrary, they always maintained that the Spanish revolution and struggle against Fascism are not only to support Spain and Spanish rights but are for the people of the whole world. Our Spanish comrades always insisted that if they succeeded in crushing Fascism in Spain it would undermine Fascism in the rest of the world. So you see, my dear, that it is not that our Spanish comrades have become nationalists instinctively so; but they are being driven at bay by friend and foe, not the least among them some of our own comrades. That has forced them to depend on their own selves and that has also created a nationalistic feeling, which I think is justified in their case. Not so the Jews who have never lifted a finger to prevent the event of Hitler in Germany or have shown the least resistance in any country. Please do not think that I feel they are getting what they deserve—no, but I cannot close my eyes to the fact that the Jews have failed miserably to defend their own grounds. I insist further that if Hitler had only persecuted the Polish Jews he would have 90% of the German Jews on his side just as Mussolini had nearly all the Jews in Italy on his side.[46] Alas, it is no good to be a coward. In the end, no one respects cowards and the price for it is just as great.

†*To Cassius Cook, Goldman writes in 2/39 that she steadfastly opposes the approaching world conflict as an imperialist war. She also foresees her likely isolation in that stand.*

. . . I cannot enthuse over what these politicians, statesmen and journalists have to say. My greater concern is what the people themselves will do. I wish I felt sure that in the coming war the peoples of Germany, Italy and now also Spain would rise to revolutionary heights and throw off the burden they are carrying and the leeches that are sapping their blood, but I have not even that hope. On the contrary, I feel certain that not only the common man who has

46. Mussolini was ambiguous in policies toward Jews until beginning an official anti-Semitic drive in 1938. Jews held posts at leading levels of the state and party, Mussolini advised Hitler in 1934 against their persecution, and to pursue his rivalry with the British in the Mediterranean he helped support resettlement of German Jewish refugees in Palestine. Until 1938, therefore, official policy toward Jews was obviously much more favorable in Italy than in Germany. However, even in the earlier years, many Jews participated alongside other Italians in the resistance movement against Italian fascism. For more details, see Esmonde M. Robertson, *Mussolini As Empire-Builder* (London: The Macmillan Press, Ltd., 1977); Ivone Kirkpatrick, *Mussolini . . .;* and Charles F. Delzell, *Mussolini's Enemies: The Italian Anti-Fascist Resistance* (Princeton, N.J.: Princeton University Press, 1961).

no social consciousness at all, but all socialists, Communists and even anarchists, not to speak of the Jews, will rush to the colors of their country the moment the slogan will be Democracy against Fascism. These people never learn anything. They certainly have not learned from the last slogan, the War to End War, the War to Save Democracy. Now too they will be deceived by it, forgetting that war has never settled anything. It is only if the people within a country rise to their stature and break their chains that war can at all be justified, but never an imperialist war—of that I am certain, and I am definitely decided to stand out against it no matter what the consequences.

†*On 2/9/39, Goldman points out to Evelyn Scott that Communist cooptation of "revolutionary" ideals for their own benefit now is effectively subverted by their efforts at common-front respectability. Thus, hopefully, the concept and vision of revolution is liberated from the Communist grasp.*

. . . You are also right in your fears that "the Revolution may also become a superstition since most of its protagonists make it a movement in their own image and the opportunity for tyrants is ever greater." You overlook one great factor, however, the change in these present day "revolutionists." They have substituted "democracy" for Revolution. While this new slogan has helped to paralyze the energies of the masses and has deliberately betrayed the struggle of the Spanish, it has also helped to rescue the very concept of Revolution from its false pretender. Those still capable of independent thinking will now be compelled to see that Revolution does not express [only] the overthrow of institutions, necessary as that may be, but also the inner growth as well of conscious intelligent understanding for the individual and collective life. The Spanish Revolution had aimed at this inner and outer transformation of man and society. But the odds against the realization of this great ideal have proven too formidable. World imperialism of the totalitarian, democratic and Russian states, all combine to crush the Spanish Revolution in the bud.

†*In a 4/27/39 Toronto speech, Goldman indicates the personal risk she is willing to take in opposing World War II.*

There is no more principle involved in the coming war than there was in 1914. The English-speaking people should take a stand against it. As the old gentlemen make war they should be sent first to the front lines. I would oppose it even if it means going to prison.

†*Against the nightmare of fascism, Goldman informs a Windsor journalist (5/19/39) that the only genuine alternative is not war, but social revolution.*

War, world war, seems inevitable. There is only one alternative to world war and that is rebellion. But I believe that this world war will come before the peoples of this world move with potent force against government.

. . . . . . . . . . . . . . . . . . . . . . . . . . . . . . . . . . . . . . . . . . . . . . . . . . .

The people do and will rise against [Fascism]. There is unrest in Fascist countries now. Fascism leads to its own defeat. War or revolution? I think war first. But I also think that in some countries, war will end with revolution.[47]

I am afraid that revolution is the only alternative to war. When the people are oppressed and rise up, there is no way of stopping them. And the democracies, by reason of the existence of Fascism, are forced to become more reactionary.

England, with its fear and panic of the Fascists and its new war measures, is placing such restrictions that mark a terrible decline in the political liberties that England has enjoyed. It is a vicious circle. One thing leads to another. The only solution that I offer is the social awakening of the masses, all people who create.

†*In an interview with a Detroit journalist on the same day, Goldman states her belief that an anti-fascist world war will produce only more fascism, regardless of who "wins" the struggle.*

I believe now that another world war is inevitable, although I think it could have been stopped last year without a shot, if the democracies had not surrendered Czechoslovakia and Spain.

But in a war between modern democracies and the Fascist powers, I do not believe that it makes much difference for the people involved who wins. The only difference is the difference between being shot and hanged.

Modern democracy is only Fascism in disguise. The liberties of the people are being constantly curtailed. The latest example is conscription in England. And, of course, the present preparation of another imperialistic war. The people always lose in such wars.

†*A few months later (10/7/39), now after the invasion of Poland and official declarations of war by Britain and France, Goldman elaborates on the same theme in a letter to British anarchist writer Herbert Read.*

My attitude in re the war is exactly the same as it was in 1917. I diverted from that stand only on behalf of the Spanish struggle because I believed it was in

47. World War II indeed produced revolution in much of eastern and central Europe, most emphatically in Yugoslavia and Greece, but also to a significant extent in Italy. It also was a major factor in moving many colonized peoples toward mass movements and insurrection against the dominant European powers.

the defense of the revolution. I have never thought that wars imposed on mankind by the powers that be for materialist designs have or ever can do any good. But that does not mean that I do not stress the need of the extermination of Nazism. It seems to me, however, that must come from within Germany and by the German people themselves. War, whoever will be victorious or vanquished, will only create a new form of madness in the world.[48] It is the same about the dictatorship in Russia. Its terrible power will never be broken and eradicated from Russian soil except by the people themselves. My position here [Canada] as a visitor makes it impossible for me to take an active stand in the present war as I had in 1917. But I am with every fibre of my being against dictatorship of every sort and I am certainly ready to carry on propaganda against it. Naturally, I also do what I can to help refugees from whatever country they come, although my interest is in our suffering Spanish refugees.

You will gather from my attitude to imperialist wars that you have not gotten me quite correctly when you say that "nothing short of war, ending in a catastrophe, will ever rouse the working classes out of their lethargy here [Britain]." Here again I insist that nothing short of a revolution in British possessions will affect the Empire.[49] In other words it must come from the bottom up and not from the top down. I see that you yourself advance the same idea. Alas, neither you nor I can have a deciding effect either one way or another. We can only contribute to our utmost in whatever way we think can bring about a fundamental change. For the present it is still possible in this part of the world to speak out in criticism of Stalin and Hitler, but it may not be long before even that will be forbidden. We already have four casualties, Italian comrades whose house was raided and they were arrested for having subversive literature. Not only is it criminal having anything dealing with the war but anything critical of the state even if written years ago.[50] We hope to base our defense on the utter absurdity of the law and its complete abrogation of civil liberties. As you see I am not permitted to rest on my laurels. I am again called upon to jump in the breach of rescuing our comrades.

†*One month later (11/6/39), Goldman emphasizes to American friend Pauline (Terkel?) her total opposition to the new world conflict, despite the growing war psychosis based in part on popular anti-fascist appeals.*

Dearest, I am unfortunately not in a position to argue the logic of the stand of people on the present war or your own reaction to it. I can only say that these

48. This new madness no doubt is best demonstrated in the international politics of terror produced by the nuclear arms race and threats of nuclear war.
49. The correctness of this assessment was proven abundantly by the impact of events in India, Ghana, Kenya and Zimbabwe for the British Empire; in Indochina and Algeria for the French Empire; and in Angola, Mozambique and Guinea-Bissau for the Portuguese.
50. See footnote 43 in Chapter VI above.

people are going through the same mistaken position that many did in the last war. I do not have to tell you that almost anybody is better than that savage, Hitler. At the same time there is no instance in the human struggle of the past that should warrant anybody, unless carried away by the war psychosis, to believe that Hitlerism can be abolished by another world conflagration. The last war was also for the purpose of ending war and for democracy. The very existence of Hitler, Mussolini and the other dictators should prove to thinking people that wars settle nothing. But as I said, I must pass this up at the present time.

## Further Footnotes for Chapter Seven

2. It should be stressed that her negative critique in this case and other such attempts was always secondary to her concern with the social tragedy of individual idealists' lives wasted by their own prior experience of oppression and by the subsequent revenge of the law. She refused to be drawn into extensive debates on the political utility of such actions and was shocked when Berkman did so in a letter from prison, following McKinley's assassination (*LL*, I, 322-25). For her, the emotional content of the event was all-important: the suffering beforehand, the desperate self-sacrifice of the act itself and subsequent vulnerability to the full fury of authorities and the mob.

6. See, for example, her *Mother Earth* article "Preparedness: The Road to Universal Slaughter," reprinted in Shulman, ed., *Red Emma Speaks*. In Goldman's eyes, as for most in the historical anarchist movement, *nationalist* revolutions for independence occupied a sort of middle ground between capitalist wars and genuine social revolutions. To the extent that "national liberation" symbolically implies emancipation from *all* structures of oppression under colonial rule, it is historically progressive, representing the genuine liberatory desires and energies of vast numbers of people. But nationalist independence movements also consistently are dominated by groups and individuals wishing to restore state hierarchy – and often capitalism itself – only now under their own leadership. Thus Goldman supported the Cuban and Filipino revolutions against Spanish colonialism (*LL*, I, 226) and Irish rebellion against the British (*LL*, II, 573), but also refused to endorse the Zionist move to establish a Jewish national state (see her remarks in the present chapter). Along the same lines, she clearly distinguished between the deep social emancipatory aspirations of the French revolution and the relatively more superficial aspects dominating the American struggle for independence. (*LL*, I, 265).

12. Anarchist insurrections also occurred in January 1932, January 1933 and December 1933. There is little point in over-extrapolating from Emma Goldman's few remarks about these developments. She was apparently too poorly informed on the details of the Spanish scene at the time to write that much about it. It thus seems futile to try to locate her in the spectrum of anarchist debate on such revolts.

17. The division among Spanish anarchists referred to in the preceding footnote also split the international movement as a whole. Many anarchists argued that the difference between liberal democracy and fascism was crucial, that is that the struggle against fascism was a struggle for literal survival. For them, the only apparently effective way to participate was to join the Allied military effort directly, however statist and authoritarian this path. By contrast, among those siding with Goldman's anti-collaborationist position were anarchists such as Prudhommeaux and Louis Lecoin in France, the *War Commentary* journal collective in Britain and David Wieck and Ammon Hennacy in the United States.

19. The governmental decree of October 10, 1936 transferred the anti-fascist militia into a central government-controlled regular army. Regular units were to be formed with a traditional hierarchical structure of officers and military rules. Despite much wavering, then growing

general acceptance of this policy by anarchist leaders, there was significant resistance to its actual implementation, including in the anarchist militias themselves (see footnote 48 in Ch. IV). Good discussion of this issue and the various stages of reaction can be found in Semprun-Maura, *Révolution et contre-révolution* . . ., ch. 5; Bolloten, part IV; Paz, pp. 394-401; and an eloquent account by an anonymous militiaman in the anarchist "Iron Column," reprinted recently as *Protestation devant les libertaires du présent et du futur sur les capitulations de 1937.*

23. The same argument was made by Goldman in her 3/24/31 letter to Henry Aalsberg (AMS-R). There, she sees passive resistance as contrary to the cultural tradition of Western humanity – "a humanity fed for centuries on the Jewish and Christian religions, both of which stand for violence, notwithstanding the theory of the other cheek." On the other hand, she sees no reason not to propagate against that cultural tradition while realistically understanding its influence in the present.

41. She refers here to the Indian National Congress movement, the main political organization in the Indian nationalist drive for independence from the British from 1885 on. Gandhi collaborated with the Congress movement in various ways from his earliest days of activism in India, including accepting the post of president in 1924-25 and generally acting over the long range as spiritual "guru." In 1930, he published the Indian Declaration of Independence, calling for a complete political break from Britain. Until that time, Gandhi had hoped that the British government might become a benevolent ruler on its own or that it could be convinced to work out its own timetable for Indian independence. From 1930 on, he personally led waves of pressure tactics on the British designed to force them to grant self-rule; at the same time he engaged in talks with British officials to discuss new stages of autonomy. In 1937, elections permitted the Congress party to lead provincial governments under overall British authority, a dominant governing role it has more or less retained to the present.

# Chapter Eight

# The Role of Women
# in the Spanish Revolution

*In the historical anarchist movement generally, emancipation of women was seen as a crucial part of overall social transformation. Though the early French anarchist theoretician Proudhon had notoriously sexist views, by the time of Bakunin's prominence in the movement and the formation of First International anarchist sections in various European countries, anarchist thinking had changed decisively. Indeed, in late 19th century Western Europe and America, anarchists more than other socialist movements encouraged female participation and espoused the ideal of female emancipation.[1] Louise Michel, Teresa Claramunt, Lucy Parsons, Voltairine de Cleyre, and Emma Goldman were only more prominent examples of female significance in anarchist ranks.[2]*

*Nevertheless, despite their general goals, past anarchists rarely articulated or on a day-to-day basis manifested that strong anarcha-feminist perspective so prominent and increasingly influential today.[3] Few were the anarchists strongly advocating and struggling for equal sharing of all domestic chores and child-rearing, the widespread option of easy birth control, equal female rights to full sexual choice and gratification, and equal participation of a couple within movement activities themselves. Despite the impressive rhetoric, most frequently male anarchists retreated to cultural orthodoxy in their personal relationships with women.[4] At the same time, they favored movement prominence for only those females fitting*

---

1. See footnote 1 at back of chapter.
2. See footnote 2 at back of chapter.
3. See footnote 3 at back of chapter.
4. Marsh article, pp. 542-45. As of the early 1890's, Jewish and Russian radical men were the only males Goldman had met who practiced the "equality of sexes" ideal which they preached (*LL*, I, 93). German male anarchists explicitly believed that female anarchists' primary task was to stay home and raise children (*LL*, I, 151). By 1929, Goldman still had met only two German anarchists, Rudolf Rocker and Max Baginski, who seemed free from this prejudice (Goldman 3/9/29 letter to "Comrade" [Max Nettlau], AMS-G).

*images of charismatic mothers or quasi-males. Both tendencies still exist in movement ranks today and justifiably are attacked by contemporary feminists as subverting the prospects of genuine social change.*

## II

*Emma Goldman linked feminism and anarchism early in her movement experience. As a young recruit to New York City anarchism in 1889, she was quickly introduced to its then most influential figure, Johann Most. As her autobiography portrays, on the one hand Most viewed Goldman as a talented enthusiastic activist, eager to contribute her obviously great energies to the movement's advance. More importantly, however, Most increasingly saw her as a young attractive female whose personal attention and love could help heal the scars of his painful activist career. But Goldman soon perceived the conflict between Most's personal expectations and her own potential as a full contributor to the movement. Interestingly also, she grew increasingly aware that the nature of their relationship caused Most to lose his own anarchist sensitivity[5] – thus potentially damaging the movement even more. She was thus not long to break the personal tie. Among Goldman's later love relationships, that with Edward Brady[6] in the late 1890's seems most to have produced eventually the same impasse. Despite her strong affection, in the face of Brady's insistence that she temporarily retire from active movement life to a domestic role in the home (including potentially to raise children), Goldman chose her independence, as she always would.*

*On issues of women's emancipation, besides serving as a strong feminist conscience within the anarchist movement, Emma Goldman was one of North America's leading propagandists generally.[7] As a young girl in Russia, she witnessed the cruel ostracism and economic abandonment of unwed pregnant servant girls. Later in New York City as a practicing nurse and midwife, she observed close at hand the suffering of mothers with babies they had not chosen to have. Motivated by both the power of her ideals and direct observation, she personally took responsibility for learning and publicizing the latest methods of birth control. And this at a time when such knowledge, all the more its distribution, was thought by most males to be just as subversive in the cultural realm as was anarchism in politics. Equally threatening was Goldman's denunciation of traditional marriage as essentially no more than legalized prostitution. Even in the anarchist movement some viewed these efforts as needlessly distracting from "the main task" of social revolution. For Goldman, as for many other feminists then and now, cultural and political concerns were inseparable.[8] Nevertheless, in contrast with the vast majority of other*

---

5. Most's increasing possessiveness toward Goldman and his envious antagonism toward Berkman, her apparent greater attraction, are described in *LL*, I, 53-54, 65, 72-75.
6. Brady was an exiled Austrian who earlier spent ten years in prison for publishing anarchist literature.
7. See five of her essays on women's emancipation in Shulman, ed., *Red Emma Speaks*. Also, see Shulman's own article "Dancing in the Revolution: Emma Goldman's Feminism" in *Socialist Review*, no. 61 (March-April 1982).
8. See footnote 8 at back of chapter.

*feminists, while Goldman praised the militance of the suffragettes, she regarded their political instincts (hoping for significant change through the vote and parliament) as hopelessly naive. For her, to link feminism with politics was indeed necessary, but meaningless when left at the level of elections and the state. The essential bond in her view was between feminist consciousness and anarchism.*

*Before comrades in the movement itself, Goldman vigorously defended her own independent life-style and her particular attention to the plight of women. There is also no doubt that she often felt special attraction toward other prominent women revolutionaries, anarchist or not.[9] It is not clear whether Goldman also consistently criticized male comrades for their own sexist practice, in movement activity or in their own daily relationships.[10] Indeed, at that same daily level, some present-day veteran female anarchists remember her as frequently less than patient or sympathetic with her sisters in the ranks.[11]*

*One might speculate that at least unconsciously one reason why Goldman persistently avoided organized movement commitment beyond the affinity-group level was precisely her dislike for the typical male personalities found therein. In her view, movement organization generally, even among anarchists, encouraged careerism, petty jealousies and new hierarchies. No doubt these tendencies were to some degree the result of male preponderance in the movement, as well as due to movement organization in itself.[12]*

# III

*On this issue, by the mid-1930's, Emma Goldman saw the Spanish anarchist movement from two contrasting perspectives, a duality which would continue through the years of revolution. On the one hand, she was irritated and repulsed by the sexist patterns typifying Spanish culture generally. She was all the more antagonized to see such patterns frequently within the Spanish anarchist movement itself. True, a Teresa Claramunt, Soledad Gustavo or Federica Montseny could attain positions of great inspirational influence. At the same time, however, the vast majority of Spanish comrades continued to expect their own "companions" to provide the emotionally supportive and submissive relationship "necessary" for the activism of the males. Also, anarchists apparently agreed only theoretically that the goal of women's emancipation was equal to and essential for transformation in the*

---

9.  Beyond the reference in footnote 2 to her encounter with Louise Michel, see Goldman's enthusiastic and moving description of meetings with Russian revolutionists Catherine Breshkovskaya, Angelica Balabanoff and Maria Spiridonovna in *LL*, I, 362-63; II, 760-62; and II, 801-04 respectively.
10. This, like many other aspects of Goldman's life, deserves far greater research.
11. Similarly, given her commitment to women's emancipation and an end to traditional sex-roles, it is surprising to find her statement in *LL* that "it is really woman's inhumanity to man that makes him what he is" (II, 557) and her stereotypical equation of bravery with "real manhood" on the same page. A further critique is articulated by Dale Spender in *Women of Ideas and What Men Have Done to Them* (Boston: Routledge and Kegan Paul, 1982), pp. 360-67.
12. As Goldman in 1925 remarked (no doubt only half-jokingly) to her friend Van Valkenburgh, when she saw what a mess males made out of Russia and the whole world, she felt more feminine than ever (4/5/25 letter, UML).

*economic and political realms. Nevertheless,* despite *the seriousness of these critiques, Goldman continued to support the Spanish anarchist movement, even sometimes herself concluding that in the midst of armed conflict and rapid economic reconstruction perhaps the women's issue would have to wait.*

*With the emergence in Spain of "Mujeres Libres," a separate anarchist women's organization, Emma Goldman was overjoyed. Truly she felt at home among these comrades, as her descriptions of their leadership and activities make clear.*[13] *Yet for all its vigor, this separate organization still never approached the overall influential role played by the FAI, the CNT, or even the Libertarian Youth.*

*Goldman enthusiastically supported the Spanish movement, despite its failures when measured by a strong feminist critique. Clearly many contemporary anarcha-feminists would not.*[14] *For the latter, either anarchism starts with a solid feminist consciousness and practice or it is doomed to just as much internal contradiction and failure as anarchists traditionally foresaw for hierarchical Marxism. Cultural collaborationism, in this perspective, is just as deadly as collaborationism in the political realm. Despite such differences, Goldman's negative critique on this issue is obviously just as relevant now as before. So also is her hearty endorsement of the separate anarchist women's organization. Certainly, the persistence (in exile) and strong re-emergence of "Mujeres Libres" in current Spain would be acclaimed strongly by Goldman now. No doubt she would praise all the more the present widespread anarcha-feminist consciousness and practice in North America and Western Europe, itself a product of concrete feminist and movement experience over the last two decades similar to Goldman's own.*

*†For several years Goldman exchanged letters with anarchist Max Nettlau on the issue of women's liberation. In this passage from her 2/8/35 letter, Goldman places her impression of Spanish women (from her earlier visit and from her U.S. experience) within the broader framework of this discussion. At both levels, this provides a solid introduction to her subsequent comments in the late 1930's.*

I have your letter of January 12th. I am terribly sorry to have hurt you. Believe me, I had no intention to do it. I understood perfectly that in referring to the "innermost wish" of the Spanish woman to have broods of children you were teasing me and that you meant it as a joke. Those who know me more intimately than you, dear comrade, know perfectly well that I appreciate humor because I have a considerably developed sense of it myself. How do you suppose I would have survived my struggle, if I lacked that sense? But there are certain things which somehow don't lend themselves to joking. And one of them is the male contention that woman loves to have broods of children. Please don't feel hurt again when I tell you that, like the rest of your sex, you really know nothing about woman. You take too much for granted. I would have to talk with Spanish women myself to get beneath the age-long

13. See footnote 13 at back of chapter.
14. See footnote 14 at back of chapter.

tradition which has put her into the sexual straightjacket. I am sure that I would get quite a different picture than you have painted of her.

You charge me with having a hasty and superficial opinion about the Spanish mother from my short visit in Spain. You forget, dear comrade, that I had been thrown together with Spanish men and women in America for over a period of thirty-five years. We had quite a Spanish movement when [Pedro] Esteve[15] was alive. Not only did I know all the comrades merely in a public way from meetings and gatherings, but I knew their private lives. I nursed their wives in childbirth and I was with them and the male comrades in a special way. Long before I went to Spain I knew the relation between Spanish men and women. As I knew the relation between the Italian men and women. My visit in Spain merely verified all that I had learned from them over many years. And what is it that I have learned? It is that all Latin men still treat their wives, or their daughters, as inferiors and consider them as mere breeding machines as the caveman did. And not only the Latin men. My connection with the German movement gave the same definite impression. In other words, with the exception of the Scandinavians and the Anglo-Saxons, the most modern is the Old Adam in his inhibitions to woman. He is something like most Gentiles are to the Jew: when you scratch deep down to their inner being you will find an anti-Semitic streak lurking somewhere in their make-up. Now, of course, dear comrade, you call that "terrible Russian rigorousness and severity." Aside of the fact that you are the only one of my friends who has discovered this trait in me, I wish to say it is nothing of the kind. When one feels deeply, one's expression sounds "rigorous and severe." And I do feel the position of woman very intensely. I have seen too, many tragedies in the relation between the sexes; I have seen too many broken bodies and maimed spirits from the sex slavery of woman not to feel the matter deeply or to express my indignation against the attitude of most of you gentlemen.

All your assurance not withstanding, I wish to say that I have yet to meet the woman who wants to have many children. That doesn't mean that I ever for a moment denied the fact that most women want to have *a child*, although that, too, has been exaggerated by the male. I have known quite a number of women, feminine to the last degree, who nevertheless lack that supposed-to-be inborn trait of motherhood or longing for the child. There is no doubt the exception. But, as you know, the exception proves the rule. Well, granted that every woman wants to become a mother. But unless she is densely ignorant with an exaggerated trait of passivity, she wants only as many children as she can decide to have and, I am sure, the Spanish woman makes no exception. Certainly habits and traditions play a tremendous part in creating artificial desires that may become a second nature. The church, especially the

15. Editor of *Cultura Obrera* (N.Y.), Esteve died in 1925.

Catholic Church, as you know yourself, has done its utmost to impress upon woman that she must live up to the dicta of God to multiply. But would it interest you to know that among the women who apply to birth control clinics the Catholics, regardless of the hold the priest has over them, represent a very large percentage? You may suggest that in America they have already become "infected with the horror of horrors" of limiting the number of offspring. Well, I would be willing to put it to a test, if it were possible to reach the women in Spain with lectures on birth control and birth control methods. Just how many would demonstrate your romantic conception of what they want or my suggestion of "artificial" limitation of offspring? I am afraid, dear comrade, you would lose the bet.

Your interpretation of matriarchy as meaning that the mother must keep her sons tied to her apron strings, accept his earnings, and act the generous godmother in giving him pocket money, was to say the least very amusing to me. To me this merely indicates the unconscious revenge of the enslaved female on the male. But it doesn't indicate the least freedom of either the man or the woman. Besides, matriarchy means more to me than this cleavage which exists between mother and son or father and daughter. Where such conditions exist no one is free. . . .

Aside from all these considerations, it is the continuation of the conservatism of woman which has undoubtedly been a great contributory force to the reaction in Spain, the complete collapse of everything worthwhile in Germany, and the continued existence of Mussolini. Or will you deny the fact that the first thing after the Spanish women were given the vote was to vote back black reaction?[16] Or will you deny the fact that the German women have been driven back to the Kirche and Kinder[17] without as much as a protest? Or that the Italian women have been hurled back at least fifty years into their old position as mere sex objects? Heaven knows, I hold no brief for the American woman. I know the majority is still as conservative and as much in the clutches of the church as the women of the countries I have mentioned. But I do insist that there is in America a large minority of women, advanced women, if you please, who will fight to the last drop of their blood for the gains which they have made, physical and intellectual, and for their rights to equality with the man. Anyway, dear comrade, it seems futile to argue this matter between us. We will never agree. It is a commentary, however, on how little theories fight inhibitions. Here you are an anarchist, firmly believing in the utmost freedom of the individual, and yet you persist in glorifying

16. The parliamentary elections of November 1933 were the first under the new Second Republic constitution which granted equal suffrage to women. Apparently there was a significant loss of strength for Republican candidates due to middle-class women following the directions of their priests rather than the preference of their husbands (Brenan, *The Spanish Labyrinth*, p. 266).
17. "Church, Children and Kitchen" was one of the basic themes of the Nazis to guide German women back to the supposed strength (and docility) of traditional culture.

woman as the cook and breeder of large families. Do you not see the inconsistency of your claims? But the inhibitions and traditions of the male are too deep set. I am afraid they will continue long after anarchism has been established. . . .

. . . . . . . . . . . . . . . . . . . . . . . . . . . . . . . . . . . . . . . . . . . . . . . . . . . . . . . . .

I know you are too generous to harbor a grievance too long. You must not be angry with me for having called you antediluvian. I meant no hurt, but I will fight you to the last stitch on the question of woman and her great desire to have broods of children.

† *In this 4/24/36 letter to a comrade, Goldman announces her first contact with the "Mujeres Libres" group in Spain.*

Yesterday I had a letter from comrade Mercedes Comaposada[18] of Madrid asking for an article to a magazine called *Free Women [Mujeres Libres].* I was not able to write an article now but I wrote her a letter [stating] how very glad I was that such a paper is being issued to emancipate the Spanish women from bondage. Do you know anything about this comrade?

† *In the midst of her first visit to revolutionary Spain, Goldman informs her niece Stella Ballantine (11/18/36) of the work that needs to be done among women and the difficulty of doing it in the midst of a civil war.*

I find my energies instead of declining are growing stronger. Especially since I came here and saw all that needs to be done among women and children for instance. You have no idea how primitive everything in this direction is. Enlightenment among women is desperately needed. But our comrades are too engrossed in winning the anti-Fascist war to devote much time to this kind of necessary labor. A beginning has been made of course. But one cannot sweep away the ignorance, prejudice and superstition of a people in four months. However, I could do much, I know, and my efforts would be welcomed. But it is again the language, in Catalonia not only Spanish but Catalan. You see then how paralyzed I feel. There is no way out, I will have to leave.

† *To comrade Harry Kelly on 12/5/36 she speaks again of important tasks for Spanish women's emancipation and their relative neglect in the past.*

18. Mercedes Comaposada was one of the founding members of the Madrid women's group of the same name, "Mujeres Libres," before 1936.

You must remember that the anti-Fascist war and the revolutionary reconstruction our Spanish comrades have before them are not all of their colossal task. There is the education and emancipation of woman, the new approach to the child, to common ordinary questions of health. All that has been sadly neglected by our comrades. Perhaps they had to concentrate all their energies on the economic struggle [so] they could not reach out into many directions. But that does not alter the low status of woman and the depressing ignorance of method of the care of woman and the child. This field alone is large enough to keep one busy. And there are others. Yes, I will go back to Spain.

†*A few days later, the* Mujeres Libres *periodical published this important Goldman appeal to Spanish women.*

Human progress is very slow. In fact it has been said that for every step upward the human race has made, it retreated two steps into the bondage it has striven to escape. It has taken centuries for man to rise from his prostrate position — his blind belief in the superstition of the church, the divine right of kings and the power of a master class. True, this vicious trinity still holds sway over many millions in every part of our planet. Still it can no longer rule with an iron rod or exact obedience at the point of torture or death, though this is still the case in Fascist lands. However, Fascism is, historically speaking, only of the hour. And even under this black pest the rumbling of the approaching storm is coming nearer and growing ever louder. In Spain Fascism is meeting its Waterloo, all along the line. On the other hand is the ever increasing volume of active protest in the world at large against the evil institutions of capitalism. Strangely enough, the average male, so ready to fight heroically for his own emancipation, is far from believing in the same for the opposite sex.

To be sure, the women of many countries have brought about a veritable Revolution in their own social, political and ethical status. They have done so through years of bitter struggle — after heartbreaking defeat and discouragement, but also final triumph.

Unfortunately this cannot be said for the women of all countries. In Spain, for instance, woman seems still to be considered very much inferior to man, a mere sex-object for his gratification and child-bearing. This attitude would not be so surprising were it only to be found among the bourgeoisie. But to find the same antediluvian conception among the workers, even among our comrades, is a very great shock indeed.

Nowhere in the world has Libertarianism so entered the very life of the worker as it has the life of the Spanish masses. The glorious victory of the Revolution, born in the pangs of the July battle, testifies to the superior

revolutionary stamina of the Catalan and Spanish working men. One would assume that their passionate love of liberty also includes that of women. Far from this being the case, most men in Spain either do not seem to understand the meaning of true emancipation, or they know, yet prefer to keep their women in ignorance of its meaning. The fact is, many men make themselves believe that women enjoy being kept in an inferior position. It was said that the Negro also enjoyed being owned by his plantation master. In point of truth, there can be no real emancipation so long as any form of mastery of one individual over another exists, or any group over another. Much less has emancipation of the human race any meaning so long as one sex dominates another.

After all, the human family presupposes both sexes. Of the two, woman is the more important because she is the bearer of the race. And the more perfect her development, the more perfect the race will be. If for no other reason, this alone should prove the importance of woman's place in society and the social struggle. There are other reasons. Foremost among them is woman's awakening to the fact that she is a personality in her own right. And that her needs and aspirations are as vital and important as those of the male.

Those who still imagine they can keep woman in a strait-jacket will no doubt say "Yes, but woman's needs and aspirations are different, because she is inferior." This only goes to prove the limitation of the male and also his arrogance. Else he would know that her very differentiation enriches life individually as well as socially.

Besides, the extraordinary achievements of woman in every walk of life have silenced forever the loose talk of woman's inferiority. Those who still cling to this fetish do so because they hate nothing so much as to see their authority challenged. That is the characteristic of all authority, whether the master over his economic slaves or man over woman. However, woman is everywhere escaping her cage, everywhere she is going ahead with free, large strides. Everywhere she is bravely taking her place in the battle for economic, social and ethical transformations. It is not likely that the Spanish women will escape much longer the trend of emancipation.

It is true of woman, as it is of the workers. Those who would be free must themselves strike the first blow. The workers of Catalonia, of all of Spain, have struck the first blow. They have freed themselves, they are shedding their blood to safeguard their freedom.

Now it is your turn, Catalan and Spanish women, to strike the blow to break your fetters. It is your turn to rise in your dignity, your self-respect, to stand proudly and firmly on your rights as women, as free individualities, as equal members of society, as comrades in battle against Fascism and for the Social Revolution. Only when you have freed yourself from the superstitions of religion — the prejudice of the double standard of morality, the degrading and enslaving obedience to a dead past, will you become a great force in the

anti-Fascist battle—in the defense of the Revolution. Only then will you be able and worthy to help build the new free society where every man, woman and child will be truly free.


†*In a published interview (1/8/37) upon her return from Spain, Goldman assesses the progress, yet long distance ahead in the effort for women's emancipation.*

So far the women in Spain have hardly been given a chance to contribute much [to the Revolution]. They are not sufficiently awakened and advanced. Nevertheless I did find a difference in women as compared with 1929 when I visited Spain. They are much more alert and are beginning to show interest in the social struggle.

Yes, most certainly [woman will find her place in the new society], but it means an enormous amount of work yet to be done for the emancipation of woman. Once that is achieved, the Spanish woman will take equal place in the constructive work.


†*In a 3/30/37 letter to Chicago anarchist and friend Jeanne Levey, Goldman first comments on the role of the "Mujeres Libres" group within the Spanish women's struggle.*

. . . Our women comrades in Barcelona . . . are publishing a wonderful paper called *Mujeres Libres* (*Free Women*). They have begun an intensive campaign to raise the status of their sex. Until '31, it was fifty years behind the status of women of any country of Western Europe or the United States, and heaven only knows that [in those places] women are still not treated as equals of men. During the ill-fated Republic, some advance was made but the bulk of the Spanish women are still frightfully benighted. Our blessed comrades have been the pioneers of a great many things in Spain and they are also in their efforts to emancipate and educate the bulk of Spanish women. The paper was started by a group of university women who have continued for two years and who are now carrying on an intensive campaign. They have asked me to get them in touch with women's organizations in England and America, which of course I am trying to carry out.[19]

†*To Ethel Mannin, then preparing a new book, Goldman writes on 10/1/37 of her contact with one of the prominent women in the Spanish anarchist movement.*

This is only to let you know that I had a talk with one of the most able women

---

19. Goldman even joined a London women's organization, the Six-Point Club, as a way of developing such contact.

Anarchists who is really the historian of the revolutionary movement in Spain.[20] She is in the movement 55 years, is 72 now and she knew the great woman Anarchist Revolutionist [Teresa] Claramunt who it seems was really the Louise Michel of Spain. She has promised to prepare some material for your purpose and to have it ready early next week. I will then send it to you without delay. It may come too late for your purpose but at least you will know that I have not forgotten my promise to you.

†*Reporting on her second trip to revolutionary Spain in an article for publication (3/4/38), Goldman provides more details on the origin and activities of "Mujeres Libres."*

Madrid is the birthplace of the "Mujeres Libres." It was there that a group of university women with our comrade, Mercedes Comaposada, began the publication of the magazine by that name, dedicated to the enlightenment and emancipation of the Spanish women. The paper has since been transferred to Barcelona, but some of the originators, together with a staff of young women, are continuing their work in Madrid; and a formidable work it is.

The "Mujeres Libres,"[21] among other tasks, also busy themselves in visiting the wounded in hospitals, inspecting the children's schools and the distribution of a tremendous amount of printed matter circulating among the civil population to acquaint them with the purpose and the importance of the anti-Fascist struggle. They have classes for children and adults which embrace all sorts of subjects, including a class for chauffeurs. The comrades told us with pride that several of them already qualified and were holding driving licences. In addition there is a class for languages.

Then there is the "Prosperidad" Group that has 90 members affiliated with the "M.L." They comprise delegates from various local federations; among them the most active is Maria Teresa who is at the same time the principal of the school and all other efforts that are being made for the enlightenment and emancipation of Spanish women and for the care of children, especially those who have become orphans by the Christian grace of Franco. They are playing their great part in the task of raising the physical and mental standard of Spanish women, held in bondage for so many centuries, and especially in their devoted care of children. No more loving attention could one possibly give one's own child than these comrades of the "Mujeres Libres" are giving to

20. Probably Soledad Gustavo, the mother of Federica Montseny.
21. The "Mujeres Libres" federation involved some 30,000 women with close to 100 branches all over republican Spain by mid-1938. Beyond this brief description by Goldman, more detailed images appear in the material indicated in footnotes 13 and 14 above. There also is considerable description of "Mujeres Libres" activity in the Spanish anarchist press of the day, as well as in the periodical of the same name as the organization itself.

the innocent victims of Franco. I was particularly moved by the children aged from two to ten years, who were crowded together in a room turned into a cinema, and were hanging on every performance of Mickey Mouse and fairy tales, and sagas by Grimm and Anderson.

## Further Footnotes for Chapter Eight

1.  As Sheila Rowbotham points out: "In the anarchist movement at the time, even more than among the socialists, there was a very strong tendency to try to live out the ideals of the future society within the existing world" (*Women, Resistance and Revolution* [N.Y.: Vintage Books, 1974], p. 96). Among stated ideals in anarchist manifestoes or programs from the early years on were "equal political, social, and economic rights, as well as equal obligations for women" and "religious and civil marriage to be replaced by *free* marriage" (from Bakunin's "Revolutionary Catechism" written in 1866; reproduced in Sam Dolgoff, ed., *The Anarchism of Michael Bakunin*, p. 93). See also Margaret S. Marsh, "The Anarchist-Feminist Response to the 'Woman Question' in Late Nineteenth Century America," *American Quarterly*, vol. 30, Fall 1978, pp. 546-47, as well as her subsequent book *Anarchist Women: 1870-1920,* for other statements of the same theme.

2.  Louise Michel was an extremely popular and courageous militant in the 1871 Paris Commune who turned anarchist at age 43 during her subsequent exile to New Caledonia. She returned a decade later and was a leading anarchist speaker and writer in France until her death in 1905. Goldman's account of a meeting with her in 1895 appears in *LL,* I, 166-68. Her memoirs were translated recently by Bullitt Lowry and Elizabeth Ellington and edited as *The Red Virgin* (University, Ala.: University of Alabama Press, 1981). An English translation of a recent biography, Edith Thomas' *Louise Michel* was published in 1980 by Black Rose Books of Montreal. Teresa Claramunt was a longtime Spanish anarchist militant, a survivor of many imprisonments including the 1896 Montjuich ordeal (mentioned in Chapter I), and another influential writer and speaker. She died in 1931. (See Goldman's references to her further on in this chapter.) Lucy Parsons (1853-1942) was one of the most influential fiery militants in the predominantly anarchist-oriented labor movement in Chicago in the early 1880's. Following the brutal repression of that movement (including the execution of her husband Albert) after the Haymarket incident of 1886 (mentioned also in Chapter I), she continued militant activity as a speaker and organizer for the remainder of her life. In later years, however, she no longer identified herself exclusively as an anarchist. See the biography of Lucy Parsons by Carolyn Ashbaugh, *Lucy Parsons: American Revolutionary,* mentioned in Chapter I, footnote 2. Voltairine de Cleyre (1866-1912) was one of the rare American-born individuals to become prominent in this country's anarchist movement in the late 19th and early 20th centuries. She also was a very influential speaker and writer. Goldman's references to personal encounters and relations with de Cleyre are found in *LL,* I, 124, 140, 157-58, 332-34. Goldman's glowing tribute to her appears in *LL,* II, 504-05 and in a short biographical sketch, *Voltairine De Cleyre* (Berkeley Heights, N.J.: Oriole Press, 1933). A detailed biography of de Cleyre is Paul Avrich, *An American Anarchist: The Life of Voltairine De Cleyre* (Princeton: Princeton University Press, 1978).

3.  A militant, communitarian, anti-hierarchical feminism is so prevalent in the contemporary movement for women's liberation, it is arbitrary to cite only certain organizations or periodicals to the exclusion of others. Nevertheless, there are by now several "classic" statements of current anarcha-feminism in the United States. Several of these, by Carol Ehrlich, Marian Leighton and Peggy Kornegger, appear in Howard Ehrlich, et al., eds., *Reinventing Anarchy,* part V. Several feminist publications, including *The Second Wave* and *Off Our Backs* have regular contributions from this same perspective. Other useful publications within the last several years have included *Anarcha-Feminist Notes, Social Anarchism* and *Zero* (London).

8. It was their emphasis on greater liberty for individuals and groups that attracted Goldman in 1890 to the *Autonomie* German anarchists, Most's direct rivals in the movement. This strong concern with developing the *individual* as well as large numbers became a consistent critique by Goldman of the entire radical movement—anarchists included—through the rest of her life. An example of this view is found in her 5/13/31 letter to Max Nettlau (HAR): "I believe that the evil in all Socialist and Anarchist ranks was the lack of understanding for the necessary preparations today for what may come tomorrow. I mean that freedom, liberty and the respect for individual rights were looked upon as something that would fall down from Heaven like manna the day after the Revolution. Not enough stress was laid on the necessity of preparing the individual as well as the mass for the control of events after the revolt. That certainly was the main error of the past."

13. In the Spring of 1936, even before the civil war and revolution began, Goldman was invited by "Mujeres Libres" (at the suggestion of Mollie Steimer) to write for their periodical (an invitation she accepted) and to visit Spain itself. A few months later she was invited to become a corresponding editor and the organization's official representative in England. (Mercedes Comaposada 4/17/36 and 6/8/37 letters to Goldman, AMS-G.) Mary Nash, ed., *Mujeres Libres* (Barcelona: Tusquets Editor, 1975) is a collection of articles from the organization's newspaper, with a lengthy introductory sketch by the editor.

14. See recent appraisals of women and the Spanish anarchist movement of the 1930's in Liz Willis, *Women in the Spanish Revolution* (London: "Solidarity" pamphlet, 1975); Temma Kaplan, "Spanish Anarchism and Women's Liberation," *Journal of Contemporary History,* vol. 6 (1971), no. 2 and "Other Scenarios: Women and Spanish Anarchism," in Renate Bridenthal and Claudia Koonz, eds., *Becoming Visible: Women in European History* (Boston: Houghton Mifflin Co., 1977); Mary Nash, *Mujer y movimiento obrero en España, 1931-39* (Barcelona: Editorial Fontamara, 1981); Lola Iturbe, *La mujer en la lucha social* (Mexico City: Editores Mexicanos Unidos, S.A., 1974); Carmen Alcalde, *La mujer en la Guerra Civil Española* (Madrid: Editorial Cambio 16, n.d.); and Martha Ackelsberg, "Revolution Begins at Home: Women's Roles in Spanish Anarchist Collectives," "'Separate But Equal'? Mujeres Libres and Anarchist Strategy for Women's Emancipation," and "Revolution and Its Discontents: Politicization and De-politicization in the Spanish Revolution" (all three manuscripts available from the author, Department of Government, Smith College).

# Chapter Nine

# *Overall Assessments of the Spanish Revolution*

*The relative success of every social revolution may be judged from at least two temporal perspectives. To what degree were its transformational goals accomplished in the* immediate period *at the expense of how much compromise? To what extent did this profound social experience contribute to the* long-range *advance of revolutionary social consciousness generally—both within that particular society and internationally as well?*

*Rarely do millions of people simultaneously become conscious that the entrenched institutions and social relations around them are only a facade, that they are merely artificial social constructions exploiting the many for the comfort of the few. In these brief revolutionary periods, not only institutions are under attack. It also is the moment to confront mechanical behavior generally. Liberation becomes simultaneously a realizable social goal and a lived personal experience. In a shared atmosphere of magical energy, the world experienced to the present seems now a relic of history, a long nightmare forever cast away. It is morning, the bright sun promises a vast new beginning, opportunity is as far as the imagination can reach.*

*It is this immensely humane experience in revolution that provides so many great creative thrusts in personal and social fields alike, that clarifies and renews the vision of a joyous, exquisite world. Releasing experiences such as these may be lived on a reduced scale in non-revolutionary times, as in the exhilaration of mass strikes and demonstrations or in the peak experiences of intimate small groups or individuals.[1] Yet for its depth and breadth of lasting influence, there is nothing in so short a time period to equal the tremendous progressive humanization of society as social revolution. After two centuries, surely the West's persistent glance backward to the French Revolution, that condensed culmination of centuries of social ferment, demonstrates how profound this experience can be.*

---

1. See my essay on this theme, "Revolutionary Realization: The Motivational Energy," in H. Ehrlich, et al., eds., *Reinventing Anarchy.*

262 Vision On Fire

*At the beginning, social revolution is thousands or even millions of previously silent individuals now stating a common will to cast off the chains, to defy at whatever cost the forces leading them to their own dreary deaths. As a common recognition of unfettered hopes and a common atmosphere of free expression, social revolution is immensely exhilarating. Not only do individuals release those liberatory instincts so long repressed in the face of outside violence. One sees such affirmation everywhere and feels the tremendous social strength in proclaiming it together. Perfect strangers become one's closest comrades in an hour.* [2]

*Alongside exhilaration is destruction, though usually the two in part coincide. Targeted are a whole range of institutions and obligations, particularly those most despotic in the past. Revolutionary rage is usually unmerciful toward those persons well known for delighting in privilege at the expense of others, those dedicated to conscious exploitation. Psychologically as well as in strategic political and economic terms, one needs finally to release one's stored-up venom on the oppressor, if one is not to be consumed by the poison oneself. By contrast, in this springtime of flourishing humanization, past oppressors not seen as consciously or viciously attached to privileged roles often gain from a high level of tolerance, a sparing from destructive rage, assuming that these persons and institutions too can have genuine, decent human purpose.* [3]

*Indeed, revolution is not exhilaration and destruction alone. There is also an impulse, desire, momentum toward creating* longer-range *liberatory alternatives—new social relationships for the first time acknowledging that individuals and voluntary groups should be responsible for their own daily life. Having tasted the joy of the first moments of liberation itself, people rightfully expect relationships now to permit, indeed to include as an essential component the festive playful side of human experience which so thoroughly complements, makes purposeful and infiltrates the side of hard effort.*

# II

*The historical anarchist movement always looked beyond the mere toppling of oppressive institutions to the greatest flourishing possible of individual and community potential. Most anarchists traditionally believed that social revolution was the only way such goals could be accomplished. Only such a context of exploding energy could bring a decisive enough break from past bonds and habits to permit a conscious humanistic new order. For anarchists and others concerned with genuine social revolution it was essential to keep both tasks in mind, the negative*

---

2. Accounts of this phenomenon appear in every sensitive description of historical revolution. For those involved on a smaller scale in various rebellious contexts during the last decades—from campus sit-ins to the massive defiance throughout thousands of institutional settings in France in May 1968—it was a lesson in "alternative consciousness" never forgotten. Indeed, knowledge of this social possibility can be a continuing sustained source of energy for years of activism afterwards. Some of the best first-hand statements on the liberatory exhilaration of May 1968 are found in Alfred Willener, *The Action-Image of Society: On Cultural Politicization* (N.Y.: Pantheon Books, 1970).

3. See footnote 3 at back of chapter.

*and positive alike. Thus, toward the beginning of the century, for example, the great anarcho-syndicalist thrust in France, Spain, and to lesser degrees elsewhere represented not only the forging of a powerful instrument to paralyze capitalist production and thus bring the entire structure to its knees. It also simultaneously was the intellectual and experiential opportunity for thousands or millions of workers to familiarize themselves with concrete forms and potentials of alternative social relationships — those based on equality, comradeship and mutually-chosen design. The more this positive consciousness accumulated before the revolution, the earlier and easier the challenge and transition would be.*

*Emma Goldman inherited this general anarchist analysis and expectation of revolution during her first years in the North American movement. Her writings on the subject, as in* Mother Earth, *follow the same overall lines indicated above. Like most other anarchists, she was thus immensely enthusiastic over prospects in Russia, once the revolution broke out in early 1917. Her own direct immersion in and reaction to this upheaval are summarized in earlier chapter introductions and are described in great detail in both her autobiography and her book* My Disillusionment In Russia.[4] *These writings, as well as those by her close comrade Berkman,[5] stood out for many years (and perhaps still remain) as the best anarchist analysis of the Russian upheaval, certainly the best in the English language.*

*Without repeating or elaborating upon earlier summaries of that analysis, three aspects need special attention, since they directly relate to Goldman's subsequent evaluation of Spain. First is a matter of form. Once in Russia itself, Goldman found herself beseiged by utterly contradictory evidence. However much she had tried to keep in contact with Russian developments over the years, she was still an outsider. That was bad enough. But she also arrived on Russian soil expecting to see a lifelong ideal finally coming to fruition. Inevitably then she was bound to be prejudiced in her first impressions and was conscious of this herself. During the first few months she purposefully avoided excessive judgement in either direction, even when Russian anarchists sharply criticized her reserve. Additionally, however, Russia was an immense society. What may have seemed true in Moscow or St. Petersburg was perhaps not so in other cities or the countryside. Goldman realized this and welcomed the opportunity to travel thousands of miles by rail in a minor official capacity in 1920 precisely to gain better bases for judgement. Having done so, she was finally ready, in several more months, to break with the regime and that version of revolution it had brought about.*

*Goldman also was disappointed to see destructive rage predominating over constructive achievement. While still admiring the momentum and essentially liberatory goals when millions were involved in the great initial stage of revolution, Goldman came to feel that in Russia this energy had been too diffuse, too easily dissipated, too susceptible to cooptation. Only a prior awareness of and concern with practical progressive alternatives, a constructive consciousness among large*

---

4. As well as in many letters in the volume by the Drinnons.
5. Berkman's critique of the Russian revolution is found in his *The Russian Tragedy, The Bolshevik Myth,* and chs. 14-18 of *What Is Communist Anarchism?* Another excellent English-language anarchist critique is Gregori Maximoff, *The Guillotine At Work.* Also see Voline, *The Unknown Revolution, 1917-1921.*

*numbers in the population* before *the initial outburst could have produced a different outcome. Such conditions simply had not existed in Russia. The lack of particular constructive channels meant that when revolutionary energies finally were released, they expressed themselves predominantly through destruction, a one-sided emphasis not required objectively by needs of revolutionary defense at that time.*

*Observing this situation led to the third major feature of Goldman's analysis. In her view, the positive humane base essential for the revolution's continued popularity and progress was soon corrupted, demoralized and forgotten. Meanwhile, the Bolsheviks were that organized political group most ready to perform the destructive tasks and to assert themselves to a position of control.*[6] *The existing context gave them powerful leverage by which to demolish all potential competitors, organized or unorganized, genuinely revolutionary or not. In Goldman's view, this opportunistic channelling of mass-based revolutionary energy by a hierarchically-organized group meant the death of the revolution.*

*To the extent of its positive direction, Goldman felt, the Russian revolution was intensely inspiring. It was one more historical example—all the more powerful because in the present era—of the enormous latent progressive energies of oppressed peoples. This forceful positive reminder, together with the negative lessons of inadequate constructive activity and thus cooptation by an organized party, constituted the immensely valuable learning from the Russian experience. To be sure, capitalist propaganda would hide the positive message. Meanwhile the magical allure of Russia from abroad and the powerful propaganda machine of the new Soviet regime would obscure the negative. Nevertheless, even if it took decades to achieve, both sets of lessons from Russia would eventually be understood.*

## III

*Like Russia earlier, Spain in the late 1930's was a place of immensely hopeful, but also confusing and contradictory imagery and experience. Having little direct involvement with Spain previously, Emma Goldman again consciously avoided hasty overall assessments. At the same time, guided by the vivid memory of her Russian experience, soon she felt free to criticize* particular *developments whenever so moved—however contradictory and thus weakened a position this seemed to some comrades. As she herself stated, it was important to take a stand however confusing the situation, because one could never hope to be wholly consistent and uncompromising in the midst of revolution. By nature, revolution was a vastly expansive outward flow of energy in all directions. It proceeded too quickly into too many realms to be fully comprehended ahead of time. It was impossible for anyone to anticipate in advance exactly at which points one needed to be uncompromising or could show restraint. Goldman pleaded with anarchists abroad to understand this nature of revolution, to be sensitive to the difficulty for Spanish comrades to judge moment by moment its course from within.*

6.   Though relying for much of their popularity on *positive appeals*, the greatest weight of their action was destructive in nature.

*Compared with her Russian experience, the Spanish revolution apparently confirmed from the* positive *side the same basic lessons she had learned before. First, the constructive efforts, so enthusiastically described by Goldman in Chapter Three, far exceeded those in Russia's upheaval, and this despite a heavier presence in Spain of armed foreign intervention. To Goldman, these Spanish efforts proved both the actuality and viability of anarchist* constructive *ideals. They demonstrated the effectiveness of generations of massive anarchist consciousness-raising as a necessary prelude to successful conscientious and socially-coordinated radical transformation.*

*Not only that. In Goldman's view, vast constructive revolution created both the tremendous courage and energy of soldiers at the front and that continued dedication in the rear* despite *sabotage and destruction by Loyalist "allies." Similarly, it was the constructive experience which maintained that degree of autonomous judgement and self-responsibility shown by grass-roots anarchists even in the face of political compromise by their own "leading comrades." Given this positive revolutionary energy and dedication among so wide a popular base, it seemed impossible to Goldman that statist political forces or even collaborationist anarchist leaders could for long impose control on the transformational process. Revolutions are made by the people, not by leaders. Though she readily admitted weaknesses of revolutionary strategy and even of consciousness itself in Spain, Goldman eventually concluded that the failure of the Spanish revolution to survive was due* primarily *to the international context. As she emphasized in Chapter Six, the Spanish war was the first stage of World War II – again demonstrating that a revolution must be judged also in broader terms than the particular national society concerned.*

*According to Goldman, the Spanish revolution was the finest example yet seen of how a revolution should be made. As for its failures, these had now made obvious that* the international dimension must be accounted for more effectively in advance. *It was also now clear that even decades of massive anarchist consciousness-raising does not automatically lead everyone (not even all anarchists) toward anarchism, once the revolution occurs. As with Russia, the Spanish revolution gave to history important negative lessons on top of the positive ones reconfirmed. As a long-range contribution, it thus potentially brought the world that much closer to the anarchist ideal. However depressing the immediate outcome, however distorted and reactionary the images of Spain conveyed by the media and politicians of Communist and capitalist worlds both, eventually the message would get out.*

*Indeed, the impressive present interest in the historical anarchist movement and the revolution in Spain is one measure of how valid her judgement has proved to be. It is certainly one of my own hopes in presenting these writings that the lessons Emma Goldman lived through and articulated do not have to be fully experienced all over again by new generations. In this sense, while produced in the heat of conflict forty-five years ago, Goldman's assessments are written directly to us in the present. They help to deliver to us this incredibly valuable gift from the Spanish people.*

---

† *Only one month after the outbreak of civil war, Goldman writes from France to her niece Stella Ballantine (8/22/36) of her enthusiasm for the constructive emphasis in Spain.*

[The CNT and the FAI are] the strongest and most revolutionary Anarchist and labor organization in the world. One that has already set to work to organize the industries constructively. That appeals to me more than even the actual fighting. It is what had been neglected in Russia. That's why the Revolution could so easily be hitched to the Bolshevik State. This will never happen in Spain so long as the CNT and the FAI remain alive. Of course that holds good only for Catalonia. The CNT is uppermost there.[7]

†*On the verge of leaving for Spain (9/13/36), Goldman already communicates to comrade Mark Mratchny a pessimistic assessment of the likely outcome.*

I am not fool enough to think the victory is on our side. The odds against our people, not only from the whites[8] but even more so from the Communists and Socialists, are too great. But whether our comrades will be victorious or fail, I want to share their lot to the last breath of my life.

†*In her first speech to anarchists in Barcelona (quoted on 9/25/36), Goldman praises their constructive activity and the positive image of anarchism they thereby offer to the world.*

I am in your midst only a few days. But thanks to the solidarity and cooperation of the CNT and FAI, I have already been placed in a position to learn that over and above your struggle to crush Fascism you are laying great stress on the constructive side of your battle. The factories I visited and the houses you have requisitioned for your great task are in perfect condition and order as if there had been no pitched battles with our enemies in Barcelona. Work and life has continued under your supervision perhaps better than under the old owners. You have thereby proven that our grand teacher Michael Bakunin was right when he said that the spirit of destruction is also the spirit of construction. And you have done more. You have branded as villainous misrepresentations the charges in many papers that Anarchism is a chaotic theory—that it has no program—that it is only bent on wreck and ruin. In the face of danger and death you have already demonstrated that Anarchism is the most constructive social philosophy worth living, fighting and, if need be, dying for.

You comrades of Barcelona and Catalonia in general are giving a shining example to the workers of the rest of the world, that you fully understand the

7. Actually, in that area of Spain not occupied by the Nationalists, the CNT was by far the strongest force in Aragón and in large parts of the Levante as well.
8. She refers here, as in the case of White Russian forces in the Russian civil war, to the *reactionary* forces of Spain—the militarists, monarchists, conservatives and explicit fascists.

meaning of revolution. For you have learned through past mistakes that unless the revolutionary forces succeed in feeding, clothing and sheltering the people during the revolutionary period, the revolution is doomed to ruin. For its strength and its security lie not in the state or in the political power of parties but in the constructive efforts during the fighting period. Your marvelous experiment will and must succeed. But whether it does or fails, you are planting new roots deeply in the soil of Spain, in the hearts and minds of your people, and in the hearts and minds of the oppressed all over the world.

† *In a briefer statement, Goldman tells Phillip (Kapp?) (9/25/36) of the enormous significance of a large-scale anarchist presence in social revolution, despite her caution still about the depth of change actually accomplished.*

Since I came here a week ago till today I have been in a trance. It seems impossible that the miracle should have happened. That the idea Sasha and I have propagated, and so many greater spirits than ours, should actually have attained a chance of expression. No, I am not foolish enough to be carried away by external things. I know that the CNT-FAI has not yet ushered in Anarchism. But to see Anarchist tendencies expressed in the midst of danger and battle, to see our own comrades guiding the economic, social and industrial life, is something I had not thought possible in many years in any country. Yet here it is a fact, a living throbbing reality. As I said in my first address at a huge meeting, copy of which I enclose, whether the CNT-FAI wins or loses, the roots will remain deep in the Spanish earth and it will sprout again and again until it comes to fruition.

† *She reiterates the same theme and contrasts Spain with Russia in this letter to comrade Alexander Schapiro four days later.*

For the present, I can already tell you that the achievements of our comrades so far are simply formidable. They have undertaken what had been so criminally neglected in the R.R. [Russian Revolution], to reorganize, reconstruct and rebuild while they are also fighting desperately to crush the Fascist conspiracy, and they are doing it with a will and a whim that requires no measures of dictatorship to compel the workers to continue the gigantic job. Believe me I am not fool enough to be carried away by surface impressions. Yet I must say I have been deeply impressed by the effort of our comrades to translate our ideas in action and to apply them to their needs.

† *Speaking to a mass meeting of anarchist youth in Barcelona on 10/18/36, Goldman again praises the lesson of positive anarchism being provided in Spain*

*and also warns against the designs of "statist" allies.*

Comrades of the FAI and CNT, anarchist youth of Catalonia and the rest of Spain, I greet you. The great Norwegian dramatist, Henrik Ibsen, who was also a revolutionist and anarchist in his opposition to the state, in his drama, "The Master Builder," wrote: *"The Young Generation is knocking at the door."* You, the youth of Catalonia and Spain not only have knocked at the door. You have crashed through it. You have broken all doors and windows behind which were hidden ignorance, superstitions and crimes.

The crimes of capitalism, of exploitation and misery, the superstitions of the church, the tyranny of militarism; you have demolished them all. You have let in the light so that all might see the abuses and injustices of the ages. You have done more. You have brought to the Spanish masses a new hope, a new confidence in its own possibilities.

You, my young comrades of the FAI and CNT, have stormed forward to destroy all false gods and all false values. It was your fiery spirit, your flaming courage that brought about your revolution and that has proceeded to build, on the ruins of the old, the new edifice we of the old generation have dreamed about and worked for.

Until July 19th no one outside of Spain knew of the existence and importance of the FAI or the CNT. Now the two have become the torch bearer for the youth of the rest of the world. Indeed they are blazoning the path that all will eventually have to take to reach the goal you have set before you.

To be sure, there have been other revolutions. The human struggle for freedom is as old as humanity itself. And always, everywhere, at all periods of the upward march of progress, it was nearly always the youth who rushed forward in every revolution made by the oppressed and disinherited to break their chains. And yet, and yet your revolution is the first of its kind. It is the first time in human history that a revolution is advanced and led by anarchists and anarcho-syndicalists, by an oppressed people. For Fascism, Monarchism, Republicanism and everyone else who demands the State all hate us and all work against us and our ideal.

The Spanish Revolution inspired by you Catalonian Youth, you of the FAI and CNT, therefore signifies so much for Spain and for the youth and the masses in all other countries.

Though only three months old your Revolution has destroyed forever the stupid idea, even among so-called intellectuals, that anarchism stands for crime and destruction. That it has no social programs or capacity for organised concerted action. You, young comrades of the FAI and CNT, have disproven this lie, have shown that you can build as well as destroy. You have demonstrated this in the face of the Fascist hordes and the deadly blockade of your so-called friends. You are going ahead in your daily task with a courage bordering on recklessness, and with an iron will to create a new conception of

human and social values, of the right of every individual to freedom and well-being. It is therein that your revolution is far ahead of any revolution in the past.

Dear comrades, you have the right to be proud of your achievement. But your pride must not obscure the fact that your enemies are always lying in ambush. Not only your Fascist enemies. There are others as well. All those who talk of the necessity of new governments, who forge new chains for your enslavement. They intend, consciously or unconsciously, to lead the revolution into a new form of dictatorship. That would mean the death of the Revolution and oppression for all.

Comrades, anarchist youth of Catalonia and all of Spain, you who are fighting heroically on the anti-Fascist front, need all your courage to destroy every effort to attack your noble goals. That is the supreme need of the moment. But also you must make ready to fight on every other front that is threatening the Spanish revolution.[9]

You, comrades of the FAI and CNT, you, the young and proud generation of Catalonia and the rest of Spain, are in the process of bringing the revolution to a glorious end!

You will not halt on the way. You will demonstrate that anarchy is the surest and strongest basis for a new free society. You have already given this example and by doing so you have instilled part of your young blood in our old arteries. Together with you, dear comrades, we of the old generation[10] want to reach the summit of our glorious ideal and see it realised in all its splendor and beauty.

> Long live the youth of the FAI and CNT!
> Long live the Social Revolution!
> Long live Anarchy!

†*Another crucial accomplishment of the anarchists was in demonstrating that revolution does not require dictatorship, as she here informs Cassius Cook (2/8/37).*

[The Spanish workers] have shown that dictatorship is not essential in a revolutionary period. It is true that those who are enjoying political freedom

9. This is one example of an early explicit warning by Goldman to the Spanish anarchists about the dangers of collaborating with those who would destroy the revolution.
10. Goldman appeared at this meeting alongside Sébastien Faure and Luigi Bertoni. Faure (1858-1942) was a very influential anarchist in the French movement from the 1890's on, due to his frequent speaking tours and steady editorship of *Le Libertaire*. Bertoni was the editor for all forty years and over 1000 numbers of the Geneva periodical, *Le Reveil Anarchiste (Il Risveglio Anarchico*, Italian Edition) (1900-40). His own account of this same meeting appears in issue no. 959 (October 31, 1936).

in Spain are taking advantage of it to an alarming extent, but I agree with the comrades that there is less danger in the abuses of freedom than in dictatorship.

*†In her 6/10/37 letter to Milly and Rudolf Rocker following the May Days in Barcelona, Goldman contrasts Russia and Spain in the international dimension and concerning the motivations of their revolutionary leaders.*

*She understands how outside comrades are now so bitter or intolerant, precisely because the Spanish revolution raised their hopes so high. But contrary to what they believe, they need to see that Lenin and the CNT-FAI had different goals. Furthermore, it was far easier to defend the Russian revolution than that in Spain. The former had a vast land area, far from the European powers and tens of thousands of experienced armed soldiers, fresh from the front. Anti-Fascist Spain had no trained soldiers and was close prey to Germany and Italy both. It also had to contend with the potential willingness of Britain and France at any time to join the others in ripping apart Spain and the revolution.*

Seen in this light there is more reason not to throw out the child with the bath as our French comrades and our dearest Mollitchka, Senia, Sania and the others are doing.

*†In her July 1937 preface to the reprint of Berkman's* What Is Communist Anarchism?, *Goldman sees his emphasis on constructive efforts in the social revolution as borne out by the Spanish example.*

There is no getting away from the fact that there is a vast difference between the mind of the Latin worker and that of his brother in the United States and in England: the former has been steeped in the revolutionary traditions and struggles for freedom and other causes, while the latter has been brought up on the "blessings" of parliamentarianism.
. . . . . . . . . . . . . . . . . . . . . . . . . . . . . . . . . . . . . . . . . . . . .
[There] was the urgent need for a new orientation of revolutionary tactics, called forth by the experience of the Russian Revolution. Anarchists as well as all Social Revolutionists had been steeped in the romantic glamor of the French Revolution. We all believed (I do not exclude myself) that the Social Revolution had magic power, not merely to destroy the old decayed order, but that it could, by its own terrific force, build up the new social edifice. The Russian Revolution demolished this romantic dream. It proved that, while it can rouse the masses to the very zenith of revolutionary fervor, it cannot maintain them in that height for very long. The very fact that Lenin and his comrades succeeded in a very brief space of time to alienate the Russian masses from the Revolution, and Stalin was able to emasculate the latter altogether, proved that mere revolutionary fervor is not enough. More was

needed to safeguard the Revolution from the political State design of the new masters of Russia. The will to constructive work, the economic and social preparation were needed in order to direct the Revolution into channels where it was meant to go.

None of the post-revolutionary Anarchist writings had attempted to deal with the new orientation. It was left to Alexander Berkman to carry out his difficult, yet most important, task. And who was there so eminently qualified, so able and with so penetrating an intellect to do justice to such a subject?

Not in his wildest fancies did Alexander Berkman anticipate that the lesson from the Russian Revolution, discussed by him so ably in this volume [*Now and After: The ABC of Communist Anarchism*], would become a living factor within six short years of its creation. The Spanish Revolution of July 19, 1936 and the part played in it by the Anarcho-Syndicalists and Anarchists imbue with much deeper meaning the ideas presented in the present volume of Alexander Berkman's *The ABC of Communist Anarchism* than its author ever dared to hope for. From the very first moment of the 19th of July, the National Confederation of Labor (the CNT) and the Anarchist Federation of Iberia (the FAI)—the most dominant, most ardent and daring organizations—were the forces that drove back the Fascist hordes from Catalonia. Their marvelous achievement is the first of its kind in any revolution. It merely bears out the truism asserted by Alexander Berkman regarding the imperative need for constructive preparedness, if the Social Revolution is not to repeat the errors of the past.

How my old pal and comrade would have gloried in the Spanish Revolution, in the heroic determination of the people to fight unto the last man against Fascism! Above all, how gratifying it would have been to him to see the Spanish people evince such profound feeling and understanding of *Comunismo Libertario*—how that would have rejuvenated our comrade and given him new strength, new hope!


†*In this moving 9/10/37 reply to her critical yet close comrade and friend Mollie Steimer, Goldman praises Spanish anarchist accomplishment and defends their right to make honest mistakes.*


. . . Anarchism in Spain, far from having failed, has actually proven consistent and realizable. I have in mind the constructive work begun by our comrades which was the greatest achievement in any revolutionary period. By their constructive efforts the CNT-FAI have demonstrated to the whole world that Anarchism is not only a theory, a wild irresponsible fancy, a destructive force. But that it applies to life and the innermost needs of the people. If the Spanish revolution had given no other proof for its justification, this one fact should convince those at all capable of thinking that Anarchism is a practical

theory of a new social order. Even if the CNT-FAI have actually lost all ground, their grand efforts temporarily destroyed, which I do not believe for a moment, they will still have given a splendid example of the work done in the face of war and Revolution.

You may suggest the price was too high. And you may ask why the Spanish comrades had learned so little from the Russian Revolution to permit Stalin's gangsters to rob them of the fruit of their wonderful beginning. Well, while it is extremely painful to admit it even to ourselves we have yet to look facts in the face. And they are that neither the people en masse nor the individual ever learn anything from the experience of another. We rarely learn from our own experience. If we did we would not go on repeating the same blunders all our lives. But we certainly never learn from the experience of others. Why then be surprised if the Spanish comrades have not learned much from the Russian revolution? Besides it is not true that they have learned nothing. In point of fact they went much further than the Russian revolution. They did what was sadly neglected in the Russian revolution. They immediately proceeded to construct whereas in Russia everybody, including the Anarchists, did nothing but destroy. I do not mean this to detract from the part played by our Russian comrades. I mean it only as a historic fact. Another important point by no means of small importance is also the fact that our comrades in Russia were never at any time surrounded by so many diverse political enemies to be forced to decide whether or not they should align themselves with them. And yet many of our best comrades justified the alignment with the Bolsheviki and defended them until the Kronstadt massacre.

You will ask if that means that I justify the alignment of our comrades with their political enemies. Of course not. Truth to tell I opposed it from the very beginning when you and Senia asked, "What should our comrades have done?" You speak of taking a stand. I have done that, dearest Mollitchka, in my article "Where I Stand."[11] I have specifically stated that I stand today where I always have. That I am just as opposed to Anarchists' participation in any government whatever its tendency and every political party whatever its pretense. But while I stand firmly on my life-long ground, I refuse to join in the condemnation of our comrades, because as I have already stated, we none of us learn from the experience of others. Whatever the price our comrades are paying in Spain they evidently had to have their own, they had to act according to their own lights and not according to ours. However I am not so sure that we in their place would have been wiser and more consistent than our comrades. Don't you agree that there is a large amount of vanity in every one of us to think that we would have acted otherwise? We insist on our superior knowledge and understanding for events in private life as well as for large social issues. We are never willing to admit

11. In *Spain and the World*, I, 15 (July 2, 1937), reproduced in near entirety in Chapter II.

that we actually do not know how we would act were we in the place of those we so readily hold up to scorn and condemnation until some emergency arises. The older I grow the surer I become that it is extremely difficult to decide a mode of action for either ourselves or others. All that we can really be sure of is that we mean to try honestly to act in keeping with our ideas and our faith.

†*Now back in revolutionary Spain on her second visit, Goldman is amazed that the comrades could maintain their constructive momentum in the midst of attacks from all sides (9/23/37 letter to* Spain and the World*).*

You will be impatient with me that I have written so little since I got to Spain. The events are too overwhelming for letters. The days are filled to overflowing with impressions. Especially is this the case here. Madrid is the wonder of centuries for there is nothing like it in fortitude and epic grandeur. One had to see it to realize its tremendous courage and spirit regardless of the danger surrounding it, regardless of what the city and the people have already endured at the hands of Fascism. Greater still is the faith of our people who go on building, creating and laboring not for the hour but for all times. One cannot help but set aside all doubts and all superficial criticism in the face of such wonderful manifestation of human endurance and determination to win come what may. I am so full of it all I cannot concentrate on any one impression or say what is more inspiring than the other. More than even last year I wish I could remain with our people right here in this heroic city and share in their struggle and their aspirations. But once again I will have to leave much sooner than I want. We are going back to Valencia tomorrow, from there Sunday or Monday to Barcelona. Perhaps I can write more coherently from there. I only wish all our comrades so ready to judge could come to Spain to see for themselves that whatever the mistakes made they are as nothing compared with the gigantic work already achieved. Whatever happens this will remain a lasting monument to the valor and the constructive genius of our comrades.

†*In this scathing 5/38 reply to Leon Trotsky intended for publication, Goldman contrasts Spanish anarchist accomplishment to the ideals and practice of his own cause.*

. . . [Trotsky] joins the howling mob and thrusts his own poisoned dagger into the vitals of the Spanish Anarchists in their most crucial hour.[12]

No doubt the Spanish Anarchists have committed a grave error. They failed to invite Leon Trotsky to take charge of the Spanish Revolution and to

12. In his article in *The New International*, vol. IV, no. 4 (April 1938).

show them how well he had succeeded in Russia that it may be repeated all over again on Spanish soil. That seems to be his chagrin.

Leon Trotsky tries a trump card when he asks "Where and when their great principles were confirmed, in practice at least partially, at least in tendency?" This card, like all the others he has already played in his life, will not win him the game. In point of fact Anarchist principles in practice and tendency have been confirmed in Spain. I agree, only partially. How could that be otherwise with all the forces conspiring against the Spanish Revolution? The constructive work undertaken by the National Confederation of Labor, the CNT, and the Anarchist Federation of Iberia, the FAI, is something never thought of by the Bolshevik regime in all the years it was in power, and yet the collectivization of the industries and the land stand out as the greatest achievement of any revolutionary period. Moreover, even if Franco should win, and the Spanish Anarchists be exterminated in rivers of blood, will the work they have started continue to live? The roots of Anarchist principles and tendencies are so deeply rooted in Spanish soil that they cannot be eradicated. Where and when has Trotsky's banner, which he claims has never compromised with the enemy and represents the revolutionary current of the future, even remotely equalled the splendid example of the men and women who are now fighting with their backs to the wall?

†*Replying on 2/3/39 to anarchist Ben Capes, Goldman points out that Spain demonstrates that the state will not disappear on its own in the midst of revolutionary social arrangements.*

My dear, I have read Proudhon's *General Idea of the Revolution in the 19th Century*,[13] and I know his attitude towards the "difference between Marx' conception of the withering away of the State, or the State dissolution in the economic organism." Nevertheless I will read it again, if only to satisfy you. It is quite true, my dear, that our people have laid the greatest stress on the economic organization during the period of the Revolution. If Proudhon is right, then that should have weakened the republican government, but as a matter of fact it has not. It was unfortunately this false belief which gave the republican government a breathing space so that they could reorganize their forces and become the dead weight of the Revolution.[14]

13. Published in July 1851. An English translation was published in London in 1923 and reprinted by Gordon Press (New York) in 1972.
14. See footnote 3 above. Though anarchists concentrated on economic organization, they also legitimized and participated in governmental institutions as well — from the local level to the national government, from the military realm to the economic, a debilitating reality which Goldman describes in detail in Chapters IV and V.

†*Following the collapse of Catalonia, in this 2/17/39 letter to American friend Lillian Nedelsohn (Mendelsohn), Goldman already presents a broad judgement of the Spanish revolution's place in history.*

The events in Catalonia and Barcelona have been too much even for my iron nerves. I feel too crushed to be able to concentrate on worthwhile writing, but I may before long pull myself together . . . .

. . . . . . . . . . . . . . . . . . . . . . . . . . . . . . . . . . . . . . . . . . . . . . . . . . .

This, my dear, is all I can tell you about the collapse of a great beginning, the greatest in history, and of a struggle that does not know its equal in many centuries.

As to what will become of central and southern Spain, that is difficult to say at this writing. I am certain that the people there are determined to fight on to the uttermost, but I have no faith whatever in the Negrín government, not that I have faith in any government, but Negrín has proven weak, ineffectual and ready to sell out. For that, too, I have documentary proofs. Nothing is so ridiculous to me than to read what Negrín or anyone else of the government say about "we will fight to the end" when the people do the fighting and pay the price. I wish I could give you more detailed description. Unfortunately the material I have cannot be disclosed until our comrades themselves have settled whether to go on or surrender their achievement.

†*A week later (2/24/39) to Cassius Cook, she again assumes a distanced perspective.*
*Though on several occasions, the Spanish anarchists could have established a dictatorship, they steadfastly refused to do so. This particular fact historians probably will assess as one of the most positive aspects of the revolution. For the present, she is too upset by the tragedy in Catalonia to pose alternative methods for protecting a revolution from its enemies.*

I know that our people have made irreparable mistakes, but also I know that one cannot learn without mistakes, so perhaps the Spanish anarchists and anarcho-syndicalists who have sacrificed so much and who are now suffering beyond belief will learn something constructive for their future struggle out of it all.

†*Three days later, in a letter to CNT leader Mariano Vázquez, Goldman stresses the decisive importance of faith and vision in maintaining revolutionary momentum and the negative impact of "realist" measures and institutions in deflating such energy. It was the latter factor, as direction of the anti-fascist struggle passed from the workers themselves to the government, which was at least as important as the lack of arms in bringing defeat. This was clear from her many conversations with comrades during her last visit to Spain. Even now, however, she still feels the spirit*

*of the Spanish people and the anarchist movement remains unconquered. Thus she cannot agree with his stress now on realism over revolutionary illusion. Without idealistic vision, so-called reality is meaningless, a sorry imitation of life.*

†*In her final public speech in London (3/24/39), Goldman asserts that it was precisely the positive nature of the anarchist example in Spain which attracted such vicious antagonism from all sides.*

. . . I was amazed at the tremendous constructive work that the Spanish workers achieved side by side with their struggle, with the loss of life, with hunger, with all sorts of things against them; and that is what was feared the most. Don't you see, don't you realise, to demonstrate that Anarchists, who are decried by all sorts of people, working men, liberals, labour people, the capitalistic class, as criminals who go about with bombs in their hands or pockets, and with knives and with poison, and who can only be appeased if they destroy the children of the capitalists and hang the priests on the nearest lamp-post—that such Anarchists, hated by everyone, condemned by everyone, attacked by everyone, were able to show a new line of procedure in revolutionary struggle—what greater crime or offence? And that is why it was necessary to do everything possible in order to destroy that marvellous beginning.

†*Though the Spanish revolution was defeated, in this 10/7/39 letter to British anarchist Herbert Read, Goldman still states her faith in its ultimate long-range triumph.*

How right you are when you say "that Spain was a turning point, and that it will probably be a century or more before we recover from that tragedy." However, I have abiding faith in the Spanish people and I feel certain they will come back and then woe be to the victors who are now in the saddle.

## Further Footnotes for Chapter Nine

3. Many anarchists would argue that in the case of Spain, concerns with maintaining the anti-fascist front as well as inadequate analysis pulled destruction of the old society far *short* of what was needed—not only politically (as in maintaining governmental institutions), but in the economic realm as well. A. De Malandier argued in the Summer of 1939 that beyond the corroding effect on the revolution caused by the more obvious state structures, equal leverage for those working to re-establish the old order came from the churches, people's tribunals (with their symbolic air of "legality"—however defined), prisons, salaries, money, and all official public and business records generally (*L'Espagne Nouvelle*, July-September 1939). By such standards, the attempt to abolish money (without alternative "exchange" replacements) in several small anarchist villages and the bold (but aborted) plan by Durruti, Santillán and others in October 1936 to confiscate the gold from the Bank of Spain to counterbalance the power of the Madrid government seem moderate indeed.

# Chapter Ten

# General Reflections on Anarchism and the Movement

*The Spanish movement of the late 1930's was greater in numbers and political influence than anywhere else in modern anarchist history. With this strength and decisive presence in the context of a massive social revolution, the experience of Spanish anarchists during this period easily might be seen as the best test to date of anarchism's viability as a political ideology and movement.*

*However valid such measures of anarchist "success" may be, it is assessible in other terms as well. Its goal is immense: to transform social consciousness of entire populations and to introduce freely-chosen social forms in place of those of existing oppression. To achieve both tasks, anarchism must reach beyond its obvious liberatory concern with the immediate social moment. Complementary long-range analysis and effort are essential, a need anarchists have been forced bitterly to accept because of the immense strength of the existing forces of domination. From this it follows that one possible and relevant alternative measure of anarchism's success is its ability to survive and grow in influence over time.*

*For this reason, from early in the movement's history, most anarchists have valued education and other small-scale efforts which gradually develop and nurture that liberatory spirit in all. Such efforts are made despite the knowledge that decades may pass before a large-scale revolution. In addition, within this same long-range perspective, anarchists tend to be far more concerned that the flame of free spirit and rebellion survive and spread than that a* particular *movement organizational structure itself persist over time.[1] In this sense, viewing the quality of human experience as a guide, not perpetuation of institutions for their own sake,*

---

1. To the extent that a long-range continuation of "the movement" as such is valued, it is more in the sense of the present book's purpose—to preserve historical consciousness of important anarchist experiences and insights from the past. This is especially needed in the face of efforts by the institutionalized Left and the Establishment to hide forever such "dangerous" examples from social memory.

*again anarchists differ considerably from other political movements.*[2]

*This leads to another relevant measure of anarchism's viability or success. Anarchism heavily emphasizes* consistent *politics in the* present. *As Chapter Four underscored, anarchists are especially sensitive to that fatal erosion of human spirit when each oppressive experience goes unchallenged in the name of "waiting for a better opportunity." Needless to say, this anarchist emphasis on consistency directly contrasts with the common short-range calculations of politicians (establishment and radical both) who sell out principles overnight at the slightest chance to gain power.*

*Given the tremendous anarchist stress on the significance of the individual, the high quality of liberation achieved by even a few in number can be seen in* one *sense as just as important at any moment as a lesser emancipation for larger numbers. Of course most anarchists would resist any type of trade-off of the many for the benefit of the few and would disagree among themselves as to how much freedom individuals can achieve, in any case, if surrounded by, let alone dependent on, others who are oppressed. Indeed, these are crucial differences between right-wing laissez-faire individualists and left-wing communitarian or social anarchists.*[3] *But in general terms, anarchists, more than others concerned with social change, traditionally have seen individual emancipation and maintenance of personal integrity as important measures of the movement's success.*

*A third alternative measure comes from the internationalist perspective of anarchism. Since any national and cultural boundaries are superficial compared to the universal needs and potentials of human nature, truly the entire global population is just as much the movement's concern as the activist's own community or nation. Naturally, because of their roots, most people are more relaxed and effective interacting with others of the same culture. This is one reason why activists tend to give more attention, when possible, to the movement in their own "home" areas, all the more if language barriers and communication over distance are significant obstacles as well. Nevertheless, generally again the anarchist movement more than others has emphasized truly international comradeship and concern.*[4]

*Let us return to the original more common criteria for success mentioned at the beginning. By the three measures of size, immediate political influence, and location in a revolutionary context, many anarchists and others over the last forty-five years have viewed the Spanish experience of the late 1930's as the greatest height and greatest collapse of the anarchist movement in history. Yet by at least the three alternative perspectives described above, the Spanish experience looks*

2.  There have been significant debates on this issue within the anarchist movement. The most relevant example for this book was in the Spanish movement-in-exile itself, from 1939 to 1975, and subsequently concerning the role of the CNT in post-Franco Spain. For more detailed discussion of this debate see the references indicated in footnote 1 of Chapter II.
3.  Current North American examples of the former current are found on the fringes of the Libertarian Party and *The Libertarian Review,* while examples of the latter are the Anarchist Association of the Americas, and the journals *Open Road* (Vancouver), *Social Anarchism* (Baltimore) and *Black Rose* (Boston).
4.  Symbolically at least, the movement's past attempts to develop the universal language Esperanto as a common means of communication exemplifies this internationalist emphasis.

*significantly different. This contrast is important. Indeed, it was precisely the presence of such competing value-criteria within the international and Spanish anarchist movements themselves in the 1930's which caused such fierce debates on many of the issues discussed in earlier chapters. Struggling over these differences in the concrete context of the Spanish revolution forced anarchists again to re-think the appropriateness of their own value priorities. This constant search for the most meaningful criteria—as well as the use of such measures once chosen—is familiar to those active today in the immensely complex and shifting circumstances of struggle. The present chapter focuses on both the general anarchist experience historically and the movement's learnings from the Spanish revolution in particular. Hopefully the manner in which both subjects are considered will reimpress those currently involved in anti-authoritarian social change with the importance of defining and clarifying appropriate purposes for our own activity.*

## II

*Emma Goldman first viewed herself as an anarchist following the trial and martyrdom of the Chicago Haymarket defendants in 1886-87. At this point in her life, Goldman already felt consumed by rage toward her domineering, physically-aggressive father, her constricting marriage, and the dehumanizing effects of daily factory existence. Together, these feelings merged with the anger she felt in witnessing the calmly brutal repression of those struggling for meaningful existence on the broader social front.*

*In the United States at that time, anarchists were a significant presence in labor battles throughout the country. Statements by the Chicago prosecutors and their newspaper allies locally and elsewhere show that anarchism was perceived here as much as in any other country as a serious political threat to the prevailing system. Worse yet, in their view, its influence was apparently growing. There seemed a real possibility that anarchists would serve a catalytic role in a massive working-class revolt.*

*It was precisely this appeal, this serious hope, which attracted Goldman as she followed from afar the Haymarket events in the press. By her own account, this allure was all the clearer once she left parents and marriage in Rochester and settled in the inflammatory atmosphere of New York's radical working-class immigrant Lower East Side. Her then almost apocalyptic image of anarchism starkly reveals itself in her own and Berkman's descriptions of their mutual plot to assassinate Frick, reinspire the steelworkers of Pittsburgh and set off a nationwide working-class upheaval which would overthrow the entire exploitative system. To be sure, for Goldman the immediate consequence of the assassination attempt was tragically disappointing. Yet the main political lesson she drew from this at the time was not so much pessimism about working-class revolutionary potential. Instead, it was more an awareness that the particular tactics chosen, at least in the United States, were too easily manipulated by the media and politicians—thus coopted to the advantage of capitalism itself. The crucial task, then, was to find the right*

*catalytic spark. Potential survivability or longevity of the movement was for her not an issue at this time. Like many activists of the 1960's, '70's and '80's, immersed in day-to-day struggle, her focus was on the present.*

*Nevertheless, her criteria for judging the success of anarchism were definitely beginning to change. Goldman's strong urge to pursue her own self-chosen path, so conscious an impulse by her early teens, had contributed much to attracting her initially to that political ideology—anarchism—which best supported this rebelliousness and gave it a socially coherent framework for expression. At first then, the imminent role of the anarchist movement in social revolution was for her the implied logical measure of its success. But after seeing bitter disputes between the anarchist circles of Most and Joseph Peukert,⁵ leading influences in the New York immigrant anarchist community, and especially after her own disillusionment with Most when he repudiated Berkman's action, Goldman insisted more strongly than before on the necessary autonomy of anarchist individuals and groups. Anything short of this, any attempt to impose a monolithic anarchist political "line" would be disastrous. This conviction was only strengthened at every subsequent stage of her life.*

*According to this principle, the anarchist movement at least partially succeeded when it assured herself and others the needed autonomy to assert and act upon their own political perspectives (whatever the overall social outcome of the movement's activity). It was unsuccessful, imitating the failures of other radical movements, to the extent that it sought to impose censorship, to appeal to misinformed non-movement public sentiments against certain disliked anarchists, or to use any other quasi-coercive measures of discipline.⁶ When some anarchists seemed scandalized by Goldman's publicized defense of the motivation of Leon Czolgosz or even by her later love relationship with Ben Reitman, she assailed such pressures, attacked the general provincialism of formally-organized movements and withdrew even her limited collaboration from such individuals and groups.⁷*

*Concerning a different criterion, at an early period, Goldman became concerned about anarchist influence beyond the United States as well.⁸ As part of the immigrant radical community herself, she well understood the need for mutual support between peoples of different national backgrounds. Indeed, the most substantial immediate praise for Berkman's act and support for him as a prisoner came from German, Italian and Jewish comrades she had already worked with in the past. From that point on, Goldman continued to follow international anarchist*

5. Joseph Peukert (1855-1910) was a longtime anarchist activist and the most influential member of the German-language *Autonomie* group in New York from 1890 on (mentioned in footnote 7, Chapter VIII). Goldman's brief description of him and the dispute with Most is in *LL*, I, 74-76. A much more detailed account of Peukert's life and the dispute with Most is found in Andrew Carlson, *Anarchism in Germany*, chs. 8, 10, 11.
6. Several decades later, in 1930, she posed to Max Nettlau the importance of issuing a statement against political violence generally—including violence committed by anarchists against anarchists, physically and in the form of slanderous charges (1/19/30 letter, AMS-G).
7. *LL*, I, 225, 316, 318; Goldman 5/14/29 letter to Berkman (quoted in Drinnon and Drinnon, eds., *Nowhere at Home*, p. 148-50); see also her comments on her own role in the anarchist movement below.
8. See footnote 8 at back of chapter.

*developments and debate through the immigrant community, the movement press, personal correspondence, and discussions with visiting foreign activists in New York. In her own subsequent journeys to Europe in 1895, 1899-1900 and 1907, she made special efforts to contact anarchists and attend international conferences of the movement. As stated in the introduction to Chapter Six, neither Goldman nor other anarchists developed a sophisticated understanding or program for successful international revolution. But she did subscribe to an internationalist perspective of movement comradeship, solidarity of the oppressed and opposition to capitalist international wars—all of which led her to take the public stands mentioned earlier. Like many anarchists, her internationalism indeed led her to consider the Russian revolution as her own struggle—even to the point of going gladly to participate in it from a far-off land.[9]*

*Following her break with comrades after McKinley's assassination, she emerged within a few months time as an increasingly popular speaking and writing attraction among certain liberal as well as radical circles across the country. In this role, Goldman seems to have accepted long-range "survival" of anarchism, as well as the other mentioned factors, as an important criterion to judge its success. At the least, this new value is implied in her choice of personal activity.[10] However defiantly radical her spoken message, her willingness to address meetings organized by liberals and intellectuals can be understood at least partly as an effort to encourage greater toleration in general for the effective propagation of radical ideas.[11] Certainly this latter motivation was much stronger than a belief in possibly organizing large numbers from this constituency to move toward revolution. She did become more optimistic about potentially radicalizing individual middle-class intellectuals and liberals. But she neither viewed that social group as replacing the role of revolutionary workers nor herself moved politically toward a reformist civil libertarian perspective.[12] Essentially she now acknowledged the need to protect the flanks of the anarchist movement[13] adequately to assure its longer-range survival and growth. By this criterion, to the extent that her own writing and speaking efforts (and the struggles against their repression) gained more tolerance generally for expression of radical ideas and self-chosen life-styles, her own activity made anarchism more of a success.[14]*

*Her experience with anarchists in Russia convinced Goldman more than ever that her own comrades too were fallible and that disputes between them inevitably would arise. Again this re-emphasized in her own mind the desirability and necessity*

---

9. As Goldman clarifies in her own autobiography, though she wanted to join the revolution in Russia, she also wanted to do so by her own free will—not as the result of forced exile by the U.S. government.
10. The remarks in footnote 8 above, on Goldman's reorientation to a predominantly U.S. concern, are relevant here as well.
11. See footnote 11 at back of chapter.
12. See footnote 12 at back of chapter.
13. Reference to the "anarchist movement" here and elsewhere is in the broad sense, not necessarily meaning any formal organization.
14. Her direct influence in this way on Margaret Sanger and the development of the birth-control movement and on Roger Baldwin and the emergence of the American Civil Liberties Union are leading examples.

*that individuals and groups within the movement be free to find their own paths.* [15]
*She insisted on such space herself, in relation to other anarchists, during her own
intense "apprenticeship" period with the Bolsheviks. A practical result of her
autonomy was that once having seen enough of Bolshevik reality, even through an
initially sympathetic perspective, she then was more committed than ever to struggle against "progressive collaborationist" or "democratic centralist" anarchist
divergences from their own ideological tradition. Personally burned by her initial
tolerance of Bolshevism, she was thus potentially all the more understood by others
then and later facing the same issue.*

*At the same time, having seen her Russian comrades so relatively isolated in the
midst of mass social upheaval, Goldman increasingly sympathized with the need
for serious attempts at large-scale movement coordination.* [16] *Following her stay in
Russia, she was indeed exposed to and admired the birth and growth of a substantial anarcho-syndicalist movement in postwar Germany. From these experiences,
Goldman became much more open to* long-range *efforts at building an effective,
non-coercive organization.*

*Goldman's experience with Russia during and after her stay likewise increased
her commitment to an active, truly supportive,* international *movement. To assist
anarchists in an ongoing revolution implied constructive criticism, physical support, and direct action against intervention by foreign governments. In turn,
solidarity for anarchist revolutionaries imprisoned by increasingly intolerant state
regimes (led by the Soviet Union) meant providing publicity and communication at
least to keep them alive and at best to cause their release.*

# III

*From the first outbreak of the Spanish revolution to its final collapse in March
1939, Emma Goldman passionately attached herself to the fate of the Spanish anarchists. She felt at home among them. She was exhilarated on seeing their popular
influence and the success of their transformational efforts in the anarchist direction. She felt crushed personally when they were sabotaged by Spanish "allies,"
wracked by bitter internal disputes, and eventually defeated militarily. Because of
this close personal identification with the rise and fall of the CNT-FAI, inevitably
Goldman's general comments on anarchism during this period reflect many of the
particular developments in Spain.*

*Despite the exhilarations and tragedies of the immediate moment, Goldman
simultaneously attempted also to judge anarchism from some of the alternative
lenses suggested above. From an internationalist revolutionary perspective, initially the Spanish drama was encouraging. At the beginning, she and many other
non-Spanish anarchists rushed to Spain to offer their talents, energies, and*

---

15. By the same logic she argued that "the majority . . . under Anarchism will no doubt be on a
higher level, but even so the individual will always be in advance of it. It is inevitable"
(Goldman 3/24/31 letter to Henry Aalsberg, AMS-R).

16. Peter Kropotkin himself also arrived at the same conclusion on the basis of this same evidence
(George Woodcock and Ivan Avakumovic, *The Anarchist Prince: Peter Kropotkin* [N.Y.:
Schocken Books, 1971], pp. 419, 425-26; *LL*, II, 864).

*lives if necessary to both fight the fascists and assist in creating the new society behind the front-lines. For thousands of exiled anarchists at the time, especially those from countries with openly reactionary regimes—most notably Bulgaria, Italy and Germany—such a choice was indeed the best they could make. By contrast, given the isolation of the Spanish Republic from international arms and supplies (especially compared to the fascist insurgents), for those anarchists in countries still permitting some political freedom it was more logical to assist the revolution by direct action at home. From that location, they could also apply their energies if the Spanish example inspired upheavals in their own lands as well.*

*Still living her forced exile from her home base in the United States and despite her intense desire to remain in the midst of a revolution, even Goldman reluctantly accepted the logic of this internationalist self-discipline. During most of the thirty-three months of the war, she thus spent her time in endlessly frustrating and relatively futile efforts to organize effective solidarity in Britain. As a measure of anarchism's success by internationalist criteria, Goldman viewed the flow of anarchists to Spain, including formation of anarchist international militia,[17] as immensely positive. At the same time, however, her own discouraging British experience was duplicated almost everywhere else in the West and was a severe indictment of the movement indeed. Despite ambitious programs defined especially by the anarcho-syndicalist International Workingmen's Association, the degree of support outside of Spain was relatively insubstantial.[18] Beyond that, as we know, there emerged in that period no new centers of revolution inspired by the Spanish example.[19] The agony all this caused Goldman is reflected in her comments below, as well as in certain earlier statements in Chapters Two and Six. At her most despairing moments, she even felt that, compared with other political movements of the day, aside from Spain and several other countries, there really was no anarchist movement in the world at all.*

*The lack of effective international anarchist support, aside from comrades who themselves came to Spain, especially contrasted with the loud criticism of the Spanish movement by many anarchists abroad. As Chapter Four reveals, Goldman was pleased that anarchist principles were strong enough for comrades to be independently critical, even in the midst of severe crisis. Yet she also felt the pain of her beseiged Spanish comrades when they were sharply attacked in public by others of their own movement abroad. For Goldman personally, so long as she felt that an anarchist-tending revolution was still in progress, she would work to support the CNT-FAI. In no case would she voice her most serious objections in public, thus preventing non-anarchists from using them to their own advantage against Spanish anarchists or anarchism in general.*

*This was discipline imposed on Goldman by herself, not by the movement. At this stage of her life,[20] she valued solidarity with beseiged comrades even more than*

17. See footnote 17 at back of chapter.
18. This remark is not meant to discredit the enormous efforts of certain anarchist individuals and groups outside of Spain during this period. It is merely comparing, in relative terms, the tremendous *needs* of outside support with the small degree to which they were fulfilled.
19. See footnote 19 at back of chapter.
20. In her remarks of Chapter IV and in one letter of the present chapter, she admitted that her position might have been different in her youth.

*how she or others perceived her own ideological purity.*[21] *At the same time, such self-imposed limits still grated against her own individualism. While she disagreed tactically with and was pained by those foreign comrades publicly criticizing Spanish anarchist leaders, she also was glad to be part of a movement which was unable and unwilling to impose any "line," despite certain half-hearted efforts in that direction.*[22] *It was crucial for the survival of the ideal that all who claimed to be anarchists respect each other's autonomy, that all be allowed to learn their own lessons. Infraction of this fundamental principle would be far more deadly to the long-range attractiveness of anarchism than temporary erroneous policy on the part of particular comrades in Spain.*

*It was this long-range perspective which in fact enabled Goldman to survive the Spanish drama with as much equanimity as she did, with indeed the energy to pursue even further anarchist defense and organizing activity in Canada during the final year of her life, at seventy years of age. However committed she had been to the Spanish struggle, to the point of being ready to sacrifice her own life within it, Goldman simultaneously perceived this upheaval as but one relatively short episode in a long historical process. Such capacity for intellectual distancing was at times quite important. It was a trait she greatly valued in those international anarchist thinkers she so admired, Rudolf Rocker and Camillo Berneri. Such a vantage point gave her the remarkable independence critically to perceive the movement she so loved as unrealistically optimistic and far ahead of its time. At the same moment, she strongly reasserted her belief that anarchist struggle was the only one worth committing herself to, whatever its difficulties and internal disputes. From her long-range perspective, anarchism had actually gained strength from the Spanish experience, since it once again boldly reminded the world of both the anarchist ideal and its genuine concrete practicality. Meanwhile, the Spanish revolution clarified for anarchists themselves the nature of certain of the immense immediate obstacles along the way. To balance the necessary long-range vision with intense personal commitment to immediate struggle is extraordinarily difficult. Yet as Emma Goldman demonstrated through her own life, culminating in the late 1930's, this balance is not only possible, it is a very powerful and thoroughly admirable combination.*

†*In this letter to Dutch anarchist William Jong two years before the outbreak of the Spanish revolution (5/11/34), Goldman distinguishes between anarchists, syndicalists and anarcho-syndicalists.*

. . . I have to disagree with your attitude toward Anarcho-Syndicalism. You refer me to the French Syndicalists, surely you must know that they are not anarchists,[23] and therefore [they are] subject to the development of

21. This was an issue to the extent that her consistency seemed tainted by avoiding public conflict on issues she felt strongly about.
22. See footnote 22 at back of chapter.
23. See footnote 23 at back of chapter.

bureaucracy and dictatorship. Besnard,[24] who is their leader, holds that Syndicalism is sufficient unto itself, and that it must play the sole part during and after the Revolution of molding the new productive forces. This has never been maintained by the able and well-informed leaders of Anarcho-Syndicalism. You are quite right that some of the young comrades in the F.A.U.D.[25] called for "all power to the soviet, no power over the soviets." I have fought that idea during my entire tour in Germany. Fortunately none of the older comrades—Rocker, Schapiro, Berkman, I or the others—believe in that. We do say that the intricate machinery of production will run smoother if it is directed by the Syndicalist forces. On the other hand we insist that Anarchism must be the very basis upon which these forces will have to operate.[26] For myself, I hold that Syndicalism is merely the clearing house for industrial planning, the distribution of the necessities of life should find their expression through the cooperatives, while the Anarchist group should act as the cultural force; these three factors federated together would safeguard society from any possibility of bureaucracy. In other words, mere groups of Anarchists who never reach the masses have not in the past and will not in the future play a decisive part in the revolutionary period. It is more likely that they will always be used by politicians to pull the chestnuts out of the fire for them. This has been done in Russia, and will be done in Spain should our comrades be foolish enough to make a united front with either the Socialists or the Communists.

†*Goldman writes to American anarchist Joe Goldman on 7/31/34, offering her opinion on various issues before an upcoming anarchist conference. She assesses the value of anarchist activity within and outside of anarcho-syndicalist organizations, the importance of harmonizing means with ends and the need for more unity within the anarchist movement itself.*

You say that the Anarchists have in the past considered their principle "too pure" to cooperate with other organizations. That is not entirely true. It is true that many comrades have insisted on sticking closely within the four walls of their groups and that they have repudiated any suggestion of propaganda on a large scale or of any cooperation with other libertarians and labor groups. However, the majority of our comrades organized along Anarcho-Syndicalist lines have certainly carried their work to the workers in shops, mines and factories—indeed everywhere where people were at work—by word of mouth and quantities of literature on every subject. And they have also participated in mass action. In times of important national issues they have never refused to cooperate with non-political organizations. These

24. See footnote 24 at back of chapter.
25. The Freie Arbeiter-Union Deutschlands (the German Free Workers Union).
26. At the heart of Goldman's explanation here is the need to avoid bureaucracy and elitism in the syndicalist organization (or confederation of "soviets" or "workers' councils") itself and to

comrades were active even during elections, not by voting for any particular candidate but by demonstrations and manifestos that pointed out the fallacy of political action. For well our comrades know that to combine with any political body would have meant a denial of their ideals and would in the end have made them ridiculous in the eyes of the workers. After all one cannot oppose government and then vote somebody into office knowing as we do that the best man in power can do nothing for the workers even [if] he would.

. . . . . . . . . . . . . . . . . . . . . . . . . . . . . . . . . . . . . . . . . . . . . . . . . . . . .

But why should the Anarchists have to go with one party or another [in a time of national emergency]? Why could they not stand on their own feet and represent their ideas to the masses? Certainly if they remain in their groups they probably will have no effect, but by strong Anarcho-Syndicalist organization they certainly could be a moral force. They could point out that both Socialism and Communism mean power inevitably used against the masses. Granted that the Communists or Socialists may be stronger and the Anarchists may again be defeated, but is there not sometimes greater success in defeat than the ordinary person realizes? Some day the workers must wake up to see that Anarchism alone represents the only safeguard for freedom and well-being. I rather think it is worth the price.

You are correct when you say that most fundamental historic changes have not been brought about by the workers themselves or any one class; the peasants too had their share; the intelligentsia also had a considerable part. The proof for that are the French Encyclopedia,[27] and certainly the entire Russian intelligentsia. The February and October revolutions[28] might yet be one hundred years behind the times if not for the intensive heroic preparatory work of these martyrs.

. . . . . . . . . . . . . . . . . . . . . . . . . . . . . . . . . . . . . . . . . . . . . . . . . . . . .

In spite of its failure in San Francisco I still insist that the general strike is the most formidable weapon labor has. The failure in California and in other American and Canadian cities years ago[29] was due to the lack of understanding

recognize that other aspects of existence, aside from the workplace, are also of critical significance for a free life. Both emphases are part of a strong *anarchist* sensitivity and conviction and imply a variety of independent self-managed organizational forms in the free community of the future.

27. The elaborate compendium of Enlightenment thought assembled by Diderot in the mid-18th century.
28. Of Russia in 1917.
29. Excellent descriptions of the 1934 San Francisco general strike, as well as similar upheavals in Seattle (1919), Milwaukee (1886), and throughout the U.S. in 1877 are found in Brecher, *Strike!*. The official workers' strike committee account of the Seattle strike is found in Root and Branch, ed., *Root and Branch: The Rise of the Workers'Movements* (Greenwich, Ct.: Fawcett Publications, Inc., 1975). Two accounts of the 1920 Winnipeg general strike are Peter Kidd, *The Winnipeg General Strike* (N.Y.: Viking Press, 1972) and David Bercuson, *Confrontation at Winnipeg* (Montreal: McGill-Queens University Press, 1974). Goldman's enthusiasm for grass-roots militant solidarity in the British general strike of 1926 is expressed in her 5/31/26 letter to Stewart Kerr (NYPL) and in *LL*, II, 983-84.

of the general strike. It is a foolish notion that one can discuss the general strike for days and weeks in advance, thus giving the enemy a chance to array the entire force of the state. A general strike can only be successful if it is spontaneous and if it is the culminating result of preliminary educational and agitational work. This is true not only of the workers but of the public as well. It is essential to bring the public to realize its relation to labor and the awareness that it depends on the producing elements and therefore must either help the workers in a strike or suffer the consequences. Yet up till now no attempt was made either in England or on the [North] American continent to educate the masses and the public about the meaning and the importance of the general strike. . . .

. . . The importance of a general strike, I repeat, is its spontaneity – and spontaneity means the culminating expression of the advance educational and agitational work done. That never having been done in Anglo-Saxon countries, it was a foregone conclusion that the general strike in San Francisco would fail.

You speak of the "art of compromise; Advisedly." Yes, my dear, the higher the art of compromise the more disintegrating it is. It means the complete loss of integrity, the need of sacrificing all one holds high. The old Jesuitic notion that the end justifies the means. Well, the Bolsheviki are following that to the very letter, and what is the result? The complete debacle of the Russian Revolution, the sickening compromise with the very powers Lenin had come to slay. I admit that as a government the Russian Communists have succeeded but as the pseudo-voice of the Revolution the Communist state is the most colossal failure the world has ever seen. Frankly I never want to live to the time when the same might be said about the Anarchist experiment. For this very reason the means must be harmonized with the end and that excludes compromise. You will suggest that we compromise on every step or we could not live. I agree. But this compromise is imposed on us by forces over which we have no control. They are not of our choosing. Whereas compromising for the sake of apparent success is of our own making. I cannot see how we can possibly engage in that and yet claim to be Anarchists.

. . . . . . . . . . . . . . . . . . . . . . . . . . . . . . . . . . . . . . . . . . . . . . . . . . .

In summing up I would say there is certainly much work to do but the first step is to bring about a united front in our own ranks. Unless the comrades eliminate their personal vanities, their desire to shine in their little groups or organizations, the ever-lasting fault-finding with each other, they will always remain a negligible quantity, and exert no influence whatever.[30]

---

†In a 2/1/35 letter to American IWW veteran J.B. Laird, Goldman again stresses

30. See footnote 30 at back of chapter.

*the importance of maintaining consistency with anarchist principles, while refusing*
*to worship dogmatically the revolutionary potential of the proletariat.*

Naturally [the younger generation of anarchists] storms ahead without any looking back. And yet, if the future is to amount to anything, it will have to be the result of the lesson given by the past.

I don't exactly understand what you mean when you say "to practice in war what we believe to be the best in peace is to jeopardize our chances of ever achieving anything."[31] I don't see why it should. . . .

I think you are wrong in one thing. That the question of freedom and voluntary action is not as important as our struggle against the utilitarian schools including the capitalists. Unless we are quite sure what we are fighting for the cooperation will lead us nowheres. And unless our objective is freedom and the recognition of the individual as the vital factor in the social struggle and social changes our efforts will only create new utilitarian schools. That is just the trouble of the various social tendencies. Their adherents seem to think they can cooperate with every Tom, Dick and Harry and then only to discover that they have been used to pull the chestnuts out of the fire. That has unfortunately happened to the anarchists time on end. So you need not blame them if they are insistent on having clear what cooperation is for.

. . . The masses have submitted and submit to the whip. Just see the last result in the Saar.[32] See the part workers have had in the crushing of the Spanish uprising.[33] See the indolent mass in America that can stand unemployment, poverty, and wretchedness for five years without as much as moving a finger. I know too well that the masses can rise to the highest revolutionary summit, but I don't think that they always have sustaining power. What is the use of closing our eyes to facts? There are just as many among the proletariat who have a bourgeois psychology and [are] ready to betray the revolution for the flesh pots of Egypt as those who come from the bourgeoisie. Don't think I am losing faith in the masses. I simply refuse to be a fanatic and see all the evils in one class and all the virtues in another. The classes are made up of individuals and individuals are not merely saints but also sinners and vice versa.

†*In this brief passage of a 10/19/36 letter, Goldman tells Rudolf Rocker of his*

---

31. Presumably the question implies that anarchists cannot hold to the same degree of consistency with their principles of internationalism, anti-militarism and anti-statism during war because this would discredit them forever in the eyes of the vast majority who favor the conflict.

32. Following World War I, the Saar region of western Germany was placed under a governing commission of the League of Nations for 15 years. At the end of that period (January 1935) a plebiscite was held to determine its future. Over 90% of the voters chose to return to Germany (though the process itself was controversial), despite the Nazi regime then in power.

33. Referring to the uprising in October 1934.

*crucial role for the international anarchist movement generally.*

. . . You are the last of our generation who has the knowledge and the ability to articulate our ideas. You will be especially necessary to interpret the super-human struggle of our marvelous comrades in Spain. *You simply must not risk your life and your chance of a place* where you can still contribute from the wealth of your mind and your heart to our movement.[34]

*† She praises foreign anarchists involved in the Spanish struggle in this 11/14/36 letter to her niece Stella Ballantine from Spain.*

[The self-sufficiency and resentment of outside interference on the part of the Spanish Anarchist movement] does not make our lot, I mean the lot of all foreign comrades here any easier. And yet they do magnificent work at all the fronts. Especially the Italian Anarchists and anti-Fascists represent a con-siderable contingent. Such splendid types too and so brave and daring.

*† In her 1/5/37 letter to Ben Capes, Goldman stresses the importance of critiques from foreign anarchists, but pleads for informed analysis. She insists that if the Spanish comrades were observed close at hand, with all their dedication, effort and integrity, others would write differently than they do. It is both stupid and cruel to slander the Spanish, as some have done on the basis of inadequate information.*

*† In a 2/16/37 letter to longtime American friend and comrade Van Valkenburgh, Goldman discusses the prospect of foreign volunteers coming to assist the Spanish anarchists. Only those who are ready, able and young enough to go to the front would be welcome. Indeed, Goldman was encouraged by the Spanish to find such comrades in Britain. Others would simply be one more burden to take care of in the rear. As to his bleak assessment of his own life and usefulness:*

Who of us has not muddled his private life? Perhaps it is impossible to serve two gods. If one gives oneself to an ideal to the uttermost one hardly ever also suc-ceeds in one's private affairs. This is true not only of those obsessed by a social ideal. It is true of every ideal, art, letters, science. . . . You will find that your failure is the failure of us all [who] are dedicated to one purpose in life.

---

34. She was especially concerned about Rocker's very tenuous immigration status in the United States, where Goldman still saw a potential for significant public appeal as well as a base for writing internationally. Rocker came to the U.S. following the Nazi rise to power in Germany.

*As for those such as Marcus Graham[35] in the anarchist movement, she finds their writings poisonous in intent. However, she has long since felt that inspiration by the ideal of anarchism and by those who defend it as in Spain are far more significant than those vengeful and cowardly elements in the ranks.*

† *Seven days later, Goldman admonishes friend and comrade Alexander Schapiro for his critical aloofness from the Spanish struggle. At the same time, she acknowledges the weakness of the international movement.*

It seems very easy indeed, my dear, to find fault with the CNT-FAI when one is safe in Paris or any other country while our people are facing daily dangers and death and are straining every nerve to fight back the enemy. But is it fair? . . . Frankly, I do not think it is. Especially since you did not find it necessary to go to Spain directly after the 19th to help in the actual battle. You who have been associated with the Spanish comrades for so long. Your presence might have affected the actions of the CNT-FAI. But since you kept aloof you cannot justly condemn every act in such sweeping manner as your letter contains.

. . . . . . . . . . . . . . . . . . . . . . . . . . . . . . . . . . . . . . . . . . . . . . . . .

You are also unfair to the FAI. But you have always been to those who did not swear completely to the syndicalist side. You refused to help me to a credential when I went to Canada[36] and offered to raise funds for our Russian politicals because you doubted my 100 percent syndicalism. Now I did not mind it for myself. I only minded the loss of large sums of money I could have raised because of your sectarianism. You justly say that the conference of the FAI will not be representative of the Anarchist movement since we have none. But let's be honest, Sania dear, just how many *bona fide* organizations did the I.A.A. [IWMA] ever have at its conferences? Actually it existed only on paper, did it not? You are right in saying we have no movement. No one can be more aware of it than I. But it is necessary for the Anarchists as individuals to be at such a conference as planned, if they will be able to get into Spain, in order to see the masses of the CNT-FAI. It might teach them how to organize. At any rate I think it wrong to throw cold water on every attempt to get the comrades together.

† *Goldman indicates to Harry Kelly (4/5/37) her plans to attend the international*

35. Marcus Graham was born in 1893 in Rumania and emigrated to Philadelphia at age 14. He became an anarchist before World War I and has continued writing and publishing from that time forward. An autobiographical essay appears in the edited anthology of articles from his earlier anarchist periodical, *Man!* (London: Cienfuegos Press, 1974). For more on the reasons for Goldman's opinion of Graham, see her 7/12/38 letter to Rudolf Rocker below.
36. Probably the trip in 1934.

*anarchist conference in Barcelona (eventually cancelled) despite her misgivings about its significance.*

I still have dates to fill here and the venture of April 25th to go through with and don't know if I will get through in time to be in Barcelona the 1st May. I am hoping the conference will be postponed. The Jewish Anarchist Federation[37] has asked me to represent them and other groups may want the same. We know that such conferences don't go very far. Its moral importance is that it will take [place] in Barcelona and it is the 1st time that Anarchism represents a great force—at least in Catalonia, Aragón and the Levante.

†*On 5/9/37, she replies to the intolerance in a previous letter from anarchist Max Nettlau.*

I confess, I do not know where to begin to answer your letter. One thing is certain: I never thought you capable of such an outbreak and such intolerance; for a man who has always stood up for the utmost liberty, even to the extent of being impatient with organizational work, your letter is certainly the most intolerant outbreak I have read in a long while. Now mind you, I agree with you that [for] the comrades in Holland to continue to be pacifist in the face of the grave dangers from the Fascist pest, is, to say the least of it, childish; so is the criticism of some of the comrades in Toronto of the things the CNT-FAI are doing. First let me set you right about Toronto, those who denounced the entry of comrades into the government were not Anarchists at all. Actually, the comrades we have got in Toronto are heart and soul with the Revolution in Spain and have demonstrated their solidarity in a number of ways. You are therefore doing them an injustice in lumping them together with a lot of outsiders who were never in our ranks. But even they should be granted the right to question the consistency of Anarchists who have repudiated governments all their lives now being in the same councils with the government.

As to the comrades in Holland, they surely are entitled to the right of criticism; they are people who have carried on anti-military work for nearly half a century. They are the direct descendents of Domela Nieuwenhuis' anti-military work.[38] They are fanatically sincere and they have proven themselves of sterling quality and courage not only in speech or press, but also by many of them going to prison again and again rather than to join the army. I must protest, therefore, against your condemnation of these people, though I, myself, am opposed to their attitude as regards Spain. Certainly, they do not deserve the "nice" names you give them.

37. Presumably of New York City.
38. See footnote 25 in Chapter VII above.

292 Vision On Fire

As regards your impatience with me — to call it mildly — I can only explain it by your complete reversal of mind and feeling. It is not so very long ago — not more than 3 or 4 years — when you showed no understanding or sympathy with Syndicalism, when you thought it more advisable for Anarchists to ally themselves with liberal democratic elements rather than to bust themselves with bringing to life large economic organizations. Now you have no patience whatever with comrades who refuse to see in the leading Anarchists in Spain demigods whose actions are not to be questioned. Don't you consider this rather a plunge from your former attitude? Your former position regarding all governments and their danger?

As to your "kindly" tribute to me for my "heinous" offense in my statement that appeared in the *Fr. Arb. St.* and *Spain and the World*, really, dear comrade, you seem to have become a regular heresy-hunter, for no one else among the hundreds of comrades and friends who have read the statement has complained of a single infraction of loyalty on my part. Far from criticizing the CNT-FAI in my statement, I go out of my way to explain them to the comrades who had asked for light on what seemed to them a breach of principle and rather a useless compromise. I was astounded, therefore, to find that you charge me with "lèse-majesté."

Granted that I were guilty of that, I should consider it a sad day for the Spanish Anarchists if their comrades no longer had the right to express their opinions frankly and honestly. I am quite certain that the comrades in Spain would repudiate such a thing, and I do not think you are rendering them very great service by putting yourself up as "judge and executioner" of everyone who does not happen to approve of every step and decision taken by prominent members of the CNT-FAI. How does that compare with your condemnation of the Bolsheviki and their dictatorship? You could not make peace with them, yet you seem to be anxious to put a gag in everybody's mouth — is that not dictatorship?

However, even if my article had contained criticism or condemnation, you as the ultra-libertarian in our movement should not attack me as you have done; but I insist that unless you have become super-sensitive in regard to the least disagreement with some of our Spanish comrades, you could not possibly have found anything objectionable on my part. As I just wrote Alexander Schapiro, I am the unfortunate orphan who was condemned for what she did not. *He* has attacked me for going back on my Anarchist ideas because I am not critical of the compromise in the CNT, and *you* attack me because I appear to have been critical. Fortunately I have never been able to be "all things to all men." I have gone my own way, though often condemned and burnt in oil by my own comrades, and I mean to continue to my last breath to uphold what I consider right and attack what seems to me to be wrong, which does not seem to me to say that I consider myself infallible, but it does mean that, in order to be true to myself, I must decide my own actions and

reactions for myself.

. . . . . . . . . . . . . . . . . . . . . . . . . . . . . . . . . . . . . . . . . . . . . . . . . .

You assume, dear comrade, that I knew nothing about the Spanish movement before I came to Spain. What do you base this assumption on? You seem to forget that we had a very strong Spanish movement in America for many years, that I was connected with the *Cultura Proletaria* all through the years when Pedro Esteve was editor,[38a] that I have read nearly everything you and Rocker have written about Spain. Not only that, but I have always held the Spanish Anarchists to be the shining example of consistency, courage and fortitude. Actually, if I had not always believed in them implicitly, I should have left Spain after that disgraceful pact between Russia and the leaders of the CNT-FAI, and certainly should not have raised a finger in aid or support. It was precisely . . . my abiding faith in the revolutionary resiliency of the Spanish Anarchists and the certainty that they will wake up soon to the danger of their compromise that gave me courage to go out and work as I have worked in England since I returned here. I do not think therefore that I deserve your censure.

. . . . . . . . . . . . . . . . . . . . . . . . . . . . . . . . . . . . . . . . . . . . . . . . . .

Do not lose any sleepless nights, dear comrade. I am not writing this to others, and I would not have written it to you had you not delivered yourself of such a ferocious attack on my poor innocent head.

I have asked you once before to write me exactly what you mean about all of us having "frittered away our libertarian ideas" and not having done enough to make Kropotkin and Bakunin known. I hope you will explain it next time you write. To me it is sheer nonsense, but speaking only for A.B. and myself, I can only say that all our years were devoted to the presentation of the ideas and writings of both Kropotkin and Bakunin. If we did less with Bakunin's works, it is only because we did not have them in English and our work was mainly in Anglo-Saxon countries, but to say that we have not done our share in popularizing our teachers' works is to be guilty of lack of understanding and appreciation of our activities.

†*Finally hearing details on the May Days confrontation in Barcelona, Goldman expresses to Rudolf Rocker (5/14/37) her grief at the news of Camillo Berneri's assassination.*

. . . I am too grieved and too shaken over Berneri's death. We were in daily communication and comradeship. I learned to admire his mind and love his personality as few comrades I found in Barcelona. It was on the day of the disgraceful demonstration with the Communists, the day of the Russian

---

38a. Actually *Cultura Proletaria* was the 1927 successor to *Cultura Obrera*, two years after Esteve's death.

Revolution [anniversary] I called a gathering in my room. Berneri was present. He brought me a statement pointing out the blunders of the CNT-FAI. I still have it. But even he was against any public stand against the leaders in our ranks. Now this clear voice and strong pen are silenced, murdered in cold blood by the butchers of Moscow. It makes me shudder.

† *Continuing her difficult dialogue with Max Nettlau in this letter of 6/1/37, Goldman again insists on the importance of a critical perspective toward Spanish anarchist compromise.*

I am not sure that it is worthwhile to continue our argument. You either cannot or will not see that your objections to criticism [of] the leaders of the CNT-FAI [by] comrades outside of Spain places you in the same position as the Bolsheviki in the early period of the Revolution. They too kept stressing the fact that they were engaged in a "death and life struggle," that they were surrounded by many counter-revolutionists and that they had to continue their compromising methods.

You will reply that Lenin and his comrades were building a State machine while our comrades in Spain are working for a free society. That is not the point, dear comrade. The point is that you not only criticize but also condemn unreservedly the compromises of the Bolsheviki. While now you justify similar compromises of our comrades. You forget, of course, that the Russian revolution at that time was as much in danger as the Spanish is. I insist that if we are willing to be critical of our opponents we should be even more critical of our own comrades. I admit it is harder to find fault with our own than it is with our enemies. But is this not the principal trait of Anarchism which differentiates us from other political groups? Imagine a Max Nettlau to write that the young comrades of the FAI have been "egged on" by the critical attitude of the French and other comrades. Really, my dear old comrade, it is ridiculous to make such charges. Do you mean to suggest that no Spanish anarchist had enough mentality to see where the concessions will lead that have been made by the leaders of the CNT-FAI? Or if the anarchists had not been "egged on" they would have [contained] themselves in the face of many mistakes made by their elders? I should give very little for the Revolution if I shared such opinion of the Spanish anarchist youth or of the FAI.

I could hardly believe my eyes when I saw the statement in your letter. Your contention that the comrades in France or Berneri have caused the tragic events in the first days of May in Barcelona is on par with the charges made in Russia against Makhno and the Russian anarchists who had dared to point out that the Revolution was being emasculated by the Communist state. Lenin also considered it the height of treason to be criticized by his political opponents.

As to your explanation about Berneri's death, I confess I was shocked. How can you of all people say that it was surprising that Berneri did not meet such an end before because he was so critical and faultfinding? I certainly never expected such poor logic from you. What if Berneri was critical? What if he was a stickler for consistency? Is that enough to damn him and even justify his murder? I agree that this is crime enough in the eyes of the Communist zealots, but why should it have surprised you? Of course I do not agree with you for a moment that Berneri was "moderate at heart" or that he had nothing "positive about him." I considered Berneri the most brilliant mind since Malatesta,[39] among the most courageous, and of extraordinary ability to work with large groups. It was he who organized the Italian anti-Fascist column. It was he who managed the supply of food, clothing and arms. It was Berneri who fought with them at every front and raised their spirit when he saw sign of discouragement and pessimism. In other words Camillo Berneri was one of the finest [types] of comrades I have ever come across in the anarchist movement and no sane human being free from hatred and fanaticism could possibly have found reason to kill Berneri. But of course he was uncompromising and relentless with the Communists. Bravely he wrote in his paper pointing out that the Revolution was sailing between two dangerous cliffs—Burgos[40] and Moscow. How very prophetic his words were the dreadful days of Barcelona proved.

I see you are still harping on my offense in my article in *Spain and the World*. I can only repeat what I wrote you in my last letter. Only one hunting for heresy in every word I wrote could possibly find the least objection to the article. In point of fact I wrote against my better conviction when I tried so hard to defend the comrades who compromised right and left. I saw only too soon that they were leading the Revolution to a precipice. I now realize that I should have said so in print. Instead I defended their actions on the grounds that they had no choice. Yet you go on reiterating that I had criticized them. It is no use going on with this part of your letter.

. . . . . . . . . . . . . . . . . . . . . . . . . . . . . . . . . . . . . . . . . . . . . . . . . .

Not for one moment have the comrades whom you so "gently" condemn lost sight of the desperate need to accept arms and food from Soviet Russia, but what they objected to were the unnecessary concessions to Stalin. Actually they submitted to a noose round their necks. If any one of us had the least doubt about this, the hand Moscow had in the plot against the CNT-FAI has quite convinced us of what we had seen at the time.

You object to criticism because of the menace of Fascism and in the same breath you maintain that you consider dictatorship as [a] greater menace.

39. For details on Malatesta, see footnote 10, Chapter I.
40. Burgos, the old capital city of Castile in north-central Spain, was made the capital of the fascist regime in the vry first days of the rebellion. It was there that Franco was installed as Head of State for Nationalist Spain on October 1, 1936.

More reason why our comrades in Spain should have refused to have trout with the banner-bearers of dictatorship. You must not think, dear comrade, that the comrades outside of Spain do not see the great danger of Franco. They have proved that they are well aware of it by the campaign they have carried on in behalf of the anti-Fascist struggle. They have worked day and night. They have held large meetings. They have raised money. In point of truth, they fairly consecrated themselves to the needs of our heroic comrades even though they could not agree with every step the latter had taken. The very fact that they were able to see and yet try to defend, explain and excuse what seemed so far afield from the revolutionary traditions of the Spanish anarchist movement proves that they realized the imminent danger of Franco and his hordes.

Regarding the Anarchist conference, you seem to think that I have been back of the call for it. Let me tell you that I knew nothing about it until I received the call. I admit it fired my imagination to see comrades from all over the world gathered in revolutionary Barcelona. I knew that there would be differences, clashes and even useless condemnations. Nevertheless I considered such a conference of moral importance to the Anarchist movement outside of Spain, but we need not quarrel about it anymore. The dastardly plot against the CNT-FAI and the Revolution has done away with the chances of an Anarchist gathering in Spain. I would not feel so grieved if that were all that the plot has accomplished. More terrible is the loss of the strategic position held by the CNT-FAI until May 3rd. I wonder whether you realize how much the CNT-FAI have lost. Barcelona seems to have been turned into a fortress that makes it impossible to get into it or out of it and all that in the small expanse of time of six months. What a tragedy. To me the tragedy is all-embracing, as deep as the untimely death of our comrade Alexander.

† *In a June 1937 report on her activities to the CNT National Committee, Goldman remarks about the decline of anarchist activity in Britain.*

I entered the anarchist ranks in 1889 and have fought for our ideas ever since. In Spain I saw my dreams and fervent hopes as a living, active force; I could therefore not bear to exchange this for the barren soil of England—barren despite the fact that this country was, in a measure, the cradle of anarchism. Its parents and foster-parents were some of the most distinguished English men and women,[41] its teachers among the greatest in the world. They were

---

41. After Gerrard Winstanley and the Diggers in the English civil war of the mid-17th century, the next prominent anarchist influences were late 18th-early 19th century writers William Blake, Mary Wollstonecraft, William Godwin and Percy Shelley. (Goldman's unpublished typescript of an article on Wollstonecraft is in the New York Public Library; Alice Wexler discusses this study in an article in *Feminist Studies*, Spring 1981.) In the later 19th century, she no doubt refers to such figures as

political refugees from every land[42] who had found a ready asylum in pre-war England. It is therefore strange that so little is left of the anarchist movement they had created.

Whether this is due to the Anglo-Saxon delusion of parliament as the channel of all social redress or to the world war that had destroyed all faith in liberating ideas or the introduction of dictatorship as the new deity all must worship, I cannot tell; but one thing is certain, . . . little of our pre-war movement has survived these devastating factors. Knowing therefore how difficult it has always proven to break new ground for Anarchism in England I cautioned the comrades in Spain not to expect wonders from our work. It was bitter hard for me to leave the revolutionary battle-field for the easy-going British isle where revolution "is simply not done."

†*In a 6/18/37 letter to the* Manchester Guardian, *Goldman underlines the essential idealism of the anarchist movement, contrary to its usual false image.*

That Anarchism and Anarchists have been a target for every sort of calumny from the ignorant as well as those who possess the banner bearers of education and culture is nothing new. Of course one does expect more from intelligent people than from those who have never had a chance to learn anything first hand. Though why one should I do not know. The utter confusion of mind and the insensibility to every wrong since the world slaughter have proved that the educated are by far less capable of independent thinking than the masses. The gravest offense today is independent thinking. A case in point is dictatorship of varied hues. Its defenders are the pseudo-cultured. They worship at its shrine. They justify every crime committed in its name. Anarchism and Anarchists still [adhere] to the "old-fashioned" idea that life without freedom is a monstrous delusion even if "trains run on time"[43] and "our beloved comrade in the Kremlin has made Russia the most comfortable and joyous in the world." Small wonder Anarchism and Anarchists should continue to be grossly misrepresented and their struggle distorted beyond belief.

The incredible reports of the recent tragic events in Barcelona demonstrate once more to what extent most scribes will go to pervert news when it concerns Anarchists and their cause.

. . . . . . . . . . . . . . . . . . . . . . . . . . . . . . . . . . . . . . . . . . . .

Oscar Wilde, Charlotte Wilson and William Morris (though the latter was not strictly an anarchist), and working-class militants Joseph Lane and Frank Kitz. Useful sources for this last period are Quail, *The Slow Burning Fuse;* Rocker, *The London Years;* and George Woodcock and Ivan Avakumovic, *The Anarchist Prince.*

42. Among such refugees, some of the most famous were Johann Most, Emile Pouget, Peter Kropotkin, Nicholas Tchaikovsky, Errico Malatesta and Rudolf Rocker.

43. "Now the trains run on time" was one of the popular slogans of those who admired Italian fascist dictator Mussolini.

. . . The naivest and most confiding people in the world are not the hard-boiled realists. They are the idealists, the romantics, and visionaries, as the Anarchists are called by our well-wishers. I suppose I am one of these incorrigibles. For I have abiding faith in the resiliency of the Spanish people. Persecution, prison, torture, suppression of their movement, their publications and their works, they overcame everything. They rebounded with new strength and new determination to go on and on until their ideas would triumph. I am certain that this will again happen in the near future despite all plots and connivance to crush them and to undermine the social edifice the CNT-FAI have begun in the glorious revolutionary days of July 19th.

† *In this 7/1/37 letter to Tom Bell, Goldman seeks to clarify distinctions between individualist and communist conceptions of anarchism through focusing on the crucial issue of work-compensation during and following a revolution. She also clarifies her own growing affinity with anarcho-syndicalism.*

I am afraid I cannot now argue the difference between your position as an individualist Anarchist and mine as an Anarchist Communist. That has always been a bone of contention between us and other dear comrades and friends of mine who were opposed to Anarchist Communism. I can only say that if ever I doubted it, the importance of a variety of payments in return for labour [in] Russia has destroyed that doubt. The cause of all the trouble that began in Russia was the thirty-three varieties of rations and of pay to the workers and all the other sections in Russian life. It undermined the faith of the masses in the justice of the Russian Revolution and it set one layer of the masses against another. I do not mean to suggest that once Anarchism is established there should not be the widest and broadest possible remuneration [for] different efforts contributed to the welfare of all. But to hold the revolutionary spirit and enthusiasm of the people it is absolutely essential that there should be no preference and no privileges. That everyone should be remunerated on an equal basis, according to the real usefulness to society of the labour contributors. For myself I consider the workers who work in sewers [as] infinitely more important to the health of the community than the novelist, the dramatist or the poet. You certainly know that I never maintained the fallacy that the economic element in human society is the only driving force of social changes. That is why I insist that the philosophy of Anarchism includes all human beings and not merely those belonging to different classes. At the same time I cannot close my eyes to the fact that in the great struggle two dominant forces play their part. The haves and the have-nots. I admit that the have-nots are often guilty of more stodgy middle-class ideas and feelings than the haves. In fact I have always maintained that the middle class is a deadlier weight on society than the aristocracy or the workers. But nevertheless it is

true that there are two opposite forces struggling for a place in the sun—the rich and the poor. There are many heirs in a kingdom and I certainly welcome all whose background is different from that of the masses. Often those who have come from wealth have been more dedicated to the struggle for freedom than the enslaved. There is no more brutal master than the slave of yesterday. We hardly need argue that. But we do need to see clearly the danger of maintaining the wage system during the Revolution or in a free society. Aside of the need of a terrific bureaucracy and government to maintain such a system it is intrinsically wrong and diametrically opposed to the system of equality. But as I said we will never agree on this point because you lean towards individualism and I have been and am an Anarchist Communist. I would say Anarchist-Syndicalist with libertarian communism as the basis of a free society.

† *In this important "political will" included as part of her 9/10/37 letter to friend and comrade Mollie Steimer before departing for her second visit to revolutionary Spain, Goldman predicts a long difficult struggle to make anarchism a living experience in the world, but also urges continuation of the effort.*

Your contention that there is something wrong with Anarchism because Kropotkin failed our ideas in the war, and because the leading comrades in Spain failed Anarchism seems to be very faulty reasoning. In the first place, the failure of one or several individuals can never take away from the depth and truth of an ideal. . . .

. . . . . . . . . . . . . . . . . . . . . . . . . . . . . . . . . . . . . . . . . . . . . . . . . . . . . . . . .

However, there is something else. Something I have been thinking about very deeply since the May events in Spain. It is whether we Anarchists have not taken the wish for the thought. Whether we have not been too optimistic in our belief that Anarchism had taken root in the masses. The war, the Revolution in Russia and Spain, and the utter failure of the masses to stand up against the annihilation in all countries of every vestige of liberty have convinced me that Anarchism, even less than any other social ideas, has not penetrated the minds and hearts of even a substantial minority, let alone the compact mass. Actually, there is no Anarchist movement anywhere in the world. What we have got is so insignificant, so piffling, it is ridiculous to speak of an Anarchist organized movement. In other words, everywhere the soil for our ideas has proven sterile. In Spain alone has the ground been fertile. But even in Spain the harvest is still small. In our enthusiasm we forgot the natural forces the young, tender plants will be subjected to, the storm and stress, the drought and winds. We admit all this in nature. But we were not willing to admit the forces that beset the social growth. My dears, my dears, think of it, in a country in the grips of feudalism and the Church almost to the moment of July 19th

we Anarchists imagined our ideas can be realized in one jump, rise from the depths of enslavement and degradation to the very heights of fulfillment, come to full fruition from the hard rocks of the past in Spain. It was our mistake and we are now paying for it in the agony of our bitter disappointment.

I don't know whether you ever read Wm. Marion Reedy's beautiful tribute to me which he called "A Daughter of A Dream." He said "there is only one thing the matter with Anarchism and Emma Goldman, they are five thousand years ahead of their time."[44] I was furious with Reedy for that. And I still am. And yet what he said contained some truth.[45] This has been borne in on me the last twenty years and even more forcibly since the Spanish events in May. Anarchism is still very much ahead of its time. And I am convinced it will take more than one revolution before our ideas will come to full growth. Until then the steps will be feeble, our ideas no doubt [will] fall from the heights many times and many will be the mistakes our comrades are bound to make.

Does that mean that I have lost faith in Anarchism, or that I think we ought to sit hands folded? Of course not. In point of truth I think now more than ever we must strain every nerve to bring our ideas before the world. Now more than ever, because we have the living proof for our claims that nothing can be gained from any association with governments or political parties. Now we also have the living proof that it is possible to build amidst destruction, amidst war and revolution, that the Anarchists have been the only ones to begin such gigantic work. However the Spanish revolution will end it has already given us marvelous material to enhance the logic of our ideas. And it should also give us greater courage to go on and on so long as there is a breath of life in us.

Moreover, whatever the fault and shortcomings of our Spanish comrades, they alone and none other in any country have created a strongly organized Anarchist body and movement that cannot but leave a lasting mark on future events. I feel therefore that though I cannot and will not reconcile myself to the compromises of the few comrades I will not raise my hand against them so long as the hand of the whole world is raised against them ready to choke the life out of our people. If that is treason against "what I have taught you," as Senia said, I am willing to be thus branded. But I am not willing to join the howl of all the wild beasts in and outside Spain who are ready to devour our people.

My going to Spain is not so much for the purpose of gathering proofs for the blunder of our people during the events of May. I have enough proof for that. It is more to get at the rank and file. To find out whether Comunismo Libertario still is the same fiery inspiration as it was last year. Every worker and

44. Reedy's essay appeared in the newspaper he edited, the *St. Louis Mirror* of November 5, 1908. Actually he estimated 8000 instead of 5000 years too soon!
45. In a 6/7/28 letter to Stewart Kerr (NYPL), she suggested that perhaps anarchist vision would be realized only in 100 or 500 years.

peasant I spoke with had assured me it is in their blood for four generations. If this is still the case, then the May events could not possibly have eradicated this sacred flame and nothing has been lost by them. If it is no longer there then it would only prove to me that even in Spain Anarchism was also a delicate plant and that therefore it could not survive the onslaught of war and all the evil forces arrayed against it. Perhaps even in Spain Anarchism must go through a process of gestation to gain strength and sustenance for the battle which is still to come.

† *To her friend Martin Gudell in Spain, Goldman on 11/15/37 writes of the importance of maintaining a constructive critical perspective.*

. . . I believe in the right of friendly and comradely criticism. It would be a great tragedy if that were no longer permitted in our ranks. We would in no way differ from those who want everybody gagged and silenced. No, I insist we must have freedom of criticism, but it must be done in a comradely tone and it must not make us so bitter that we do not see the good for the bad.

† *Writing to Ethel Mannin on the latter's Marxist beliefs (11/18/37), Goldman reveals her characteristic attraction to free-spirited, concerned individuals, despite formal ideological differences.*

As to your Marxism, my sweet Ethel, I am sure the time will come when you will realize that "it is not the abuse of the thing which is wrong. It is the thing itself." It matters not what kind of a Marxist one is, it is the theory itself which tends to annihilate all freedom and initiative. No matter the best intentions, all Marxists in power have proven alike, except that one set became aggressively centralistic, hence dictatorial.[46] And the other set beginning as revolutionists ended in the muddy waters of parliamentarism. But both cases have proven deadly and the tactics impatient of everyone else in the social struggle. If ever I doubted this the years since the world war and since the ascendency of Socialists in whatever country[47] gave me overwhelming proofs. However, I believe too much in personal freedom, I would not for anything impose my views of Marxism on you. But I feel certain you will outgrow it. I love you for your fine spirit, your revolutionary zeal and above all for your loving nature. Nothing else matters.

46. At this date, the Bolsheviks in Russia were the only example of this latter type in power, though her comments about the Communists in the Caballero and Negrín governments in Spain are equally appropriate. No doubt she similarly would have criticized the various Communist regimes throughout the world today.
47. As in Germany, Britain and France.

†*In an 11/19/37 letter to Milly and Rudolf Rocker upon her return from Spain, Goldman clarifies the factor that sets her apart from the critique by Schapiro and others. Given that the Spanish movement is under deadly attack, it is hardly surprising that foreign comrades cannot restrain themselves from vocalizing their feelings toward concessions of the movement which they see as responsible. Schapiro is sincere in his appraisal, though dogmatic in his own way. But it is the bitter and vindictive tone which seems to her totally inappropriate while the Spanish comrades are under such assault.*

*Returning to the English context was a depressing experience. Self-proclaimed anarchists here are a hopeless lot. Rumors, petty fights and egoism are the only traits to be found. The younger persons who approach her efforts are 'miserable material' as well.*

*The forthcoming December congress of the IWMA will be a nasty encounter. The foreign comrades are very upset that fundraising for Spain is being shifted from the IWMA to the new SIA. But the Spanish are also angry that secretary-general Besnard circulated a critique of their strategy to the other members without informing the CNT. Further issues between Rüdiger, representing the IWMA, and Souchy, for the CNT, only have made things worse. Though requested to stay in Paris for the meeting, she refused since she is not a member and it would be too agonizing to be in the midst of such disputes at this time.*

†*To Schapiro himself, on 12/2/37, Goldman pleas that a bitter split be avoided in the IWMA.*

If I believed in the efficacy of prayer I would pray most devoutly that the conference of the I.A.A. [IWMA] will not end in a break-up. It would really be a great disaster if our people will not be large enough to set aside their misunderstandings for the bigger issue of maintaining and strengthening morally at [least] the supreme importance of the CNT, regardless of what the [National] Committee may be guilty of or not.

†*A day later, Goldman returns to her dialogue with Ethel Mannin, further clarifying her statement of two weeks before.*

Darling, don't ever think that I will feel "fed up" with anything you write me. I wish I could put you at ease about this and other things. For instance, with your sticking to the I.L.P. My love for you and my regard has nothing to do with your political adherence. It has to do with yourself, with your passionate hatred of sham and hypocrisy and with your revolutionary spirit. I admit I was a bit surprised when you write that "the very name of your movement [the Anarchists] frightens people away." My sweet Ethel, since when does one join a movement when it is already a success? Since when are revolutionists deterred from joining a movement because it is still anathema? It seems to me

that would just be the time to throw oneself into it with all one's intensity. Besides the first motivation of joining a movement should be one's passionate faith that it stands for real changes and not merely for political scene-shifting which even the most sincere parties represent. But as I wrote before I would not want you to join the A. movement unless you reached the point that it is the only ideal of a new social order. So do not let this worry you about whether you should or should not leave the I.L.P. Yes, dearest, I know your party stands for more advanced ideas than the other labor parties. But also it stands for dictatorship, true proletarian dictatorship. The trouble is that dictatorship is deadly no matter who dictates. But let us not worry about our differences on this issue. We have so much in common, our sweet friendship among them, we need not discuss our political differences. Only one thing more. I do not doubt the sincere and good people in the ranks of the I.L.P. I only doubt their revolutionary fiber.

† *Writing to Helmut Rüdiger the next day in response to his advance report for the coming IWMA congress,*[48] *Goldman urges an end to personal-level disputes in the movement. While she finds his overall description very informative and complete, she regrets the insertion of so much individual hostility. She points out that his own attacks on Souchy and Martin Gudell for being subservient to the CNT are in fact echoed by other critical comrades toward himself because he has not openly condemned its National Committee.*

*One point in his report is entirely correct, the absolute need for foreign comrades who support the Spanish struggle to act independently, not as puppets of the CNT. In fact she just reiterated this need in a letter to Vázquez yesterday and said that she would resign her post as official representative of the movement if such autonomy was unacceptable.*

*She also adds a despairing comment on the Anarcho-Syndicalist Union she founded,*[49] *which merely reflects the state of the movement in England more generally.*

. . . The people who joined the [Anarcho-Syndicalist] Union were so unknowledgeable and so incapable that they were unable to do anything in the way of new activities; instead of for propaganda, they used the weekly meetings for chattering and personal arguments. . . . The spiritual poverty and the sorry state of the anarchists in England, of whom all the talk cannot create an anarchist or anarcho-syndicalist movement, is what makes my work here so difficult and so nerve-wracking.

*Finally, she adds her regrets that Rudolf Rocker will not be able to attend the*

48. Rüdiger's report details his own role as IWMA representative in Barcelona and his observations on the activities and policy of the CNT.
49. See footnote 49 at back of chapter.

*December IWMA congress, since she thinks he personally could have a moderating influence on both sides of the growing dispute.*[50]

†*From Paris where she suddenly rushed to participate in the IWMA congress, Goldman expresses her despair to Ethel Mannin (12/11/37) at the bitter antagonism within the movement.*

You will be surprised to get this letter from here. I am myself surprised to be here. I was called to Paris by wire to the congress of the International Workingmen's Association and the CNT. I hated to rush away from London when we had just begun to get things organized. Also I know the dreadful things that will happen at the congress, the personal recriminations, the bitter antagonism between my Spanish comrades and those of other countries, comrades who neither know nor understand the danger the CNT-FAI find themselves [in] and the concessions forced on them. But I have to follow the call; though not being a member either of the CNT or the I.W.M.A., I knew I would have no say or a vote. I arrived Wed. and I am all broken up from what I have already listened to. I shall probably not remain until the end. It is only that my Spanish comrades politically lean on me to explain the iron necessity of their action. Oh, my darling, when the Spanish Revolution happened I wept for the loss of my Sasha. He would have regained his strength through the inspiring event. I no longer regret he is gone. I only regret that I am not in his place.

†*In this passage from Goldman's mid-December address to the IWMA congress, she pleas for more tolerance from both sides, especially given the relative isolation of anarchists in the world generally.*

I am inclined to believe that the critics in our ranks outside of Spain would be less rigid in their appraisal if they too had come closer to the life-and-death struggle of the CNT-FAI—not that I do not agree with their criticism. I think them 95% right. However, I insist that independent thinking and the right of criticism have ever been our proudest Anarchist boast, indeed, the very bulwark of Anarchism. The trouble with our Spanish comrades is their marked sensitivity to criticism, or even to advice from any comrade outside of Spain. But for that, they would understand that their critics are moved not by villainy, but by their deepest concern for the fate of the CNT-FAI.

The Spanish Anarcho-Syndicalist and Anarchist movements until very

50. Rudolf Rocker was one of the founders of the IWMA in Berlin in 1922. Until forced to leave Germany in 1933, he served as its general secretary and through the late 1930's still retained great moral influence, though exiled to the United States.

recently have held out the most glaring fulfillment of all our dreams and aspirations. I cannot therefore blame those of our comrades who see in the compromises of the Spanish Anarchists a reversal of all they had held high for well nigh seventy years. Naturally some comrades have grown apprehensive and have begun to cry out against the slippery road which the CNT-FAI entered on. I have known these comrades for years. They are among my dearest friends. I know it is their revolutionary integrity which makes them so critical, and not any ulterior motive. If our Spanish comrades could only understand this, they would be less indignant [and not] consider their critics their enemies.

Also, I fear that the critics too are very much at fault. They are no less dogmatic than the Spanish comrades. They condemn every step made in Spain unreservedly. In their sectarian attitude they have overlooked the motive element recognized in our time even in capitalist courts. Yet it is a fact that one can never judge human action unless one has discovered the motive back of the action.

When I have pointed this out to our critical comrades they have insisted that Lenin and his group were also moved by the best intentions, "and see what they have made of the Revolution." I fail to see even the remotest similarity. Lenin aimed at a formidable State machine, a deadly dictatorship. From the very beginning, this spelled the death of the Russian Revolution — whereas the CNT-FAI not only aimed at, but actually gave life to, libertarian economic reconstructions. From the very moment they had driven the Fascists and militarists out of Catalonia, this herculean task was never lost sight of. The work achieved, considering the insurmountable obstacles, was extraordinary.

. . . . . . . . . . . . . . . . . . . . . . . . . . . . . . . . . . . . . . . . . . . . . . . . . . . .

Strangely enough, the very comrades of the civil war in Russia who had explained every step of the dictatorship as "revolutionary necessity" are now the most unyielding opponents of the CNT-FAI. "We have learned our lesson from the Russian Revolution," they say. But as no one learns anything from the experience of others, we must, whether we like it or not, give our Spanish comrades a chance to find their bearings through their own experience. Surely our own flesh and blood are entitled to the same patient help and solidarity some of us have given generously to our arch-enemies, the Communists.

. . . . . . . . . . . . . . . . . . . . . . . . . . . . . . . . . . . . . . . . . . . . . . . . . . . .

It has been suggested that our comrades in every country have contributed handsomely in men and money to the Spanish struggle, and that they alone should have been appealed to.

Well, comrades, we are members of the same family and we are among ourselves. We therefore need not beat around the bush. The deplorable fact is that there is no Anarchist or Anarcho-Syndicalist movement of any great

consequence outside of Spain, and in a smaller degree France, with the exception of Sweden. Whatever Anarchist movements there are in other countries consist of small groups. In all England, for instance, there is no organized movement—only a few groups.

*†Reflecting on the paucity of genuine revolutionaries in Britain in this 12/30/37 letter to Rudolf Rocker, Goldman despairs at the organizing prospects for the new branch of the SIA. The Spanish comrades will want her to seek support beyond the level of revolutionary appeals.*

That means I will have to appeal to some of the middle class in this country. God knows it is without stamina everywhere when it comes to real revolutionary fighters; but it is sickening here. 95% of the intellectuals have been caught in the Communist trap including so great a mind as Paul Robeson,[51] and the remaining 5% wishy-washy pacifists—well-meaning I am sure.

*†Writing to Rüdiger on the same day, Goldman conveys her pained feelings about the IWMA congress just attended.*

I'm still all sick and discouraged from the sessions—the petty frictions and the demented incapacity to understand man and events in a generous way. . . . I'm not used to giving "diplomatic" speeches.[52] My whole life I truly spoke out what I thought and felt. I never thought that in my old age I would become a tightrope walker. I was so depressed during the congress I could have cried. It was difficult, very difficult to find the right words which would hurt neither [side] . . . .

*At the same time, she felt as if she were gagged since she had no official voice or influence to confront the upsetting spectacle before her eyes.[53]*

*She refers again to her sense that some degree of personal dispute was involved in Rüdiger's judgement of Souchy's activities for the CNT. She has no doubt as to Rüdiger's sincerity. It's just that she knows how deep in the psyche one's*

51. See footnote 51 at back of chapter.
52. At the last moment, CNT leaders convinced a reluctant Goldman to come from London to participate as a friendly observer (since she was not a member or delegate from any official anarcho-syndicalist organization belonging to the IWMA), thus hopefully to add moral weight on the Spanish side in the face of their hostile international critics in the movement. Goldman did so and was permitted to make her own verbal observations on one occasion, in which she appealed to both sides to come to some sort of conciliation. Passages from her speech appear two items above and in Chapters III-VII. The full speech is also reproduced in Shulman, ed., *Red Emma Speaks*.
53. Goldman made her one speech at the objection of the French delegation. Likewise, she was attacked by her previously-close comrade Schapiro for allowing the CNT to use her as a moral crutch (Goldman 6/2/38 letter to Rüdiger, AMS-G).

*judgements are based, however conscious or not this may be.*

†*She communicates to Harry Kelly (1/1/38) similar impressions of the congress and states her torment at not openly speaking her mind to the public.*

I was called to the congress of the IWMA in Paris. I really had no business there, as I am not affiliated with any of their sections, and I was not sent as a delegate; but Vázquez wired me to come, so I went, and I sat through a week's procedure which was certainly the most agonizing I have ever experienced, and you also know that anarchists' congresses have never been pleasant affairs.

At the instance of the Spanish and Swedish delegations I was given the floor. I am just in the midst of writing out my notes. I will send you a copy; but of course it will not be for publication. I should hate to make the washing of anarchist soiled linen a spectacle for the world.

For the present I am sending you a copy of my letter to Rudolf. Please bear in mind that this too is not to be circulated.

Yes, my dear, we have come to a point [where] I never expected to arrive: to have two opinions. One for the outside world and one for intimate comrades and friends. How I upbraided Bob Minor[54] when he refused to divulge to the public the horrors of the Soviet regime he disclosed to Sasha and me. How naive and childish we were to believe that a revolution brought about by anarchists will not impose measures wide of the mark of our ideas.

†*Three days later, she explains to Ethel Mannin the significance of individual idealists pursuing the struggle outside of political parties.*

Darling, don't you understand that one individual may often have greater moral force than a whole party, especially a political party? I am not unaware that since the World War and the advent of Fascism and Russian Communism, the mass looks to the strong armed man or the strong political party. That is the tragedy of our time. It has destroyed all moral and ethical revolutionary values. As far as I am concerned, I feel that just because of the void of all social and moral values in all the political parties, I must grind on to hold high the banner of [the] ideals of freedom and mutual help. They are the lasting values, my dear, never mind whether they have already taken "roots in the British workers" or not.

---

54. An American political artist and journalist, Bob Minor attended the 3rd congress of the Red Trade Union International in mid-1921. (See Goldman's account in *LL*, 910-14, 917.) Though an anarchist and collaborator in the publications of Goldman and Berkman during the decade before, he was a founder of the American Communist Party and one of its leaders for 35 years, for a time editing its newspaper *The Daily Worker*.

†*Reaching for close, trusting friendship with a European movement comrade in the vacuum from 1936 on, Goldman expresses her gratitude to Helmut Rüdiger in a letter of 1/24/38. With the death of Berkman and the breakdown of communication with Schapiro, Steimer and Fleshin, developing a closer relationship with him is for her a real treasure.*

†*Concerned with U.S. anarchist Abe Bluestein's intent to publicize a critique of the Spanish anarchists following his lengthy stay in that country, Goldman explains to him (1/25/38) the nature of her own disciplined solidarity and gently urges reconsideration of his plans.*

Thank you for giving me credit for having been an outstanding person in our movement who was "never tied by limits of organizations." Though you may not believe it, I want you to know that if I did not feel with all my passion and intensity the dire need of standing up by our Spanish comrades, by their battle, no discipline they might want to impose [on] me would have any value. Whatever discipline I am following is the one I have imposed upon myself. I grant you that in my younger days I might have been as impatient as you and the comrades [working] on the underground activities in Spain. You see, the Spanish anarchist traditions are the first to come in my long active life that gave me faith in the triumphant outcome of the struggle regardless of the mistakes our people are making. Also I have learned through experience that ideas are one thing and life another. Whether we want it or not life imposes certain changes in our outlook or simply passes us by.

I do not think it's any use going on with arguments. I am afraid I will not convince you, and I might as well tell you frankly, you will not swerve me from my position to do what I can to help our Spanish people, actively as I have so far, or if the sad moment should arrive when I should no longer be able to speak on their behalf, to keep silent until the struggle will be over.

Yes I heard about the Santillán book; but as I have not read it I am not in a position to know why it was stopped.[55] In any event I do not think that Santillán's life was threatened by the CNT-FAI. On the day of my departure from Valencia I saw Santillán, and he told me his life was threatened by the Communists and that's why he kept under cover. Could you not have sent out a copy of Santillán's book and copies of the underground papers?[56] I tried my utmost to get the latter when I was still in Spain but failed.

No doubt Schapiro, Voline and the others are getting these papers. I suppose because the comrades think that they are safer than I.

55. See footnote 55 at back of chapter.
56. See footnote 19 in Chapter II.

I should like to hear from you, Abe, what you intend to do now that you have had a long time to consider the advisability of an open campaign. It seems that Brand has definitely changed his mind about an open criticism of what you call the "Official Anarchists" whom you consider Bolsheviks. His criticism of the real enemies of the Revolution, the Communists and the Negrín government, is very valuable[56a] I am waiting anxiously to see what your stand will be. Of course you must do what you can reconcile with your integrity.

† *In a 2/1/38 letter to her niece, Goldman explains her effort to create an attractive publicity headquarters for the Spanish anarchist cause in London.*[57] *In this she differs from the usual anarchist attitude in the U.S. and Britain that the appearance of a place makes no difference for propaganda.*

The new place will be the first the Anarchists ever had which will show that our ideas are not what they are popularly believed to be . . . . . . . One thing I am definitely set on [is] to permit no hanging around of all sorts of people who for some unknown reason to me call themselves Anarchists when they have never attempted to realize it in their own life [or] to do anything for it that would require effort.

† *In this brief 2/16/38 message to British writer Aldous Huxley, Goldman welcomes him to the anarchist movement.*

Without wishing to be pushing, I cannot refrain from assuring you that this statement of yours [endorsing the anarchist political creed][58] is an event in my life of first-rate importance: indeed, I feel that it was worth fighting for fifty years to be able to call one a comrade who is so outstanding as a creative artist and who comes from a family of libertarians. Really, you have given me much encouragement which one needs fighting for an ideal in this country. Thank you again.

† *Writing to Rudolf Rocker on 2/22/38, Goldman assesses the nature and significance of European anarchist attitudes toward the Spanish movement.*

56a Brand's critiques, written from Spain, appeared in the New York anarchist publication *Cultura Proletaria* during 1937 and early 1938. In a recent letter to me, Brand maintains that Goldman misunderstood his stance, that in fact he opposed open criticism of the Spanish anarchists from the beginning. He felt that some degree of anti-fascist collaboration was essential. Otherwise, the anarchists would have had to give up the struggle against Franco, since they didn't have the weapons to win on their own.

57. The new London office of the CNT-FAI was at 21 Frith Street, in the Soho district just off of Charing Cross Road and Shaftesbury Avenue, near Picadilly Square.

58. See footnote 58 at back of chapter.

. . . Who are our comrades in Europe? With the exception of CH [Schapiro] and Besnard and possibly Voline, there is not one of any consequence and even these three are able to reach only a small number. So in the last analysis, although their criticism was harmful, it did not carry much weight. The rank and file of the comrades in France went with the CNT-FAI. As far as Sweden is concerned the comrades there absolutely stood by our Spanish people.[59]

*† To Rüdiger on 3/12/38, Goldman expresses her continued frustration and exhaustion with the few numbers, poor energy and squabbling personalities in the anarchist movement in Britain. Constantly she has to convince herself to continue her publicity efforts for Spain, despite the absence of any significant constructive support from comrades. The London "Freedom" group has been sleeping and quarreling for years. The Anarcho-Syndicalist Union is still inactive, though presently there is an effort to revive it.*

. . . There is another person here [Guy Aldred] who is not only dumb but also unbelievably conceited. . . . Rudolf [Rocker] could tell you things about him.[60] This is the type like Pierre Ramus.[61] All his life Guy Aldred has been using the comrades and the movement only to fulfill his pathological conceit. He has slandered Rudolf in the most destructive way and not even I have been able to avoid his anger,[62] even though I met him only once in my life and that for only a few minutes.

*Aldred's behavior succeeded in splitting the Glasgow Anti-Parliamentary Group into three parts, one of which, the Anarchist-Communist group, invited her for a series of five meetings. Unfortunately the eight members of this group could probably do more if it were not for the incessant meddling of Aldred. Though quite capable, he is impossible to work with. He also has his followers present at every meeting here to confuse the audience with obscure issues.*

*† In this 3/21/38 letter to Canadian comrade Dorothy Rogers, Goldman describes*

59. Goldman goes on to state that the Swedish movement raised about 200,000 Swedish kronan (or US $90,740). More on support efforts by the 32,000-member Swedish anarcho-syndicalist organization (the S.A.C.) can be found in *I.W.M.A. Press Service* (Paris), no. 4 (May 15, 1938).
60. Meltzer gives more details on Aldred generally and on the latter's attack on Rocker in *The Anarchists in London*, pp. 16, 24. A biographical sketch of Aldred appears in the American anarchist periodical, *The Match* (Tucson), January 1975.
61. See footnote 61 at back of chapter.
62. One example was Aldred's depiction of Goldman as a representative of the Valencia government and thus a likely defender of censorship against CNT and POUM critics (*Regeneracion!* [Glasgow], March 14, 1937). Another example was his attack on Goldman and Rocker as defenders of the "corrupt degenerate Spanish bureaucracy" and on Goldman's role in London in particular, published in the Trotskyist periodical, *The New International*, vol. 4, no. 3 (March 1938). More on the long-range dispute is found in Aldred's autobiography, *No Traitor's Gait!* (Glasgow: Strickland Press, 1947), vol. II.

*the unfortunate tendency of Jewish anarchists to isolate themselves from the struggle of the broader population around them.*

First of all, I want you to get over your anxiety of thinking you annoy me with your personal life. One cannot separate one's personal self entirely from the movement. I have always taken a keen interest in the personal struggles, tragedies and comedies of my friends. Not that I ever pry into their lives; but I was always glad they shared whatever was disturbing their minds and was making life difficult, so you need never hesitate to tell me all you feel you need.

I was also interested in what you write me about the Jewish group. It is unfortunately true that our Jewish comrades on the American continent have always kept aloof from our activities in English. Even while Sasha and I were in the States and publishing *Mother Earth*, we received small help from our Jewish comrades, although there were exceptions to the rule. Some of the groups were helpful in organizing meetings when I came to their cities; but even then they concentrated more on the Jewish meetings than the English. It is tragic, but speaking generally, in the past our people have never acquired the language of the country they lived in, and for ought they knew of the life and psychology of the natives, they might just have remained in their small Jewish or Polish towns. The deeper tragedy to me is that they have done nothing to acquaint their children with the ideas for which they were willing to sacrifice so much. The irony of it is that the younger generation have drifted away and certainly never acquired the Yiddish. Consequently they don't know what is going on in the *Freie Arbeiter Stimme* or formerly in the *Arbeiter Freund*.[63] Of late the Jewish comrades have become more Jewish than they were thirty years ago. That seems to me to lie in the terrible situation of the Jews in the whole world. The mad persecution of millions of people, the denial of asylum and shelter has again brought the wandering Jew to the fore. All this does not help us in our work; but the tragedy must be understood nevertheless.

†*In this moving 3/38 preface to a published selection of Camillo Berneri's writings,[64] Goldman conveys her detailed impressions of Berneri and their common perspective on Spain.*

Camillo Berneri, lofty idealist, sweet singer of revolt, lover of all mankind, was foully murdered in Barcelona, May 7th, 1937. By his daring opposition to the insidious activities in Spain of Stalin's henchmen, Camillo had incurred

63. The *Arbeiter Freund* was the London Yiddish-language anarchist equivalent of the *Freie Arbeiter Stimme* publication in New York. Rudolf Rocker was for a number of years editor of the former and there were a number of individuals who worked on both papers over time.
64. Camillo Berneri, *Pensieri e battaglie* (Paris: Comitato Camillo Berneri, 1938).

the wrath of the Soviet torquemada and so he had to die. The gruesome story of his end is related in the tributes paid our martyred comrade by several writers, now gathered with some of his letters in this book. There is no need for me to elaborate on it. I want rather to write of my recollections and impressions of Camillo Berneri, of our camaraderie in Barcelona when we both worked almost side by side to help our comrades in their struggle for the Spanish Revolution and against Fascism.

I had heard much about Professor Berneri, his fine personality and his gentle spirit, before I met him in Paris. The meeting was very fleeting; we could but exchange a few words. It was enough, however, to give me a definite impression of the man and his aims. I was particularly carried away by the sensitiveness of his face and the charm of his manner. We promised each other to meet again soon when we would have time really to get acquainted. Little did either one of us dream that we would meet so soon in Spain and be joined in our passionate desire to help our Spanish comrades.

Comrade Berneri had preceded me to Barcelona by two months. On my arrival there in September, 1936, I already found him in the thick of the struggle: at the Huesca front as the delegate of the Italian column[65] — every hour taken up with various tasks on his return from the front — discussing with young comrades until daybreak. That and many other things kept our comrade busy and absorbed.

Frail and evidently worn from the strain of his labors, Camillo yet responded generously to every call on his energies. Extremely sensitized as he was, he easily sensed the needs of others, often imaginary needs hardly worth the waste of our comrade's strength. He was not unaware of the advantages taken of his gentle nature, but he continued to give out of his rich fount of sympathy and compassion.

The amazing thing to me was that though always in the midst of crowds, Camillo Berneri could yet hold aloof his own integrity as well as his independence of mind. He never hesitated to bring both into play the moment anybody attempted to encroach upon what he considered the most sacred part of his being. How he did it, he explains in one of the beautiful letters to his wife . . . .

In this as in many other circumstances Camillo Berneri proved his keen sense of the comic side of life and the understanding of the small and trifling affairs that loom so high to little people.

The multitude of jobs imposed upon our comrade are also set forth by him in another letter to his family . . . .

I saw his crowded days and I hesitated to become one of the many who dogged his steps. It was he who sought me out when back from the front one day, and I had returned from my tours of inspection of collective industries and

65. Of Italian emigré refugees, especially anarchist in orientation.

farms. As I have already stated, Camillo Berneri had preceded me to Spain by two months. His experience of the heights and depths of the revolutionary situation was therefore invaluable to me. In addition was the fact that I was inarticulate in Spanish. He spoke that language as well as French, outside his own Italian, and he was therefore of great help to me.

Our exchange of thoughts was grateful to my hopes and fears for the future of the Revolution and the continued strength of the CNT and the FAI. We soon found that we shared these fears. In fact we struck up a harmonious chord before we had been together an hour. I was touched by Camillo's concern in my needs and his thoughtfulness in offering help to find me comfortable quarters and anything else I might want. This was the more moving because he himself, while living in the same hotel with me, was taking his meals in the poorest of proletarian restaurants. This sweet solidarity and kindness revived the memory of one whom I had sought out during the first agonized conflict after my arrival in Russia – Maxime Gorki.

He had been the idol of my youthful days – he, the poet of the Song of the Falcon and the Snake, and so many other stirring songs; Gorki who had articulated the tragedies of the lower depths, who had been the clarion voice in the dreadful silence of the pre-revolutionary Russia . . . . He would understand my inner turmoil, the revolutionary incongruities that haunted my waking and sleeping hours. I went to him for some light in the dark horizon of the inexorable Bolshevik regime.

Maxime Gorki regarded me with unseeing eyes. He did not understand my quest. He had become a cog in the Soviet machine. He had nothing left of his former self to give.[66]

I thought of this episode while talking with Camillo about the contrasts between the Spanish and Russian Revolutions, the contrasts, too, in the protagonists of both world events. In my own mind I also contrasted the two men, Maxime Gorki and Camillo Berneri. There was a whole world between them.

The most outstanding day of the camaraderie with Camillo Berneri remained vividly in my mind. It was the 7th of November, 1936 – the [nineteenth] anniversary of the Russian Revolution. Barcelona was in festive attire. Vast masses of workers marched through the streets; the CNT-FAI and the Libertarian Youth represented the largest contingent. Proudly they carried the red and black banner and the air resounded with their triumphant cry: "CNT-FAI! CNT-FAI! CNT-FAI!" In these letters the Spanish revolutionary workers have put all their aspirations, all their dreams of the new world they had begun to build on the 19th of July.

Inspired by the memory of the Russian Revolution, by the valiant workers, peasants, soldiers and sailors who *alone* had brought about the world-stirring

66. See more on this disillusioning encounter in *LL*, II, 738, 741-45.

event, our comrades in Barcelona joyously participated in the festivities. They were blissfully ignorant of the fact that the celebration of the Russian Revolution organized by Stalin's vassals was a travesty of the Revolution.

In point of truth it had been hurled from its lofty zenith in the early days of 1917[67], kicked about by Lenin's experiment until it bled from a thousand wounds. The final thrust that ended the agony of the Russian Revolution was left to Stalin. It was this man whose virtue and desert were to be expressed in a paeon song, November 7th, 1936, in revolutionary Spain—a travesty indeed.

We of the foreign section[68] and especially the Russians who had witnessed the slow death of the Russian Revolution were of course not deceived. For us the 7th of November was a day of mourning. We resented the participation of our Spanish comrades in this event. Some of them even condemning the CNT-FAI as having gone back on their Russian comrades languishing in Soviet concentration camps. My heart was heavy with sadness, yet I could not sit in judgement over our comrades of the CNT-FAI.

Franco and his hordes were slowly creeping up to the gates of Madrid. Arms were desperately needed. It was a matter of life and death. In their own high idealism and revolutionary ethical traditions, the Spanish Anarchists accepted Stalin's proffered hand on its face value. It never occured to them that along with arms he will also send his blessings that had turned Russia into a vale of tears and had covered her soil with rivers of blood.

Camillo Berneri came to see me. He brought with him a statement he had prepared dealing with the many puzzling questions confronting us all. Not reading Italian and on the eternal move from place to place and country to country, I had been unable to follow the life and work of our comrade. In point of truth the statement, which fortunately was in French, was the first piece of writing by Camillo I had read. Through our numerous talks I had come to appreciate the clarity of his mind and the lucidity in presenting his thoughts, but his written form was even more impressive and convincing. Above everything else the statement contained the purity that motivated his criticism of the leading comrades in the CNT-FAI. It shone like a light through every line. This and our long discussion after I had read his criticism brought our comrade near to me as one of the truly great souls in our ranks, as well as one of the ablest of his generation.

The letter to Federica Montseny in this volume[69] grew out of the statement I had read on the 7th of November, 1936. In the light of subsequent events in May, the destruction of some of the constructive achievements of the CNT-FAI, the political persecution of real revolutionists, Camillo Berneri proved himself astonishingly prophetic—clairvoyant, I would say. Not that I agreed

67. Presumably she means 1918 here.
68. The foreign propaganda section of the CNT-FAI.
69. See footnote 35 in Chapter IV.

with him in what he wrote about the decline of the Spanish Revolution. I am only too aware that the Revolution had received a jolt through the alignment of the anti-Fascist forces with their Russian ally. True, it might even have been done to death by Stalin's satraps as the Russian Revolution had been destroyed, were it not for the continued moral strength of the CNT-FAI and the fact that the adherents of Moscow had overreached themselves. They had counted without their hosts, they had overlooked the Spanish people and their libertarian ideas woven into the very texture of their being.

Had Camillo Berneri lived he would have seen as I have, on my second visit to Spain, that the Revolution is still very much alive and that the increased constructive work goes on regardless of all obstacles. Moreover there is the indestructible quality of the Spanish people and their determination to fight to the bitter end. These were the matters Camillo and I differed on, but for the rest we felt deeply in everything concerning Spain, and we too were determined to serve the Revolution and the people to the uttermost.

Among the many horrors the world war brought in its wake and increased by Fascism, Nazism and Bolshevism, is the man-hunt of political refugees. They are indeed the modern Ahasuerus[70] — nowhere wanted, driven from frontier to frontier — often into death. Camillo Berneri did not escape this tragic fate of the political refugee. His letters describing the persecution, the arrests, the brutal treatment, the imprisonment to which he had been subjected in every country, are a scathing indictment of the post-war world turned into a fortress for those who will not bend their knees to the dictator's commands or become a party to their crimes.

The sufferings Camillo Berneri had endured had impaired his health. It failed utterly to affect his spirit. All through his terrible experiences his revolutionary zeal and flaming ideal burned like red-white heat. Even his rich humor never left him for long. The story of the policeman whose heart Camillo softened for a brief moment by his detection of the picture of Voltaire on the officer's pipe, and another story, bear witness to Camillo Berneri's humanity. It is when he invites the policeman sent to watch his house to have real, strong, hot Italian coffee to save him from the cold. Camillo Berneri, professor of philosophy, dangerous anarchist, showing kindness and compassion to an officer who had been sent to watch him day and night — how should the dull of mind and empty of heart know that it was precisely Camillo Berneri's love for mankind and his feeling with all human suffering that made him the anarchist he was?

Camillo Berneri's letters to his family are moving in their beauty and their devotion. He adored his wife, he idolized his two daughters and he revered his mother. Again and again he pours out his loving heart to them — to Giliane,

70. The legendary "wandering Jew."

his ten-year-old, and Maria Louise,[71] the elder one. They were the very apple of his eye. Yet his supremist love was his ideal. That had first call on him. Often Camillo found it painful to choose because of the pain his choice might cause his loved ones, but he never wavered or stopped in the path that led him to the fulfillment of his ideals. It was uppermost in his mind, and the complete dedication to it his strongest, most compelling force. In one of his letters to his wife he assures her that if he could save Bilbao with his life he would give it gladly. No one who knew Camillo could possibly doubt this. Alas, it was not given to our comrade to lay down his beautiful life as he willed. Instead he was murdered in cold blood: arbitrarily arrested on the night of 6th May together with his comrade, Barbieri. Their bodies were found riddled by bullets on the following morning in front of the Generalidad.

It is not so much how one dies that counts in the ultimate evaluation of one's worth. It is how one lives; and the life of Camillo Berneri stands out in all its inner strength and radiant beauty.

† *Goldman provides a fascinating direct link to presentday ecological discussion in a 4/5/38 letter to Rudolf Rocker.*

Who [are] Ralph Borsodi and Kettering? – also Abbot? A letter from Aldous Huxley maintains much is to be learned from the theoretical and practical work of Ralph Borsodi and the inventions of Kettering – Kettering's work on small Diesel power plants for domestic purposes, Abbot's work on a machine for making direct use of solar energy.[72]

I wish you would enlighten me on this.

*Though Huxley claims that anarchism could be achieved through intelligent use of such writings, she finds it hard to believe that basic social change can be accomplished through small numbers engaged in technological experimentation.*

† *Writing to Rüdiger two months later (6/2/38), Goldman comments on the importance of Spain for her hopes concerning anarchism in general.*

. . . Spain was our one and only glowing hope. And if that too will be crushed where will our Idea [anarchism] rise again? However, like you I cling to the hopes that all is not yet lost, as a drowning person clings to a straw. My disillusionment in Russia was terrible enough, it paralysed me for years. Defeat of

71. See the earlier reference to her in Chapter IV, footnote 15. A biographical sketch of her life and her work as an anarchist is *Marie Louise Berneri, 1918-1949: A Tribute* (London: Marie Louise Berneri Memorial Committee, 1949). See also the comments in Meltzer, *The Anarchists in London.*

72. See footnote 72 at back of chapter.

our ideas in Spain would kill me. I don't think I shall want to go on after such a blow.

† *Despite Rudolf Rocker's praise of certain Italian-American comrades,*[73] *Goldman writes to him (7/12/38) of her frustration and anger with their devisive approach. It is their willingness to engage in sectarian attacks which defeats their purpose. Specifically, she is angered by their earlier publication of Marcus Graham's dogmatic critique of her autobiography*[74] *and now a critical letter about her written to Vernon Richards, editor of* Spain and the World.

I must say that I have no patience with comrades who set themselves up as moral censors and judges of their comrades without investigating whether they have the right to do so or not. However, the methods of *L'Adunata* are nothing new in the anarchist ranks. Instead of fighting a common enemy, each one is at the other fellow's throat.

† *A week later (7/19/38), Goldman sets forth her views on "Christian anarchism" in this letter to prominent U.S. writer Edward Dahlberg.*

To come back to your letter. It contains several statements which rather startle me. One is your reference to Peter Kropotkin as a "christian Anarchist." That is certainly news to me. Kropotkin was a revolutionist from his early beginnings to his death and an atheist. He repudiated christianity *in toto*, unless you mean one's humanity and one's compassion for other human beings in pain represents christianity. At any rate, it is erroneous to call Kropotkin a christian anarchist. In point of fact christianity and anarchism are opposite poles. The christian believes in the state. Even Christ is credited with saying "Give unto Caesar that which is Caesar's and unto the Lord that which is the Lord's." No better justification for the power of the State and the Church they have practiced so long. There was nothing of that in Peter Kropotkin.

† *Goldman here offers a cautious critique (7/28/38 letter) for Abe Bluestein's new anarchist periodical* Challenge.

There are other things about *Challenge* about which I would like to write; but I do not want to take too much liberty to tell you and the other comrades how

---

73. Those in the anarchist group producing the periodical *L'Adunata dei Refrattari*.
74. Her reaction to Graham's article at the time was that it was "full of lies and misrepresentations," especially insulting in its insinuation that she had supported the Bolsheviks in their attack on Kronstadt in 1921 (Goldman 12/31/32 letter to Milly Rocker, AMS-R). Berkman attacked it for its Jesuitry, in a letter to the U.S. anarchist publication *Freedom* (2/11/33).

your paper should be gotten up or what it should contain. I have never taken that liberty even in my younger days and when I was in the States, much less do I want to sermonize you and the comrades now when I am so far away. I do not wish to tell, like all people reaching a formidable age, the young generation what is good for it; but I do believe *Challenge* can stand improvement especially in the get-up. You have no idea how much the appearance of a paper helps its sales.

† *With the growing international impact of fascism and the slide toward new world conflict, Goldman tells Rudolf Rocker (9/13/38) of her reduced faith in potential mass political awareness.*

. . . It is hard to live in this insane world. Last night all of Paris was on [its] feet hanging on every word that came out from Hitler's foul mouth.[75] What a horrible commentary on human intelligence and even more so on the integrity of the masses . . . . . . Yet you and I still believe the masses will ultimately learn to understand our ideal and be strong enough to realize it. I have begun to doubt this of late, dear Rudolf.

† *In this 11/22/38 letter to British writer Evelyn Scott, Goldman assesses the great significance of social revolution and the even greater importance of individual growth.*

I do not deny that revolution, like war, often brings worse evils in its wake than immediate good. It is impossible to conceive that a terrific storm should not wash up a lot of debris and driftwood. So, too, it is impossible to expect that revolution should do away over night, as it were, with all the mean and violent traits accumulated in man over centuries. I frankly admit that I have seen many things in Spain hard to bear and often making me ask myself whether all the pain and blood and death is worthwhile; but also I have seen the most wonderful human traits, heroism beyond belief and the spirit to bring out the best in man and that leads me to believe that revolution is the harbinger of new life and new social values. However, you are right a thousand times when you say that the first requisite is "the cultivation of individual standards."

† *Similarly, to Ethel Mannin in 12/38, Goldman explains her commitment to remain independent of any political organization.*

75. She refers to the September 12, 1938 speech of Hitler at the Nazi Nuremburg rally, containing a significant escalation of his threats toward Czechoslovakia.

Darling, did you think you could hobnob with EG, preside at CNT-FAI [meetings] and approve "Fury Over Spain"[76] without being called on the carpet by the I.L.P.? You are naive. Still it is "amusing," to use Auntie's favorite expression. I am curious to know whether your party really means business.

Oh, my dearest, all political parties are stupid, narrow and visionless. That's why I have never belonged to any—not even Anarchist groups. That's why I stand alone. I admit it is often most trying. But at least one keeps one's independence.


†*In a 2/9/39 letter to a "dear good friend," Goldman addresses the issue of how anarchist consciousness might spread.*

My dear friend, I deserve no thanks for the literature I have sent you. I am only too glad when those who are my friends express interest in the ideas that have been and are the *raison d'etre* of my life. I have never imposed my ideas on people and I could never bear people who talked shop in and out of season. But if I see the least interest I am happy to help those who are seeking for information. I am very glad also that you liked the *Life of Bakunin*[77]. It is by no means a deep work, but then my friend, Dr. Kaminski, does not pretend anything more than first-rate journalism, and as you say it is written in such a simple style that anyone who knows even little of French can easily understand it.

In attempting to make a "convert" of you I felt quite safe that you would not develop a sense of "intellectual and spiritual superiority" over the unconverted. I shouldn't want such a convert, but I had enough faith in you to know that as far as your time and energy will permit, you will use whatever knowledge and conviction you have gained from the literature I sent you to impart both to others who, like you, have been Anarchists all their lives but did not know it. As you see, I knew you better than you knew yourself. There is more fact than fiction in the contention I have maintained that Anarchists are born rather than made. I frankly own up to my ignorant belief in my youth that all that was necessary to make everyone of the thousands of people who heard me an Anarchist was to speak to them with my heart in my throat. But I soon climbed down from this self-sufficiency. I realized that all that one can do whether by word of mouth or pen is to awaken whatever is inherent in man, namely the longing for freedom and self-expression. I don't know how much I have succeeded in that through a half century of effort. It is already much to have awakened the interest in people of your caliber and some of the

76. A film on the Spanish revolution and civil war produced by the CNT-FAI.
77. H.E. Kaminski, *Michel Bakounine: la vie d'un révolutionnaire* (Paris: Aubier, 1938).

other individual minds who have come my way.

† *On the same day she writes to Evelyn Scott on the very contemporary theme of* "*human scale technology.*"

. . . You are entirely right, dear Evelyn, when you say that the "simplification introduced by the machine is useful for manipulating thousands" and that "changes wrought by machine intervention are completely on the external side and leave the real battle which has to be fought from within the person." Certainly the machine has become a fetish eulogized by every shade of Marxian schools. We Anarchists have realized this modern superstition long ago. That is why we have insisted that . . . instead of [man] being subjugated to the machine, [the latter] must be so directed as to take very little time from man so that he may gain time and leisure for his inner growth and development. Above all, the use of the machine must be so directed as to take very little time from man so that he may learn to appreciate the quality and beauty of things he produces.

† *With the collapse in Spain, Goldman feels more isolated than ever. For her, steady communication from Rudolf Rocker is essential, as she states in a letter of 3/17/39.*

. . . You do not know how frightfully cut off I am from everybody and everything I know in the States, and my isolation and loneliness here. I never felt that way so long as Sasha was alive. . . . I miss Sasha more since the Spanish struggle and its defeat. . . . In point of fact, you are taking Sasha's place because I know you feel as I do about our heroic people, and because you have understood their heights and now their depths.

† *To both Milly and Rudolf Rocker a month later (4/19/39), she expresses her general dismay in a world now without any significant movement context.*

. . . The fact of the matter is I feel so uprooted I do not belong anywhere. Yes, I know nearly everybody feels that way now. But in my case it is not due to the difficulties of getting about, rather is it because there is no movement anywhere and no new blood to give it life. The tragedy is that having dedicated fifty years to one thing, one becomes unfit for anything else.

† *To a reporter in Windsor, Canada one month later (5/19/39), Goldman defines the nature and purpose of anarchist agitation.*

We don't believe in foisting anything on any country. Any change must take place from within. Otherwise, it is a grievous mistake. If social and economic conditions arise where millions are without work and suffer a drab and miserable life, they will arise from within.

Why do I lecture? Why do I travel through Canada? Why do I travel through those countries that will admit me?

Because people are so burdened with their worries and troubles that they have no time to think of action to remedy them. I, and others with me, merely awaken them. We do not force any violent change upon them. The change must come from the soil and needs of the country.

That is what happened in Spain at the time of the revolution. That was merely a bursting of forces that had accumulated.

My definition of revolution is nothing else but the bursting point of the accumulated evolutionary forces that have preceded it.

†*A separate reporter on the same day quotes her comments on the anarchist move-ment and the potential for success.*

Anarchism will win, but not with kid gloves. We do not preach the theory of violence, but we do not believe in fighting violence by temperate measures.

The Libertarians are not really an organization. We do not believe in organization. It is impossible to tell how many members there are as there are no dues paid and no lists of members.

†*A third newspaper account at the same time again reflects her public confidence in ultimate anarchist success, despite the growing reactionary trends.*

We are in a period of reaction. I don't know how long it will last. The world has been in such periods before, and has come out of them. My faith in anarchy is unshaken. I think that the behavior of modern imperialistic govern-ments and their leaders will help convince the mass of people that chances for happiness and prosperity do not lie with political parties and political govern-ments. And like Lincoln, I do not believe that you can fool the people all the time.

†*Writing an open letter from Toronto to comrades and friends in the United States on her 70th birthday (6/27/39), Goldman reflects back on her life and expresses the same basic faith.*

As you see I am now very near to you in the United States, yet still very far away. Fortunately, there are no spiritual boundaries or to the all-embracing

force of comradeship and solidarity. I, therefore, feel very close to all of you regardless of the arbitrary frontier divisions.[78] And I feel certain that you also feel close to me.

August 15, '39 will be exactly a half century since I entered our ranks and took up the battle for Anarchism. Far from regretting this step, I can say honestly I am more convinced than in August 1889 of the logic and justice of our ideal. True, we are passing through a period of the blackest reaction in every country. The Fascists, the so-called democracies and even "the workers' fatherland" are competing with each other to further forge the chains of economic and political slavery and so destroy the individual altogether. By this very scramble for power, the state in every country has proven its utter inability to meet the needs of the people and to maintain even a modicum of freedom and well-being.

† *To Helmut Rüdiger on 8/4/39, Goldman expresses her ultimate frustrating assessment of the value of her work in England. Despite her years of activity there from 1924 on, she feels she never aroused interest in anarchism or even gathered together old veterans of the movement. Instead they persistently complained about her "dictatorial" approach in developing the Spanish campaign. Thus, only several non-anarchist personal friends in that country even bothered to send her greetings for her 70th birthday. But she's too experienced with cold treatment within the movement to let this disturb her.*

† *On the same day, she writes a similar statement to Milly and Rudolf Rocker and refers bitterly to attacks on her own personal integrity.*

. . . There really is no reason to rejoice in living under the present ghastly conditions in the world, but those of us who cannot die before their time, must go on against all odds and make what they can of whatever years left them until the final moment arrives to pay their toll. I frankly admit that I shouldn't continue but for the fact of the tragic situation of our Spanish comrades.

*At least she can try to raise money to help some of the comrades in the refugee camps.*
*"Shop-keeper traits"[79] are as typical of English radicals as they are of that population generally. This probably best explains her failure to create interest in the Spanish cause during her 2½ years in England. Indeed, she even made enemies there — to the point where now her financial integrity is being challenged. Some of her supposed friends there now want the SIA books to be audited by a public*

78. She was still barred from entry into the United States.
79. The petty-bourgeois individualism oriented almost exclusively toward affairs of one's own private, daily realm.

*accountant. She has nothing to hide,*[80] *but this cannot be done since this was not a business operation; indeed some of the money went to purposes which could not be revealed to outsiders. In any case, her responsibility was to the Spanish movement, not to anyone else.*

†*In her 10/7/39 letter to Rudolf Rocker, Goldman reflects both the distancing of a seasoned veteran and her continued determination to find new hope and struggle on.*

. . . I admit those were naive days when we still had some hope and like babes in the woods we were dreaming of all the work we were going to accomplish.[81] It seems so long ago.

. . . . . . . . . . . . . . . . . . . . . . . . . . . . . . . . . . . . . . . . . . . . . . . . . . . .

. . . [Nevertheless] I feel that now more than ever our work is desperately needed. Our trouble is that we have no movement and very few comrades who can see clearly even now. That is what makes our efforts so futile and seemingly useless.

*She now has an invitation to address four meetings in Winnipeg. If she doesn't go on from there to other cities in the West, she'll probably return to Toronto and begin writing.*[82] *A potential obstacle is that the Canadian government is now arresting certain anarchist militants, the most outstanding of which is Arthur Bortolotti.*[83] *She doesn't care if she's sent to prison, though she would hate the prospect of being sent back to England where the last several years were more painful to her than all her previous time in the U.S. Yet one cannot give up pursuing an ideal one has advocated for a lifetime.*

†*In this 11/20/39 letter to Herbert Read, Goldman again states her commitment to anarchism of spirit and action, instead of mere words.*

It is just as well that you have time now to attend to other things in the way of writing, which you can do so magnificently. By the way, our attorney [J.L. Cohen] borrowed your *Poetry and Anarchism*[84] and he has been raving about

80. In fact, Goldman's accounting of receipts and expenditures for the SIA and CNT-FAI London office seems meticulous and conscientious, as any reading of her correspondence with the Spanish comrades makes clear. She was continuously exasperated with the Spanish failure to provide certified receipts for money sent and other acknowledgements, though it is clear that the comrades with whom she had contact had every confidence in her financial decisions.
81. She recalls here the visit of Milly and Rudolf Rocker to her cottage at St. Tropez, France, in the late 1920's or early 1930's.
82. Presumably articles or a book on Spain, reflecting the same basic perspectives and images found in the present work.
83. See footnote 43 in Chapter VI.
84. Herbert Read, *Poetry and Anarchism* (London: Faber and Faber, 1938). This lengthy essay appears also in a larger collection of Read's writings, *Anarchy and Order: Essays in Politics* (1954; rpt., Boston: Beacon Press, 1971).

it. He told me that he has never read anything so profound and beautifully written.[85] So you may yet have the satisfaction of doing what I have failed to do, making an Anarchist of J.L. Actually he is such a grand person that I don't care what particular political tendencies he has. You see I am a heathen. I feel that the humanity of people is infinitely more important at times than their theories.

*She far prefers those who act and live anarchistically to those who give it lip service alone.*

85. Goldman herself was delighted to find someone in Britain willing to write so eloquently in favor of anarchism, though she felt his concepts of anarchism and anarcho-syndicalism needed better thought and formulation (Goldman 6/10/38 letter to Milly Rocker, AMS-R; Goldman 7/1/38 letter to Herbert Read, NYU).

## Further Footnotes for Chapter Ten

8. Actually, her first prominent sign of internationalism was when she and Berkman decided to refocus their attention from Russian developments back to the country they were living in. due to the Homestead strike. From that time on, she "adopted" the United States as her primary target of activist concern. She was convinced that other immigrant anarchists, like herself, would best serve their cause by trying to nurture anarchist consciousness in the native-born American population rather than remaining, as she critically observed, in their relatively isolated enclave communities or looking back to the old country. She herself took the former direction, in the process reaching out to ever-broader audiences of those with budding libertarian instincts, though who never took on the anarchist label themselves. In this sense, Goldman was a crucial intellectual link between the European anarchist tradition and that libertarianism evolving in relative isolation on North American soil.

11. An excellent example of this rationale is in her discussion of her role in organizing a Free Speech League among liberal circles in New York in 1903. Her immediate goal was to prevent English anarchist John Turner from deportation. But equally she sought to rouse a broader campaign against the Anti-Anarchist Law under which federal authorities sought to prevent *any* anarchist from entering the U.S. She also wished to educate the public generally about the absence of reality of the formal liberties supposedly guaranteed by their political system. The result of this particular campaign was both a revelation of the latter limitations (even the Supreme Court upheld the deportation order) and much greater opportunity for anarchist propaganda (through the speeches of herself and Turner). (*LL*, I, 335, 347-49, 357.)

12. The latter interpretation of her perspective unfortunately seems implied in stressing her move from personal participation in violence to that of free-speech activities, an emphasis at some points more clearly stated than at others in Richard Drinnon's well-known biography of Goldman. Liberals then and now may well have viewed Goldman as contributing to their own reformist cause—within the constitutional framework. However, Goldman herself was committed only to the libertarian part of civil libertarianism, that is rejecting the notion that such liberties could be achieved or for long protected through governmental machinery. The misreading of her orientation by British liberals no doubt played a part in their rapid reluctance to be linked to Goldman after initially greeting her warmly upon her arrival in 1924.

17. The overall number of foreign anarchist militia volunteers is hard to determine. Some joined the Communist-organized International Brigades. In addition, Thomas estimates that some 5000 foreigners fought in other anti-fascist units, especially in Catalonia (Hugh Thomas, *The Spanish Civil War*, p. 637). No doubt a large percentage of these were anarchists, especially from Italy, Germany and France. (Sam Dolgoff estimates that no more than two dozen American anarchists—meaning those of non-Spanish origin—fought in Spain [*Soil of Liberty*,

Spring 1982].) French anarchists, for example, formed a "Sébastien Faure" *centurie* (a unit of about 100 men), as part of the anarchist Durruti column on the Saragossa front. Though indeed greatly outnumbered by non-anarchists of the International Brigades (Thomas estimates the latter total at approximately 40,000; Broué and Témime suggest 25,000-30,000 as more likely [*The Revolution. . . ,* pp. 377-78]), the experience and contribution of these anarchist volunteers has been disproportionately neglected. One account concerning such experience is in Camillo Berneri, *Guerre de classes en Espagne.*

19. Nevertheless, reverberations of consciousness from the Spanish experience were felt in revolutionary movements in Italy and Yugoslavia (during and shortly after World War II), Algeria, Latin America, and now back again in Western Europe. It is impossible in so short a space to explore these various lines of influence. Among sources to consult on this question are Donald Hodges, ed., *Philosophy of the Urban Guerrilla: The Revolutionary Writings of Abraham Guillén* (N.Y.: William Morrow and Co., Inc., 1973); Alberola and Gransac, *L'Anarchisme espagnol . . .*; and Meltzer, ed., *The International Revolutionary Solidarity Movement.* The Algerian connection may be more difficult to prove than the others. I am unaware, for example, of any accounts on the role of Spanish and Italian anarchist influence on or within that struggle. However, Donald Hodges states that Yugoslav Communists in Spain were strongly influenced by the revolution's example of self-managed collectivization (p.40). The subsequent Yugoslav model, in turn, influenced to some degree the particular design of workers' self-management in the first years of post-independence Algeria.

22. Examples in the international movement during the late 1930's were the CNT-FAI leadership's withdrawal of subsidies from the increasingly critical *L'Espagne Anti-Fasciste* and *Guerra di classe* in early 1937 and similar efforts by the Spanish in late 1937 to dominate the proceedings and organization of the international anarcho-syndicalist IWMA, thus to prevent any criticism within movement ranks. (The clash these efforts produced at the December 1937 Paris meeting of the IWMA is set forth clearly in the official minutes of this gathering. A copy exists in that organization's archives at the International Institute of Social History in Amsterdam. Excerpts from these minutes were reproduced in *L'Espagne Nouvelle* [the successor to *L'Espagne Anti-Fasciste*], no 63 [March 15, 1939].)

23. Syndicalists aim their hopes and efforts for drastic social change toward a trade union movement free from any bonds to government or political party. However, there is a critical distinction between those syndicalists who also (though not their primary effort) vote for and support a reformist political party (as the French Socialists, British Labour Party or Democrats in the United States) and those who believe that *no* significant social change can be accomplished or assisted by electoral means and the state. Many among this latter revolutionary persuasion are anarchists. Quite often, the same syndicalist organization (as the IWW in the United States or the CNT in Spain) will contain individuals from each perspective, though all believe that revolution will be accomplished through the syndicalist organization's strength in the working class and that it should be the main force for coordinating economic production afterward. In the Spanish case, as opposed to the U.S. and French syndicalist movements, anarcho-syndicalists were persistently more influential than non-anarchists in leading and shaping the basic direction of the syndicalist organization. Distinctions between the two tendencies are pointed out by Goldman below. Anarcho-syndicalists differ from other types of anarchists in that they give *primary* attention to contradictions of the work place and devote their effort for social transformation primarily through revolutionary trade unions of the working class. For another attempt to define the last distinction, see Nicholas Walter, "About Anarchism," *Anarchy* (London), no. 100 (June 1969), subsequently reproduced as a separate pamphlet by Freedom Press (London). The distinction may seem clearer if the parallel is made with present-day "anarcha-feminism," which emphasizes the problem of sexism as the most critical social contradiction and thus gives primary attention and effort to organizing grass-roots, anti-authoritarian revolutionary groups of women.

24. Pierre Besnard was a railroad worker and union leader who was influential in the struggle to move French trade unions back to the anarcho-syndicalist orientation of the early 20th century. Breaking from the reformist CGT in 1922 and then from the Communist-dominated CGTU in the following year, Besnard and others founded the anarcho-syndicalist CGTSR (the Social Revolutionary General Confederation of Labor) in 1926, affiliating as well with the

326 Vision On Fire

IWMA. Besnard became secretary-general of the CGTSR in 1929. By a decade later, this organization had about 4000 members. (Maitron, *Le mouvement anarchiste en France*,II.) Following Rudolf Rocker's exile to the United States from Germany, Besnard became secretary-general of the IWMA and served in this capacity until the 1937 clash with the Spanish CNT (described in the text below).

30. In response to the disappointing outcome of the Stelton, N.J. anarchist conference this letter was written for, she reminded Harry Kelly (9/1/34 letter, NYPL) that she had often said anarchism would arrive eventually – "in spite of many anarchists." Similar observations on attempts at communes in the United States led her to oppose such efforts in the present society unless clearly based on "harmonious temperaments and common tastes in their daily life and habits," *as well as* a common theory (Goldman 9/12/34 letter to Joseph Ishill, HAR).

49. Goldman tried to launch an Anarcho-Syndicalist Union in London after her first visit to Spain, but the effort continued to frustrate her for the next two years. (Regular accounts of the goals and activities of the A.S.U. appeared in *Spain and the World*.) One target of her attack in this passage was Albert Meltzer, who has continued anarchist activism to the present day, most recently as one of several involved with the anarchist Cienfuegos Press in Scotland. His own strong feelings against Goldman's role in the 1930's also have continued to the present, as seen in his historical account, *The Anarchists in London, 1935-1955* (Sanday, Orkney Islands, Scotland: Cienfuegos Press, 1976). Goldman praises, however, Ralph Barr, a working-class London anarchist, also mentioned in Meltzer's account.

51. Paul Robeson (1898-1976), the great Afro-American singer, identified with and shared his talents on behalf of progressive campaigns from the 1930's on. Though never joining the Communist Party, he supported much of its work, and openly praised and lived in the Soviet Union for a number of years following the racist and McCarthyite attacks on him in the United States. Goldman did succeed in persuading him to appear at one fund-raising program (4/25/37) she organized in London (gaining 200£), despite the fact that the Communists organized a competing affair for the same date. He also gave a strongly supportive public statement for another solidarity meeting organized by Goldman and others later the same year (*Spain and the World*, July 2, 1937), despite the Communist *Daily Worker*'s refusal to accept an advertisement for this event.

55. Santillán's written critique of his own early collaborationist position and that of the CNT-FAI, titled "Revolution and War in Spain: Preliminary Notes for Its History," appeared in print in several stages after being initially suppressed when published in September 1937. By August 1938, he was publishing major sections of this critique within Spain in the Barcelona anarchist theoretical periodical he edited, *Timón*. (Passages from this were reproduced at the time in French in *L'Espagne Nouvelle*, no.'s 60 [September 13, 1938] and 61 [January 15, 1939] and in English in *Challenge* [N.Y.] in its four issues of September 1938.) His thoughts were finally published in a single volume in *Por qué perdimos la guerra* (Buenos Aires: Ediciones Iman, 1940).

58. Aldous Huxley (1894-1963) was the British writer, social critic, and decentralist communitarian most famous for his view of negative utopia in *Brave New World* (1932) and positive utopia in *Island*, his last novel (1962). He was very active in the British pacifist Peace Pledge Union founded in 1936. He identified himself explicitly with the anarchist model in a letter to the London *Left Review*, published with other authors' replies in their *Authors Take Sides on the Spanish War* (1937). This and similar decentralist statements of his during the same period are found in Grover Smith, ed., *Letters of Aldous Huxley* (New York: Harper and Row, 1969). The same letter to the *Left Review* also is reproduced in *Spain and the World*, December 10, 1937.

61. Pierre Ramus (Rudolf Grossmann) was an Austrian anarchist born in 1878. Over several decades, he wrote numerous articles in the international anarchist press and many books and pamphlets of his own. During World War I he was imprisoned because of his antiwar propaganda and his refusal to enter the military. He died in 1942 while crossing the Atlantic to Mexico in an effort to escape fascist Europe. (Jean Maitron and G. Haupt, *Dictionnaire biographique du mouvement international*, vol. I-*l'Autriche* [Paris: Editions Sociales, 1971], p. 243)

72. Ralph Borsodi was one of the original public advocates for the back-to-the-land, subsistence homesteading and decentralist cooperative community movement in the 1920's. His 1933

*Flight from the City* (New York: Harper and Brothers) was the first of a whole series of books, periodicals and pamphlets he produced from his base in Brookville and Yellow Springs, Ohio. In this capacity, he and the "School of Living" he helped organize in 1936 definitely were major precursors of the North American anti-authoritarian, counter-culture, commune and ecology movements of the 1960's, '70's and '80's. Huxley met with Borsodi in Suffern, New York at the beginning of his permanent residency in the United States in mid-1937 and was immensely fascinated with his practical attempts to actualize broad decentralist principles, in a manner similar to the later E.F. Schumacher. Presumably Huxley's references to Abbot and Kettering were derived from this same encounter with Borsodi. Charles Greeley Abbot was a prominent American astrophysicist and secretary of the Smithsonian Institution. Far before it became fashionable, he studied solar radiation as a potential energy source for humans, as shown in his 1929 book, *The Sun and the Welfare of Man*. Charles F. Kettering was a prominent American inventor and engineer who directed the central research laboratory for General Motors between 1919 and 1947.

This particular passage is a rare and intriguing linkage between the turn-of-the-century anarchist traditions of Goldman's generation and the decentralist, ecology-oriented, alternative technology, counter-culture aspect of contemporary anti-authoritarianism in the West. Good further linkages of these two phases of anti-authoritarian thought and practice are found in Laurence Veysey, *The Communal Experience: Anarchist and Mystical Counter-Cultures in America* (including specific reference to Huxley's role in California); Theodore Roszak, *Person/Planet: The Creative Disintegration of Industrial Society*; various works of Paul Goodman; and various writings by Murray Bookchin, especially *Post-Scarcity Anarchism*, *Toward An Ecological Society*, and *The Ecology of Freedom*.

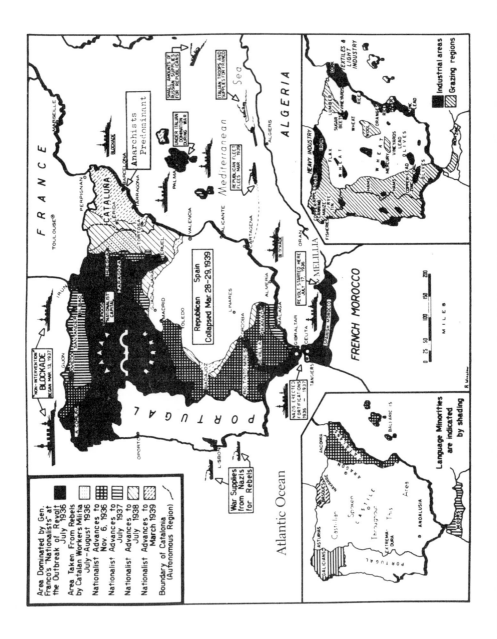

**Legend (main map):**

- Area Dominated by Gen. Franco's Nationalists at the Outbreak of Revolt July 1936
- Area Taken From Rebels by Catalan Workers Militia July–August 1936
- Nationalist Advances to Nov. 6, 1936
- Nationalist Advances to July 1937
- Nationalist Advances to July 1938
- Nationalist Advances to March 1939
- Boundary of Catalonia (Autonomous Region)

Atlantic Ocean

War Supplies from Nazis for Rebels

NON-INTERVENTION BLOCKADE BEGAN MAR. 13, 1937

NAZIS ERECTED FORTIFICATIONS 1936 – 1937

REVOLT STARTED HERE JULY 17, 1936

Republican Spain Collapsed Mar. 28–29, 1939

NATIONALIST CAPITAL

Anarchists Predominant

UNDER ITALIAN DOMINATION DURING WAR

SMALL AMOUNTS OF RUSSIAN SUPPLIES FOR REPUBLICANS

ITALIAN TROOPS AND SUPPLIES FOR FRANCO

REPUBLICAN FLEET FLEES MAR. 1939

Mediterranean Sea

BLOCKADE

FRANCE

PORTUGAL

ALGERIA

FRENCH MOROCCO

SPANISH MOROCCO

**Inset (upper right):**

Industrial areas

Grazing regions

HEAVY INDUSTRY

TEXTILES & LIGHT INDUSTRY

**Inset (lower right):**

Language Minorities are indicated by shading

Castilian Spoken Throughout This Area

Galicians / Basques / Catalans / Andalusia

MILES 0 25 50 100 150 200

# Sources

To save space I have chosen not to include an additional topical list of sources. Much of this list would duplicate citations already in the footnotes. For those who skipped over the latter, a quick glance through them now would reveal numerous relevant works to consult for further understanding of Spanish anarchism, the Spanish civil war and revolution, Emma Goldman's evolution and the anarchist movement generally.

Goldman's articles, manuscripts, reported speeches and published letters to the editor on Spain amount to at least seventy items. All of the more important of these have been quoted extensively in the present volume. Because Goldman wrote at least hundreds of letters every year, inevitably more will be discovered in the future. However, to my knowledge, all of the important archives containing Goldman letters during the late 1930's have been used for this project. On the basis of the extensive collection of letters and other materials consulted, I am certain that the basic positions of Goldman on the various issues identified here are accurately represented in this book.

The following list indicates the precise source of Goldman texts used in this book. All entries here follow the same consecutive order as within the chapters themselves. They easily can be matched with the proper texts through the dates indicated in the transition passages before each Goldman quotation and through the order in which they appear. All items indicated below are letters from Emma Goldman, unless indicated otherwise.

The following abbreviations are used to signify the particular archival locations of letters and manuscripts cited:

| | |
|---|---|
| NYPL | (New York Public Library, Rare Books and Manuscripts Division, Emma Goldman Papers) |
| UML | (University of Michigan Library, Labadie Collection) |
| NYU | (New York University, Tamiment Library, Emma Goldman Collection) |
| YAL | (Yale University Library, Harry Weinberger Papers) |
| RAD | (Radcliffe College, Schlesinger Library, Emma Goldman Papers) |
| HAR | (Harvard University, Houghton Library, Joseph Ishill Papers) |
| AMS | (International Institute of Social History, Amsterdam) |
| -G | (Goldman Archives) |
| -R | (Rocker Archives) |
| -F | (Fleshin Archives) |
| ARC | (private collection of Federico Arcos) |

## Ch. II

10/28/36, NYPL
11/14/36, NYPL
12/8/36, NYPL
12/16/36, NYPL
6/29/37, NYPL
"Where I Stand," *Spain and the World*
  (henceforth *SW*), 7/2/37
10/24/37, UML
1/25/38, NYPL
8/16/38, UML
11/11/38, AMS-R
3/31/39, AMS-R
8/4/39, AMS-R
11/18/39, ARC
10/17/36, NYPL
"Durruti," *SW*, 11/24/37
9/?/36, NYPL
11/3/36, NYPL
2/8/37, UML
5/4/37, AMS-R
5/9/37, ARC
5/14/37, ARC
11/3/36, NYPL
2/23/37, NYPL
9/2/39, AMS-R
7/27/37, AMS-G
"My Second Visit to Spain" (typescript,
  3/4/38), UML; most of the article (though
  not this paragraph) was published as "Emma
  Goldman on Spain," *Spanish Revolution*
  (henceforth *SR*), 3/21/38.
11/11/38, AMS-R
"Attending the POUM Trial" (unpublished
  typescript, 12/38), UML
4/24/39, AMS-R
6/27/39, AMS-R
8/31/39, AMS-R
12/27/37, NYPL
"Visiting the Fronts" (unpublished typescript,
  12/38), UML
8/4/39, AMS-R

## Ch. III

8/26/36, AMS-R
9/19/36, NYPL
11/30/36, NYPL
11/11/37, YAL; all but the last sentence
  reproduced in "Emma Goldman Reports on
  Spain," *SR*, 12/6/37
"Address to the IWMA" (12/37 typescript),
  NYPL
"The Lure of the Spanish People" (typescript,
  12/9/38), UML; most of this passage
  appears in an article of the same title in
  *Challenge* (N.Y.), 1/7/39
11/18/36, NYPL
10/4/36, NYPL
1/25/38, NYPL
"Emma Goldman on Spain," *SR*, 3/21/38;
  "My Second Visit to Spain " is the 3/4/38
  typescript for this article, UML
12/9/38 typescript, "The Lure of the Spanish
  People," UML

"Albalate de Cinca," *SW*, 3/5/37
First three paragraphs from "Emma
  Goldman on Spain," *SR*, 3/21/38; remainder
  from continuation of the article in *SR*,
  5/1/38
12/9/38 typescript, "The Lure of the Spanish
  People," UML
10/10/36, NYPL
12/9/38 typescript, "The Lure of the Spanish
  People," UML
"Emma Goldman on Spain," *SR*, 5/1/38;
  typescript completed 3/4/38, UML
7/15/38, AMS-G
"A Visit to Durruti-Ascaso Orphans Colony,"
  *SW*, 12/10/37
2/14/38, AMS-G
12/9/38 typescript, "The Lure of the Spanish
  People," UML; first two paragraphs of this
  passage appear in the article of the same
  title, *Challenge* (N.Y.), 1/7/39
1/14/40, NYPL

## Ch. IV

6/5/34, NYU
4/2/36, YAL
5/1/36, ARC; most of this same text appeared
  later as an article, "Anarchists and
  Elections," *Vanguard*, 6-7/36.
9/11/36, NYPL
10/3/36, NYPL
10/4/36, NYPL
10/28/36, NYPL
11/3/36, NYPL
11/14/36, NYPL
12/16/36, NYPL
1/1/37, AMS-G
1/5/37, NYPL; almost the same wording,
  but in a letter dated 1/25/37 also was
  reproduced in *SW*, 2/5/37
"Emma Goldman on the United Front in
  Spain," *SR*, 1/8/37
1/19/37, NYU
2/17/37, NYPL
2/23/37, NYPL
3/6/37, AMS-G
3/9/37, AMS-R
4/5/37, NYPL
5/2/37, AMS-G
5/14/37, ARC
6/8/37, UML
7/1/37, RAD
7/8/37, AMS-G
7/13/37, AMS-R
9/27/37, NYPL
10/11/37, AMS-G
11/11/37, YAL; part of this passage also
  appears in "Emma Goldman Reports on
  Spain," *SR*, 12/6/37
"Address to the IWMA Congress" (12/37
  typescript), NYPL
12/21/37, NYPL
12/22/37, AMS-G
12/30/37, AMS-G (transl. from German)
1/1/38, NYPL

1/20/38, UML
1/19/38, AMS-G
1/24/38, AMS-G (transl. from German)
2/10/38, AMS-G
3/3/38, AMS-G
"Emma Goldman and the Alliance Proposals," *SW*, 3/4/38
4/5/38, AMS-R
5/6/38, NYPL
11/29/38, AMS-R
3/17/39, AMS-R
5/10/39, AMS-R

## Ch. V

9/29/36, NYPL
10/1/36, NYPL
1/4/37, AMS-G
1/5/37, NYPL
1/5/37, AMS-R
2/9/37, NYPL
3/2/37, NYPL; also reproduced in *SW*, 5/19/37
4/1/37, NYPL
5/9/37, ARC
"The Soviet Political Machine," *SW*, 6/4/37 (this second half of the article completed on 5/22/37)
6/37, NYPL
"Callousness or Indifference?" *SW*, 7/2/37
8/10/37, AMS-R
9/12/37, NYPL
11/18/37, NYPL
11/19/37, AMS-R
"Political Persecution in Republican Spain," *SW*, 12/10/37
"Address to the IWMA Congress" (12/37 typescript), NYPL
1/4/38, YAL
1/4/38, NYU
1/10/38, NYPL
"The Betrayal of the Spanish People," *SW*, 1/21/38 (these remarks quoted from her 1/14/38 public speech in London)
4/28/38, NYPL
5/3/38, NYPL
5/24/38, AMS-G
6/2/38, AMS-G
11/11/38, AMS-R
11/15/38, NYU
"POUM Frameup Fails," *Vanguard*, 2/39 and "The POUM Trial in Barcelona" (typescript written by 11/24/38), NYU; the article is a slightly shorter version of the typescript, with several word changes but not in essential content; this quotation is derived from both versions
"Attending the POUM Trial" (12/38 unpublished typescript), UML
2/10/39, AMS-R
3/21/39, NYU
"Report of Miss Emma Goldman's Address at the Memorial Hall," London, 3/24/39 (typescript), NYU
8/4/39, AMS-R

9/19/39 Toronto speech, "The Stalin-Hitler Pact" (typescript), NYU
10/18/39, NYPL
10/19/39, AMS-R

## Ch. VI

7/31/36, NYPL
"Whom the Gods Would Destroy," *Vanguard*, 10-11/36 (transcript of her 9/30/36 radio talk from Barcelona); also reproduced in the *CNT-FAI Information Bulletin* (English edition) (Barcelona), 10/6/36
11/14/36, NYPL
"Which Flag, Madrid or Moscow?" *CNT-FAI Information Bulletin* (English edition) (Barcelona), 12/1/36
2/8/37, UML
2/26/37, NYPL
Introduction to reproductions of her letters to several newspapers, *SW*, 5/19/37
"Emma Goldman Reports on Spain," *SR*, 12/6/37 (from the text of her 11/11/37 letter to "Comrade," YAL)
11/24/37, AMS-G
12/30/37, AMS-G
2/14/38, AMS-G
3/24/38, AMS-G
"The Black Spectre of War," *SW*, 5/38
5/3/38, AMS-G
5/5/38, AMS-G
6/17/38, NYPL
6/22/38, AMS-G
1/30/39, UML
2/9/39, ARC
2/17/39, YAL
2/27/39, AMS-R
2/28/39, AMS-R
"Report of Miss Emma Goldman's Address at the Memorial Hall," London, 3/24/39 (typescript), NYU
4/27/39 Toronto speech, quoted in *Toronto Evening Telegram*, 4/28/39
Interview quoted in *Windsor Star*, 5/19/39
9/2/39, AMS-R
9/7/39, AMS-R
10/7/39, NYU
10/7/39, AMS-R
12/19/39, ARC
9/23/36 radio talk from Barcelona, quoted in *CNT-FAI Information Bulletin* (English edition) (Barcelona), 9/25/36; same text also reproduced in *SR*, 10/19/36
4/2/37, NYPL
"An Appeal to the Workers," manifesto written by the London Committee of the CNT-FAI (Goldman and several others) and distributed to British trade union locals; reproduced in *SW*, 4/2/37
"Address to the IWMA Congress" (12/37 typescript), NYPL
12/21/37, NYPL
12/29/37, NYPL
"Emma Goldman and the Alliance Proposals, *SW*, 3/4/38

"Emma Goldman Appeals for Support of
SIA," *SW*, 3/18/38
4/14/38, AMS-G
7/19/38, NYPL
5/19/39 speech in Windsor, Canada, quoted
in the *Windsor Star*, 5/20/39

## Ch. VII

5/19/35, RAD
9/23/36 radio talk from Barcelona, quoted in
*CNT-FAI Information Bulletin* (English edition) (Barcelona), 9/25/36; same text
reproduced also in *SR*, 10/19/36
10/4/36, NYPL
10/7/36, NYPL
11/12/36, NYPL
"Emma Goldman's Impressions," *SW*, 1/8/37
2/8/37, NYPL
2/8/37, UML
2/10/37, NYPL
3/8/37, NYPL
4/28/37, published in the *Manchester Guardian*
6/1/37, UML
6/37, NYPL
6/10/37, AMS-R
7/1/37, RAD
"Address to the IWMA Congress" (12/37
typescript), NYPL
1/24/38, AMS-G (translated from German)
"My Second Visit to Spain" (3/4/38
typescript), UML; most of this passage was
reproduced in "Emma Goldman on Spain,"
*SR*, 3/21/38
3/4/38, UML
"The Black Spectre of War," *SW*, 5/38
5/20/38, AMS-G
5/27/38, NYPL
9/10/38 letter, reproduced in *Anarchy*
(London), 8/70
11/11/38, AMS-R
11/15/38, NYU
11/22/38, NYU
1/30/39, UML
2/39, UML
2/9/39, NYU
4/27/39 speech in Toronto, quoted in *The
Evening Telegraph* (Toronto), 4/28/39
Interview quoted in the *Windsor Star*, 5/19/39
Interview quoted in *The Detroit News*, 5/19/39
10/7/39, NYU
11/6/39, ARC

## Ch. VIII

2/8/35 letter, reproduced in R. Drinnon and
A. Drinnon, eds., *Nowhere at Home* (N.Y.:
Schocken Books, 1975), pp. 185-87.
4/24/36, UML
11/18/36, NYPL
12/5/36, NYPL
"The Place of Women in Society: An Appeal
to the Spanish Women during the Revolution" (typescript), NYU; the Spanish translation of this article was published as
"Situacíon social de la mujer," *Mujeres*

Libres (mid-December 1936), and was
reproduced in Mary Nash, ed., *Mujeres
Libres* (Barcelona: Tusquets Editor, 1975)
"Emma Goldman's Impressions," *SW*, 1/8/37
3/30/37, UML
10/1/37, NYPL
"Emma Goldman Reports on Spain," *SR*,
5/1/38; typescript completed 3/4/38

## Ch. IX

8/22/36, NYPL
9/13/36, UML
First speech to anarchists in Barcelona, quoted
in *CNT-FAI Information Bulletin* (English
edition) (Barcelona), 9/25/36
9/25/36, ARC
9/29/36, NYPL
10/18/36 speech to mass meeting of anarchist
youth in Barcelona, as quoted in *Cultura
Proletaria* (N.Y.), 11/21/36 (translated from
Spanish)
2/8/37, NYPL
6/10/37, AMS-R
7/37 preface to reprint of Alexander Berkman's *What Is Communist Anarchism?* under
new title of *Now and After: The ABC of
Communist Anarchism* (N.Y.: Freie
Arbeiter Stimme, 1937)
9/10/37, NYPL
9/23/37 letter to *SW*, published 10/13/37
"Trotsky Protests Too Much!" (typescript
completed by 5/13/38), NYPL; this portion
of the typescript was not included in the article of the same title published in *Vanguard*,
7/19/38
2/3/39, NYU
2/17/39, YAL
2/24/39, AMS-R
2/27/39. AMS-R
"Report of Miss Emma Goldman's Address
at the Memorial Hall," London, 3/24/39
(typescript), NYU
10/7/39, NYU

## Ch. X

5/11/34, NYU
7/31/34, HAR
2/1/35, UML
10/19/36 letter to Milly and Rudolf Rocker,
AMS-R
11/14/36, NYPL
1/5/37, AMS-R
2/16/37, AMS-G
2/23/37, NYPL
4/5/37, NYPL
5/9/37, ARC
5/14/37, ARC
6/1/37, UML
6/37, NYPL
6/18/37, NYPL
7/1/37, RAD
9/10/37, NYPL

11/15/37, AMS-G
11/18/37, NYPL
11/19/37, AMS-R
12/2/37, AMS-G
12/3/37, NYPL
12/4/37, AMS-G (translated from German)
12/11/37, NYPL
"Address to the IWMA Congress" (12/37
  typescript), NYPL
12/30/37, AMS-G
12/30/37, AMS-G (translated from German)
1/1/38, NYPL
1/4/38, NYU
1/24/38, AMS-G (translated from German)
1/25/38, NYPL
2/1/38, AMS-G
2/16/38, RAD
2/22/38, AMS-G
3/12/38, AMS-G (translated from German)
3/21/38, ARC
3/38 typescript, NYPL; the Italian translation
  of this essay appears as the preface to
  Camillo Berneri, *Pensieri e battaglie* (Paris:
  Comitato Camillo Berneri, 1938)
4/5/38, AMS-R

6/2/38, AMS-G
7/12/38, AMS-G
7/19/38, NYPL
7/28/38, ARC
9/13/38, AMS-R
11/22/38, NYU
12/38, NYPL
2/9/39, ARC
2/9/39, NYU
3/17/39, AMS-R
4/19/39, AMS-R
Interview quoted in the *Windsor Star*, 5/19/39
Quoted in the *Detroit Times*, 5/19/39
Interview quoted in *The Detroit News*, 5/19/39
6/27/39 letter, reprinted in a "70th Birthday
  Commemorative Edition" pamphlet by the
  Los Angeles Libertarian Committee, 1939
8/4/39, AMS-R
8/4/39, AMS-R
10/7/39, AMS-R
11/20/39, NYU

(My thanks to Merrill Goldstein and Ales
Susteric for their assistance in translating from
German those items mentioned above and
other related material.)

# Index of Cited Periodicals

*(page numbers in italics indicate references in Goldman text)*

# General Index

(Page numbers in italics indicate a reference by Goldman to the indexed subject
concerned *or* letters, speeches and interviews comprising the Goldman text)

Ghana, 245n
Gide, André, *152*
Giral, José, government of, 50n, 52n, 102n
Gironella, Enrique, *160-65*
Glasgow Anarchist-Communist group, *310*
Glasgow Anti-Parliamentary group, *310*
Godwin, William, 296n
Goldberg, H.J., 125n
Golding, Louis, 205n
Goldman, Emma,
activism in U.S., 2-8, 24n, 84, *195*, 215, 249-50, *252*, 279-81, *293*, *311*, *319*, 324n; childhood and early years in Russia, 1-2, 249; collaboration with non-anarchists in U.S., 5-7, 84, 281; courage in face of great danger, 6-7, 21n, 35n, *145-46*; death of, 24n; exile activities in Europe (1922-36), 9, 85, *118*, 126n, *137*, 174, 282, *285*; experience in the Soviet Union, 8-9, 21n, 85, *105-06*, 125n, 126n, 134, 263, *307*; final year of life in Canada, xi(n), 14n, 16, 24n, *197*, 208n, *245*, 284, *321-24*; first years in U.S., 2, 279; interviews in Windsor, Ontario (1939), *194*, *244*, *320-21*; involvement in assassination attempt against Frick, 3, 54, 84, 211, 212n, 279; language ability, 16, *106*, *254*, *313*; letters to unidentified friends and comrades, *165*, *180-83*, *188*, *254*, *319-22*; love relationships, 2, 6, 26, 249, 280; notoriety of, 54;
organizing efforts in Britain for the Spanish anarchists, 16, *76*, 86, *113-14*, *119*, *180*, *183-84*, *186*, *200-01*, *203-05*, 257n, 260n, 283, *291*, *296-97*, *303-04*, *306*, *309-10*, *322-23*:
collaboration with non-anarchists for, 86n, *103-05*, *106*, *115-19*, 129n, *137-38*, *306*
threats to resign from, *107*, *109*, *114*, *120*, *303*, *308*;
perspectives on:
anarchism and anarchists (see main entries)
birth control, 5, 7, 20n, 249, *252-54*, 281n
Britain, 9, 16, *183*, *191*, *322*
callousness of world public opinion, *144-45*, *152*, 174, *203*, *297*, *299*, *307*, *318*
colonialism, 5, 11, *113*, 173, *192*, 241n, 245, 246n
communes, 326n
Communists (see main entry and her perspectives on Marxism; the Russian revolution; and Soviet dictatorship)
democracy in the West, 2, 7n, *31*, *113*, 175, *182*, *190*, 192, *200*, 207n, 225, *244*, 281, 324n
direct action, 175, *184*, *186*, *201-05*, *225-26*, *286-87*
elections, 84, 89, *91*, 250, *286*
fascism, *31-2*, *99*, *113*, *176-79*, *194*, 207n, 214-15, *218*, 222, *234-35*, *244-46*, 255
impact of technology, *316*, *320*
importance of the individual, *34*, *38-9*,

*45-6*, *241*, *243*, 260n, 280, *282n*, 284, *288*, *298*, *301-03*, *307*, *318*, *320*
inadequacy of economic struggle alone, *159*, *240*, *243*, 274, *286*, *298-99*
Jewish conditions, *197*, *241-42*, *252*, *311*
liberals, generally, 88, *115*, *118*, *190*, *196-97*, *203*, *225-26*, 281, *306*, 324n
Marxism (see also her perspectives on Communists; Socialists; the Russian revolution; and Soviet dictatorship), *45*, *103*, 132, *154*, *157-58*, *165*, *168-69*, 274, *301*, *320*
mass media, generally, *47*, *217*, 265
militarism and war, 5, *31-2*, 173, *195*, 212, 215, *216*, *218-20*, 225, *230*, *239-40*, *243-46*, 246n, 281
need to avoid assisting anti-Communist reactionaries, *196-98*
pacifism, 215, *219-22*, *225-26*, *231*, *235-38*, 247n, *291*, *306*
revolutionary potential of the proletariat, *240-41*, *270*, 279, 281, *286-88*, *298-99*
role of women, generally, 5, 249-51, *251-57*
Russian revolution (see entry on comparison of Russian revolution with Spanish revolution), 8-9, 12, 21n, *30*, 54-5, 84-5, *90*, *102*, 134, 212-13, 215, *238-39*, 263-65, *266*, *270-71*, 281, *286*, *294*, *299*, *301*, *313-14*
Socialists (see main entry)
social revolution, generally, 54-5, *60*, 87, *93*, *96*, 127n, *174-75*, *190-91*, 212-15, *216-22*, 225, 227, *231*, *234-41*, *243*, 246n, 260n, 263-65, *266-72*, *274-76*, 279-81, *285*, *318*, *321*
Soviet dictatorship, *31*, *88-90*, *97*, *103*, 106n, *113*, *116*, *118*, 134, *152*, *157*, *168*, 174, *192*, *238*, *245*, 282, *287*, *298*, *314*
Spanish anarchists (see main entry)
Spanish civil war (see main entry)
Spanish revolution (see main entry)
use of violence for self-defense, *55*, 174, 213, 215, *216-22*, 225, *229-38*, *241*, *244*, *291*
violence as a political tactic, generally, 54, 210-15, *216-22*, 225, *227-39*, *241*, 246n, 279-80, *321*
World War I, 7, *31*, 174, *181*, *184*, *190*, *216*, *234-35*, *243-46*, *315*
World War II, 175, *176-78*, *181*, *184-85*, *190-92*, *194*, *196*, *204*, 215, *216*, *239-40*, *242-46*, 265;
plans for book on Spain, xv(n), *323*; "political will" of, 135, *146*, *299-301*; prison experience, 4, 7-8, 215, *220*, *225*; publications in Spain, 12n, *255-57*; published prefaces to others' books, *270-71*, *311-16*; reaction to Berkman death, 14-15, 85, *144*, *296*, *304*, *320*; speech at IWMA meeting (1937), *58*, *112-13*, 116, *152-53*, *201-03*, *230-31*, *304-06*; speeches in Barcelona (1936), *176-78*, *198-99*, *216-17*, *266-69*; speeches in London (1938-39), *155-56*, *166-67*, *191-93*, 276; speeches in Toronto

*40-41, 61, 89, 99, 108*
participation in Anti-Fascist Militia Committee (Barcelona), 28n, *39*
participation in Catalan regional government, 28n, 51n, 129n
participation in national government, *31, 39*, 50n, 52n, *95*, 80n, *98-9, 101, 112,* 123n, *138*
political "realism" of, 27, 86, *190-91*
relative insignificance, *29, 45, 57;*
lies about, *104, 118-19, 121, 141, 146, 149-50, 181-82, 191, 198, 223-26, 232-34,* 265; in Mexican exile, 36n, *79-80, 167-68*; naivete, 27, *28-9, 47, 105, 107, 114,* 135, 175, *226, 314*; official praise of Soviet Union, *40-41*, 95-6, *103, 110-12, 125;*
opposition to collaboration:
  from foreign anarchists, *30-32, 59-60*, 86, *97-8, 102, 105, 108, 111-13, 124,* 126n, 127n, *164*, 175, 209n, 215, *220-22, 228-29*, 242, 264, *270, 272-73,* 283-84, *289-92, 294-96, 301-06, 310, 314-15,* 325n, 326n
  from French anarchists, 24n, *30*, 126n, *294*, 306n
  reaction against, *43, 98*, 127n, *242, 289, 292, 304-05*, 325n
  from within the Spanish anarchist movement, 24n, *28, 33*, 35-6, 50n, 86-7, 114n, 247n, *294, 308*;
organization of, 23n, 27, *27-48*; in post-Franco period, 25, 26n, 84, 134, 251; pre-1936 background, 10-12, 21n, 23n, *30,* 49n, 51n, *87*, 214, 246n, *298*; role of women, *77*, 250-51, *254-59*, 259n, 260n; self-discipline, *28, 37, 219*; World War II, attitudes toward and activities within, 215, *239*
Spanish civil war (1936-39),
  antifascist military effort, generally:
    anarchist contribution to (see entry on international anarchist volunteers in the civil war), *28, 37, 46-7*, 47n, 48n, 52n, *55, 104, 109, 118, 123, 166, 202, 206, 218-25, 230-36*, 242, 265, *269, 271*
    military organization of, *104*
    sabotage of, by the anarchists' "allies", *28*, 50n, *98, 109, 117-18*, 118n, *121, 125,* 131n, *132, 136-42, 146-47, 152-53, 155-59, 165-67*, 170n, 171n, *275*;
    Aragón front, *28*, 28n, *37*, 52n, 123n, 130n, *147, 153, 223-24, 230, 235, 312,* 325n; Belchite, battle of, *46, 118, 123, 156*; Bilbao, bombing of, *228*;
    Catalonia:
      collapse of, *165-67, 188*, 189n, *275* support for rest of republican Spain, *138, 223-24*
      vulnerability from the sea, *139*;
    development of conventional battlelines, 94n; fall of republican Spain, 36n; Guadalajara, battle of, 52n; Guernica, bombing of, *228*; international anarchist volunteers, *95,*

126n, *143, 145*, 145n, *147, 149-50, 223, 289, 295, 312*, 324n, 325n; International Brigades (see main entry); Madrid, battle of, *28*, 94n, *98*, 131n, *138-39, 142, 147*, 170n, *181, 223-24, 228, 233, 273, 314*; Málaga, exodus from, *224*; outbreak of, 14, 94n, *221*; Port Bou, bombing of, *139*; reprisals against the Right in republican Spain, *216-17, 220, 222*; Teruel, battle of, *46, 123, 156*
Spanish Inquisition, 140n, *151*
Spanish monarchy, 11, *143*
Spanish revolution, educational transformation in, *72-3, 76*, 81n, excellent model for rest of world, *30, 56, 60, 66, 136, 177, 179, 216, 221, 238-9, 241*, 265, *266-76, 284, 290, 300*; international solidarity with, 76n, *99, 114, 119, 201*, 283; sabotage of, 44, 50n, *57-8, 63, 72*, 80n, *87, 92-5, 98, 100, 107, 112, 116-22*, 132-33, 135, *136-65*, 170n, 171n, *182, 192*, 214, *226*, 282, *298, 314-15*;
  social and economic transformation, generally, 15, *28, 32-4*, 55, *55-79*, 80n, 81n, *238, 266-76*, 276n, 282, *305, 315*:
    in Andalusia, *59*
    in Aragón, *57-9, 64-6*, 80n, *236*
    in Castile, *59, 67-9, 73-4, 273*
    in Catalonia, *56*, 57n, *59, 61-2, 70-73, 224, 236, 254, 257, 266*
    in the Levante, *57, 59, 62-3*;
  social relief by anarchists, *75-9, 205, 258-59*
Spender, Dale, 250n
Spiridonova, Maria, *157*, 250n
Stalin, Joseph, *31, 41*, 51n, *113, 116-17, 119, 124-25*, 127n, 132, *136-38, 140-46, 152, 154-58, 160, 166-69*, 170n, 171n, *178, 182, 189-90, 194-98, 240, 270, 314*
Steimer, Mollie, *42, 96, 104*, 120n, 260n, *270, 308*;
  Goldman letters to, *100-01*, 135n, *271-73, 299-301*; letters to Goldman, 24n, 51n, 100n; biographical note, 51n
Stein, Louis, 215n
Stein, Modest (Fedya), 2-4
Sundelwitch, Nicolas, *150*
Swinton, John, 4
syndicalists, *284-85*, 325n
Tajuelo, Telesforo, 49n
Tchaikovsky, Nicholas, 297n
Tellez, Antonio, 49n
Telmes, agricultural collective of, *69-70*
Témime, Emile, 118n, 128n, 131n, 169n, 217n, 325n
10th Army Corps, 47n
Terkel, Pauline,
  Goldman letter to, *245-46*
30th Division, 80n
Thomas, Edith, 259n
Thomas, Hugh, 49n, 128n, 325n
Thomas, Paul, 171n
Tietz, Richard, *150*